C++ Templates

C++ Templates
The Complete Guide

David Vandevoorde
Nicolai M. Josuttis

✦✦Addison-Wesley

Boston • San Francisco • New York • Toronto
Montreal • London • Munich • Paris • Madrid
Capetown • Sydney • Tokyo • Singapore • Mexico City

To Karina
—David

To those who help and love
—Nico

The publisher offers discounts on this book when ordered in quantity for special sales. For more information, please contact:

U.S. Corporate and Government Sales
(800) 382-3419
corpsales@pearsontechgroup.com

For sales outside of the United States, please contact:

International Sales
(317) 581-3793
international@pearsontechgroup.com

Visit Addison-Wesley on the Web: www.awprofessional.com

Library of Congress Cataloging-in-Publication Data

Vandevoorde, David.
   C++ templates : the complete guide / David Vandevoorde, Nicolai M. Josuttis.
     p.   cm.
   Includes bibliographical references and index.
   ISBN 0-201-73484-2 (alk. paper)
    1. Microsoft Visual C++. 2. C++ (Computer program language) 3. Standard template
library. I. Josuttis, Nicolai M. II. Title.

   QA76.73.C153 V37 2003
   005.26'8—dc21   2002027933

For information on obtaining permission for use of material from this work, please submit a written request to:

Pearson Education, Inc.
Rights and Contracts Department
75 Arlington Street, Suite 300
Boston, MA 02116
Fax: (617) 848-7047

ISBN 0201734842

Text printed in the United States on recyled paper at RR Donnelley Crawfordsville in Crawfordsville, Indiana.

8th Printing   August 2006

Contents

Preface   **xv**

Acknowledgments   **xvii**

1   About This Book   **1**

    1.1   What You Should Know Before Reading This Book   2

    1.2   Overall Structure of the Book   2

    1.3   How to Read This Book   3

    1.4   Some Remarks About Programming Style   3

    1.5   The Standard versus Reality   5

    1.6   Example Code and Additional Informations   5

    1.7   Feedback   5

Part I: The Basics   **7**

2   Function Templates   **9**

    2.1   A First Look at Function Templates   9

        2.1.1   Defining the Template   9

        2.1.2   Using the Template   10

    2.2   Argument Deduction   12

    2.3   Template Parameters   13

    2.4   Overloading Function Templates   15

    2.5   Summary   19

3   Class Templates   **21**

    3.1   Implementation of Class Template `Stack`   21

        3.1.1   Declaration of Class Templates   22

     3.1.2   Implementation of Member Functions 24

3.2   Use of Class Template `Stack` 25

3.3   Specializations of Class Templates 27

3.4   Partial Specialization 29

3.5   Default Template Arguments 30

3.6   Summary 33

4   Nontype Template Parameters   **35**

4.1   Nontype Class Template Parameters 35

4.2   Nontype Function Template Parameters 39

4.3   Restrictions for Nontype Template Parameters 40

4.4   Summary 41

5   Tricky Basics   **43**

5.1   Keyword `typename` 43

5.2   Using `this->` 45

5.3   Member Templates 45

5.4   Template Template Parameters 50

5.5   Zero Initialization 56

5.6   Using String Literals as Arguments for Function Templates . . . 57

5.7   Summary 60

6   Using Templates in Practice   **61**

6.1   The Inclusion Model 61

     6.1.1   Linker Errors 61

     6.1.2   Templates in Header Files 63

6.2   Explicit Instantiation 65

     6.2.1   Example of Explicit Instantiation 65

     6.2.2   Combining the Inclusion Model and Explicit Instantiation 67

6.3   The Separation Model 68

     6.3.1   The Keyword `export` 68

     6.3.2   Limitations of the Separation Model 70

     6.3.3   Preparing for the Separation Model 70

6.4   Templates and `inline` 72

6.5   Precompiled Headers 72

6.6   Debugging Templates 74

	6.6.1	Decoding the Error Novel	75
	6.6.2	Shallow Instantiation	77
	6.6.3	Long Symbols	79
	6.6.4	Tracers	79
	6.6.5	Oracles	84
	6.6.6	Archetypes	85
6.7	Afternotes		85
6.8	Summary		85

7   Basic Template Terminology   87

7.1	"Class Template" or "Template Class"?	87
7.2	Instantiation and Specialization	88
7.3	Declarations versus Definitions	89
7.4	The One-Definition Rule	90
7.5	Template Arguments versus Template Parameters	90

Part II: Templates in Depth   93

8   Fundamentals in Depth   95

8.1	Parameterized Declarations		95
	8.1.1	Virtual Member Functions	98
	8.1.2	Linkage of Templates	99
	8.1.3	Primary Templates	100
8.2	Template Parameters		100
	8.2.1	Type Parameters	101
	8.2.2	Nontype Parameters	101
	8.2.3	Template Template Parameters	102
	8.2.4	Default Template Arguments	103
8.3	Template Arguments		104
	8.3.1	Function Template Arguments	105
	8.3.2	Type Arguments	108
	8.3.3	Nontype Arguments	109
	8.3.4	Template Template Arguments	111
	8.3.5	Equivalence	113
8.4	Friends		113
	8.4.1	Friend Functions	114

8.4.2   Friend Templates 117

8.5   Afternotes 117

9   Names in Templates   **119**

9.1   Name Taxonomy 119

9.2   Looking Up Names 121

9.2.1   Argument-Dependent Lookup 123

9.2.2   Friend Name Injection 125

9.2.3   Injected Class Names 126

9.3   Parsing Templates 127

9.3.1   Context Sensitivity in Nontemplates 127

9.3.2   Dependent Names of Types 130

9.3.3   Dependent Names of Templates 132

9.3.4   Dependent Names in Using-Declarations 133

9.3.5   ADL and Explicit Template Arguments 135

9.4   Derivation and Class Templates 135

9.4.1   Nondependent Base Classes 135

9.4.2   Dependent Base Classes 136

9.5   Afternotes 139

10 Instantiation   **141**

10.1   On-Demand Instantiation 141

10.2   Lazy Instantiation 143

10.3   The C++ Instantiation Model 146

10.3.1   Two-Phase Lookup 146

10.3.2   Points of Instantiation 146

10.3.3   The Inclusion and Separation Models 149

10.3.4   Looking Across Translation Units 150

10.3.5   Examples 151

10.4   Implementation Schemes 153

10.4.1   Greedy Instantiation 155

10.4.2   Queried Instantiation 156

10.4.3   Iterated Instantiation 157

10.5   Explicit Instantiation 159

10.6   Afternotes 163

11 Template Argument Deduction   167

11.1 The Deduction Process 167

11.2 Deduced Contexts 169

11.3 Special Deduction Situations 171

11.4 Allowable Argument Conversions 172

11.5 Class Template Parameters 173

11.6 Default Call Arguments 173

11.7 The Barton-Nackman Trick 174

11.8 Afternotes 177

12 Specialization and Overloading   179

12.1 When "Generic Code" Doesn't Quite Cut It 179

12.1.1 Transparent Customization 180

12.1.2 Semantic Transparency 181

12.2 Overloading Function Templates 183

12.2.1 Signatures 184

12.2.2 Partial Ordering of Overloaded Function Templates 186

12.2.3 Formal Ordering Rules 188

12.2.4 Templates and Nontemplates 189

12.3 Explicit Specialization 190

12.3.1 Full Class Template Specialization 190

12.3.2 Full Function Template Specialization 194

12.3.3 Full Member Specialization 197

12.4 Partial Class Template Specialization 200

12.5 Afternotes 203

13 Future Directions   205

13.1 The Angle Bracket Hack 205

13.2 Relaxed `typename` Rules 206

13.3 Default Function Template Arguments 207

13.4 String Literal and Floating-Point Template Arguments 209

13.5 Relaxed Matching of Template Template Parameters 211

13.6 Typedef Templates 212

13.7 Partial Specialization of Function Templates 213

13.8 The `typeof` Oprcrator 215

13.9   Named Template Arguments 216

13.10 Static Properties 218

13.11 Custom Instantiation Diagnostics 218

13.12 Overloaded Class Templates 221

13.13 List Parameters 222

13.14 Layout Control 224

13.15 Initializer Deduction 225

13.16 Function Expressions 226

13.17 Afternotes 228

Part III: Templates and Design   229

14 The Polymorphic Power of Templates   **231**

14.1   Dynamic Polymorphism 231

14.2   Static Polymorphism 234

14.3   Dynamic versus Static Polymorphism 238

14.4   New Forms of Design Patterns 239

14.5   Generic Programming 240

14.6   Afternotes 243

15 Traits and Policy Classes   **245**

15.1   An Example: Accumulating a Sequence 245

       15.1.1   Fixed Traits 246

       15.1.2   Value Traits 250

       15.1.3   Parameterized Traits 254

       15.1.4   Policies and Policy Classes 255

       15.1.5   Traits and Policies: What's the Difference? 258

       15.1.6   Member Templates versus Template Template Parameters 259

       15.1.7   Combining Multiple Policies and/or Traits 261

       15.1.8   Accumulation with General Iterators 262

15.2   Type Functions 263

       15.2.1   Determining Element Types 264

       15.2.2   Determining Class Types 266

       15.2.3   References and Qualifiers 268

       15.2.4   Promotion Traits 271

15.3 Policy Traits 275
    15.3.1 Read-only Parameter Types 276
    15.3.2 Copying, Swapping, and Moving 279
15.4 Afternotes 284

16 Templates and Inheritance   **285**
16.1 Named Template Arguments 285
16.2 The Empty Base Class Optimization (EBCO) 289
    16.2.1 Layout Principles 290
    16.2.2 Members as Base Classes 293
16.3 The Curiously Recurring Template Pattern (CRTP) 295
16.4 Parameterized Virtuality 298
16.5 Afternotes 299

17 Metaprograms   **301**
17.1 A First Example of a Metaprogram 301
17.2 Enumeration Values versus Static Constants 303
17.3 A Second Example: Computing the Square Root 305
17.4 Using Induction Variables 309
17.5 Computational Completeness 312
17.6 Recursive Instantiation versus Recursive Template Arguments 313
17.7 Using Metaprograms to Unroll Loops 314
17.8 Afternotes 318

18 Expression Templates   **321**
18.1 Temporaries and Split Loops 322
18.2 Encoding Expressions in Template Arguments 328
    18.2.1 Operands of the Expression Templates 328
    18.2.2 The `Array` Type 332
    18.2.3 The Operators 334
    18.2.4 Review 336
    18.2.5 Expression Templates Assignments 338
18.3 Performance and Limitations of Expression Templates 340
18.4 Afternotes 341

Part IV: Advanced Applications   345

19 Type Classification   **347**

  19.1 Determining Fundamental Types 347

  19.2 Determining Compound Types 350

  19.3 Identifying Function Types 352

  19.4 Enumeration Classification with Overload Resolution 356

  19.5 Determining Class Types 359

  19.6 Putting It All Together 359

  19.7 Afternotes 363

20 Smart Pointers   **365**

  20.1 Holders and Trules 365

      20.1.1 Protecting Against Exceptions 366

      20.1.2 Holders 368

      20.1.3 Holders as Members 370

      20.1.4 Resource Acquisition Is Initialization 373

      20.1.5 `Holder` Limitations 373

      20.1.6 Copying Holders 375

      20.1.7 Copying Holders Across Function Calls 375

      20.1.8 Trules 376

  20.2 Reference Counting 379

      20.2.1 Where Is the Counter? 380

      20.2.2 Concurrent Counter Access 381

      20.2.3 Destruction and Deallocation 382

      20.2.4 The `CountingPtr` Template 383

      20.2.5 A Simple Noninvasive Counter 386

      20.2.6 A Simple Invasive Counter Template 388

      20.2.7 Constness 390

      20.2.8 Implicit Conversions 390

      20.2.9 Comparisons 393

  20.3 Afternotes 394

21 Tuples   **395**

  21.1 Duos 395

  21.2 Recursive Duos 401

      21.2.1 Number of Fields 401

      21.2.2 Type of Fields 403

      21.2.3 Value of Fields 404

  21.3 Tuple Construction 410

  21.4 Afternotes 415

22 Function Objects and Callbacks   **417**

  22.1 Direct, Indirect, and Inline Calls 418

  22.2 Pointers and References to Functions 421

  22.3 Pointer-to-Member Functions 423

  22.4 Class Type Functors 426

      22.4.1 A First Example of Class Type Functors 426

      22.4.2 Type of Class Type Functors 428

  22.5 Specifying Functors 429

      22.5.1 Functors as Template Type Arguments 429

      22.5.2 Functors as Function Call Arguments 430

      22.5.3 Combining Function Call Parameters and Template Type Parameters 431

      22.5.4 Functors as Nontype Template Arguments 432

      22.5.5 Function Pointer Encapsulation 433

  22.6 Introspection 436

      22.6.1 Analyzing a Functor Type 436

      22.6.2 Accessing Parameter Types 437

      22.6.3 Encapsulating Function Pointers 439

  22.7 Function Object Composition 445

      22.7.1 Simple Composition 446

      22.7.2 Mixed Type Composition 450

      22.7.3 Reducing the Number of Parameters 454

  22.8 Value Binders 457

      22.8.1 Selecting the Binding 458

      22.8.2 Bound Signature 460

      22.8.3 Argument Selection 462

      22.8.4 Convenience Functions 468

  22.9 Functor Operations: A Complete Implementation 471

  22.10 Afternotes 474

Appendixes   475

A   The One-Definition Rule   475

A.1   Translation Units 475

A.2   Declarations and Definitions 476

A.3   The One-Definition Rule in Detail 477

    A.3.1   One-per-Program Constraints 477

    A.3.2   One-per-Translation Unit Constraints 479

    A.3.3   Cross-Translation Unit Equivalence Constraints 481

B   Overload Resolution   487

B.1   When Does Overload Resolution Kick In? 488

B.2   Simplified Overload Resolution 488

    B.2.1   The Implied Argument for Member Functions 490

    B.2.2   Refining the Perfect Match 492

B.3   Overloading Details 493

    B.3.1   Prefer Nontemplates 493

    B.3.2   Conversion Sequences 494

    B.3.3   Pointer Conversions 494

    B.3.4   Functors and Surrogate Functions 496

    B.3.5   Other Overloading Contexts 497

Bibliography   499

Newsgroups 499

Books and Web Sites 500

Glossary   507

Index   517

Preface

The idea of templates in C++ is more than ten years old. C++ templates were already documented in 1990 in the "Annotated C++ Reference Manual" or so-called "ARM" (see [*EllisStroustrupARM*]) and they had been described before that in more specialized publications. However, well over a decade later we found a dearth of literature that concentrates on the fundamental concepts and advanced techniques of this fascinating, complex, and powerful C++ feature. We wanted to address this issue and decided to write *the* book about templates (with perhaps a slight lack of humility).

However, we approached the task with different backgrounds and with different intentions. David, an experienced compiler implementer and member of the C++ Standard Committee Core Language Working Group, was interested in an exact and detailed description of all the power (and problems) of templates. Nico, an "ordinary" application programmer and member of the C++ Standard Committee Library Working Group, was interested in understanding all the techniques of templates in a way that he could use and benefit from them. In addition, we both wanted to share this knowledge with you, the reader, and the whole community to help to avoid further misunderstanding, confusion, or apprehension.

As a consequence, you will see both conceptual introductions with day-to-day examples and detailed descriptions of the exact behavior of templates. Starting from the basic principles of templates and working up to the "art of template programming," you will discover (or rediscover) techniques such as static polymorphism, policy classes, metaprogramming, and expression templates. You will also gain a deeper understanding of the C++ standard library, in which almost all code involves templates.

We learned a lot and we had much fun while writing this book. We hope you will have the same experience while reading it. Enjoy!

Acknowledgments

This book presents ideas, concepts, solutions, and examples from many sources. We'd like to thank all the people and companies who helped and supported us during the past few years.

First, we'd like to thank all the reviewers and everyone else who gave us their opinion on early manuscripts. These people endow the book with a quality it would never have had without their input. The reviewers for this book were Kyle Blaney, Thomas Gschwind, Dennis Mancl, Patrick Mc Killen, and Jan Christiaan van Winkel. Special thanks to Dietmar Kühl, who meticulously reviewed and edited the whole book. His feedback was an incredible contribution to the quality of this book.

We'd also like to thank all the people and companies who gave us the opportunity to test our examples on different platforms with different compilers. Many thanks to the Edison Design Group for their great compiler and their support. It was a big help during the standardization process and the writing of this book. Many thanks also go to all the developers of the free GNU and egcs compilers (Jason Merrill was especially responsive), and to Microsoft for an evaluation version of Visual C++ (Jonathan Caves, Herb Sutter, and Jason Shirk were our contacts there).

Much of the existing "C++ wisdom" was collectively created by the online C++ community. Most of it comes from the moderated Usenet groups `comp.lang.c++.moderated` and `comp.std.c++`. We are therefore especially indebted to the active moderators of those groups, who keep the discussions useful and constructive. We also much appreciate all those who over the years have taken the time to describe and explain their ideas for us all to share.

The Addison-Wesley team did another great job. We are most indebted to Debbie Lafferty (our editor) for her gentle prodding, good advice, and relentless hard work in support of this book. Thanks also go to Tyrrell Albaugh, Bunny Ames, Melanie Buck, Jacquelyn Doucette, Chanda Leary-Coutu, Catherine Ohala, and Marty Rabinowitz. We're grateful as well to Marina Lang, who first sponsored this book within Addison-Wesley. Susan Winer contributed an early round of editing that helped shape our later work.

Nico's Acknowledgments

My first personal thanks go with a lot of kisses to my family: Ulli, Lucas, Anica, and Frederic supported this book with a lot of patience, consideration, and encouragement.

In addition, I want to thank David. His expertise turned out to be incredible, but his patience was even better (sometimes I ask really silly questions). It is a lot of fun to work with him.

David's Acknowledgments

My wife, Karina, has been instrumental in this book coming to a conclusion, and I am immensely grateful for the role that she plays in my life. Writing "in your spare time" quickly becomes erratic when many other activities vie for your schedule. Karina helped me to manage that schedule, taught me to say "no" in order to make the time needed to make regular progress in the writing process, and above all was amazingly supportive of this project. I thank God every day for her friendship and love.

I'm also tremendously grateful to have been able to work with Nico. Besides his directly visible contributions to the text, his experience and discipline moved us from my pitiful doodling to a well-organized production.

John "Mr. Template" Spicer and Steve "Mr. Overload" Adamczyk are wonderful friends and colleagues, but in my opinion they are (together) also the ultimate authority regarding the core C++ language. They clarified many of the trickier issues described in this book, and should you find an error in the description of a C++ language element, it is almost certainly attributable to my failing to consult with them.

Finally, I want to express my appreciation to those who were supportive of this project without necessarily contributing to it directly (the power of cheer cannot be understated). First, my parents: Their love for me and their encouragement made all the difference. And then there are the numerous friends inquiring: "How is the book going?" They, too, were a source of encouragement: Michael Beckmann, Brett and Julie Beene, Jarran Carr, Simon Chang, Ho and Sarah Cho, Christophe De Dinechin, Ewa Deelman, Neil Eberle, Sassan Hazeghi, Vikram Kumar, Jim and Lindsay Long, R.J. Morgan, Mike Puritano, Ragu Raghavendra, Jim and Phuong Sharp, Gregg Vaughn, and John Wiegley.

Chapter 1

About This Book

Although templates have been part of C++ for well over a decade (and available in various forms for almost as long), they still lead to misunderstanding, misuse, or controversy. At the same time, they are increasingly found to be powerful instruments for the development of cleaner, faster, and smarter software. Indeed, templates have become the cornerstone of several new C++ programming paradigms.

Yet we have found that most existing books and articles are at best superficial in their treatment of the theory and application of C++ templates. Even those few books that do an excellent job of surveying various template-based techniques fail to describe accurately how these techniques are supported by the language. As a result, beginning and advanced C++ programmers alike are finding themselves wrestling with templates, attempting to decide why their code is handled unexpectedly.

This observation was one of the main motivations for us to write this book. However, we both came up with the topic independently and had somewhat distinct approaches in mind:

- David's goal was to provide a complete reference to the details of the C++ template language mechanism and the major advanced programming techniques that templates enable. His focus was on precision and completeness.
- Nico's interest was to have a book that helps himself and others use templates in the day-to-day life of a programmer. This implies that the book should present the material in an intuitive manner, while dealing with the practical aspects of templates.

In a sense, you could see us as a scientist-engineer pair: We both deal with the same discipline, but our emphasis is somewhat different (with much overlap, of course).

Addison-Wesley brought us together and as a result you get what we think is a solid combination of a careful C++ template tutorial with a detailed reference. The tutorial aspect covers not only an introduction to the language elements, but also aims at developing a sense for design methods that lead to practical solutions. Similarly, the book is not only a reference for the details of C++ template syntax and semantics, but also a compendium of well-known and lesser known idioms and techniques.

1.1   What You Should Know Before Reading This Book

To get the most from this book you should already know C++: We describe the details of a particular language feature, not the fundamentals of the language itself. You should be familiar with the concepts of classes and inheritance, and you should be able to write C++ programs using components such as IOstreams and containers from the C++ standard library. In addition, we review more subtle issues as the need arises, even when such issues aren't directly related to templates. This ensures that the text is accessible to experts and intermediate programmers alike.

We deal mostly with the C++ language as standardized in 1998 (see [*Standard98*]), plus the clarifications provided by the C++ Standardization Committee in its first *technical corrigendum* (see [*Standard02*]). If you feel your understanding of the basics of C++ is rusty or out-of-date, we recommend [*StroustrupC++PL*], [*JosuttisOOP*], and [*JosuttisStdLib*] to refresh your knowledge. These books are excellent introductions to the modern language and its standard library. Additional publications are listed in Appendix B.3.5.

1.2   Overall Structure of the Book

Our goal is to provide the information necessary for starting to use templates and benefit from their power, as well as to provide information that will enable experienced programmers to push the limits of the state-of-the-art. To achieve this, we decided to organize our text in *parts*:

- Part I introduces the basic concepts underlying templates. It is written in a tutorial style.
- Part II presents the language details and is a handy reference to template-related constructs.
- Part III explains fundamental design techniques supported by C++ templates. They range from near-trivial ideas to sophisticated idioms that may not have been published elsewhere.
- Part IV builds on the previous two parts and adds a discussion of various popular applications for templates.

Each of these parts consists of several chapters. In addition, we provide a few appendixes that cover material not exclusively related to templates (for example, an overview of overload resolution in C++).

The chapters of Part I are meant to be read in sequence. For example, Chapter 3 builds on the material covered in Chapter 2. In the other parts, however, the connection between chapters is considerably looser. For example, it would be entirely natural to read the chapter about *functors* (Chapter 22) before the chapter about *smart pointers* (Chapter 20).

Last, we provide a rather complete index that encourages additional ways to read this book out of sequence.

1.3   How to Read This Book

If you are a C++ programmer who wants to learn or review the concepts of templates, carefully read Part I, The Basics. Even if you're quite familiar with templates already, it may help to skim through this part quickly to familiarize yourself with the style and terminology that we use. This part also covers some of the logistical aspects of organizing your source code when it contains templates.

Depending on your preferred learning method, you may decide to absorb the many details of templates in Part II, or instead you could read about practical coding techniques in Part III (and refer back to Part II for the more subtle language issues). The latter approach is probably particularly useful if you bought this book with concrete day-to-day challenges in mind. Part IV is somewhat similar to Part III, but the emphasis is on understanding how templates can contribute to specific applications rather than design techniques. It is therefore probably best to familiarize yourself with the topics of Part III before delving into Part IV.

The appendixes contain much useful information that is often referred to in the main text. We have also tried to make them interesting in their own right.

In our experience, the best way to learn something new is to look at examples. Therefore, you'll find a lot of examples throughout the book. Some are just a few lines of code illustrating an abstract concept, whereas others are complete programs that provide a concrete application of the material. The latter kind of examples will be introduced by a C++ comment describing the file containing the program code. You can find these files at the Web site of this book at `http://www.josuttis.com/tmplbook/`.

1.4   Some Remarks About Programming Style

C++ programmers use different programming styles, and so do we: The usual questions about where to put whitespace, delimiters (braces, parentheses), and so forth came up. We tried to be consistent in general, although we occasionally make concessions to the topic at hand. For example, in tutorial sections we may prefer generous use of whitespace and concrete names to help visualize code, whereas in more advanced discussions a more compact style could be more appropriate.

We do want to draw your attention to one slightly uncommon decision regarding the declaration of types, parameters, and variables. Clearly, several styles are possible:

```
void foo (const int &x);
void foo (const int& x);
void foo (int const &x);
void foo (int const& x);
```

Although it is a bit less common, we decided to use the order `int const` rather than `const int` for "constant integer." We have two reasons for this. First, it provides for an easier answer to the question, "*What* is constant?" It's always what is in front of the `const` qualifier. Indeed, although

```
const int N = 100;
```

is equivalent to

```
int const N = 100;
```

there is no equivalent form for

```
int* const bookmark;        // the pointer cannot change, but the
                            // value pointed to can change
```

that would place the `const` qualifier before the pointer operator `*`. In this example, it is the pointer itself that is constant, not the `int` to which it points.

Our second reason has to do with a syntactical substitution principle that is very common when dealing with templates. Consider the following two type definitions[1]:

```
typedef char* CHARS;
typedef CHARS const CPTR;   // constant pointer to chars
```

The meaning of the second declaration is preserved when we textually replace `CHARS` with what it stands for:

```
typedef char* const CPTR;   // constant pointer to chars
```

However, if we write `const` *before* the type it qualifies, this principle doesn't apply. Indeed, consider the alternative to our first two type definitions presented earlier:

```
typedef char* CHARS;
typedef const CHARS CPTR;   // constant pointer to chars
```

Textually replacing `CHARS` results in a type with a different meaning:

```
typedef const char* CPTR;   // pointer to constant chars
```

The same observation applies to the `volatile` specifier, of course.

Regarding whitespaces, we decided to put the space between the ampersand and the parameter name:

```
void foo (int const& x);
```

By doing this, we emphasize the separation between the parameter type and the parameter name. This is admittedly more confusing for declarations such as

```
char* a, b;
```

where, according to the rules inherited from C, `a` is a pointer but `b` is an ordinary `char`. To avoid such confusion, we simply avoid declaring multiple entities in this way.

This is not a book about the C++ standard library, but we do make use of that library in some of our examples. In general, we use the C++-specific headers (for example, `<iostream>` rather than `<stdio.h>`). The exception is `<stddef.h>`. We use it instead of `<cstddef>` and therefore do not qualify `size_t` and `ptrdiff_t` with the `std::` prefix because this is still more portable and there is no advantage in using `std::size_t` instead of `size_t`.

---

[1] Note that in C++ a type definition defines a "type alias" rather than a new type. For example:
```
typedef int Length; // define Length as an alias for int
int i = 42;
Length l = 88;
i = l;              // OK
l = i;              // OK
```

1.5 The Standard versus Reality

The C++ standard has been available since late 1998. However, it was not until 2002 that a publically available compiler could make the claim to "conform fully to the standard." Thus, compilers still differ in their support of the language. Several will compile most of the code in this book, but a few fairly popular compilers may not be able to handle many of our examples. We often present alternative techniques that may help cobble together a full or partial solution for these substandard C++ implementations, but some techniques are currently beyond their reach. Still, we expect that this problem will largely be resolved as programmers everywhere demand standard support from their vendors.

Even so, the C++ programming language is likely to evolve as time passes. Already the experts of the C++ community (regardless of whether they participate in the C++ Standardization Committee) are discussing various ways to improve the language, and several candidate improvements affect templates. Chapter 13 presents some trends in this area.

1.6 Example Code and Additional Informations

You can access all example programs and find more information about this book from its Web site, which has the following URL:

```
http://www.josuttis.com/tmplbook
```

Also, you can find a lot of additional information about this topic at David Vandevoorde's Web site at `http://www.vandevoorde.com/Templates` and on the Web in general. See the Bibliography on page 499 for suggestions on where to start.

1.7 Feedback

We welcome your constructive input—both the negative and the positive. We worked very hard to bring you what we hope you'll find to be an excellent book. However, at some point we had to stop writing, reviewing, and tweaking so we could "release the product." You may therefore find errors, inconsistencies, and presentations that could be improved, or topics that are missing altogether. Your feedback gives us a chance to inform all readers through the book's Web site and to improve any subsequent editions.

The best way to reach us is by e-mail:

```
tmplbook@josuttis.com
```

Be sure to check the book's Web site for the currently known errata before submitting reports.

Many thanks.

Part I

The Basics

This part introduces the general concept and language features of C++ templates. It starts with a discussion of the general goals and concepts by showing examples of function templates and class templates. It continues with some additional fundamental template techniques such as nontype template parameters, the keyword `typename`, and member templates. It ends with some general hints regarding the use and application of templates in practice.

This introduction to templates is also partially used in Nicolai M. Josuttis's book *Object-Oriented Programming in C++*, published by John Wiley and Sons Ltd, ISBN 0-470-84399-3. This book teaches all language features of C++ and the C++ standard library and explains their practical usage in a step-by-step tutorial.

Why Templates?

C++ requires us to declare variables, functions, and most other kinds of entities using specific types. However, a lot of code looks the same for different types. Especially if you implement algorithms, such as *quicksort*, or if you implement the behavior of data structures, such as a linked list or a binary tree for different types, the code looks the same despite the type used.

If your programming language doesn't support a special language feature for this, you only have bad alternatives:

1. You can implement the same behavior again and again for each type that needs this behavior.
2. You can write general code for a common base type such as `Object` or `void*`.
3. You can use special preprocessors.

If you come from C, Java, or similar languages, you probably have done some or all of this before. However, each of these approaches has its drawbacks:

1. If you implement a behavior again and again, you reinvent the wheel. You make the same mistakes and you tend to avoid complicated but better algorithms because they lead to even more mistakes.

2. If you write general code for a common base class you lose the benefit of type checking. In addition, classes may be required to be derived from special base classes, which makes it more difficult to maintain your code.

3. If you use a special preprocessor such as the C/C++ preprocessor, you lose the advantage of formatted source code. Code is replaced by some "stupid text replacement mechanism" that has no idea of scope and types.

Templates are a solution to this problem without these drawbacks. They are functions or classes that are written for one or more types not yet specified. When you use a template, you pass the types as arguments, explicitly or implicitly. Because templates are language features, you have full support of type checking and scope.

In today's programs, templates are used a lot. For example, inside the C++ standard library almost all code is template code. The library provides sort algorithms to sort objects and values of a specified type, data structures (so-called *container classes*) to manage elements of a specified type, strings for which the type of a character is parameterized, and so on. However, this is only the beginning. Templates also allow us to parameterize behavior, to optimize code, and to parameterize information. This is covered in later chapters. Let's first start with some simple templates.

Chapter 2

Function Templates

This chapter introduces function templates. Function templates are functions that are parameterized so that they represent a family of functions.

2.1 A First Look at Function Templates

Function templates provide a functional behavior that can be called for different types. In other words, a function template represents a family of functions. The representation looks a lot like an ordinary function, except that some elements of the function are left undetermined: These elements are parameterized. To illustrate, let's look at a simple example.

2.1.1 Defining the Template

The following is a function template that returns the maximum of two values:

```cpp
// basics/max.hpp

template <typename T>
inline T const& max (T const& a, T const& b)
{
    // if a < b then use b else use a
    return  a < b ? b : a;
}
```

This template definition specifies a family of functions that returns the maximum of two values, which are passed as function parameters a and b. The type of these parameters is left open as *template parameter* T. As seen in this example, template parameters must be announced with syntax of the following form:

```
template < comma-separated-list-of-parameters >
```

In our example, the list of parameters is `typename` T. Note how the less-than and the greater-than symbols are used as brackets; we refer to these as *angle brackets*. The keyword `typename` introduces a so-called *type parameter*. This is by far the most common kind of template parameter in C++ programs, but other parameters are possible, and we discuss them later (see Chapter 4).

Here, the type parameter is T. You can use any identifier as a parameter name, but using T is the convention. The type parameter represents an arbitrary type that is specified by the caller when the caller calls the function. You can use any type (fundamental type, class, and so on) as long as it provides the operations that the template uses. In this case, type T has to support operator < because a and b are compared using this operator.

For historical reasons, you can also use `class` instead of `typename` to define a type parameter. The keyword `typename` came relatively late in the evolution of the C++ language. Prior to that, the keyword `class` was the only way to introduce a type parameter, and this remains a valid way to do so. Hence, the template `max()` could be defined equivalently as follows:

```
template <class T>
inline T const& max (T const& a, T const& b)
{
    // if a < b then use b else use a
    return  a < b ? b : a;
}
```

Semantically there is no difference in this context. So, even if you use `class` here, *any* type may be used for template arguments. However, because this use of `class` can be misleading (not only class types can be substituted for T), you should prefer the use of `typename` in this context. Note also that unlike class type declarations, the keyword `struct` cannot be used in place of `typename` when declaring type parameters.

2.1.2   Using the Template

The following program shows how to use the `max()` function template:

```
// basics/max.cpp

#include <iostream>
#include <string>
#include "max.hpp"

int main()
{
    int i = 42;
    std::cout << "max(7,i):   " << ::max(7,i) << std::endl;

    double f1 = 3.4;
```

```
        double f2 = -6.7;
        std::cout << "max(f1,f2): " << ::max(f1,f2) << std::endl;

        std::string s1 = "mathematics";
        std::string s2 = "math";
        std::cout << "max(s1,s2): " << ::max(s1,s2) << std::endl;
    }
```

Inside the program, max() is called three times: once for two ints, once for two doubles, and once for two std::strings. Each time, the maximum is computed. As a result, the program has the following output:

```
    max(7,i):    42
    max(f1,f2): 3.4
    max(s1,s2): mathematics
```

Note that each call of the max() template is qualified with ::. This is to make sure that our max() template is found in the global namespace. There is also an std::max() template in the standard library, which under some circumstances may be called or may lead to ambiguity.[1]

Normally, templates aren't compiled into single entities that can handle any type. Instead, different entities are generated from the template for every type for which the template is used.[2] Thus, max() is compiled for each of these three types. For example, the first call of max()

```
    int i = 42;
    ... max(7,i) ...
```

uses the function template with int as template parameter T. Thus, it has the semantics of calling the following code:

```
    inline int const& max (int const& a, int const& b)
    {
        // if a < b then use b else use a
        return  a < b ? b : a;
    }
```

The process of replacing template parameters by concrete types is called *instantiation*. It results in an *instance* of a template. Unfortunately, the terms *instance* and *instantiate* are used in a different context in object-oriented programming—namely, for a concrete object of a class. However, because this book is about templates, we use this term for the "use" of templates unless otherwise specified.

Note that the mere use of a function template can trigger such an instantiation process. There is no need for the programmer to request the instantiation separately.

---

[1] For example, if one argument type is defined in namespace std (such as strings), according to the lookup rules of C++, both the global and the std max() template are found.

[2] The "one-entity-fits-all" alternative is conceivable but rare in practice. All language rules are based on the concept that different entities are generated.

Similarly, the other calls of `max()` instantiate the `max` template for `double` and `std::string` as if they were declared and implemented individually:

```
const double& max (double const&, double const&);
const std::string& max (std::string const&, std::string const&);
```

An attempt to instantiate a template for a type that doesn't support all the operations used within it will result in a compile-time error. For example:

```
std::complex<float> c1, c2;      // doesn't provide operator <
...
max(c1,c2);                       // ERROR at compile time
```

Thus, templates are compiled twice:

1. Without instantiation, the template code itself is checked for correct syntax. Syntax errors are discovered, such as missing semicolons.

2. At the time of instantiation, the template code is checked to ensure that all calls are valid. Invalid calls are discovered, such as unsupported function calls.

This leads to an important problem in the handling of templates in practice: When a function template is used in a way that triggers its instantiation, a compiler will (at some point) need to see that template's definition. This breaks the usual compile and link distinction for ordinary functions, when the declaration of a function is sufficient to compile its use. Methods of handling this problem are discussed in Chapter 6. For the moment, let's take the simplest approach: Each template is implemented inside a header file by using inline functions.

2.2   Argument Deduction

When we call a function template such as `max()` for some arguments, the template parameters are determined by the arguments we pass. If we pass two `int`s to the parameter types `T const&`, the C++ compiler must conclude that `T` must be `int`. Note that no automatic type conversion is allowed here. Each `T` must match exactly. For example:

```
template <typename T>
inline T const& max (T const& a, T const& b);
...
max(4,7)      // OK: T is int for both arguments
max(4,4.2)    // ERROR: first T is int, second T is double
```

There are three ways to handle such an error:

1. Cast the arguments so that they both match:
   ```
   max(static_cast<double>(4),4.2)      // OK
   ```

2. Specify (or qualify) explicitly the type of T:
   ```
   max<double>(4,4.2)                    // OK
   ```

3. Specify that the parameters may have different types.

For a detailed discussion of these topics, see the next section.

2.3   Template Parameters

Function templates have two kinds of parameters:

1. *Template parameters*, which are declared in angle brackets before the function template name:

       template <typename T>   // T *is template parameter*

2. *Call parameters*, which are declared in parentheses after the function template name:

       ... max (T const& a, T const& b)   // a *and* b *are call parameters*

You may have as many template parameters as you like. However, in function templates (unlike class templates) no default template arguments can be specified.[3] For example, you could define the max() template for call parameters of two different types:

```
template <typename T1, typename T2>
inline T1 max (T1 const& a, T2 const& b)
{
    return  a < b ? b : a;
}
...
```

max(4,4.2)   // *OK, but type of first argument defines return type*

This may appear to be a good method to enable passing two call parameters of different types to the max() template, but in this example it has drawbacks. The problem is that the return type must be declared. If you use one of the parameter types, the argument for the other parameter might get converted to this type, regardless of the caller's intention. C++ does not provide a means to specify choosing "the more powerful type" (however, you can provide this feature by some tricky template programming, see Section 15.2.4 on page 271). Thus, depending on the call argument order the maximum of 42 and 66.66 might be the double 66.66 or the int 66. Another drawback is that converting the type of the second parameter into the return type creates a new, local temporary object. As a consequence, you cannot return the result by reference.[4] In our example, therefore, the return type has to be T1 instead of T1 const&.

Because the types of the call parameters are constructed from the template parameters, template and call parameters are usually related. We call this concept *function template argument deduction*. It allows you to call a function template as you would an ordinary function.

However, as mentioned earlier, you can instantiate a template explicitly for certain types:

---

[3] This restriction is mainly the result of a historical glitch in the development of function templates. There are probably no technical hindrances to implementing such a feature in modern C++ compilers, and in the future it will probably be available (see Section 13.3 on page 207).

[4] You are not allowed to return values by reference if they are local to a function because you'd return something that doesn't exist when the program leaves the scope of this function.

```
template <typename T>
inline T const& max (T const& a, T const& b);

...

max<double>(4,4.2)        // instantiate T as double
```

In cases when there is no connection between template and call parameters and when template parameters cannot be determined, you must specify the template argument explicitly with the call. For
example, you can introduce a third template argument type to define the return type of a function
template:

```
template <typename T1, typename T2, typename RT>
inline RT max (T1 const& a, T2 const& b);
```

However, template argument deduction does not match up return types,[5] and RT does not appear in
the types of the function call parameters. Therefore, RT cannot be deduced. As a consequence, you
have to specify the template argument list explicitly. For example:

```
template <typename T1, typename T2, typename RT>
inline RT max (T1 const& a, T2 const& b);

...

max<int,double,double>(4,4.2)      // OK, but tedious
```

So far, we have looked at cases in which either all or none of the function template arguments were
mentioned explicitly. Another approach is to specify only the first arguments explicitly and to allow
the deduction process to derive the rest. In general, you must specify all the argument types up to
the last argument type that cannot be determined implicitly. Thus, if you change the order of the
template parameters in our example, the caller needs to specify only the return type:

```
template <typename RT, typename T1, typename T2>
inline RT max (T1 const& a, T2 const& b);

...

max<double>(4,4.2)       // OK: return type is double
```

In this example, the call to max<double> explicitly sets RT to double, but the parameters T1 and T2
are deduced to be int and double from the arguments.

Note that all of these modified versions of max() don't lead to significant advantages. For the
one-parameter version you can already specify the parameter (and return) type if two arguments of a
different type are passed. Thus, it's a good idea to keep it simple and use the one-parameter version
of max() (as we do in the following sections when discussing other template issues).

See Chapter 11 for details of the deduction process.

---

[5] Deduction can be seen as part of overload resolution—a process that is not based on selection of return types
either. The sole exception is the return type of conversion operator members.

2.4 Overloading Function Templates

Like ordinary functions, function templates can be overloaded. That is, you can have different function definitions with the same function name so that when that name is used in a function call, a C++ compiler must decide which one of the various candidates to call. The rules for this decision may become rather complicated, even without templates. In this section we discuss overloading when templates are involved. If you are not familiar with the basic rules of overloading without templates, please look at Appendix B, where we provide a reasonably detailed survey of the overload resolution rules.

The following short program illustrates overloading a function template:

```cpp
// basics/max2.cpp

// maximum of two int values
inline int const& max (int const& a, int const& b)
{
    return  a < b ? b : a;
}


// maximum of two values of any type
template <typename T>
inline T const& max (T const& a, T const& b)
{
    return  a < b ? b : a;
}


// maximum of three values of any type
template <typename T>
inline T const& max (T const& a, T const& b, T const& c)
{
    return ::max (::max(a,b), c);
}


int main()
{
    ::max(7, 42, 68);       // calls the template for three arguments
    ::max(7.0, 42.0);       // calls max<double> (by argument deduction)
    ::max('a', 'b');        // calls max<char> (by argument deduction)
    ::max(7, 42);           // calls the nontemplate for two ints
    ::max<>(7, 42);         // calls max<int> (by argument deduction)
    ::max<double>(7, 42);   // calls max<double> (no argument deduction)
    ::max('a', 42.7);       // calls the nontemplate for two ints
}
```

As this example shows, a nontemplate function can coexist with a function template that has the same name and can be instantiated with the same type. All other factors being equal, the overload resolution process normally prefers this nontemplate over one generated from the template. The fourth call falls under this rule:

    ::max(7, 42)   // both int values match the nontemplate function perfectly

If the template can generate a function with a better match, however, then the template is selected. This is demonstrated by the second and third call of max():

    ::max(7.0, 42.0)   // calls the max<double> (by argument deduction)
    ::max('a', 'b')   // calls the max<char> (by argument deduction)

It is also possible to specify explicitly an empty template argument list. This syntax indicates that only templates may resolve a call, but all the template parameters should be deduced from the call arguments:

    ::max<>(7, 42)   // calls max<int> (by argument deduction)

Because automatic type conversion is not considered for templates but is considered for ordinary functions, the last call uses the nontemplate function (while 'a' and 42.7 both are converted to int):

    ::max('a', 42.7)   // only the nontemplate function allows different argument types

A more useful example would be to overload the maximum template for pointers and ordinary C-strings:

    // basics/max3.cpp

```
#include <iostream>
#include <cstring>
#include <string>


// maximum of two values of any type
template <typename T>
inline T const& max (T const& a, T const& b)
{
    return  a < b  ?  b  : a;
}


// maximum of two pointers
template <typename T>
inline T* const& max (T* const& a, T* const& b)
{
    return  *a < *b  ?  b  : a;
}
```

```cpp
// maximum of two C-strings
inline char const* const& max (char const* const& a,
                               char const* const& b)
{
    return  std::strcmp(a,b) < 0 ? b : a;
}

int main ()
{
    int a=7;
    int b=42;
    ::max(a,b);         // max() for two values of type int

    std::string s="hey";
    std::string t="you";
    ::max(s,t);         // max() for two values of type std::string

    int* p1 = &b;
    int* p2 = &a;
    ::max(p1,p2);       // max() for two pointers

    char const* s1 = "David";
    char const* s2 = "Nico";
    ::max(s1,s2);       // max() for two C-strings
}
```

Note that in all overloaded implementations, we pass all arguments by reference. In general, it is a good idea not to change more than necessary when overloading function templates. You should limit your changes to the number of parameters or to specifying template parameters explicitly. Otherwise, unexpected effects may happen. For example, if you overload the `max()` template, which passes the arguments by reference, for two C-strings passed by value, you can't use the three-argument version to compute the maximum of three C-strings:

```cpp
// basics/max3a.cpp

#include <iostream>
#include <cstring>
#include <string>

// maximum of two values of any type (call-by-reference)
template <typename T>
```

```
inline T const& max (T const& a, T const& b)
{
    return  a < b  ?  b : a;
}
```

```
// maximum of two C-strings (call-by-value)
inline char const* max (char const* a, char const* b)
{
    return  std::strcmp(a,b) < 0  ?  b : a;
}
```

```
// maximum of three values of any type (call-by-reference)
template <typename T>
inline T const& max (T const& a, T const& b, T const& c)
{
    return max (max(a,b), c);   // error, if max(a,b) uses call-by-value
}
```

```
int main ()
{
    ::max(7, 42, 68);      // OK

    const char* s1 = "frederic";
    const char* s2 = "anica";
    const char* s3 = "lucas";
    ::max(s1, s2, s3);     // ERROR

}
```

The problem is that if you call max() for three C-strings, the statement

```
    return max (max(a,b), c);
```

becomes an error. This is because for C-strings, max(a,b) creates a new, temporary local value that may be returned by the function by reference.

This is only one example of code that might behave differently than expected as a result of detailed overload resolution rules. For example, the fact that not all overloaded functions are visible when a corresponding function call is made may or may not matter. In fact, defining a three-argument version of max() without having seen the declaration of a special two-argument version of max() for ints causes the two-argument template to be used by the three-argument version:

```
// basics/max4.cpp
```

```
// maximum of two values of any type
template <typename T>
inline T const& max (T const& a, T const& b)
{
    return  a < b ? b : a;
}
```

```
// maximum of three values of any type
template <typename T>
inline T const& max (T const& a, T const& b, T const& c)
{
    return max (max(a,b), c);   // uses the template version even for ints
}                               // because the following declaration comes
                                // too late:
// maximum of two int values
inline int const& max (int const& a, int const& b)
{
    return  a < b ? b : a;
}
```

We discuss details in Section 9.2 on page 121, but for the moment, as a rule of thumb you should always have all overloaded versions of a function declared before the function is called.

2.5   Summary

- Function templates define a family of functions for different template arguments.
- When you pass template arguments, function templates are instantiated for these argument types.
- You can explicitly qualify the template parameters.
- You can overload function templates.
- When you overload function templates, limit your changes to specifying template parameters explicitly.
- Make sure you see all overloaded versions of function templates before you call them.

Chapter 3

Class Templates

Similar to functions, classes can also be parameterized with one or more types. Container classes, which are used to manage elements of a certain type, are a typical example of this feature. By using class templates, you can implement such container classes while the element type is still open. In this chapter we use a stack as an example of a class template.

3.1   Implementation of Class Template `Stack`

As we did with function templates, we declare and define class Stack<> in a header file as follows (we discuss the separation of declaration and definition in different files in Chapter 6):

```
// basics/stack1.hpp

#include <vector>
#include <stdexcept>

template <typename T>
class Stack {
  private:
    std::vector<T> elems;       // elements

  public:
    void push(T const&);        // push element
    void pop();                 // pop element
    T top() const;              // return top element
    bool empty() const {        // return whether the stack is empty
        return elems.empty();
    }
};
```

```
template <typename T>
void Stack<T>::push (T const& elem)
{
    elems.push_back(elem);      // append copy of passed elem
}


template<typename T>
void Stack<T>::pop ()
{
    if (elems.empty()) {
        throw std::out_of_range("Stack<>::pop(): empty stack");
    }
    elems.pop_back();               // remove last element
}


template <typename T>
T Stack<T>::top () const
{
    if (elems.empty()) {
        throw std::out_of_range("Stack<>::top(): empty stack");
    }
    return elems.back();        // return copy of last element
}
```

As you can see, the class template is implemented by using a class template of the C++ standard library: vector<>. As a result, we don't have to implement memory management, copy constructor, and assignment operator, so we can concentrate on the interface of this class template.

3.1.1   Declaration of Class Templates

Declaring class templates is similar to declaring function templates: Before the declaration, a statement declares an identifier as a type parameter. Again, T is usually used as an identifier:

```
template <typename T>
class Stack {
    ...
};
```

Here again, the keyword `class` can be used instead of `typename`:

```
template <class T>
class Stack {
    ...
};
```

Inside the class template, T can be used just like any other type to declare members and member functions. In this example, T is used to declare the type of the elements as vector of Ts, to declare push() as a member function that gets a constant T reference as an argument, and to declare top() as a function that returns a T:

```
template <typename T>
class Stack {
  private:
    std::vector<T> elems;     // elements

  public:
    Stack();                  // constructor
    void push(T const&);      // push element
    void pop();               // pop element
    T top() const;            // return top element
};
```

The type of this class is Stack<T>, with T being a template parameter. Thus, you have to use Stack<T> whenever you use the type of this class in a declaration. If, for example, you have to declare your own copy constructor and assignment operator, it looks like this[1]:

```
template <typename T>
class Stack {
    ...
    Stack (Stack<T> const&);                  // copy constructor
    Stack<T>& operator= (Stack<T> const&);    // assignment operator
    ...
};
```

However, when the name and not the type of the class is required, only Stack has to be used. This is the case when you specify the name of the class, the constructors, and the destructor.

---

[1] According to the standard, there are some exceptions to this rule (see Section 9.2.3 on page 126). However, to be sure, you should always write the full type when the type is required.

3.1.2   Implementation of Member Functions

To define a member function of a class template, you have to specify that it is a function template, and you have to use the full type qualification of the class template. Thus, the implementation of the member function push() for type Stack<T> looks like this:

```
template <typename T>
void Stack<T>::push (T const& elem)
{
    elems.push_back(elem);      // append copy of passed elem
}
```

In this case, push_back() of the element vector is called, which appends the element at the end of the vector.

Note that pop_back() of a vector removes the last element but doesn't return it. The reason for this behavior is exception safety. It is impossible to implement a completely exception-safe version of pop() that returns the removed element (this topic was first discussed by Tom Cargill in [*CargillExceptionSafety*] and is discussed as Item 10 in [*SutterExceptional*]). However, ignoring this danger, we could implement a pop() that returns the element just removed. To do this, we simply use T to declare a local variable of the element type:

```
template<typename T>
T Stack<T>::pop ()
{
    if (elems.empty()) {
        throw std::out_of_range("Stack<>::pop(): empty stack");
    }
    T elem = elems.back();      // save copy of last element
    elems.pop_back();           // remove last element
    return elem;                // return copy of saved element
}
```

Because back() (which returns the last element) and pop_back() (which removes the last element) have undefined behavior when there is no element in the vector, we have to check whether the stack is empty. If it is empty, we throw an exception of type std::out_of_range. This is also done in top(), which returns but does not remove the top element:

```
template<typename T>
T Stack<T>::top () const
{
    if (elems.empty()) {
        throw std::out_of_range("Stack<>::top(): empty stack");
    }
    return elems.back();        // return copy of last element
}
```

Of course, as for any member function, you can also implement member functions of class templates as an inline function inside the class declaration. For example:

```
template <typename T>
class Stack {
    ...
    void push (T const& elem) {
        elems.push_back(elem);      // append copy of passed elem
    }
    ...
};
```

3.2   Use of Class Template `Stack`

To use an object of a class template, you must specify the template arguments explicitly. The following example shows how to use the class template Stack<>:

```
// basics/stack1test.cpp

#include <iostream>
#include <string>
#include <cstdlib>
#include "stack1.hpp"

int main()
{
    try {
        Stack<int>         intStack;       // stack of ints
        Stack<std::string> stringStack;    // stack of strings

        // manipulate int stack
        intStack.push(7);
        std::cout << intStack.top() << std::endl;

        // manipulate string stack
        stringStack.push("hello");
        std::cout << stringStack.top() << std::endl;
        stringStack.pop();
        stringStack.pop();
    }
```

```
    catch (std::exception const& ex) {
        std::cerr << "Exception: " << ex.what() << std::endl;
        return EXIT_FAILURE;    // exit program with ERROR status
    }
}
```

By declaring type `Stack<int>`, int is used as type T inside the class template. Thus, `intStack` is created as an object that uses a vector of `ints` as elements and, for all member functions that are called, code for this type is instantiated. Similarly, by declaring and using `Stack<std::string>`, an object that uses a vector of strings as elements is created, and for all member functions that are called, code for this type is instantiated.

Note that code is instantiated only for *member functions that are called*. For class templates, member functions are instantiated only if they are used. This, of course, saves time and space. It has the additional benefit that you can instantiate a class even for those types that cannot perform all the operations of all the member functions, as long as these member functions are not called. As an example, consider a class in which some member functions use the operator < to sort elements. If you refrain from calling these member functions, you can instantiate the class template for types for which operator < is not defined.

In this example, the default constructor, `push()`, and `top()` are instantiated for both int and strings. However, `pop()` is instantiated only for strings. If a class template has static members, these are instantiated once for each type.

An instantiated class template's type can be used just like any other type. You can qualify it with `const` or `volatile`, or derive array and reference types from it. You can even use it as a type parameter when building another template type:

```
    void foo (Stack<int> const& s)    // parameter s is int stack
    {
        Stack<int> istack[10];        // istack is array of 10 int stacks
        ...
    }
```

By using a type definition, you can make using a class template more convenient:

```
    typedef Stack<int> IntStack;

    void foo (IntStack const& s)     // s is stack of ints
    {
        IntStack istack[10];         // istack is array of 10 stacks of ints
        ...
    }
```

Note that in C++ a type definition defines a "type alias" rather than a new type. Thus, after the type definition

```
typedef Stack<int> IntStack;
```

IntStack and Stack<int> are the same type and can be used for and assigned to each other.

Template arguments may be any type, such as pointers to floats or even stacks of ints:

```
Stack<float*>        floatPtrStack;     // stack of float pointers
Stack<Stack<int> > intStackStack;       // stack of stack of ints
```

The only requirement is that any operation that is called is possible according to this type.

Note that you have to put whitespace between the two closing template brackets. If you don't do this, you are using operator >>, which results in a syntax error:

```
Stack<Stack<int>> intStackStack;     // ERROR: >> is not allowed
```

3.3 Specializations of Class Templates

You can specialize a class template for certain template arguments. Similar to the overloading of function templates (see page 15), specializing class templates allows you to optimize implementations for certain types or to fix a misbehavior of certain types for an instantiation of the class template. However, if you specialize a class template, you must also specialize all member functions. Although it is possible to specialize a single member function, once you have done so, you can no longer specialize the whole class.

To specialize a class template, you have to declare the class with a leading template<> and a specification of the types for which the class template is specialized. The types are used as a template argument and must be specified directly following the name of the class:

```
template<>
class Stack<std::string> {
    ...
};
```

For these specializations, any definition of a member function must be defined as an "ordinary" member function, with each occurrence of T being replaced by the specialized type:

```
void Stack<std::string>::push (std::string const& elem)
{
    elems.push_back(elem);     // append copy of passed elem
}
```

Here is a complete example of a specialization of Stack<> for type std::string:

```
// basics/stack2.hpp

#include <deque>
```

```cpp
#include <string>
#include <stdexcept>
#include "stack1.hpp"

template<>
class Stack<std::string> {
  private:
    std::deque<std::string> elems;   // elements

  public:
    void push(std::string const&);   // push element
    void pop();                      // pop element
    std::string top() const;         // return top element
    bool empty() const {             // return whether the stack is empty
        return elems.empty();
    }
};

void Stack<std::string>::push (std::string const& elem)
{
    elems.push_back(elem);      // append copy of passed elem
}

void Stack<std::string>::pop ()
{
    if (elems.empty()) {
        throw std::out_of_range
                ("Stack<std::string>::pop(): empty stack");
    }
    elems.pop_back();               // remove last element
}

std::string Stack<std::string>::top () const
{
    if (elems.empty()) {
        throw std::out_of_range
                ("Stack<std::string>::top(): empty stack");
    }
    return elems.back();        // return copy of last element
}
```

In this example, a deque instead of a vector is used to manage the elements inside the stack. Although this has no particular benefit here, it does demonstrate that the implementation of a specialization might look very different from the implementation of the primary template.[2]

3.4 Partial Specialization

Class templates can be partially specialized. You can specify special implementations for particular circumstances, but some template parameters must still be defined by the user. For example, for the following class template

```
template <typename T1, typename T2>
class MyClass {
    ...
};
```

the following partial specializations are possible:

```
// partial specialization: both template parameters have same type
template <typename T>
class MyClass<T,T> {
    ...
};
```

```
// partial specialization: second type is int
template <typename T>
class MyClass<T,int> {
    ...
};
```

```
// partial specialization: both template parameters are pointer types
template <typename T1, typename T2>
class MyClass<T1*,T2*> {
    ...
};
```

---

[2] In fact, there is a benefit for using a deque instead of a vector to implement a stack: A deque frees memory when elements are removed, and it can't happen that elements have to be moved as a result of reallocation. However, this is no particular benefit for strings. For this reason it is probably a good idea to use a deque in the primary class template (as is the case in class std::stack<> of the C++ standard library).

The following example shows which template is used by which declaration:

```
MyClass<int,float> mif;      // uses MyClass<T1,T2>
MyClass<float,float> mff;    // uses MyClass<T,T>
MyClass<float,int> mfi;      // uses MyClass<T,int>
MyClass<int*,float*> mp;     // uses MyClass<T1*,T2*>
```

If more than one partial specialization matches equally well, the declaration is ambiguous:

```
MyClass<int,int> m;          // ERROR: matches MyClass<T,T>
                             //        and MyClass<T,int>
MyClass<int*,int*> m;        // ERROR: matches MyClass<T,T>
                             //        and MyClass<T1*,T2*>
```

To resolve the second ambiguity, you can provide an additional partial specialization for pointers of the same type:

```
template <typename T>
class MyClass<T*,T*> {
   ...
};
```

For details, see Section 12.4 on page 200.

3.5   Default Template Arguments

For class templates you can also define default values for template parameters. These values are called *default template arguments*. They may even refer to previous template parameters. For example, in class Stack<> you can define the container that is used to manage the elements as a second template parameter, using std::vector<> as the default value:

```
// basics/stack3.hpp

#include <vector>
#include <stdexcept>

template <typename T, typename CONT = std::vector<T> >
class Stack {
  private:
    CONT elems;                 // elements

  public:
    void push(T const&);        // push element
    void pop();                 // pop element
    T top() const;              // return top element
```

```
        bool empty() const {          // return whether the stack is empty
            return elems.empty();
        }
};

template <typename T, typename CONT>
void Stack<T,CONT>::push (T const& elem)
{
    elems.push_back(elem);      // append copy of passed elem
}

template <typename T, typename CONT>
void Stack<T,CONT>::pop ()
{
    if (elems.empty()) {
        throw std::out_of_range("Stack<>::pop(): empty stack");
    }
    elems.pop_back();           // remove last element
}

template <typename T, typename CONT>
T Stack<T,CONT>::top () const
{
    if (elems.empty()) {
        throw std::out_of_range("Stack<>::top(): empty stack");
    }
    return elems.back();        // return copy of last element
}
```

Note that we now have two template parameters, so each definition of a member function must be defined with these two parameters:

```
template <typename T, typename CONT>
void Stack<T,CONT>::push (T const& elem)
{
    elems.push_back(elem);      // append copy of passed elem
}
```

You can use this stack the same way it was used before. Thus, if you pass a first and only argument as an element type, a vector is used to manage the elements of this type:

```cpp
template <typename T, typename CONT = std::vector<T> >
class Stack {
  private:
    CONT elems;      // elements

  ...
};
```

In addition, you could specify the container for the elements when you declare a Stack object in your program:

```cpp
// basics/stack3test.cpp

#include <iostream>
#include <deque>
#include <cstdlib>
#include "stack3.hpp"

int main()
{
    try {
        // stack of ints:
        Stack<int> intStack;

        // stack of doubles which uses a std::deque<> to manage the elements
        Stack<double,std::deque<double> > dblStack;

        // manipulate int stack
        intStack.push(7);
        std::cout << intStack.top() << std::endl;
        intStack.pop();

        // manipulate double stack
        dblStack.push(42.42);
        std::cout << dblStack.top() << std::endl;
        dblStack.pop();
        dblStack.pop();
    }
    catch (std::exception const& ex) {
        std::cerr << "Exception: " << ex.what() << std::endl;
        return EXIT_FAILURE;   // exit program with ERROR status
    }
}
```

With

```
Stack<double,std::deque<double> >
```

you declare a stack for `doubles` that uses a `std::deque<>` to manage the elements internally.

3.6 Summary

- A class template is a class that is implemented with one or more type parameters left open.
- To use a class template, you pass the open types as template arguments. The class template is then instantiated (and compiled) for these types.
- For class templates, only those member functions that are called are instantiated.
- You can specialize class templates for certain types.
- You can partially specialize class templates for certain types.
- You can define default values for class template parameters. These may refer to previous template parameters.

Chapter 4

Nontype Template Parameters

For function and class templates, template parameters don't have to be types. They can also be ordinary values. As with templates using type parameters, you define code for which a certain detail remains open until the code is used. However, the detail that is open is a value instead of a type. When using such a template, you have to specify this value explicitly. The resulting code then gets instantiated. This chapter illustrates this feature for a new version of the stack class template. In addition, we show an example of nontype function template parameters and discuss some restrictions to this technique.

4.1 Nontype Class Template Parameters

In contrast to the sample implementations of a stack in previous chapters, you can also implement a stack by using a fixed-size array for the elements. An advantage of this method is that the memory management overhead, whether performed by you or by a standard container, is avoided. However, determining the best size for such a stack can be challenging. The smaller the size you specify, the more likely it is that the stack will get full. The larger the size you specify, the more likely it is that memory will be reserved unnecessarily. A good solution is to let the user of the stack specify the size of the array as the maximum size needed for stack elements.

To do this, define the size as a template parameter:

```
// basics/stack4.hpp

#include <stdexcept>

template <typename T, int MAXSIZE>
class Stack {
  private:
    T elems[MAXSIZE];        // elements
    int numElems;            // current number of elements
```

```cpp
  public:
    Stack();                    // constructor
    void push(T const&);        // push element
    void pop();                 // pop element
    T top() const;              // return top element
    bool empty() const {        // return whether the stack is empty
        return numElems == 0;
    }
    bool full() const {         // return whether the stack is full
        return numElems == MAXSIZE;
    }
};

// constructor
template <typename T, int MAXSIZE>
Stack<T,MAXSIZE>::Stack ()
  : numElems(0)                 // start with no elements
{
    // nothing else to do
}

template <typename T, int MAXSIZE>
void Stack<T,MAXSIZE>::push (T const& elem)
{
    if (numElems == MAXSIZE) {
        throw std::out_of_range("Stack<>::push(): stack is full");
    }
    elems[numElems] = elem;     // append element
    ++numElems;                 // increment number of elements
}

template<typename T, int MAXSIZE>
void Stack<T,MAXSIZE>::pop ()
{
    if (numElems <= 0) {
        throw std::out_of_range("Stack<>::pop(): empty stack");
    }
    --numElems;                 // decrement number of elements
}
```

```
template <typename T, int MAXSIZE>
T Stack<T,MAXSIZE>::top () const
{
    if (numElems <= 0) {
        throw std::out_of_range("Stack<>::top(): empty stack");
    }
    return elems[numElems-1];   // return last element
}
```

The new second template parameter, MAXSIZE, is of type int. It specifies the size of the array of stack elements:

```
template <typename T, int MAXSIZE>
class Stack {
  private:
    T elems[MAXSIZE];       // elements
    ...
};
```

In addition, it is used in push() to check whether the stack is full:

```
template <typename T, int MAXSIZE>
void Stack<T,MAXSIZE>::push (T const& elem)
{
    if (numElems == MAXSIZE) {
        throw std::out_of_range("Stack<>::push(): stack is full");
    }
    elems[numElems] = elem;     // append element
    ++numElems;                 // increment number of elements
}
```

To use this class template you have to specify both the element type and the maximum size:

```
// basics/stack4test.cpp

#include <iostream>
#include <string>
#include <cstdlib>
#include "stack4.hpp"

int main()
{
```

```
    try {
        Stack<int,20>         int20Stack;      // stack of up to 20 ints
        Stack<int,40>         int40Stack;      // stack of up to 40 ints
        Stack<std::string,40> stringStack;     // stack of up to 40 strings

        // manipulate stack of up to 20 ints
        int20Stack.push(7);
        std::cout << int20Stack.top() << std::endl;
        int20Stack.pop();

        // manipulate stack of up to 40 strings
        stringStack.push("hello");
        std::cout << stringStack.top() << std::endl;
        stringStack.pop();
        stringStack.pop();
    }
    catch (std::exception const& ex) {
        std::cerr << "Exception: " << ex.what() << std::endl;
        return EXIT_FAILURE;   // exit program with ERROR status
    }
}
```

Note that each template instantiation is its own type. Thus, `int20Stack` and `int40Stack` are two different types, and no implicit or explicit type conversion between them is defined. Thus, one cannot be used instead of the other, and you cannot assign one to the other.

Again, default values for the template parameters can be specified:

```
template <typename T = int, int MAXSIZE = 100>
class Stack {

   ...

};
```

However, from a perspective of good design, this may not be appropriate in this example. Default values should be intuitively correct. But neither type `int` nor a maximum size of 100 seems intuitive for a general stack type. Thus, it is better when the programmer has to specify both values explicitly so that these two attributes are always documented during a declaration.

4.2 Nontype Function Template Parameters

You can also define nontype parameters for function templates. For example, the following function template defines a group of functions for which a certain value can be added:

```
// basics/addval.hpp

template <typename T, int VAL>
T addValue (T const& x)
{
    return x + VAL;
}
```

These kinds of functions are useful if functions or operations in general are used as parameters. For example, if you use the Standard Template Library (STL) you can pass an instantiation of this function template to add a value to each element of a collection:

```
std::transform (source.begin(), source.end(),    // start and end of source
                dest.begin(),                    // start of destination
                addValue<int,5>);                // operation
```

The last argument instantiates the function template `addValue()` to add 5 to an `int` value. The resulting function is called for each element in the source collection `source`, while it is translated into the destination collection `dest`.

Note that there is a problem with this example: `addValue<int,5>` is a function template instance, and function template instances are considered to name a set of overloaded functions (even if the set has only one member). However, according to the current standard, sets of overloaded functions cannot be used for template parameter deduction. Thus, you have to cast to the exact type of the function template argument:

```
std::transform (source.begin(), source.end(),    // start and end of source
                dest.begin(),                    // start of destination
                (int(*)(int const&)) addValue<int,5>);  // operation
```

There is a proposal for the standard to fix this behavior so that the cast isn't necessary in this context (see [*CoreIssue115*] for details), but until then the cast may be necessary to be portable.

4.3   Restrictions for Nontype Template Parameters

Note that nontype template parameters carry some restrictions. In general, they may be constant integral values (including enumerations) or pointers to objects with external linkage.

Floating-point numbers and class-type objects are not allowed as nontype template parameters:

```
template <double VAT>           // ERROR: floating-point values are not
double process (double v)       //            allowed as template parameters
{
    return v * VAT;
}


template <std::string name>     // ERROR: class-type objects are not
class MyClass {                 //            allowed as template parameters
   ...
};
```

Not being able to use floating-point literals (and simple constant floating-point expressions) as template arguments has historical reasons. Because there are no serious technical challenges, this may be supported in future versions of C++ (see Section 13.4 on page 210).

Because string literals are objects with internal linkage (two string literals with the same value but in different modules are different objects), you can't use them as template arguments either:

```
template <char const* name>
class MyClass {
   ...
};


MyClass<"hello"> x;     // ERROR: string literal "hello" not allowed
```

You cannot use a global pointer either:

```
template <char const* name>
class MyClass {
   ...
};


char const* s = "hello";


MyClass<s> x;               // ERROR: s is pointer to object with internal linkage
```

However, the following is possible:

```
template <char const* name>
class MyClass {
   ...
};

extern char const s[] = "hello";

MyClass<s> x;           // OK
```

The global character array s is initialized by "hello" so that s is an object with external linkage.

See Section 8.3.3 on page 109 for a detailed discussion and Section 13.4 on page 209 for a discussion of possible future changes in this area.

4.4 Summary

- Templates can have template parameters that are values rather than types.
- You cannot use floating-point numbers, class-type objects, and pointers to objects with internal linkage (such as string literals) as arguments for nontype template parameters.

Chapter 5

Tricky Basics

This chapter covers some further basic aspects of templates that are relevant to the practical use of templates: an additional use of the typename keyword, defining member functions and nested classes as templates, template template parameters, zero initialization, and some details about using string literals as arguments for function templates. These aspects can be tricky at times, but every day-to-day programmer should have heard of them.

5.1 Keyword `typename`

The keyword typename was introduced during the standardization of C++ to clarify that an identifier inside a template is a type. Consider the following example:

```
template <typename T>
class MyClass {
    typename T::SubType * ptr;
    ...
};
```

Here, the second typename is used to clarify that SubType is a type defined within class T. Thus, ptr is a pointer to the type T::SubType.

Without typename, SubType would be considered a static member. Thus, it would be a concrete variable or object. As a result, the expression

```
T::SubType * ptr
```

would be a multiplication of the static SubType member of class T with ptr.

In general, typename has to be used whenever a name that depends on a template parameter is a type. This is discussed in detail in Section 9.3.2 on page 130.

A typical application of typename is the access to iterators of STL containers in template code:

```cpp
// basics/printcoll.hpp

#include <iostream>

// print elements of an STL container
template <typename T>
void printcoll (T const& coll)
{
    typename T::const_iterator pos;   // iterator to iterate over coll
    typename T::const_iterator end(coll.end());   // end position

    for (pos=coll.begin(); pos!=end; ++pos) {
        std::cout << *pos << ' ';
    }
    std::cout << std::endl;
}
```

In this function template, the call parameter is an STL container of type T. To iterate over all elements of the container, the iterator type of the container is used, which is declared as type `const_iterator` inside each STL container class:

```cpp
class stlcontainer {
  ...
  typedef ...  iterator;        // iterator for read/write access
  typedef ...  const_iterator;  // iterator for read access
  ...
};
```

Thus, to access type `const_iterator` of template type T, you have to qualify it with a leading typename:

```cpp
typename T::const_iterator pos;
```

The `.template` Construct

A very similar problem was discovered after the introduction of `typename`. Consider the following example using the standard `bitset` type:

```cpp
template<int N>
void printBitset (std::bitset<N> const& bs)
{
    std::cout << bs.template to_string<char,char_traits<char>,
                                       allocator<char> >();
}
```

The strange construct in this example is .template. Without that extra use of template, the compiler does not know that the less-than token (<) that follows is not really "less than" but the beginning of a template argument list. Note that this is a problem only if the construct before the period depends on a template parameter. In our example, the parameter bs depends on the template parameter N.

In conclusion, the .template notation (and similar notations such as ->template) should be used only inside templates and only if they follow something that depends on a template parameter. See Section 9.3.3 on page 132 for details.

5.2 Using `this->`

For class templates with base classes, using a name x by itself is not always equivalent to this->x, even though a member x is inherited. For example:

```
template <typename T>
class Base {
  public:
    void bar();
};

template <typename T>
class Derived : Base<T> {
  public:
    void foo() {
        bar();    // calls external bar() or error
    }
};
```

In this example, for resolving the symbol bar inside foo(), bar() defined in Base is *never* considered. Therefore, either you have an error, or another bar() (such as a global bar()) is called.

We discuss this issue in Section 9.4.2 on page 136 in detail. For the moment, as a rule of thumb, we recommend that you always qualify any symbol that is declared in a base that is somehow dependent on a template parameter with this-> or Base<T>::. If you want to avoid all uncertainty, you may consider qualifying all member accesses (in templates).

5.3 Member Templates

Class members can also be templates. This is possible for both nested classes and member functions. The application and advantage of this ability can again be demonstrated with the Stack<> class template. Normally you can assign stacks to each other only when they have the same type, which implies that the elements have the same type. However, you can't assign a stack with elements of any other type, even if there is an implicit type conversion for the element types defined:

```
Stack<int>    intStack1, intStack2;    // stacks for ints
Stack<float> floatStack;               // stack for floats
...
intStack1 = intStack2;    // OK: stacks have same type
floatStack = intStack1;   // ERROR: stacks have different types
```

The default assignment operator requires that both sides of the assignment operator have the same type, which is not the case if stacks have different element types.

By defining an assignment operator as a template, however, you can enable the assignment of stacks with elements for which an appropriate type conversion is defined. To do this you have to declare Stack<> as follows:

```
// basics/stack5decl.hpp

template <typename T>
class Stack {
  private:
    std::deque<T> elems;    // elements

  public:
    void push(T const&);    // push element
    void pop();             // pop element
    T top() const;          // return top element
    bool empty() const {    // return whether the stack is empty
        return elems.empty();
    }

    // assign stack of elements of type T2
    template <typename T2>
    Stack<T>& operator= (Stack<T2> const&);
};
```

The following two changes have been made:

1. We added a declaration of an assignment operator for stacks of elements of another type T2.
2. The stack now uses a deque as an internal container for the elements. Again, this is a consequence of the implementation of the new assignment operator.

The implementation of the new assignment operator looks like this:

```
// basics/stack5assign.hpp

template <typename T>
 template <typename T2>
Stack<T>& Stack<T>::operator= (Stack<T2> const& op2)
{
    if ((void*)this == (void*)&op2) {      // assignment to itself?
        return *this;
    }

    Stack<T2> tmp(op2);                     // create a copy of the assigned stack

    elems.clear();                          // remove existing elements
    while (!tmp.empty()) {                  // copy all elements
        elems.push_front(tmp.top());
        tmp.pop();
    }
    return *this;
}
```

First let's look at the syntax to define a member template. Inside the template with template parameter T, an inner template with template parameter T2 is defined:

```
template <typename T>
 template <typename T2>
 ...
```

Inside the member function you may expect simply to access all necessary data for the assigned stack op2. However, this stack has a different type (if you instantiate a class template for two different types, you get two different types), so you are restricted to using the public interface. It follows that the only way to access the elements is by calling top(). However, each element has to become a top element, then. Thus, a copy of op2 must first be made, so that the elements are taken from that copy by calling pop(). Because top() returns the last element pushed onto the stack, we have to use a container that supports the insertion of elements at the other end of the collection. For this reason, we use a deque, which provides push_front() to put an element on the other side of the collection.

Having this member template, you can now assign a stack of ints to a stack of floats:

```
Stack<int>   intStack;    // stack for ints
Stack<float> floatStack;  // stack for floats
 ...
floatStack = intStack;    // OK: stacks have different types,
                          //      but int converts to float
```

Of course, this assignment does not change the type of the stack and its elements. After the assignment, the elements of the `floatStack` are still `float`s and therefore `top()` still returns a `float`.

It may appear that this function would disable type checking such that you could assign a stack with elements of any type, but this is not the case. The necessary type checking occurs when the element of the (copy of the) source stack is moved to the destination stack:

```
elems.push_front(tmp.top());
```

If, for example, a stack of strings gets assigned to a stack of `float`s, the compilation of this line results in an error message stating that the string returned by `tmp.top()` cannot be passed as an argument to `elems.push_front()` (the message varies depending on the compiler, but this is the gist of what is meant):

```
Stack<std::string> stringStack;   // stack of strings
Stack<float>       floatStack;    // stack of floats
...
floatStack = stringStack;   // ERROR: std::string doesn't convert to float
```

Note that a template assignment operator doesn't replace the default assignment operator. For assignments of stacks of the same type, the default assignment operator is still called.

Again, you could change the implementation to parameterize the internal container type:

```
// basics/stack6decl.hpp

template <typename T, typename CONT = std::deque<T> >
class Stack {
  private:
    CONT elems;                 // elements

  public:
    void push(T const&);     // push element
    void pop();              // pop element
    T top() const;           // return top element
    bool empty() const {     // return whether the stack is empty
        return elems.empty();
    }

    // assign stack of elements of type T2
    template <typename T2, typename CONT2>
    Stack<T,CONT>& operator= (Stack<T2,CONT2> const&);
};
```

Then the template assignment operator is implemented like this:

```
// basics/stack6assign.hpp
template <typename T, typename CONT>
 template <typename T2, typename CONT2>
Stack<T,CONT>&
Stack<T,CONT>::operator= (Stack<T2,CONT2> const& op2)
{
    if ((void*)this == (void*)&op2) {      // assignment to itself?
        return *this;
    }

    Stack<T2,CONT2> tmp(op2);              // create a copy of the assigned stack

    elems.clear();                         // remove existing elements
    while (!tmp.empty()) {                 // copy all elements
        elems.push_front(tmp.top());
        tmp.pop();
    }
    return *this;
}
```

Remember, for class templates, only those member functions that are called are instantiated. Thus, if you avoid assigning a stack with elements of a different type, you could even use a vector as an internal container:

```
// stack for ints using a vector as an internal container
Stack<int,std::vector<int> > vStack;
...
vStack.push(42);
vStack.push(7);
std::cout << vStack.top() << std::endl;
```

Because the assignment operator template isn't necessary, no error message of a missing member function push_front() occurs and the program is fine.

For the complete implementation of the last example, see all the files with a name that starts with "stack6" in the subdirectory basics.[1]

---

[1] Don't be surprised if your compiler reports errors with these sample files. In the samples, we use almost every important template feature. Thus, you need a compiler that conforms closely to the standard.

5.4   Template Template Parameters

It can be useful to allow a template parameter itself to be a class template. Again, our stack class template can be used as an example.

To use a different internal container for stacks, the application programmer has to specify the element type twice. Thus, to specify the type of the internal container, you have to pass the type of the container *and* the type of its elements again:

```
Stack<int,std::vector<int> > vStack;   // integer stack that uses a vector
```

Using template template parameters allows you to declare the Stack class template by specifying the type of the container without respecifying the type of its elements:

```
Stack<int,std::vector> vStack;              // integer stack that uses a vector
```

To do this you must specify the second template parameter as a template template parameter. In principle, this looks as follows[2]:

```
// basics/stack7decl.hpp

template <typename T,
          template <typename ELEM> class CONT = std::deque >
class Stack {
  private:
    CONT<T> elems;              // elements

  public:
    void push(T const&);        // push element
    void pop();                 // pop element
    T top() const;              // return top element
    bool empty() const {        // return whether the stack is empty
        return elems.empty();
    }
};
```

The difference is that the second template parameter is declared as being a class template:

```
template <typename ELEM> class CONT
```

The default value has changed from `std::deque<T>` to `std::deque`. This parameter has to be a class template, which is instantiated for the type that is passed as the first template parameter:

```
CONT<T> elems;
```

---

[2] There is a problem with this version that we explain in a minute. However, this problem affects only the default value `std::deque`. Thus, we can illustrate the general features of template template parameters with this example.

This use of the first template parameter for the instantiation of the second template parameter is particular to this example. In general, you can instantiate a template template parameter with any type inside a class template.

As usual, instead of `typename` you could use the keyword `class` for template parameters. However, CONT is used to define a class and must be declared by using the keyword `class`. Thus, the following is fine:

```
template <typename T,
          template <class ELEM> class CONT = std::deque>  // OK
class Stack {
    ...
};
```

but the following is not:

```
template <typename T,
          template <typename ELEM> typename CONT = std::deque>
class Stack {                                                      // ERROR
    ...
};
```

Because the template parameter of the template template parameter is not used, you can omit its name:

```
template <typename T,
          template <typename> class CONT = std::deque >
class Stack {
    ...
};
```

Member functions must be modified accordingly. Thus, you have to specify the second template parameter as the template template parameter. The same applies to the implementation of the member function. The `push()` member function, for example, is implemented as follows:

```
template <typename T, template <typename> class CONT>
void Stack<T,CONT>::push (T const& elem)
{
    elems.push_back(elem);     // append copy of passed elem
}
```

Template template parameters for function templates are not allowed.

Template Template Argument Matching

If you try to use the new version of `Stack`, you get an error message saying that the default value `std::deque` is not compatible with the template template parameter CONT. The problem is that a template template argument must be a template with parameters that *exactly* match the parameters of the template template parameter it substitutes. Default template arguments of template template arguments are not considered, so that a match cannot be achieved by leaving out arguments that have default values.

The problem in this example is that the `std::deque` template of the standard library has more than one parameter: The second parameter (which describes a so-called *allocator*) has a default value, but this is not considered when matching `std::deque` to the `CONT` parameter.

There is a workaround, however. We can rewrite the class declaration so that the `CONT` parameter expects containers with two template parameters:

```
template <typename T,
          template <typename ELEM,
                    typename ALLOC = std::allocator<ELEM> >
                    class CONT = std::deque>
class Stack {
  private:
    CONT<T> elems;              // elements

    ...
};
```

Again, you can omit `ALLOC` because it is not used.

The final version of our `Stack` template (including member templates for assignments of stacks of different element types) now looks as follows:

```
// basics/stack8.hpp

#ifndef STACK_HPP
#define STACK_HPP

#include <deque>
#include <stdexcept>
#include <memory>

template <typename T,
          template <typename ELEM,
                    typename = std::allocator<ELEM> >
                    class CONT = std::deque>
class Stack {
  private:
    CONT<T> elems;              // elements

  public:
    void push(T const&);       // push element
```

```cpp
        void pop();              // pop element
        T top() const;           // return top element
        bool empty() const {     // return whether the stack is empty
            return elems.empty();
        }

        // assign stack of elements of type T2
        template<typename T2,
                 template<typename ELEM2,
                          typename = std::allocator<ELEM2>
                         >class CONT2>
        Stack<T,CONT>& operator= (Stack<T2,CONT2> const&);
};

template <typename T, template <typename,typename> class CONT>
void Stack<T,CONT>::push (T const& elem)
{
    elems.push_back(elem);      // append copy of passed elem
}

template<typename T, template <typename,typename> class CONT>
void Stack<T,CONT>::pop ()
{
    if (elems.empty()) {
        throw std::out_of_range("Stack<>::pop(): empty stack");
    }
    elems.pop_back();           // remove last element
}

template <typename T, template <typename,typename> class CONT>
T Stack<T,CONT>::top () const
{
    if (elems.empty()) {
        throw std::out_of_range("Stack<>::top(): empty stack");
    }
    return elems.back();        // return copy of last element
}
```

```
template <typename T, template <typename,typename> class CONT>
 template <typename T2, template <typename,typename> class CONT2>
Stack<T,CONT>&
Stack<T,CONT>::operator= (Stack<T2,CONT2> const& op2)
{
    if ((void*)this == (void*)&op2) {       // assignment to itself?
        return *this;
    }

    Stack<T2,CONT2> tmp(op2);                // create a copy of the assigned stack

    elems.clear();                          // remove existing elements
    while (!tmp.empty()) {                  // copy all elements
        elems.push_front(tmp.top());
        tmp.pop();
    }
    return *this;
}


#endif // STACK_HPP
```

The following program uses all features of this final version:

```
// basics/stack8test.cpp

#include <iostream>
#include <string>
#include <cstdlib>
#include <vector>
#include "stack8.hpp"

int main()
{
    try {
        Stack<int>   intStack;       // stack of ints
        Stack<float> floatStack;     // stack of floats

        // manipulate int stack
        intStack.push(42);
        intStack.push(7);
```

```
          // manipulate float stack
          floatStack.push(7.7);

          // assign stacks of different type
          floatStack = intStack;

          // print float stack
          std::cout << floatStack.top() << std::endl;
          floatStack.pop();
          std::cout << floatStack.top() << std::endl;
          floatStack.pop();
          std::cout << floatStack.top() << std::endl;
          floatStack.pop();
    }
    catch (std::exception const& ex) {
          std::cerr << "Exception: " << ex.what() << std::endl;
    }

    // stack for ints using a vector as an internal container
    Stack<int,std::vector> vStack;
    ...
    vStack.push(42);
    vStack.push(7);
    std::cout << vStack.top() << std::endl;
    vStack.pop();
}
```

The program has the following output:

```
7
42
Exception: Stack<>::top(): empty stack
7
```

Note that template template parameters are one of the most recent features required for compilers to conform to the standard. Thus, this program is a good evaluation of the conformity of your compiler regarding template features.

For further discussions and examples of template template parameters, see Section 8.2.3 on page 102 and Section 15.1.6 on page 259.

5.5   Zero Initialization

For fundamental types such as `int`, `double`, or pointer types, there is no default constructor that initializes them with a useful default value. Instead, any noninitialized local variable has an undefined value:

```
void foo()
{
    int x;       // x has undefined value
    int* ptr;    // ptr points to somewhere (instead of nowhere)
}
```

Now if you write templates and want to have variables of a template type initialized by a default value, you have the problem that a simple definition doesn't do this for built-in types:

```
template <typename T>
void foo()
{
    T x;       // x has undefined value if T is built-in type
}
```

For this reason, it is possible to call explicitly a default constructor for built-in types that initializes them with zero (or `false` for `bool`). That is, `int()` yields zero. As a consequence you can ensure proper default initialization even for built-in types by writing the following:

```
template <typename T>
void foo()
{
    T x = T();     // x is zero (or false) if T is a built-in type
}
```

To make sure that a member of a class template, for which the type is parameterized, gets initialized, you have to define a default constructor that uses an initializer list to initialize the member:

```
template <typename T>
class MyClass {
  private:
    T x;
  public:
    MyClass() : x() {   // ensures that x is initialized even for built-in types
    }
    ...
};
```

5.6 Using String Literals as Arguments for Function Templates

Passing string literal arguments for reference parameters of function templates sometimes fails in a surprising way. Consider the following example:

```
// basics/max5.cpp

#include <string>

// note: reference parameters
template <typename T>
inline T const& max (T const& a, T const& b)
{
    return  a < b  ?  b : a;
}

int main()
{
    std::string s;

    ::max("apple","peach");     // OK: same type
    ::max("apple","tomato");    // ERROR: different types
    ::max("apple",s);           // ERROR: different types
}
```

The problem is that string literals have different array types depending on their lengths. That is, `"apple"` and `"peach"` have type `char const[6]` whereas `"tomato"` has type `char const[7]`. Only the first call is possible because the template expects both parameters to have the same type. However, if you declare nonreference parameters, you can substitute them with string literals of different size:

```
// basics/max6.cpp

#include <string>

// note: nonreference parameters
template <typename T>
inline T max (T a, T b)
{
    return  a < b  ?  b : a;
}
```

```
int main()
{
    std::string s;

    ::max("apple","peach");     // OK: same type
    ::max("apple","tomato");    // OK: decays to same type
    ::max("apple",s);           // ERROR: different types
}
```

The explanation for this behavior is that during argument deduction array-to-pointer conversion (often called *decay*) occurs only if the parameter does not have a reference type. This is demonstrated by the following program:

```
// basics/refnonref.cpp

#include <typeinfo>
#include <iostream>

template <typename T>
void ref (T const& x)
{
    std::cout << "x in ref(T const&): "
              << typeid(x).name() << '\n';
}

template <typename T>
void nonref (T x)
{
    std::cout << "x in nonref(T):      "
              << typeid(x).name() << '\n';
}

int main()
{
    ref("hello");
    nonref("hello");
}
```

The example passes a string literal to function templates that declare their parameter to be a reference or nonreference respectively. Both function templates use the typeid operator to print the type of the instantiated parameters. The `typeid` operator returns an lvalue of type `std::type_info`, which encapsulates a representation of the type of the expression passed to the `typeid` operator. The member function `name()` of `std::type_info` is intended to return a human-readable text representation of the latter type. The C++ standard doesn't actually say that `name()` must return something meaningful, but on good C++ implementations, you should get a string that gives a good description of the type of the expression passed to `typeid` (with some implementations this string is *mangled*, but a *demangler* is available to turn it into human-readable text). For example, the output might be as follows:

```
x in ref(T const&):  char [6]
x in nonref(T):      const char *
```

If you encounter a problem involving a mismatch between an array of characters and a pointer to characters, you might have stumbled on this somewhat surprising phenomenon.[3] There is unfortunately no general solution to address this problem. Depending on the context, you can

- use nonreferences instead of references (however, this can lead to unnecessary copying)
- overload using both reference and nonreference parameters (however, this might lead to ambiguities; see Section B.2.2 on page 492)
- overload with concrete types (such as `std::string`)
- overload with array types, for example:

```
template <typename T, int N, int M>
T const* max (T const (&a)[N], T const (&b)[M])
{
    return  a < b  ?  b : a;
}
```

- force application programmers to use explicit conversions

In this example it is best to overload `max()` for strings (see Section 2.4 on page 16). This is necessary anyway because without overloading in cases where the call to `max()` is valid for string literals, the operation that is performed is a pointer comparison: a < b compares the addresses of the two string literals and has nothing to do with lexicographical order. This is another reason why it is usually preferable to use a string class such as `std::string` instead of C-style strings.

See Section 11.1 on page 168 for details.

---

[3] In fact, this is the reason that you cannot create a pair of values initialized with string literals using the original C++ standard library (see [*Standard98*]):

```
std::make_pair("key","value")  // ERROR according to [Standard98]
```

This was fixed with the first technical corrigendum by replacing the reference parameters of `make_pair()` by nonreference parameters (see [*Standard02*]).

5.7   Summary

- To access a type name that depends on a template parameter, you have to qualify the name with a leading `typename`.
- Nested classes and member functions can also be templates. One application is the ability to implement generic operations with internal type conversions. However, type checking still occurs.
- Template versions of assignment operators don't replace default assignment operators.
- You can also use class templates as template parameters, as so-called *template template parameters*.
- Template template arguments must match exactly. Default template arguments of template template arguments are ignored.
- By explicitly calling a default constructor, you can make sure that variables and members of templates are initialized by a default value even if they are instantiated with a built-in type.
- For string literals there is an array-to-pointer conversion during argument deduction if and only if the parameter is not a reference.

Chapter 6

Using Templates in Practice

Template code is a little different from ordinary code. In some ways templates lie somewhere between macros and ordinary (nontemplate) declarations. Although this may be an oversimplification, it has consequences not only for the way we write algorithms and data structures using templates, but also for the day-to-day logistics of expressing and analyzing programs involving templates.

In this chapter we address some of these practicalities without necessarily delving into the technical details that underlie them. Many of these details are explored in Chapter 10. To keep the discussion simple, we assume that our C++ compilation systems consist of fairly traditional compilers and linkers (C++ systems that don't fall in this category are quite rare).

6.1 The Inclusion Model

There are several ways to organize template source code. This section presents the most popular approach as of the time of this writing: the inclusion model.

6.1.1 Linker Errors

Most C and C++ programmers organize their nontemplate code largely as follows:
- Classes and other types are entirely placed in *header files*. Typically, this is a file with a `.hpp` (or `.H`, `.h`, `.hh`, `.hxx`) filename extension.
- For global variables and (noninline) functions, only a declaration is put in a header file, and the definition goes into a so-called *dot-C file*. Typically, this is a file with a `.cpp` (or `.C`, `.c`, `.cc`, or `.cxx`) filename extension.

This works well: It makes the needed type definition easily available throughout the program and avoids duplicate definition errors on variables and functions from the linker.

With these conventions in mind, a common error about which beginning template programmers complain is illustrated by the following (erroneous) little program. As usual for "ordinary code," we declare the template in a header file:

```
// basics/myfirst.hpp
```

```
#ifndef MYFIRST_HPP
#define MYFIRST_HPP
```

```
// declaration of template
template <typename T>
void print_typeof (T const&);
```

```
#endif // MYFIRST_HPP
```

`print_typeof()` is the declaration of a simple auxiliary function that prints some type information. The implementation of the function is placed in a dot-C file:

```
// basics/myfirst.cpp
```

```
#include <iostream>
#include <typeinfo>
#include "myfirst.hpp"
```

```
// implementation/definition of template
template <typename T>
void print_typeof (T const& x)
{
    std::cout << typeid(x).name() << std::endl;
}
```

The example uses the `typeid` operator to print a string that describes the type of the expression passed to it (see Section 5.6 on page 58).

Finally, we use the template in another dot-C file, into which our template declaration is `#include`d:

```
// basics/myfirstmain.cpp
```

```
#include "myfirst.hpp"
```

```
// use of the template
int main()
{
```

```
      double ice = 3.0;
      print_typeof(ice);     // call function template for type double
}
```

A C++ compiler will most likely accept this program without any problems, but the linker will probably report an error, implying that there is no definition of the function `print_typeof()`.

The reason for this error is that the definition of the function template `print_typeof()` has not been instantiated. In order for a template to be instantiated, the compiler must know which definition should be instantiated and for what template arguments it should be instantiated. Unfortunately, in the previous example, these two pieces of information are in files that are compiled separately. Therefore, when our compiler sees the call to `print_typeof()` but has no definition in sight to instantiate this function for `double`, it just assumes that such a definition is provided elsewhere and creates a reference (for the linker to resolve) to that definition. On the other hand, when the compiler processes the file `myfirst.cpp`, it has no indication at that point that it must instantiate the template definition it contains for specific arguments.

6.1.2   Templates in Header Files

The common solution to the previous problem is to use the same approach that we would take with macros or with inline functions: We include the definitions of a template in the header file that declares that template. For our example, we can do this by adding

```
#include "myfirst.cpp"
```

at the end of `myfirst.hpp` or by including `myfirst.cpp` in every dot-C file that uses the template. A third way, of course, is to do away entirely with `myfirst.cpp` and rewrite `myfirst.hpp` so that it contains all template declarations *and* template definitions:

```
// basics/myfirst2.hpp

#ifndef MYFIRST_HPP
#define MYFIRST_HPP

#include <iostream>
#include <typeinfo>

// declaration of template
template <typename T>
void print_typeof (T const&);

// implementation/definition of template
template <typename T>
void print_typeof (T const& x)
```

```
{
    std::cout << typeid(x).name() << std::endl;
}
```

#endif // *MYFIRST_HPP*

This way of organizing templates is called the *inclusion model.* With this in place, you should find that our program now correctly compiles, links, and executes.

There are a few observations we can make at this point. The most notable is that this approach has considerably increased the cost of including the header file `myfirst.hpp`. In this example, the cost is not the result of the size of the template definition itself, but the result of the fact that we must also include the headers used by the definition of our template—in this case `<iostream>` and `<typeinfo>`. You may find that this amounts to tens of thousands of lines of code because headers like `<iostream>` contain similar template definitions.

This is a real problem in practice because it considerably increases the time needed by the compiler to compile significant programs. We will therefore examine some possible ways to approach this problem in upcoming sections. However, real-world programs quickly end up taking hours to compile and link (we have been involved in situations in which it literally took days to build a program completely from its source code).

Despite this build-time issue, we do recommend following this inclusion model to organize your templates when possible. We examine two alternatives, but in our opinion their engineering deficiencies are more serious than the build-time issue discussed here. They may have other advantages not directly related to the engineering aspects of software development, however.

Another (more subtle) observation about the inclusion approach is that noninline function templates are distinct from inline functions and macros in an important way: They are not expanded at the call site. Instead, when they are instantiated, they create a new copy of a function. Because this is an automatic process, a compiler could end up creating two copies in two different files, and some linkers could issue errors when they find two distinct definitions for the same function. In theory, this should not be a concern of ours: It is a problem for the C++ compilation system to accommodate. In practice, things work well most of the time, and we don't need to deal with this issue at all. For large projects that create their own library of code, however, problems occasionally show up. A discussion of instantiation schemes in Chapter 10 and a close study of the documentation that came with the C++ translation system (compiler) should help address these problems.

Finally, we need to point out that what applies to the ordinary function template in our example also applies to member functions and static data members of class templates, as well as to member function templates.

6.2 Explicit Instantiation

The inclusion model ensures that all the needed templates are instantiated. This happens because the C++ compilation system automatically generates those instantiations as they are needed. The C++ standard also offers a construct to instantiate templates manually: the *explicit instantiation directive*.

6.2.1 Example of Explicit Instantiation

To illustrate manual instantiation, let's revisit our original example that leads to a linker error (see page 62). To avoid this error we add the following file to our program:

```
// basics/myfirstinst.cpp

#include "myfirst.cpp"

// explicitly instantiate print_typeof() for type double
template void print_typeof<double>(double const&);
```

The explicit instantiation directive consists of the keyword template followed by the fully substituted declaration of the entity we want to instantiate. In our example, we do this with an ordinary function, but it could be a member function or a static data member. For example:

```
// explicitly instantiate a constructor of MyClass<> for int
template MyClass<int>::MyClass();

// explicitly instantiate a function template max() for int
template int const& max (int const&, int const&);
```

You can also explicitly instantiate a class template, which is short for requesting the instantiation of all its instantiatable members. This excludes members that were previously specialized as well as those that were already instantiated:

```
// explicitly instantiate class Stack<> for int:
template class Stack<int>;

// explicitly instantiate some member functions of Stack<> for strings:
template Stack<std::string>::Stack();
template void Stack<std::string>::push(std::string const&);
template std::string Stack<std::string>::top() const;

// ERROR: can't explicitly instantiate a member function of a
//        class that was itself explicitly instantiated:
template Stack<int>::Stack();
```

There should be, at most, one explicit instantiation of each distinct entity in a program. In other words, you could explicitly instantiate both `print_typeof<int>` and `print_typeof<double>`, but each directive should appear only once in a program. Not following this rule usually results in linker errors that report duplicate definitions of the instantiated entities.

Manual instantiation has a clear disadvantage: We must carefully keep track of which entities to instantiate. For large projects this quickly becomes an excessive burden; hence we do not recommend it. We have worked on several projects that initially underestimated this burden, and we came to regret our decision as the code matured.

However, explicit instantiation also has a few advantages because the instantiation can be tuned to the needs of the program. Clearly, the overhead of large headers is avoided. The source code of template definition can be kept hidden, but then no additional instantiations can be created by a client program. Finally, for some applications it can be useful to control the exact location (that is, the object file) of a template instance. With automatic instantiation, this may not be possible (see Chapter 10 for details).

```
stack.hpp:

    #ifndef STACK_HPP
    #define STACK_HPP

    #include <vector>

    template <typename T>
    class Stack {
      private:
        std::vector<T> elems;
      public:
        Stack();
        void push (T const&);
        void pop();
        T top() const;
    };

    #endif
```

```
stackdef.hpp:

    #ifndef STACKDEF_HPP
    #define STACKDEF_HPP

    #include "stack.hpp"

    template <typename T>
    void Stack<T>::push (T const& elem)
    {
        elems.push_back(elem);
    }
    ...

    #endif
```

Figure 6.1. Separation of template declaration and definition

6.2.2   Combining the Inclusion Model and Explicit Instantiation

To keep the decision open whether to use the inclusion model or explicit instantiation, we can provide the declaration and the definition of templates in two different files. It is common practice to have both files named as header files (using an extension ordinarily used for files that are intended to be #included), and it is probably wise to stick to this convention. (Thus, myfirst.cpp of our motivating example becomes myfirstdef.hpp, with preprocessor guards around the code inserted.) Figure 6.1 demonstrates this for a Stack<> class template.

Now if we want to use the inclusion model, we can simply include the definition header file stackdef.hpp. Alternatively, if we want to instantiate the templates explicitly, we can include the declaration header stack.hpp and provide a dot-C file with the necessary explicit instantiation directives (see Figure 6.2).

```
stacktest1.cpp:

    #include "stack.hpp"
    #include <iostream>
    #include <string>

    int main()
    {
        Stack<int> intStack;
        intStack.push(42);
        std::cout << intStack.top() << std::endl;
        intStack.pop();

        Stack<std::string> stringStack;
        stringStack.push("hello");
        std::cout << stringStack.top() << std::endl;
    }


stack_inst.cpp:

    #include "stackdef.hpp"
    #include <string>

    // instantiate class Stack<> for int
    template Stack<int>;

    // instantiate some member functions of Stack<> for strings
    template Stack<std::string>::Stack();
    template void Stack<std::string>::push(std::string const&);
    template std::string Stack<std::string>::top() const;
```

Figure 6.2. Explicit instantiation with two template header files

6.3   The Separation Model

Both approaches advocated in the previous sections work well and conform entirely to the C++ standard. However, this same standard also provides the alternative mechanism of *exporting* templates. This approach is sometimes called the C++ template *separation model*.

6.3.1   The Keyword `export`

In principle, it is quite simple to make use of the `export` facility: Define the template in just one file, and mark that definition and all its nondefining declarations with the keyword `export`. For the example in the previous section, this results in the following function template declaration:

```
// basics/myfirst3.hpp

#ifndef MYFIRST_HPP
#define MYFIRST_HPP

// declaration of template
export
template <typename T>
void print_typeof (T const&);

#endif // MYFIRST_HPP
```

Exported templates can be used without their definition being visible. In other words, the point where a template is being used and the point where it is defined can be in two different translation units. In our example, the file `myfirst.hpp` now contains only the *declaration* of the member functions of the class template, and this is sufficient to use those members. Comparing this with the original code that was triggering linker errors, we had to add only one `export` keyword in our code and things now work just fine.

Within a preprocessed file (that is, within a translation unit), it is sufficient to mark the first declaration of a template with `export`. Later redeclarations, including definitions, implicitly keep that attribute. This is why `myfirst.cpp` does not need to be modified in our example. The definitions in this file are implicitly exported because they were so declared in the `#included` header file. On the other hand, it is perfectly acceptable to provide redundant `export` keywords on template definitions, and doing so may improve the readability of the code.

The keyword `export` really applies to function templates, member functions of class templates, member function templates, and static data members of class templates. `export` can also be applied to a class template declaration. It implies that every one of its exportable members is exported, but class templates themselves are not actually exported (hence, their definitions still appear in header files). You can still have implicitly or explicitly defined inline member functions. However, these inline functions are not exported:

```
export template <typename T>
class MyClass {
  public:
    void memfun1();        // exported
    void memfun2() {       // not exported because implicitly inline
        ...
    }
    void memfun3();        // not exported because explicitly inline
    ...
};

template <typename T>
inline void MyClass<T>::memfun3 ()
{
    ...
}
```

However, note that the keyword export cannot be combined with inline and must always precede the keyword template. The following is invalid:

```
template <typename T>
class Invalid {
  public:
    export void wrong(T);      // ERROR: export not followed by template
};

export template<typename T>    // ERROR: both export and inline
inline void Invalid<T>::wrong(T)
{
}

export template<typename T>    // ERROR: both export and inline
inline T const& max (T const& a, T const& b)
{
    return  a < b ? b : a;
}
```

6.3.2   Limitations of the Separation Model

At this point it is reasonable to wonder why we're still advocating the inclusion approach when exported templates seem to offer just the right magic to make things work. There are a few different aspects to this choice.

First, even four years after the standard came out, only one company has actually implemented support for the `export` keyword.[1] Therefore, experience with this feature is not as widespread as other C++ features. Clearly, this also means that at this point experience with exported templates is fairly limited, and all our observations will ultimately have to be taken with a grain of salt. It is possible that some of our misgivings will be addressed in the future (and we show how to prepare for that eventuality).

Second, although `export` may seem quasi-magical, it is not *actually* magical. Ultimately, the instantiation process has to deal with both the place where a template is instantiated and the place where its definition appears. Hence, although these two seem neatly decoupled in the source code, there is an invisible coupling that the system establishes behind the scenes. This may mean, for example, that if the file containing the definition changes, both that file and all the files that instantiate the templates in that file may need to be recompiled. This is not substantially different from the inclusion approach, but it is no longer obviously visible in the source code. As a consequence, dependency management tools (such as the popular `make` and `nmake` programs) that use traditional source-based techniques no longer work. It also means that quite a few bits of extra processing by the compiler are needed to keep all the bookkeeping straight; and in the end, the build times may not be better than those of the inclusion approach.

Finally, exported templates may lead to surprising semantic consequences, the details of which are explained in Chapter 10.

A common misconception is that the `export` mechanism offers the potential of being able to ship libraries of templates without revealing the source code for their definitions (just like libraries of nontemplate entities).[2] This is a misconception in the sense that hiding code is not a language issue: It would be equally possible to provide a mechanism to hide included template definitions as to hide exported template definitions. Although this may be feasible (the current implementations do not support this model), it unfortunately creates new challenges in dealing with template compilation errors that need to refer to the hidden source code.

6.3.3   Preparing for the Separation Model

One workable idea is to prepare our sources in such a way that we can easily switch between the inclusion and export models using a harmless dose of preprocessor directives. Here is how it can be done for our simple example:

---

[1] As far as we know, Edison Design Group, Inc. (EDG) is still that company (see [*EDG*]). Their technology is available through other vendors, however.

[2] Not everybody considers this *closed-source* approach a plus.

```
// basics/myfirst4.hpp

#ifndef MYFIRST_HPP
#define MYFIRST_HPP

// use export if USE_EXPORT is defined
#if defined(USE_EXPORT)
#define EXPORT export
#else
#define EXPORT
#endif

// declaration of template
EXPORT
template <typename T>
void print_typeof (T const&);

// include definition if USE_EXPORT is not defined
#if !defined(USE_EXPORT)
#include "myfirst.cpp"
#endif

#endif // MYFIRST_HPP
```

By defining or omitting the preprocessor symbol USE_EXPORT, we can now select between the two models. If a program defines USE_EXPORT before it includes myfirst.hpp, the separation model is used:

```
// use separation model:
#define USE_EXPORT
#include "myfirst.hpp"
...
```

If a program does not define USE_EXPORT, the inclusion model is used because in this case myfirst.hpp automatically includes the definitions in myfirst.cpp:

```
// use inclusion model:
#include "myfirst.hpp"
...
```

Despite this flexibility, we should reiterate that besides the obvious logistical differences, there can be subtle semantic differences between the two models.

Note that we can also explicitly instantiate exported templates. In this case the template definition can be in another file. To be able to choose between the inclusion model, the separation model, and explicit instantion, we can combine the organization controlled by USE_EXPORT with the conventions described in Section 6.2.2 on page 67.

6.4   Templates and `inline`

Declaring short functions to be inline is a common tool to improve the running time of programs. The `inline` specifier indicates to the implementation that inline substitution of the function body at the point of call is preferred over the usual function call mechanism. However, an implementation is not required to perform this inline substitution at the point of call.

Both function templates and inline functions can be defined in multiple translation units. This is usually achieved by placing the definition in a header file that is included by multiple dot-C files.

This may lead to the impression that function templates are inline by default. However, they're not. If you write function templates that should be handled as inline functions, you should use the `inline` specifier (unless the function is inline already because it is defined inside a class definition).

Therefore, many short template functions that are not part of a class definition should be declared with `inline`.[3]

6.5   Precompiled Headers

Even without templates, C++ header files can become very large and therefore take a long time to compile. Templates add to this tendency, and the outcry of waiting programmers has in many cases driven vendors to implement a scheme usually known as *precompiled headers*. This scheme operates outside the scope of the standard and relies on vendor-specific options. Although we leave the details on how to create and use precompiled header files to the documentation of the various C++ compilation systems that have this feature, it is useful to gain some understanding of how it works.

When a compiler translates a file, it does so starting from the beginning of the file and works through to the end. As it processes each token from the file (which may come from #included files), it adapts its internal state, including such things as adding entries to a table of symbols so they may be looked up later. While doing so, the compiler may also generate code in object files.

The precompiled header scheme relies on the fact that code can be organized in such a manner that many files start with the same lines of code. Let's assume for the sake of argument that every file to be compiled starts with the same N lines of code. We could compile these N lines and save the complete state of the compiler at that point in a so-called *precompiled header*. Then, for every file in our program, we could reload the saved state and start compilation at line $N+1$. At this point it is worthwhile to note that reloading the saved state is an operation that can be orders of magnitude

---

[3] We may not always apply this rule of thumb because it may distract from the topic at hand.

faster than actually compiling the first N lines. However, saving the state in the first place is typically more expensive than just compiling the N lines. The increase in cost varies roughly from 20 to 200 percent.

The key to making effective use of precompiled headers is to ensure that—as much as possible— files start with a maximum number of common lines of code. In practice this means the files must start with the same #include directives, which (as mentioned earlier) consume a substantial portion of our build time. Hence, it can be very advantageous to pay attention to the order in which headers are included. For example, the following two files

```
#include <iostream>
#include <vector>
#include <list>
...
```

and

```
#include <list>
#include <vector>
...
```

inhibit the use of precompiled headers because there is no common initial state in the sources.

Some programmers decide that it is better to #include some extra unnecessary headers than to pass on an opportunity to accelerate the translation of a file using a precompiled header. This decision can considerably ease the management of the inclusion policy. For example, it is usually relatively straightforward to create a header file named std.hpp that includes all the standard headers[4]:

```
#include <iostream>
#include <string>
#include <vector>
#include <deque>
#include <list>
...
```

This file can then be precompiled, and every program file that makes use of the standard library can then simply be started as follows:

```
#include "std.hpp"
...
```

Normally this would take a while to compile, but given a system with sufficient memory, the precompiled header scheme allows it to be processed significantly faster than almost any single standard header would require without precompilation. The standard headers are particularly convenient in

---

[4] In theory, the standard headers do not actually need to correspond to physical files. In practice, however, they do, and the files are very large.

this way because they rarely change, and hence the precompiled header for our std.hpp file can be built once.[5] Otherwise, precompiled headers are typically part of the dependency configuration of a project (for example, they are updated as needed by the popular make tool).

One attractive approach to manage precompiled headers is to create *layers* of precompiled headers that go from the most widely used and stable headers (for example, our std.hpp header) to headers that aren't expected to change all the time and therefore are still worth precompiling. However, if headers are under heavy development, creating precompiled headers for them can take more time than what is saved by reusing them. A key concept to this approach is that a precompiled header for a more stable layer can be reused to improve the precompilation time of a less stable header. For example, suppose that in addition to our std.hpp header (which we have precompiled), we also define a core.hpp header that includes additional facilities that are specific to our project but nonetheless achieve a certain level of stability:

```
#include "std.hpp"
#include "core_data.hpp"
#include "core_algos.hpp"
...
```

Because this file starts with #include "std.hpp", the compiler can load the associated precompiled header and continue with the next line without recompiling all the standard headers. When the file is completely processed, a new precompiled header can be produced. Applications can then use #include "core.hpp" to provide access quickly to large amounts of functionality because the compiler can load the latter precompiled header.

6.6   Debugging Templates

Templates raise two classes of challenges when it comes to debugging them. One set of challenges is definitely a problem for writers of templates: How can we ensure that the templates we write will function for *any* template arguments that satisfy the conditions we document? The other class of problems is almost exactly the opposite: How can a user of a template find out which of the template parameter requirements it violated when the template does not behave as documented?

Before we discuss these issues in depth, it is useful to contemplate the kinds of constraints that may be imposed on template parameters. In this section we deal mostly with the constraints that lead to compilation errors when violated, and we call these constraints *syntactic constraints*. Syntactic constraints can include the need for a certain kind of constructor to exist, for a particular function call to be unambiguous, and so forth. The other kind of constraint we call *semantic constraints*.

---

[5] Some committee members find the concept of a comprehensive std.hpp header so convenient that they have suggested introducing it as a standard header. We would then be able to write #include <std>. Some even suggest that it should be implicitly included so that all the standard library facilities become available without #include.

These constraints are much harder to verify mechanically. In the general case, it may not even be practical to do so. For example, we may require that there be a < operator defined on a template type parameter (which is a syntactic constraint), but usually we'll also require that the operator actually defines some sort of ordering on its domain (which is a semantic constraint).

The term *concept* is often used to denote a set of constraints that is repeatedly required in a template library. For example, the C++ standard library relies on such concepts as *random access iterator* and *default constructible*. Concepts can form hierarchies in the sense that one concept can be a refinement of another. The more refined concept includes all the constraints of the other concept but adds a few more. For example, the concept *random access iterator* refines the concept *bidirectional iterator* in the C++ standard library. With this terminology in place, we can say that debugging template code includes a significant amount of determining how concepts are violated in the template implementation and in their use.

6.6.1 Decoding the Error Novel

Ordinary compilation errors are normally quite succinct and to the point. For example, when a compiler says "class X has no member 'fun'," it usually isn't too hard to figure out what is wrong in our code (for example, we might have mistyped run as fun). Not so with templates. Consider the following relatively simple code excerpt using the C++ standard library. It contains a fairly small mistake: list<string> is used, but we are searching using a greater<int> function object, which should have been a greater<string> object:

```
std::list<std::string> coll;
...
// Find the first element greater than "A"
std::list<std::string>::iterator pos;
pos = std::find_if(coll.begin(),coll.end(),          // range
                 std::bind2nd(std::greater<int>(),"A")); // criterion
```

This sort of mistake commonly happens when cutting and pasting some code and forgetting to adapt parts of it.

A version of the popular GNU C++ compiler reports the following error:

```
/local/include/stl/_algo.h: In function 'struct _STL::_List_iterator<_STL::basic
_string<char,_STL::char_traits<char>,_STL::allocator<char> >,_STL::_Nonconst_tra
its<_STL::basic_string<char,_STL::char_traits<char>,_STL::allocator<char> > > >
_STL::find_if<_STL::_List_iterator<_STL::basic_string<char,_STL::char_traits<cha
r>,_STL::allocator<char> >,_STL::_Nonconst_traits<_STL::basic_string<char,_STL::
char_traits<char>,_STL::allocator<char> > > >, _STL::binder2nd<_STL::greater<int
> > >(_STL::_List_iterator<_STL::basic_string<char,_STL::char_traits<char>,_STL:
:allocator<char> >,_STL::_Nonconst_traits<_STL::basic_string<char,_STL::char_tra
its<char>,_STL::allocator<char> > > >, _STL::_List_iterator<_STL::basic_string<c
har,_STL::char_traits<char>,_STL::allocator<char> >,_STL::_Nonconst_traits<_STL:
:basic_string<char,_STL::char_traits<char>,_STL::allocator<char> > > >, _STL::bi
nder2nd<_STL::greater<int> >, _STL::input_iterator_tag)':
```

```
/local/include/stl/_algo.h:115:    instantiated from '_STL::find_if<_STL::_List_i
terator<_STL::basic_string<char,_STL::char_traits<char>,_STL::allocator<char> >,
_STL::_Nonconst_traits<_STL::basic_string<char,_STL::char_traits<char>,_STL::all
ocator<char> > > >, _STL::binder2nd<_STL::greater<int> > >(_STL::_List_iterator<
_STL::basic_string<char,_STL::char_traits<char>,_STL::allocator<char> >,_STL::_N
onconst_traits<_STL::basic_string<char,_STL::char_traits<char>,_STL::allocator<c
har> > > >, _STL::_List_iterator<_STL::basic_string<char,_STL::char_traits<char>
,_STL::allocator<char> >,_STL::_Nonconst_traits<_STL::basic_string<char,_STL::ch
ar_traits<char>,_STL::allocator<char> > > >, _STL::binder2nd<_STL::greater<int>
>)'
testprog.cpp:18:    instantiated from here
/local/include/stl/_algo.h:78: no match for call to '(_STL::binder2nd<_STL::grea
ter<int> >) (_STL::basic_string<char,_STL::char_traits<char>,_STL::allocator<cha
r> > &)'
/local/include/stl/_function.h:261: candidates are: bool _STL::binder2nd<_STL::g
reater<int> >::operator ()(const int &) const
```

A message like this starts looking more like a novel than a diagnostic. It can also be overwhelming to the point of discouraging novice template users. However, with some practice, messages like this become manageable, and the errors are relatively easily located.

The first part of this error message says that an error occurred in a function template instance (with a horribly long name) deep inside the /local/include/stl/_algo.h header. Next, the compiler reports why it instantiated that particular instance. In this case it all started on line 18 of testprog.cpp (which is the file containing our example code), which caused the instantiation of a find_if template on line 115 of the _algo.h header. The compiler reports all this in case we simply were not expecting all these templates to be instantiated. It allows us to determine the chain of events that caused the instantiations.

However, in our example we're willing to believe that all kinds of templates needed to be instantiated, and we just wonder why it didn't work. This information comes in the last part of the message: The part that says "no match for call" implies that a function call could not be resolved because the types of the arguments and the parameter types didn't match. Furthermore, just after this, the line containing "candidates are" explains that there was a single candidate type expecting an integer type (parameter type const int&). Looking back at line 18 of the program, we see std::bind2nd(std::greater<int>(),"A"), which does indeed contain an integer type (<int>) that is not compatible with the string type objects for which we're looking in our example. Replacing <int> with <std::string> makes the problem go away.

There is no doubt that the error message could be better structured. The actual problem could be emitted before the history of the instantiation, and instead of using fully expanded template instantiation names like MyTemplate<YourTemplate<int> >, decomposing the instance as in MyTemplate<T> with T=YourTemplate<int> can reduce the overwhelming length of names. However, it is also true that all the information in this diagnostic could be useful in some situations. It is therefore not surprising that other compilers provide similar information (although some use the structuring techniques mentioned).

Note that STLFilt by Leor Zolman provides a way to decrypt the STL error messages for several compilers (see http://www.bdsoft.com/tools/stlfilt.html).

6.6.2 Shallow Instantiation

Diagnostics such as those discussed earlier arise when errors are found after a long chain of instantiations. To illustrate this, consider the following somewhat contrived code:

```
template <typename T>
void clear (T const& p)
{
    *p = 0;   // assumes T is a pointer-like type
}

template <typename T>
void core (T const& p)
{
    clear(p);
}

template <typename T>
void middle (typename T::Index p)
{
    core(p);
}

template <typename T>
void shell (T const& env)
{
    typename T::Index i;
    middle<T>(i);
}

class Client {
  public:
    typedef int Index;
};

Client main_client;

int main()
{
    shell(main_client);
}
```

This example illustrates the typical layering of software development: High-level function templates like shell() rely on components like middle(), which themselves make use of basic facilities like core(). When we instantiate shell(), all the layers below it also need to be instantiated. In this example, a problem is revealed in the deepest layer: core() is instantiated with type int (from the use of Client::Index in middle()) and attempts to dereference a value of that type, which is an error. A good generic diagnostic includes a trace of all the layers that led to the problems, but we observe that so much information can appear unwieldy.

An excellent discussion of the core ideas surrounding this problem can be found in [*StroustrupDnE*], in which Bjarne Stroustrup identifies two classes of approaches to determine earlier whether template arguments satisfy a set of constraints: through a language extension or through earlier parameter use. We cover the former option to some extent in Section 13.11 on page 218. The latter alternative consists of forcing any errors in *shallow instantiations*. This is achieved by inserting unused code with no other purpose than to trigger an error if that code is instantiated with template arguments that do not meet the requirements of deeper levels of templates.

In our previous example we could add code in shell() that attempts to dereference a value of type T::Index. For example:

```
template <typename T>
inline void ignore(T const&)
{
}


template <typename T>
void shell (T const& env)
{
    class ShallowChecks {
        void deref(T::Index ptr) {
            ignore(*ptr);
        }
    };
    typename T::Index i;
    middle(i);
}
```

If T is a type such that T::Index cannot be dereferenced, an error is now diagnosed on the local class ShallowChecks. Note that because the local class is not actually used, the added code does not impact the running time of the shell() function. Unfortunately, many compilers will warn about the fact that ShallowChecks is not used (and neither are its members). Tricks such as the use of the ignore() template can be used to inhibit such warnings, but they add to the complexity of the code.

Clearly, the development of the dummy code in our example can become as complex as the code that implements the actual functionality of the template. To control this complexity it is natural to attempt to collect various snippets of dummy code in some sort of library. For example, such a library could contain macros that expand to code that triggers the appropriate error when a template parameter substitution violates the concept underlying that particular parameter. The most popular such library is the *Concept Check Library*, which is part of the Boost distribution (see [*BCCL*]).

Unfortunately, the technique isn't particularly portable (the way errors are diagnosed differs considerably from one compiler to another) and sometimes masks issues that cannot be captured at a higher level.

6.6.3 Long Symbols

The error message analyzed in Section 6.6.1 on page 75 demonstrates another problem of templates: Instantiated template code can result in very long symbols. For example, in the implementation used earlier `std::string` is expanded to

```
_STL::basic_string<char,_STL::char_traits<char>,
                        _STL::allocator<char> >
```

Some programs that use the C++ standard library produce symbols that contain more than 10,000 characters. These very long symbols can also cause errors or warnings in compilers, linkers, and debuggers. Modern compilers use compression techniques to reduce this problem, but in error messages this is not apparent.

6.6.4 Tracers

So far we have discussed bugs that arise when compiling or linking programs that contain templates. However, the most challenging task of ensuring that a program behaves correctly at run time often *follows* a successful build. Templates can sometimes make this task a little more difficult because the behavior of generic code represented by a template depends uniquely on the client of that template (certainly much more so than ordinary classes and functions). A tracer is a software device that can alleviate that aspect of debugging by detecting problems in template definitions early in the development cycle.

A tracer is a user-defined class that can be used as an argument for a template to be tested. Often, it is written just to meet the requirements of the template and no more than those requirements. More important, however, a tracer should generate a *trace* of the operations that are invoked on it. This allows, for example, to verify experimentally the efficiency of algorithms as well as the sequence of operations.

Here is an example of a tracer that might be used to test a sorting algorithm:

```
// basics/tracer.hpp

#include <iostream>

class SortTracer {
  private:
```

```cpp
    int value;              // integer value to be sorted
    int generation;         // generation of this tracer
    static long n_created;  // number of constructor calls
    static long n_destroyed; // number of destructor calls
    static long n_assigned; // number of assignments
    static long n_compared; // number of comparisons
    static long n_max_live; // maximum of existing objects

    // recompute maximum of existing objects
    static void update_max_live() {
        if (n_created-n_destroyed > n_max_live) {
            n_max_live = n_created-n_destroyed;
        }
    }

  public:
    static long creations() {
        return n_created;
    }
    static long destructions() {
        return n_destroyed;
    }
    static long assignments() {
        return n_assigned;
    }
    static long comparisons() {
        return n_compared;
    }
    static long max_live() {
        return n_max_live;
    }

  public:
    // constructor
    SortTracer (int v = 0) : value(v), generation(1) {
        ++n_created;
        update_max_live();
        std::cerr << "SortTracer #" << n_created
                  << ", created generation " << generation
```

```
                 << " (total: " << n_created - n_destroyed
                 << ")\n";
}

// copy constructor
SortTracer (SortTracer const& b)
 : value(b.value), generation(b.generation+1) {
    ++n_created;
    update_max_live();
    std::cerr << "SortTracer #" << n_created
              << ", copied as generation " << generation
              << " (total: " << n_created - n_destroyed
              << ")\n";
}

// destructor
~SortTracer() {
    ++n_destroyed;
    update_max_live();
    std::cerr << "SortTracer generation " << generation
              << " destroyed (total: "
              << n_created - n_destroyed << ")\n";
}

// assignment
SortTracer& operator= (SortTracer const& b) {
    ++n_assigned;
    std::cerr << "SortTracer assignment #" << n_assigned
              << " (generation " << generation
              << " = " << b.generation
              << ")\n";
    value = b.value;
    return *this;
}

// comparison
friend bool operator < (SortTracer const& a,
                        SortTracer const& b) {
    ++n_compared;
```

```
            std::cerr << "SortTracer comparison #" << n_compared
                      << " (generation " << a.generation
                      << " < " << b.generation
                      << ")\n";
            return a.value < b.value;
        }

        int val() const {
            return value;
        }
};
```

In addition to the value to sort, `value`, the tracer provides several members to trace an actual sort: `generation` traces for each object how many copies it is from the original. The other static members trace the number of creations (constructor calls), destructions, assignment comparisons, and the maximum number of objects that ever existed.

The static members are defined in a separate dot-C file:

// basics/tracer.cpp

```
#include "tracer.hpp"

long SortTracer::n_created = 0;
long SortTracer::n_destroyed = 0;
long SortTracer::n_max_live = 0;
long SortTracer::n_assigned = 0;
long SortTracer::n_compared = 0;
```

This particular tracer allows us to track the pattern of entity creation and destruction as well as assignments and comparisons performed by a given template. The following test program illustrates this for the `std::sort` algorithm of the C++ standard library:

// basics/tracertest.cpp

```
#include <iostream>
#include <algorithm>
#include "tracer.hpp"

int main()
{
    // prepare sample input:
    SortTracer input[] = { 7, 3, 5, 6, 4, 2, 0, 1, 9, 8 };
```

```
// print initial values:
for (int i=0; i<10; ++i) {
    std::cerr << input[i].val() << ' ';
}
std::cerr << std::endl;

// remember initial conditions:
long created_at_start = SortTracer::creations();
long max_live_at_start = SortTracer::max_live();
long assigned_at_start = SortTracer::assignments();
long compared_at_start = SortTracer::comparisons();

// execute algorithm:
std::cerr << "---[ Start std::sort() ]-------------------\n";
std::sort<>(&input[0], &input[9]+1);
std::cerr << "---[ End std::sort() ]---------------------\n";

// verify result:
for (int i=0; i<10; ++i) {
    std::cerr << input[i].val() << ' ';
}
std::cerr << "\n\n";

// final report:
std::cerr << "std::sort() of 10 SortTracer's"
          << " was performed by:\n "
          << SortTracer::creations() - created_at_start
          << " temporary tracers\n "
          << "up to "
          << SortTracer::max_live()
          << " tracers at the same time ("
          << max_live_at_start << " before)\n "
          << SortTracer::assignments() - assigned_at_start
          << " assignments\n "
          << SortTracer::comparisons() - compared_at_start
          << " comparisons\n\n";
}
```

Running this program creates a considerable amount of output, but much can be concluded from the "final report." For one implementation of the `std::sort()` function, we find the following:

```
std::sort() of 10 SortTracer's was performed by:
  15 temporary tracers
  up to 12 tracers at the same time (10 before)
  33 assignments
  27 comparisons
```

For example, we see that although 15 temporary tracers were created in our program while sorting, at most two additional tracers existed at any one time.

Our tracer thus fulfills two roles: It proves that the standard `sort()` algorithm requires no more functionality than our tracer (for example, operators `==` and `>` were not needed), and it gives us a sense of the cost of the algorithm. It does not, however, reveal much about the correctness of the sorting template.

6.6.5 Oracles

Tracers are relatively simple and effective, but they allow us to trace the execution of templates only for specific input data and for a specific behavior of its related functionality. We may wonder, for example, what conditions must be met by the comparison operator for the sorting algorithm to be meaningful (or correct), but in our example we have only tested a comparison operator that behaves exactly like less-than for integers.

An extension of tracers is known in some circles as *oracles* (or *run-time analysis oracles*). They are tracers that are connected to a so-called *inference engine*—a program that can remember assertions and reasons about them to infer certain conclusions. One such system that was applied to certain parts of a standard library implementation is called *MELAS* and is discussed in [*MusserWangDynaVeri*].[6]

Oracles allow us, in some cases, to verify template algorithms dynamically without fully specifying the substituting template arguments (the oracles are the arguments) or the input data (the inference engine may request some sort of input assumption when it gets stuck). However, the complexity of the algorithms that can be analyzed in this way is still modest (because of the limitations of the inference engines), and the amount of work is considerable. For these reasons, we do not delve into the development of oracles, but the interested reader should examine the publication mentioned earlier (and the references contained therein).

---

[6] One author, David Musser, was also a key figure in the development of the C++ standard library. Among other things, he designed and implemented the first associative containers.

6.6.6 Archetypes

We mentioned earlier that tracers often provide an interface that is the minimal requirement of the template they trace. When such a minimal tracer does not generate run-time output, it is sometimes called an *archetype*. An archetype allows us to verify that a template implementation does not require more syntactic constraints than intended. Typically, a template implementer will want to develop an archetype for every concept identified in the template library.

6.7   Afternotes

The organization of source code in header files and dot-C files is a practical consequence of various incarnations of the so-called *one-definition rule* or *ODR*. An extensive discussion of this rule is presented in Appendix A.

The inclusion versus separation model debate has been a controversial one. The inclusion model is a pragmatic answer dictated largely by existing practice in C++ compiler implementations. However, the first C++ implementation was different: The inclusion of template definitions was implicit, which created a certain illusion of *separation* (see Chapter 10 for details on this original model).

[*StroustrupDnE*] contains a good presentation of Stroustrup's vision for template code organization and the associated implementation challenges. It clearly wasn't the inclusion model. Yet, at some point in the standardization process, it seemed as if the inclusion model was the only viable approach after all. After some intense debates, however, those envisioning a more decoupled model garnered sufficient support for what eventually became the separation model. Unlike the inclusion model, this was a theoretical model not based on any existing implementation. It took more than five years to see its first implementation published (May 2002).

It is sometimes tempting to imagine ways of extending the concept of precompiled headers so that more than one header could be loaded for a single compilation. This would in principle allow for a finer grained approach to precompilation. The obstacle here is mainly the preprocessor: Macros in one header file can entirely change the meaning of subsequent header files. However, once a file has been precompiled, macro processing is completed, and it is hardly practical to attempt to patch a precompiled header for the preprocessor effects induced by other headers.

A fairly systematic attempt to improve C++ compiler diagnostics by adding dummy code in high-level templates can be found in Jeremy Siek's *Concept Check Library* (see [BCCL]). It is part of the Boost library (see [Boost]).

6.8   Summary

- Templates challenge the classic compiler-plus-linker model. Therefore there are different approaches to organize template code: the inclusion model, explicit instantiation, and the separation model.
- Usually, you should use the inclusion model (that is, put all template code in header files).

- By separating template code into different header files for declarations and definitions, you can more easily switch between the inclusion model and explicit instantiation.
- The C++ standard defines a separate compilation model for templates (using the keyword `export`). It is not yet widely available, however.
- Debugging code with templates can be challenging.
- Template instances may have very long names.
- To take advantage of precompiled headers, be sure to keep the same order for `#include` directives.

Chapter 7

Basic Template Terminology

So far we have introduced the basic concept of templates in C++. Before we go into details, let's look at the terms of the concepts we use. This is necessary because, inside the C++ community (and even in the standard), there is a lack of precision regarding concepts and terminology.

7.1 "Class Template" or "Template Class"?

In C++, structs, classes, and unions are collectively called *class types*. Without additional qualification, the word "class" in plain text type is meant to include class types introduced with either the keyword `class` or the keyword `struct`.[1] Note specifically that "class type" includes unions, but "class" does not.

There is some confusion about how a class that is a template is called:

- The term *class template* states that the class is a template. That is, it is a parameterized description of a family of classes.
- The term *template class* on the other hand has been used
  - as a synonym for class template.
  - to refer to classes generated from templates.
  - to refer to classes with a name that is a template-id.

  The difference between the second and third meaning is somewhat subtle and unimportant for the remainder of the text.

Because of this imprecision, we avoid the term *template class* in this book.

Similarly, we use *function template* and *member function template*, but avoid *template function* and *template member function*.

---

[1] In C++, the only difference between `class` and `struct` is that the default access for `class` is `private` whereas the default access for `struct` is `public`. However, we prefer to use `class` for types that use new C++ features, and we use `struct` for ordinary C data structure that can be used as "plain old data" (POD).

7.2 Instantiation and Specialization

The process of creating a regular class, function, or member function from a template by substituting actual values for its arguments is called *template instantiation*. This resulting entity (class, function, or member function) is generically called a *specialization*.

However, in C++ the instantiation process is not the only way to produce a specialization. Alternative mechanisms allow the programmer to specify explicitly a declaration that is tied to a special substitution of template parameters. As we introduced in Section 3.3 on page 27, such a specialization is introduced by `template<>`:

```
template <typename T1, typename T2>        // primary class template
class MyClass {
  ...
};


template<>                                 // explicit specialization
class MyClass<std::string,float> {
  ...
};
```

Strictly speaking, this is called a so-called *explicit specialization* (as opposed to an *instantiated* or *generated specialization*).

As introduced in Section 3.4 on page 29, specializations that still have template parameters are called *partial specializations*:

```
template <typename T>                      // partial specialization
class MyClass<T,T> {
  ...
};


template <typename T>                      // partial specialization
class MyClass<bool,T> {
  ...
};
```

When talking about (explicit or partial) specializations, the general template is also called the *primary template*.

7.3 Declarations versus Definitions

So far, the words *declaration* and *definition* have been used only a few times in this book. However, these words carry with them a rather precise meaning in standard C++, and that is the meaning that we use.

A *declaration* is a C++ construct that introduces or reintroduces a name into a C++ scope. This introduction always includes a partial classification of that name, but the details are not required to make a valid declaration. For example:

```
class C;          // a declaration of C as a class
void f(int p);    // a declaration of f() as a function and p as a named parameter
extern int v;     // a declaration of v as a variable
```

Note that even though they have a "name," macro definitions and `goto` labels are not considered declarations in C++.

Declarations become *definitions* when the details of their structure are made known or, in the case of variables, when storage space must be allocated. For class type and function definitions, this means a brace-enclosed body must be provided. For variables, initializations as well as a missing `extern` lead to definitions. Here are examples that complement the preceding nondefinition declarations:

```
class C {};           // definition (and declaration) of class C

void f(int p) {       // definition (and declaration) of function f()
    std::cout << p << std::endl;
}

extern int v = 1;     // an initializer makes this a definition for v

int w;                // global variable declarations not preceded by
                      // extern are also definitions
```

By extension, the declaration of a class template or function template is called a definition if it has a body. Hence,

```
template <typename T>
void func (T);
```

is a declaration that is not a definition, whereas

```
template <typename T>
class S {};
```

is in fact a definition.

7.4   The One-Definition Rule

The C++ language definition places some constraints on the redeclaration of various entities. The totality of these constraints is known as the *one-definition rule* or *ODR*. The details of this rule are quite complex and span a large variety of situations. Later chapters illustrate the various resulting facets in each applicable context, and you can find a complete description of the ODR in Appendix A. For now, it suffices to remember the following ODR basics:

- Noninline functions and member functions, as well as global variables and static data members should be defined only once across the whole *program*.
- Class types (including structs and unions) and inline functions should be defined at most once per *translation unit*, and all these definitions should be identical.

A *translation unit* is what results from preprocessing a source file; that is, it includes the contents named by #include directives.

   In the remainder of this book, *linkable entity* means one of the following: a noninline function or member function, a global variable or a static data member, including any such things generated from a template.

7.5   Template Arguments versus Template Parameters

Compare the following class template

```
template <typename T, int N>
class ArrayInClass {
  public:
    T array[N];
};
```

with a similar plain class:

```
class DoubleArrayInClass {
  public:
    double array[10];
};
```

The latter becomes essentially equivalent to the former if we replace the parameters T and N by double and 10 respectively. In C++, the name of this replacement is denoted as

```
ArrayInClass<double,10>
```

Note how the name of the template is followed by so-called *template arguments* in angle brackets.

   Regardless of whether these arguments are themselves dependent on template parameters, the combination of the template name, followed by the arguments in angle brackets, is called a *template-id*.

This name can be used much like a corresponding nontemplate entity would be used. For example:

```
int main()
{
    ArrayInClass<double,10> ad;
    ad.array[0] = 1.0;
}
```

It is essential to distinguish between *template parameters* and *template arguments*. In short, you can say that you "pass *arguments* to become *parameters*."[2] Or more precisely:

- *Template parameters* are those names that are listed after the keyword `template` in the template declaration or definition (`T` and `N` in our example).
- *Template arguments* are the items that are substituted for template parameters (`double` and 10 in our example). Unlike template parameters, template arguments can be more than just "names."

The substitution of template parameters by template arguments is explicit when indicated with a template-id, but there are various situations when the substitution is implicit (for example, if template parameters are substituted by their default arguments).

A fundamental principle is that any template argument must be a quantity or value that can be determined at compile time. As becomes clear later, this requirement translates into dramatic benefits for the run-time costs of template entities. Because template parameters are eventually substituted by compile-time values, they can themselves be used to form compile-time expressions. This was exploited in the `ArrayInClass` template to size the member array `array`. The size of an array must be a so-called *constant-expression*, and the template parameter `N` qualifies as such.

We can push this reasoning a little further: Because template parameters are compile-time entities, they can also be used to create valid template arguments. Here is an example:

```
template <typename T>
class Dozen {
  public:
    ArrayInClass<T,12> contents;
};
```

Note how in this example the name `T` is both a template parameter and a template argument. Thus, a mechanism is available to enable the construction of more complex templates from simpler ones. Of course, this is not fundamentally different from the mechanisms that allow us to assemble types and functions.

---

[2] In the academic world, *arguments* are sometimes called *actual parameters* whereas *parameters* are called *formal parameters*.

Part II

Templates in Depth

The first part of this book provided a tutorial for most of the language concepts underlying C++ templates. That presentation is sufficient to answer the majority of questions that may arise in everyday C++ programming. The second part of this book provides a reference that answers even the more unusual questions that arise when pushing the envelope of the language to achieve some advanced software effect. If desired, you can skip this part on a first read and return to specific topics as prompted by references in later chapters or after looking up a concept in the index.

Our goal is to be clear and complete, but also to keep the discussion concise. To this end, our examples are short and often somewhat artificial. This also ensures that we don't stray from the topic at hand to unrelated issues.

In addition, we look at possible future changes and extensions for the templates language feature in C++. Topics include:

- Fundamental template declaration issues
- The meaning of names in templates
- The C++ template instantiation mechanisms
- The template argument deduction rules
- Specialization and overloading
- Future possibilities

Chapter 8

Fundamentals in Depth

In this chapter we review some of the fundamentals introduced in the first part of this book *in depth*: the declaration of templates, the restrictions on template parameters, the constraints on template arguments, and so forth.

8.1   Parameterized Declarations

C++ currently supports two fundamental kinds of templates: class templates and function templates (see Section 13.6 on page 212 for a possible future change in this area). This classification includes member templates. Such templates are declared much like ordinary classes and functions, except for being introduced by a *parameterization clause* of the form

```
template<... parameters here... >
```

or perhaps

```
export template<... parameters here... >
```

(see Section 6.3 on page 68 and Section 10.3.3 on page 149 for a detailed explanation of the keyword `export`).

We'll come back to the actual template parameter declarations in a later section. An example illustrates the two kinds of templates, both as class members and as ordinary namespace scope declarations:

```
template <typename T>
class List {                        // a namespace scope class template
  public:
    template <typename T2>          // a member function template
    List (List<T2> const&);         // (constructor)

    ...
};
```

```
template <typename T>
 template <typename T2>
List<T>::List (List<T2> const& b)   // an out-of-class member function
{                                   // template definition

    ...

}


template <typename T>
int length (List<T> const&);        // a namespace scope function template

class Collection {
    template <typename T>           // an in-class member class template
    class Node {                    // definition

        ...

    };

    template <typename T>           // another member class template,
    class Handle;                   // without its definition

    template <typename T>           // an in-class (and therefore implicitly
    T* alloc() {                    // inline) member function template
        ...                         // definition
    }
    ...
};

template <typename T>               // an out-of-class member class
class Collection::Handle {          // template definition

    ...

};
```

Note how member templates defined outside their enclosing class can have multiple template<...> parameterization clauses: one for the template itself and one for every enclosing class template. The clauses are listed starting from the outermost class template.

Union templates are possible too (and they are considered a kind of class template):

```
template <typename T>
union AllocChunk {
    T object;
    unsigned char bytes[sizeof(T)];
};
```

Function templates can have default call arguments just like ordinary function declarations:

```
template <typename T>
void report_top (Stack<T> const&, int number = 10);

template <typename T>
void fill (Array<T>*, T const& = T());   // T() is zero for built-in types
```

The latter declaration shows that a default call argument could depend on a template parameter. When the `fill()` function is called, the default argument is not instantiated if a second function call argument is supplied. This ensures that no error is issued if the default call argument cannot be instantiated for a particular T. For example:

```
class Value {
  public:
    Value(int);              // no default constructor
};

void init (Array<Value>* array)
{
    Value zero(0);

    fill(array, zero);   // OK: = T() is not used
    fill(array);         // ERROR: = T() is used, but not valid for T = Value
}
```

In addition to the two fundamental kinds of templates, three other kinds of declarations can be parameterized using a similar notation. All three correspond to definitions of members of class templates[1]:

1. Definitions of member functions of class templates
2. Definitions of nested class members of class templates
3. Definitions of static data members of class templates

Although they can be parameterized, such definitions aren't quite first-class templates. Their parameters are entirely determined by the template of which they are members. Here is an example of such definitions:

```
template <int I>
class CupBoard {
    void open();
    class Shelf;
    static double total_weight;
    ...
};
```

---

[1] They are much like ordinary class members, but they are occasionally (erroneously) referred to as *member templates*.

```
template <int I>
void CupBoard<I>::open()
{
    ...
}

template <int I>
class CupBoard<I>::Shelf {
    ...
};

template <int I>
double CupBoard<I>::total_weight = 0.0;
```

Although such parameterized definitions are commonly called *templates*, there are contexts when the term doesn't quite apply to them.

8.1.1 Virtual Member Functions

Member function templates cannot be declared virtual. This constraint is imposed because the usual implementation of the virtual function call mechanism uses a fixed-size table with one entry per virtual function. However, the number of instantiations of a member function template is not fixed until the entire program has been translated. Hence, supporting virtual member function templates would require support for a whole new kind of mechanism in C++ compilers and linkers.

In contrast, the ordinary members of class templates can be virtual because their number is fixed when a class is instantiated:

```
template <typename T>
class Dynamic {
  public:
    virtual ~Dynamic();   // OK: one destructor per instance of Dynamic<T>

    template <typename T2>
    virtual void copy (T2 const&);
                          // ERROR: unknown number of instances of copy()
                          //         given an instance of Dynamic<T>
};
```

8.1.2   Linkage of Templates

Every template must have a name and that name must be unique within its scope, except that function templates can be overloaded (see Chapter 12). Note especially that, unlike class types, class templates cannot share a name with a different kind of entity:

```
int C;

class C;   // OK: class names and nonclass names are in a different ''space''

int X;

template <typename T>
class X;   // ERROR: conflict with variable X

struct S;

template <typename T>
class S;   // ERROR: conflict with struct S
```

Template names have linkage, but they cannot have *C linkage*. Nonstandard linkages may have an implementation-dependent meaning (however, we don't know of an implementation that supports nonstandard name linkages for templates):

```
extern "C++" template <typename T>
void normal();
    // this is the default: the linkage specification could be left out

extern "C" template <typename T>
void invalid();
    // ERROR: templates cannot have C linkage

extern "Xroma" template <typename T>
void xroma_link();
    // nonstandard, but maybe some compiler will some day
    // support linkage compatible with the Xroma language
```

Templates usually have external linkage. The only exceptions are namespace scope function templates with the `static` specifier:

```
template <typename T>
void external();                    // refers to the same entity as a declaration of
                                    // the same name (and scope) in another file
```

```
template <typename T>
static void internal();    // unrelated to a template with the same name in
                           // another file
```

Note that templates cannot be declared in a function.

8.1.3 Primary Templates

Normal declarations of templates declare so-called *primary templates*. Such template declarations are declared without adding template arguments in angle brackets after the template name:

```
template<typename T> class Box;           // OK: primary template

template<typename T> class Box<T>;        // ERROR

template<typename T> void translate(T*);  // OK: primary template

template<typename T> void translate<T>(T*); // ERROR
```

Nonprimary class templates occur when declaring so-called *partial specializations* which are discussed in Chapter 12. Function templates must always be primary templates (but see Section 13.7 on page 213 for a potential future language change).

8.2   Template Parameters

There are three kinds of template parameters:

1. Type parameters (these are by far the most common)
2. Nontype parameters
3. Template template parameters

Template parameters are declared in the introductory parameterization clause of a template declaration. Such declarations do not necessarily need to be named:

```
template <typename, int>
class X;
```

A parameter name is, of course, required if the parameter is referred to later in the template. Note also that a template parameter name can be referred to in a subsequent parameter declaration (but not before):

```
template <typename T,              // the first parameter is used in the
          T* Root,                 // declaration of the second one and
          template<T*> class Buf>  // the third one
class Structure;
```

8.2.1   Type Parameters

Type parameters are introduced with either the keyword `typename` or the keyword `class`: The two are entirely equivalent.[2] The keyword must be followed by a simple identifier and that identifier must be followed by a comma to denote the start of the next parameter declaration, a closing angle bracket (`>`) to denote the end of the parameterization clause, or an equal sign (`=`) to denote the beginning of a default template argument.

Within a template declaration, a type parameter acts much like a *typedef name*. For example, it is not possible to use an elaborated name of the form `class T` when T is a template parameter, even if T were to be substituted by a class type:

```
template <typename Allocator>
class List {
    class Allocator* allocator;   // ERROR
    friend class Allocator;       // ERROR
    ...
};
```

It is possible that a mechanism to enable such a friend declaration will be added in the future.

8.2.2   Nontype Parameters

Nontype template parameters stand for constant values that can be determined at compile or link time.[3] The type of such a parameter (in other words, the type of the value for which it stands) must be one of the following:

- An integer type or an enumeration type
- A pointer type (including regular object pointer types, function pointer types, and pointer-to-member types)
- A reference type (both references to objects and references to functions are acceptable)

All other types are currently excluded (although floating-point types may be added in the future, see Section 13.4 on page 210).

Perhaps surprisingly, the declaration of a nontype template parameter can in some cases also start with the keyword `typename`:

```
template<typename T,                          // a type parameter
         typename T::Allocator* Allocator> // a nontype parameter
class List;
```

---

[2] The keyword `class` does *not* imply that the substituting argument should be a class type. It could be almost any accessible type. However, class types that are defined in a function (*local classes*) cannot be used as template arguments (independent of whether the parameter was declared with `typename` or `class`).

[3] Template template parameters do not denote types either; however, they are not considered when talking about *nontype* parameters.

The two cases are easily distinguished because the first is followed by a simple identifier, whereas the second is followed by a *qualified name* (in other words, a name containing a double colon, `::`). Section 5.1 on page 43 and Section 9.3.2 on page 130 explain the need for the keyword `typename` in the nontype parameter.

Function and array types can be specified, but they are implicitly adjusted to the pointer type to which they decay:

```
template<int buf[5]> class Lexer;          // buf is really an int*
template<int* buf> class Lexer;            // OK: this is a redeclaration
```

Nontype template parameters are declared much like variables, but they cannot have nontype specifiers like `static`, `mutable`, and so forth. They can have `const` and `volatile` qualifiers, but if such a qualifier appears at the outermost level of the parameter type, it is simply ignored:

```
template<int const length> class Buffer; // const is useless here
template<int length> class Buffer;         // same as previous declaration
```

Finally, nontype parameters are always *rvalues*: Their address cannot be taken, and they cannot be assigned to.

8.2.3   Template Template Parameters

Template template parameters are placeholders for class templates. They are declared much like class templates, but the keywords `struct` and `union` cannot be used:

```
template <template<typename X> class C>  // OK
void f(C<int>* p);


template <template<typename X> struct C> // ERROR: struct not valid here
void f(C<int>* p);


template <template<typename X> union C>  // ERROR: union not valid here
void f(C<int>* p);
```

In the scope of their declaration, template template parameters are used just like other class templates.

The parameters of template template parameters can have default template arguments. These default arguments apply when the corresponding parameters are not specified in uses of the template template parameter:

```
template <template<typename T,
                   typename A = MyAllocator> class Container>
class Adaptation {
    Container<int> storage;   // implicitly equivalent to
                              // Container<int, MyAllocator>

    ...
};
```

The name of a template parameter of a template template parameter can be used only in the declaration of other parameters of that template template parameter. The following contrived template illustrates this concept:

```
template <template<typename T, T*> class Buf>
class Lexer {
    static char storage[5];
    Buf<char, &Lexer<Buf>::storage[0]> buf;
    ...
};


template <template<typename T> class List>
class Node {
    static T* storage;    // ERROR: a parameter of a template template
                          //        parameter cannot be used here
    ...
};
```

Usually however, the names of the template parameters of a template template parameter are not used. As a result, the former parameters are often left unnamed altogether. For example, our earlier Adaptation template could be declared as follows:

```
template <template <typename,
                    typename = MyAllocator> class Container>
class Adaptation {
    Container<int> storage;   // implicitly equivalent to
                              // Container<int, MyAllocator>
    ...
};
```

8.2.4 Default Template Arguments

Currently, only class template declarations can have default template arguments (see Section 13.3 on page 207 for likely changes in this area). Any kind of template parameter can be equipped with a default argument, although it must match the corresponding parameter. Clearly, a default argument should not depend on its own parameter. However, it may depend on previous parameters:

```
template <typename T, typename Allocator = allocator<T> >
class List;
```

Similar to default function call arguments, a template parameter can have a default template argument only if default arguments were also supplied for the subsequent parameters. The subsequent default values are usually provided in the same template declaration, but they could also have been declared in a previous declaration of that template. The following example makes this clear:

```
template <typename T1, typename T2, typename T3,
          typename T4 = char, typename T5 = char>
class Quintuple;   // OK

template <typename T1, typename T2, typename T3 = char,
          typename T4, typename T5>
class Quintuple;   // OK: T4 and T5 already have defaults

template <typename T1 = char, typename T2, typename T3,
          typename T4, typename T5>
class Quintuple;   // ERROR: T1 cannot have a default argument
                   // because T2 doesn't have a default
```

Default template arguments cannot be repeated:

```
template<typename T = void>
class Value;

template<typename T = void>
class Value;   // ERROR: repeated default argument
```

8.3   Template Arguments

Template arguments are the "values" that are substituted for template parameters when instantiating a template. These values can be determined using several different mechanisms:

- Explicit template arguments: A template name can be followed by explicit template argument values enclosed in angle brackets. The resulting name is called a *template-id*.
- Injected class name: Within the scope of a class template X with template parameters P1, P2, ..., the name of that template (X) can be equivalent to the template-id X<P1, P2, ...>. See Section 9.2.3 on page 126 for details.
- Default template arguments: Explicit template arguments can be omitted from class template instances if default template arguments are available. However, even if all template parameters have a default value, the (possibly empty) angle brackets must be provided.
- Argument deduction: Function template arguments that are not explicitly specified may be deduced from the types of the function call arguments in a call. This is described in detail in Chapter 11. Deduction is also done in a few other situations. If all the template arguments can be deduced, no angle brackets need to be specified after the name of the function template.

8.3.1 Function Template Arguments

Template arguments for a function template can be specified explicitly or deduced from the way the template is used. For example:

```
// details/max.cpp

template <typename T>
inline T const& max (T const& a, T const& b)
{
    return  a < b ? b : a;
}

int main()
{
    max<double>(1.0, -3.0);   // explicitly specify template argument
    max(1.0, -3.0);           // template argument is implicitly deduced
                              // to be double
    max<int>(1.0, 3.0);       // the explicit <int> inhibits the deduction;
                              // hence the result has type int
}
```

Some template arguments can never be deduced (see Chapter 11). The corresponding parameters are best placed at the beginning of the list of template parameters so they can be specified explicitly while allowing the other arguments to be deduced. For example:

```
// details/implicit.cpp

template <typename DstT, typename SrcT>
inline DstT implicit_cast (SrcT const& x)   // SrcT can be deduced,
{                                           // but DstT cannot
    return x;
}

int main()
{
    double value = implicit_cast<double>(-1);
}
```

If we had reversed the order of the template parameters in this example (in other words, if we had written template<typename SrcT, typename DstT>), a call of implicit_cast would have to specify both template arguments explicitly.

Because function templates can be overloaded, explicitly providing all the arguments for a function template may not be sufficient to identify a single function: In some cases, it identifies a *set* of functions. The following example illustrates a consequence of this observation:

```
template <typename Func, typename T>
void apply (Func func_ptr, T x)
{
    func_ptr(x);
}

template <typename T> void single(T);

template <typename T> void multi(T);
template <typename T> void multi(T*);

int main()
{
    apply(&single<int>, 3);   // OK
    apply(&multi<int>, 7);    // ERROR: no single multi<int>
}
```

In this example, the first call to `apply()` works because the type of the expression `&single<int>` is unambiguous. As a result, the template argument value for the `Func` parameter is easily deduced. In the second call, however, `&multi<int>` could be one of two different types and therefore `Func` cannot be deduced in this case.

Furthermore, it is possible that explicitly specifying the template arguments for a function template results in an attempt to construct an invalid C++ type. Consider the following overloaded function template (RT1 and RT2 are unspecified types):

```
template<typename T> RT1 test(typename T::X const*);
template<typename T> RT2 test(...);
```

The expression `test<int>` makes no sense for the first of the two function templates because type `int` has no member type `X`. However, the second template has no such problem. Therefore, the expression `&test<int>` identifies the address of a single function. The fact that the substitution of `int` into the first template fails does not make the expression invalid.

This "substitution-failure-is-not-an-error" (SFINAE) principle is clearly an important ingredient to make the overloading of function templates practical. However, it also enables remarkable compile-time techniques. For example, assuming that types RT1 and RT2 are defined as follows:

```
typedef char RT1;
typedef struct { char a[2]; } RT2;
```

We can check *at compile time* (in other words, as a so-called *constant-expression*) whether a given type T has a member type X:

```
#define type_has_member_type_X(T)          \
        (sizeof(test<T>(0)) == 1)
```

To understand the expression in this macro, it is convenient to analyze from the outside to the inside. First, the `sizeof` expression will equal one if the first `test` template (which returns a `char` of size one) is selected. The other template returns a structure with a size that is at least two (because it contains an array of size two). In other words, this is a device to determine as a constant-expression whether the first or second template was selected for the call `test<T>(0)`. Clearly, the first template cannot be selected if the given type T has no member type X. However, if the given type *has* a member type X, then the first template is preferred because overload resolution (see Appendix B) prefers the conversion from zero to a null pointer constant over binding an argument to an ellipsis parameter (ellipsis parameters are the weakest kind of binding from an overload resolution perspective). Similar techniques are explored in Chapter 15.

The SFINAE principle protects only against attempts to create invalid types but not against attempts to evaluate invalid expressions. The following example is therefore invalid C++:

```
template<int I> void f(int (&)[24/(4-I)]);
template<int I> void f(int (&)[24/(4+I)]);

int main()
{
    &f<4>;     // ERROR: division by zero (SFINAE doesn't apply)
}
```

This example is an error even though the second template supports the substitution without leading to a division by zero. This sort of error must occur in the expression itself and not in binding of an expression to a template parameter. Indeed, the following example is valid:

```
template<int N>  int g() { return N; }
template<int* P> int g() { return *P; }

int main()
{
    return g<1>(); // 1 cannot be bound to int* parameter,
}                  // but SFINAE principle applies
```

See Section 15.2.2 on page 266 and Section 19.3 on page 353 for further applications of the SFINAE principle.

8.3.2   Type Arguments

Template type arguments are the "values" specified for template type parameters. Most commonly used types can be used as template arguments, but there are two exceptions:

1. Local classes and enumerations (in other words, types declared in a function definition) cannot be involved in template type arguments.

2. Types that involve unnamed class types or unnamed enumeration types cannot be template type arguments (unnamed classes or enumerations that are given a name through a typedef declaration are OK).

An example illustrates these two exceptions:

```
template <typename T> class List {
    ...
};

typedef struct {
    double x, y, z;
} Point;

typedef enum { red, green, blue } *ColorPtr;

int main()
{
    struct Association
    {
        int* p;
        int* q;
    };
    List<Association*> error1; // ERROR: local type in template argument
    List<ColorPtr> error2;     // ERROR: unnamed type in template
                               //          argument
    List<Point> ok;            // OK: unnamed class type named through
                               //      a typedef
}
```

Although other types can, in general, be used as template arguments, their substitution for the template parameters must lead to valid constructs:

```
template <typename T>
void clear (T p)
{
    *p = 0;       // requires that the unary * be applicable to T
}
```

```
int main()
{
    int a;
    clear(a);   // ERROR: int doesn't support the unary *
}
```

8.3.3 Nontype Arguments

Nontype template arguments are the values substituted for nontype parameters. Such a value must be one of the following things:

- Another nontype template parameter that has the right type
- A compile-time constant value of integer (or enumeration) type. This is acceptable only if the corresponding parameter has a type that matches that of the value, or a type to which the value can be implicitly converted (for example, a char can be provided for an int parameter).
- The name of an external variable or function preceded by the built-in unary & ("address of") operator. For functions and array variables, & can be left out. Such template arguments match nontype parameters of a pointer type.
- The previous kind of argument but without a leading & operator is a valid argument for a nontype parameter of reference type.
- A pointer-to-member constant; in other words, an expression of the form &C::m where C is a class type and m is a nonstatic member (data or function). This matches nontype parameters of pointer-to-member type only.

When matching an argument to a parameter that is a pointer or reference, *user-defined conversions* (constructors for one argument and conversion operators) and derived-to-base conversions are not considered, even though in other circumstances they would be valid implicit conversions. Implicit conversions that make an argument more const or more volatile are fine.

Here are some valid examples of nontype template arguments:

```
template <typename T, T nontype_param>
class C;

C<int, 33>* c1;        // integer type

int a;
C<int*, &a>* c2;       // address of an external variable

void f();
void f(int);
C<void (*)(int), f>* c3;
                       // name of a function: overload resolution selects
                       // f(int) in this case; the & is implied
```

```
class X {
  public:
    int n;
    static bool b;
};
```

```
C<bool&, X::b>* c4;    // static class members are acceptable variable
                       // and function names
```

```
C<int X::*, &X::n>* c5;
                       // an example of a pointer-to-member constant
```

```
template<typename T>
void templ_func();
```

```
C<void (), &templ_func<double> >* c6;
                       // function template instantiations are functions too
```

A general constraint of template arguments is that a compiler or a linker must be able to express their value when the program is being built. Values that aren't known until a program is run (for example, the address of local variables) aren't compatible with the notion that templates are instantiated when the program is built.

Even so, there are some constant values that are, perhaps surprisingly, not currently valid:

- Null pointer constants
- Floating-point numbers
- String literals

One of the problems with string literals is that two identical literals can be stored at two distinct addresses. An alternative (but cumbersome) way to express templates instantiated over constant strings involves introducing an additional variable to hold the string:

```
template <char const* str>
class Message;
```

```
extern char const hello[] = "Hello World!";
```

```
Message<hello>* hello_msg;
```

Note the need for the `extern` keyword because otherwise a `const` array variable would have internal linkage.

See Section 4.3 on page 40 for another example and Section 13.4 on page 209 for a discussion of possible future changes in this area.

Here are few other (less surprising) invalid examples:

```
template<typename T, T nontype_param>
class C;

class Base {
  public:
    int i;
} base;

class Derived : public Base {
} derived_obj;

C<Base*, &derived_obj>* err1;   // ERROR: derived-to-base conversions are
                                //          not considered


C<int&, base.i>* err2;          // ERROR: fields of variables aren't
                                //          considered to be variables

int a[10];
C<int*, &a[0]>* err3;           // ERROR: addresses of individual array
                                //          elements aren't acceptable either
```

8.3.4 Template Template Arguments

A template template argument must be a class template with parameters that *exactly* match the parameters of the template template parameter it substitutes. Default template arguments of a template template *argument* are ignored (but if the template template *parameter* has default arguments, they are considered during the instantiation of the template).

This makes the following example invalid:

```
#include <list>
    // declares:
    // namespace std {
    //      template <typename T,
    //                typename Allocator = allocator<T> >
    //      class list;
    // }
```

```
template<typename T1,
         typename T2,
         template<typename> class Container>
                                // Container expects templates with only
                                // one parameter
class Relation {
  public:
    ...
  private:
    Container<T1> dom1;
    Container<T2> dom2;
};

int main()
{
    Relation<int, double, std::list> rel;
        // ERROR: std::list has more than one template parameter
    ...
}
```

The problem in this example is that the std::list template of the standard library has more than one parameter. The second parameter (which describes a so-called *allocator*) has a default value, but this is not considered when matching std::list to the Container parameter.

Sometimes, such situations can be worked around by adding a parameter with a default value to the template template parameter. In the case of the previous example, we may rewrite the Relation template as follows:

```
#include <memory>

template<typename T1,
         typename T2,
         template<typename T,
                  typename = std::allocator<T> > class Container>
            // Container now accepts standard container templates
class Relation {
  public:
    ...
  private:
    Container<T1> dom1;
    Container<T2> dom2;
};
```

Clearly this isn't entirely satisfactory, but it enables the use of standard container templates. Section 13.5 on page 211 discusses possible future changes of this topic.

The fact that syntactically only the keyword `class` can be used to declare a template template parameter is not to be construed as an indication that only class templates declared with the keyword `class` are allowed as substituting arguments. Indeed, "struct templates" and "union templates" are valid arguments for a template template parameter. This is similar to the observation that (just about) any type can be used as an argument for a template type parameter declared with the keyword `class`.

8.3.5 Equivalence

Two sets of template arguments are equivalent when values of the arguments are identical one-for-one. For type arguments, typedef names don't matter: It is the type ultimately underlying the typedef that is compared. For integer nontype arguments, the value of the argument is compared; how that value is expressed doesn't matter. The following example illustrates this concept:

```
template <typename T, int I>
class Mix;

typedef int Int;

Mix<int, 3*3>* p1;
Mix<Int, 4+5>* p2;   // p2 has the same type as p1
```

A function generated from a function template is never equivalent to an ordinary function even though they may have the same type and the same name. This has two important consequences for class members:

1. A function generated from a member function template never overrides a virtual function.
2. A constructor generated from a constructor template is never a default copy constructor. (Similarly, an assignment generated from an assignment template is never a copy-assignment operator. However, this is less prone to problems because implicit calls of copy-assignment operators are less common.)

8.4 Friends

The basic idea of friend declarations is a simple one: Identify classes or functions that have a privileged connection with the class in which the friend declaration appears. Matters are somewhat complicated, however, by two facts:

1. A friend declaration may be the only declaration of an entity.
2. A friend function declaration can be a definition.

Friend class declarations cannot be definitions and therefore are rarely problematic. In the context of templates, the only new facet of friend class declarations is the ability to name a particular instance of a class template as a friend:

```
template <typename T>
class Node;

template <typename T>
class Tree {
    friend class Node<T>;
    ...
};
```

Note that the class template must be visible at the point where one of its instances is made a friend of a class or class template. With an ordinary class, there is no such requirement:

```
template <typename T>
class Tree {
    friend class Factory;    // OK, even if first declaration of Factory
    friend class Node<T>;    // ERROR if Node isn't visible
};
```

Section 9.2.2 on page 125 has more to say about this.

8.4.1   Friend Functions

An instance of a function template can be made a friend by making sure the name of the friend function is followed by angle brackets. The angle brackets can contain the template arguments, but if the arguments can be deduced, the angle brackets can be left empty:

```
template <typename T1, typename T2>
void combine(T1, T2);

class Mixer {
    friend void combine<>(int&, int&);
                        // OK: T1 = int&, T2 = int&
    friend void combine<int, int>(int, int);
                        // OK: T1 = int, T2 = int
    friend void combine<char>(char, int);
                        // OK: T1 = char T2 = int
    friend void combine<char>(char&, int);
                        // ERROR: doesn't match combine() template
    friend void combine<>(long, long) { ... }
                        // ERROR: definition not allowed!
};
```

Note that we cannot *define* a template instance (at most, we can define a specialization), and hence a friend declaration that names an instance cannot be a definition.

If the name is not followed by angle brackets, there are two possibilities:

1. If the name isn't qualified (in other words, it doesn't contain a double colon), it never refers to a template instance. If no matching nontemplate function is visible at the point of the friend declaration, the friend declaration is the first declaration of that function. The declaration could also be a definition.

2. If the name *is* qualified (it contains : :), the name must refer to a previously declared function or function template. A matching function is preferred over a matching function template. However, such a friend declaration cannot be a definition.

An example may help clarify the various possibilities:

```
void multiply(void*);       // ordinary function

template <typename T>
void multiply(T);           // function template

class Comrades {
    friend void multiply(int) {}
                            // defines a new function ::multiply(int)

    friend void ::multiply(void*);
                            // refers to the ordinary function above;
                            // not to the multiply<void*> instance

    friend void ::multiply(int);
                            // refers to an instance of the template

    friend void ::multiply<double*>(double*);
                            // qualified names can also have angle brackets
                            // but a template must be visible.

    friend void ::error() {}
                            // ERROR: a qualified friend cannot be a definition
};
```

In our previous examples, we declared the friend functions in an ordinary class. The same rules apply when we declare them in class templates, but the template parameters may participate in identifying the function that is to be a friend:

```
template <typename T>
class Node {
    Node<T>* allocate();
    ...
};
```

```
template <typename T>
class List {
    friend Node<T>* Node<T>::allocate();
    ...
};
```

However, an interesting effect occurs when a friend function is *defined* in a class template because anything that is only declared in a template isn't a concrete entity until the template is instantiated. Consider the following example:

```
template <typename T>
class Creator {
    friend void appear() {    // a new function ::appear(), but it doesn't
        ...                   // exist until Creator is instantiated
    }
};
```

```
Creator<void> miracle;    // ::appear() is created at this point
Creator<double> oops;     // ERROR: ::appear() is created a second time!
```

In this example, two different instantiations create two identical definitions—a direct violation of the *ODR* (see Appendix A).

We must therefore make sure the template parameters of the class template appear in the type of any friend function defined in that template (unless we want to prevent more than one instantiation of a class template in a particular file, but this is rather unlikely). Let's apply this to a variation of our previous example:

```
template <typename T>
class Creator {
    friend void feed(Creator<T>*){    // every T generates a different
        ...                           // function ::feed()
    }
};
```

```
Creator<void> one;      // generates ::feed(Creator<void>*)
Creator<double> two;    // generates ::feed(Creator<double>*)
```

In this example, every instantiation of `Creator` generates a different function. Note that even though these functions are generated as part of the instantiation of a template, the functions themselves are ordinary functions, not instances of a template.

Also note that because the body of these functions is defined inside a class definition, they are implicitly inline. Hence, it is not an error for the same function to be generated in two different translation units. Section 9.2.2 on page 125 and Section 11.7 on page 174 have more to say about this topic.

8.4.2   Friend Templates

Usually when declaring a friend that is an instance of a function or a class template, we can express exactly which entity is to be the friend. Sometimes it is nonetheless useful to express that all instances of a template are friends of a class. This requires a so-called *friend template*. For example:

```
class Manager {
    template<typename T>
        friend class Task;
    template<typename T>
        friend void Schedule<T>::dispatch(Task<T>*);
    template<typename T>
        friend int ticket() {
            return ++Manager::counter;
        }
    static int counter;
};
```

Just as with ordinary friend declarations a friend template can be a definition only if it names an unqualified function name that is not followed by angle brackets.

A friend template can declare only primary templates and members of primary templates. Any partial specializations and explicit specializations associated with a primary template are automatically considered friends too.

8.5   Afternotes

The general concept and syntax of C++ templates have remained relatively stable since their inception in the late 1980s. Class templates and function templates were part of the initial template facility. So were type parameters and nontype parameters.

However, there were also some significant additions to the original design, mostly driven by the needs of the C++ standard library. Member templates may well be the most fundamental of those additions. Curiously, only member *function* templates were formally voted into the C++ standard. Member *class* templates became part of the standard by an editorial oversight.

Friend templates, default template arguments, and template template parameters are also relatively recent additions to the language. The ability to declare template template parameters is sometimes called *higher-order genericity*. They were originally introduced to support a certain allocator model in the C++ standard library, but that allocator model was later replaced by one that does not rely on template template parameters. Later, template template parameters came close to being removed from the language because their specification had remained incomplete until very late in the standardization process. Eventually a majority of committee members voted to keep them and their specifications were completed.

Chapter 9

Names in Templates

Names are a fundamental concept in most programming languages. They are the means by which a programmer can refer to previously constructed entities. When a C++ compiler encounters a name, it must "look it up" to identify the entity being referred. From an implementer's point of view, C++ is a hard language in this respect. Consider the C++ statement x*y;. If x and y are the names of variables, this statement is a multiplication, but if x is the name of a type, then the statement declares y as a pointer to an entity of type x.

This small example demonstrates that C++ (like C) is a so-called *context-sensitive language*: A construct cannot always be understood without knowing its wider context. How does this relate to templates? Well, templates are constructs that must deal with multiple wider contexts: (1) the context in which the template appears, (2) the context in which the template is instantiated, and (3) the contexts associated with the template arguments for which the template is instantiated. Hence it should not be totally surprising that "names" must be dealt with quite carefully in C++.

9.1 Name Taxonomy

C++ classifies names in a variety of ways—a large variety of ways in fact. To help cope with this abundance of terminology, we provide Table 9.1 and Table 9.2, which describe these classifications. Fortunately, you can gain good insight into most C++ template issues by familiarizing yourself with two major naming concepts:

1. A name is a *qualified name* if the scope to which it belongs is explicitly denoted using a scope-resolution operator (::) or a member access operator (. or ->). For example, this->count is a qualified name, but count is not (even though the plain count might actually refer to a class member).

2. A name is a *dependent name* if it depends in some way on a template parameter. For example, std::vector<T>::iterator is a dependent name if T is a template parameter, but it is a nondependent name if T is a known typedef (for example, of int).

Classification	Explanation and Notes
Identifier	A name that consists solely of an uninterrupted sequences of letters, underscores (_) and digits. It cannot start with a digit, and some identifiers are reserved for the implementation: You should not introduce them in your programs (as a rule of thumb, avoid leading underscores and double underscores). The concept of "letter" should be taken broadly and includes special *universal character names* (*UCNs*) that encode glyphs from nonalphabetical languages.
Operator-function-id	The keyword `operator` followed by the symbol for an operator—for example, `operator new` and `operator []`. Many operators have alternative representations. For example, `operator &` can equivalently be written as `operator bitand` even when it denotes the unary *address of* operator.
Conversion-function-id	Used to denote a user-defined implicit conversion operator—for example `operator int&`, which could also be obfuscated as `operator int bitand`.
Template-id	The name of a template followed by template arguments enclosed in angle brackets; for example, `List<T, int, 0>`. (Strictly speaking, the C++ standard allows only simple identifiers for the template name of a template-id. However, this is probably an oversight and an operator-function-id should be allowed too; e.g. `operator+<X<int> >`.)
Unqualified-id	The generalization of an identifier. It can be any of the above (identifier, operator-function-id, conversion-function-id or template-id) or a "destructor name" (for example, notations like `~Data` or `~List<T, T, N>`).
Qualified-id	An unqualified-id that is qualified with the name of a class or namespace, or just with the global scope resolution operator. Note that such a name itself can be qualified. Examples are `::X`, `S::x`, `Array<T>::y`, and `::N::A<T>::z`.
Qualified name	This term is not defined in the standard, but we use it to refer to names that undergo so-called *qualified lookup*. Specifically, this is a qualified-id or an unqualified-id that is used after an explicit member access operator (`.` or `->`). Examples are `S::x`, `this->f`, and `p->A::m`. However, just `class_mem` in a context that is implicitly equivalent to `this->class_mem` is not a qualified name: The member access must be explicit.
Unqualified name	An unqualified-id that is not a qualified name. This is not a standard term but corresponds to names that undergo what the standard calls *unqualified lookup*.

Table 9.1. Name Taxonomy (part one)

Classification	Explanation and Notes
Name	Either a qualified or an unqualified name.
Dependent name	A name that depends in some way on a template parameter. Certainly any qualified or unqualified name that explicitly contains a template parameter is dependent. Furthermore, a qualified name that is qualified by a member access operator (. or ->) is dependent if the type of the expression on the left of the access operator depends on a template parameter. In particular, b in this->b is a dependent name when it appears in a template. Finally, the identifier ident in a call of the form ident(x, y, z) is a dependent name if and only if any of the argument expressions has a type that depends on a template parameter.
Nondependent name	A name that is not a dependent name by the above description.

Table 9.2. Name Taxonomy (part two)

It is useful to read through the tables to gain some familiarity with the terms that are sometimes used to describe C++ template issues, but it is not essential to remember the exact meaning of every term. Should the need arise, they can be found easily in the index.

9.2 Looking Up Names

There are many small details to looking up names in C++, but we will focus only on a few major concepts. The details are necessary to ensure only that (1) normal cases are treated intuitively, and (2) pathological cases are covered in some way by the standard.

Qualified names are looked up in the scope implied by the qualifying construct. If that scope is a class, then base classes may also be searched. However, enclosing scopes are not considered when looking up qualified names. The following illustrates this basic principle:

```
int x;

class B {
  public:
    int i;
};

class D : public B {
};
```

```
void f(D* pd)
{
    pd->i = 3;   // finds B::i
    D::x = 2;    // ERROR: does not find ::x in the enclosing scope
}
```

In contrast, unqualified names are typically looked up in successively more enclosing scopes (although in member function definitions the scope of the class and its base classes is searched before any other enclosing scopes). This is called *ordinary lookup*. Here is a basic example showing the main idea underlying ordinary lookup:

```
extern int count;                  // (1)

int lookup_example(int count)      // (2)
{
    if (count < 0) {
        int count = 1;             // (3)
        lookup_example(count);     // unqualified count refers to (3)
    }
    return count + ::count;        // the first (unqualified) count refers to (2);
}                                  // the second (qualified) count refers to (1)
```

A more recent twist to the lookup of unqualified names is that—in addition to ordinary lookup—they may sometimes undergo so-called *argument-dependent lookup* (*ADL*).[1] Before proceeding with the details of ADL, let's motivate the mechanism with our perennial max() template:

```
template <typename T>
inline T const& max (T const& a, T const& b)
{
    return  a < b ? b : a;
}
```

Suppose now that we need to apply this template to a type defined in another namespace:

```
namespace BigMath {
    class BigNumber {

        ...
    };
    bool operator < (BigNumber const&, BigNumber const&);
    ...
}
```

---

[1] This is also called *Koenig lookup* (or *extended Koenig lookup*) after Andrew Koenig, who first proposed a variation of this mechanism.

```
using BigMath::BigNumber;

void g (BigNumber const& a, BigNumber const& b)
{
    ...
    BigNumber x = max(a,b);
    ...
}
```

The problem here is that the max() template is unaware of the BigMath namespace, but ordinary lookup would not find the operator < applicable to values of type BigNumber. Without some special rules, this greatly reduces the applicability of templates in the context of C++ namespaces. ADL is the C++ answer to those "special rules."

9.2.1 Argument-Dependent Lookup

ADL applies only to unqualified names that look like they name a nonmember function in a function call. If ordinary lookup finds the name of a member function or the name of a type, then ADL does not happen. ADL is also inhibited if the name of the function to be called is enclosed in parentheses.

Otherwise, if the name is followed by a list of argument expressions enclosed in parentheses, ADL proceeds by looking up the name in namespaces and classes "associated with" the types of the call arguments. The precise definition of these *associated namespaces* and *associated classes* is given later, but intuitively they can be thought as being all the namespaces and classes that are fairly directly connected to a given type. For example, if the type is a pointer to a class X, then the associated classes and namespace would include X as well as any namespaces or classes to which X belongs.

The precise definition of the set of *associated namespaces* and *associated classes* for a given type is determined by the following rules:

- For built-in types, this is the empty set.
- For pointer and array types, the set of associated namespaces and classes is that of the underlying type.
- For enumeration types, the associated namespace is the namespace in which the enumeration is declared.
- For class members, the enclosing class is the associated class.
- For class types (including union types) the set of associated classes is the type itself, the enclosing class, and any direct and indirect base classes. The set of associated namespaces is the namespaces in which the associated classes are declared. If the class is a class template instantiation, then the types of the template type arguments and the classes and namespaces in which the template template arguments are declared are also included.
- For function types, the sets of associated namespaces and classes comprise the namespaces and classes associated with all the parameter types and those associated with the return type.

- For pointer-to-member-of-class-X types, the sets of associated namespaces and classes include those associated with X in addition to those associated with the type of the member. (If it is a pointer-to-member-function type, then the parameter and return types can contribute too.)

ADL then looks up the name in all the associated namespaces as if the name had been qualified with each of these namespaces in turn, except that using-directives are ignored. The following example illustrates this:

```cpp
// details/adl.cpp

#include <iostream>

namespace X {
    template<typename T> void f(T);
}

namespace N {
    using namespace X;
    enum E { e1 };
    void f(E) {
        std::cout << "N::f(N::E) called\n";
    }
}

void f(int)
{
    std::cout << "::f(int) called\n";
}

int main()
{
    ::f(N::e1);   // qualified function name: no ADL
    f(N::e1);     // ordinary lookup finds ::f() and ADL finds N::f(),
}                 // the latter is preferred
```

Note that in this example, the using-directive in namespace N is ignored when ADL is performed. Hence X::f() is never even a candidate for the call in main().

9.2.2 Friend Name Injection

A friend function declaration can be the first declaration of the nominated function. If this is the case, then the function is assumed to be declared in the nearest namespace scope (or perhaps the global scope) enclosing the class containing the friend declaration. A relatively controversial issue is whether that declaration should be visible in the scope in which it is "injected." It is mostly a problem with templates. Consider the following example:

```
template<typename T>
class C {
    ...
    friend void f();
    friend void f(C<T> const&);
    ...
};

void g (C<int>* p)
{
    f();       // Is f() visible here?
    f(*p);     // Is f(C<int> const&) visible here?
}
```

The trouble is that if friend declarations are visible in the enclosing namespace, then instantiating a class template may make visible the declaration of ordinary functions. Some programmers find this surprising, and the C++ standard therefore specifies that friend declarations do not ordinarily make the name visible in the enclosing scope.

However, there is an interesting programming technique that depends on declaring (and defining) a function in a friend declaration only (see Section 11.7 on page 174). Therefore the standard also specifies that friend functions are found when the class of which they are a friend is among the associated classes considered by ADL.

Reconsider our last example. The call f() has no associated classes or namespaces because there are no arguments: It is an invalid call in our example. However, the call f(*p) does have the associated class C<int> (because this is the type of *p), and the global namespace is also associated (because this is the namespace in which the type of *p is declared). Therefore the second friend function declaration could be found provided the class C<int> was actually fully instantiated prior to the call. To ensure this, it is assumed that a call involving a lookup for friends in associated classes actually causes the class to be instantiated (if not done already).[2]

---

[2] Although this was clearly intended by those who wrote the C++ standard, it is not clearly spelled out in the standard.

9.2.3   Injected Class Names

The name of a class is "injected" inside the scope of that class itself and is therefore accessible as an unqualified name in that scope. (However, it is not accessible as a qualified name because this is the notation used to denote the constructors.) For example:

```
// details/inject.cpp

#include <iostream>

int C;

class C {
  private:
    int i[2];
  public:
    static int f() {
        return sizeof(C);
    }
};

int f()
{
    return sizeof(C);
}

int main()
{
    std::cout << "C::f() = " << C::f() << ","
              << " ::f() = " << ::f() << std::endl;
}
```

The member function `C::f()` returns the size of type `C` whereas the function `::f()` returns the size of the variable `C` (in other words, the size of an `int` object).

Class templates also have injected class names. However, they're stranger than ordinary injected class names: They can be followed by template arguments (in which case they are injected class *template* names), but if they are not followed by template arguments they represent the class with its parameters as its arguments (or, for a partial specialization, its specialization arguments). This explains the following situation:

```
template<template<typename> class TT> class X {
};

template<typename T> class C {
    C* a;         // OK: same as ''C<T>* a;''
    C<void> b;    // OK
    X<C> c;       // ERROR: C without a template argument list
                  //          does not denote a template
    X<::C> d;     // ERROR: <: is an alternative token for [
    X< ::C> e;    // OK: the space between < and :: is required
};
```

Note how the unqualified name refers to the injected name and is not considered the name of the template if it is not followed by a list of template arguments. To compensate, we can force the name of the template to be found by using the file scope qualifier ::. This works, but we must then be careful not to create a so-called *digraph* token <:, which is interpreted as a left bracket. Although relatively rare, such errors result in perplexing diagnostics.

9.3 Parsing Templates

Two fundamental activities of compilers for most programming languages are *tokenization*—also called *scanning* or *lexing*—and parsing. The tokenization process reads the source code as a sequence of characters and generates a sequence of tokens from it. For example, on seeing the sequence of characters int* p = 0;, the "tokenizer" will generate token descriptions for a keyword int, a symbol/operator *, an identifier p, a symbol/operator =, an integer literal 0, and a symbol/operator ;.

A parser will then find known patterns in the token sequence by recursively reducing tokens or previously found patterns into higher level constructs. For example, the token 0 is a valid expression, the combination * followed by an identifier p is a valid declarator, and that declarator followed by "=" followed by the expression "0" is also a valid declarator. Finally, the keyword int is a known type name, and, when followed by the declarator *p = 0, you get the initializing declaration of p.

9.3.1 Context Sensitivity in Nontemplates

As you may know or expect, tokenizing is easier than parsing. Fortunately, parsing is a subject for which a solid theory has been developed, and many useful languages are not hard to parse using this theory. However, the theory works best for so-called *context-free languages*, and we have already noted that C++ is context sensitive. To handle this, a C++ compiler will couple a symbol table to the tokenizer and parser: When a declaration is parsed, it is entered in the symbol table. When the tokenizer finds an identifier, it looks it up and annotates the resulting token if it finds a type.

For example, if the C++ compiler sees

```
x*
```

the tokenizer looks up x. If it finds a type, the parser sees

```
identifier, type, x
symbol, *
```

and concludes that a declaration has started. However, if x is not found to be a type, then the parser receives from the tokenizer

```
identifier, nontype, x
symbol, *
```

and the construct can be parsed validly only as a multiplication. The details of these principles are dependent on the particular implementation strategy, but the gist should be there.

Another example of context sensitivity is illustrated in the following expression:

```
X<1>(0)
```

If X is the name of a class template, then the previous expression casts the integer 0 to the type X<1> generated from that template. If X is not a template, then the previous expression is equivalent to

```
(X<1)>0
```

In other words, X is compared with 1, and the result of that comparison—true or false, implicitly converted to 1 or 0 in this case—is compared with 0. Although code like this is rarely used, it is valid C++ (and valid C, for that matter). A C++ parser will therefore look up names appearing before a < and treat the < as an angle bracket only if the name is that of a template; otherwise, the < is an ordinary "less than" operator.

This form of context sensitivity is an unfortunate consequence of having chosen angle brackets to delimit template argument lists. Here is another such consequence:

```
template<bool B>
class Invert {
  public:
    static bool const result = !B;
};

void g()
{
    bool test = Invert<(1>0)>::result;   // parentheses required!
}
```

If the parentheses in `B<(1>0)>` were omitted, the "greater than" symbol would be mistaken for the closing of the template argument list. This would make the code invalid because the compiler would read it to be equivalent to `((B<1>)0>::result`.[3]

The tokenizer isn't spared problems with the angle-bracket notation either. We have already cautioned (see Section 3.2 on page 27) to introduce whitespace when nesting template-ids, as in

```
List<List<int> > a;
        // ^-- whitespace is not optional!
```

Indeed, the whitespace between the two closing angle brackets is not optional: Without this whitespace, the two `>` characters combine into a right shift token `>>`, and hence are never treated as two separate tokens. This is a consequence of the so-called *maximum munch* tokenization principle: A C++ implementation must collect as many consecutive characters as possible into a token.

This particular issue is a very common stumbling block for beginning template users. Several C++ compiler implementations have therefore been modified to recognize this situation and treat the `>>` as two separate `>` *in this particular situation* (and with a warning that it is not really valid C++). The C++ committee is also considering mandating this behavior in a revision of the standard (see Section 13.1 on page 205).

Another example of the maximum munch principle is the less known fact that the scope resolution operator (`::`) must also be used carefully with angle brackets:

```
class X {
    ...
};
```

```
List<::X> many_X;     // SYNTAX ERROR!
```

The problem in the previous example is that the sequence of characters `<:` is a so-called *digraph*[4]: an alternative representation for the symbol `[`. Hence, the compiler really sees the equivalent of `List[:X> many_X;`, which makes no sense at all. Again, the solution is to add some whitespace:

```
List< ::X> many_X;
     // ^-- whitespace is not optional!
```

---

[3] Note the double parentheses to avoid parsing `(B<1>)0` as a cast operation—yet another source of syntactic ambiguity.

[4] Digraphs were added to the language to ease the input of C++ source with international keyboards that lack certain characters (such as `#`, `[`, and `]`).

9.3.2   Dependent Names of Types

The problem with names in templates is that they cannot always be sufficiently classified. In particular, one template cannot look into another template because the contents of that other template can be made invalid by an *explicit specialization* (see Chapter 12 for details). The following contrived example illustrates this:

```
template<typename T>
class Trap {
  public:
    enum { x };          // (1) x is not a type here
};


template<typename T>
class Victim {
  public:
    int y;
    void poof() {
        Trap<T>::x*y;    // (2) declaration or multiplication?
    }
};


template<>
class Trap<void> {       // evil specialization!
  public:
    typedef int x;       // (3) x is a type here
};


void boom(Victim<void>& bomb)
{
    bomb.poof();
}
```

As the compiler is parsing line (2), it must decide whether it is seeing a declaration or a multiplication. This decision in turn depends on whether the dependent qualified name Trap<T>::x is a type name. It may be tempting to look in the template Trap at this point and find that, according to line (1), Trap<T>::x is not a type, which would leave us to believe that line (2) is a multiplication. However, a little later the source corrupts this idea by overriding the generic Trap<T>::x for the case where T is void. In this case, Trap<T>::x is in fact type int.

The language definition resolves this problem by specifying that in general a dependent qualified name does *not* denote a type unless that name is prefixed with the keyword typename. If it turns out, after substituting template arguments, that the name is not the name of a type, the program is invalid and your C++ compiler should complain at instantiation time. Note that this use of typename is different from the use to denote template type parameters. Unlike type parameters, you cannot equivalently replace typename with class. The typename prefix to a name is *required* when the name

1. Appears in a template
2. Is qualified
3. Is not used as in a list of base class specifications or in a list of member initializers introducing a constructor definition
4. Is dependent on a template parameter

Furthermore, the typename prefix is *not allowed* unless at least the first three previous conditions hold. To illustrate this, consider the following erroneous example[5]:

```
template<typename₁ T>
struct S: typename₂ X<T>::Base {
    S(): typename₃ X<T>::Base(typename₄ X<T>::Base(0)) {}
    typename₅ X<T> f() {
        typename₆ X<T>::C * p;    // declaration of pointer p
        X<T>::D * q;              // multiplication!
    }
    typename₇ X<int>::C * s;
};


struct U {
    typename₈ X<int>::C * pc;
};
```

Each occurrence of typename—correct or not—is numbered with a subscript for easy reference. The first, $typename_1$, indicates a template parameter. The previous rules do not apply to this first use. The second and third typenames are disallowed by the third item in the previous rules. Names of base classes in these two contexts cannot be preceded by typename. However, $typename_4$ is required. Here, the name of the base class is not used to denote what is being initialized or derived from. Instead, the name is part of an expression to construct a temporary X<T>::Base from its argument 0 (a sort of conversion, if you will). The fifth typename is prohibited because the name that follows it, X<T>, is not a qualified name. The sixth occurrence is required if this statement is to declare a pointer. The next line omits the typename keyword and is, therefore, interpreted by the compiler as a multiplication. The seventh typename is optional because it satisfies all the previous rules except the last. Finally, $typename_8$ is prohibited because it is not used inside a template.

---

[5] From [*VandevoordeSolutions*], proving once and for all that C++ promotes code reuse.

9.3.3   Dependent Names of Templates

A problem very similar to the one encountered in the previous section occurs when a name of a template is dependent. In general, a C++ compiler is required to treat a < following the name of a template as the beginning of a template argument list; otherwise, it is a "less than" operator. As is the case with type names, a compiler has to assume that a dependent name does not refer to a template unless the programmer provides extra information using the keyword `template`:

```
template<typename T>
class Shell {
  public:
    template<int N>
    class In {
      public:
        template<int M>
        class Deep {
            public:
            virtual void f();
        };
    };
};


template<typename T, int N>
class Weird {
  public:
    void case1 (typename Shell<T>::template
                        In<N>::template Deep<N>* p) {
        p->template Deep<N>::f();   // inhibit virtual call
    }
    void case2 (typename Shell<T>::template
                        In<N>::template Deep<N>& p) {
        p.template Deep<N>::f();   // inhibit virtual call
    }
};
```

This somewhat intricate example shows how all the operators that can qualify a name (`::`, `->`, and `.`) may need to be followed by the keyword `template`. Specifically, this is the case whenever the type of the name or expression preceding the qualifying operator is dependent on a template parameter, and the name that follows the operator is a template-id (in other words, a template name followed by template arguments in angle brackets). For example, in the expression

```
p.template Deep<N>::f()
```

the type of p depends on the template parameter T. Consequently, a C++ compiler cannot look up Deep to see if it is a template, and we must explicitly indicate that Deep is the name of a template by inserting the prefix `template`. Without this prefix, `p.Deep<N>::f()` is parsed as `((p.Deep)<N>>f()`. Note also that this may need to happen multiple times within a qualified name because qualifiers themselves may be qualified with a dependent qualifier. (This is illustrated by the declaration of the parameters of `case1` and `case2` in the previous example.)

If the keyword `template` is omitted in cases such as these, the opening and closing angle brackets are parsed as "less than" and "greater than" operators. However, if the keyword is not strictly needed, it is in fact not allowed at all.[6] You cannot "just sprinkle" template qualifiers throughout your code.

9.3.4   Dependent Names in Using-Declarations

Using-declarations can bring in names from two places: namespaces and classes. The namespace case is not relevant in this context because there are no such things as *namespace templates*. Using-declarations that bring in names from classes can, in fact, bring in names only from a base class to a derived class. Such using-declarations behave like "symbolic links" or "shortcuts" in the derived class to the base declaration, thereby allowing the members of the derived class to access the nominated name as if it were actually a member declared in that derived class. A short nontemplate example illustrates the idea better than mere words:

```
class BX {
  public:
    void f(int);
    void f(char const*);
    void g();
};

class DX : private BX {
  public:
    using BX::f;
};
```

The previous using-declaration brings in the name `f` of the base class `BX` into the derived class `DX`. In this case, this name is associated with two different declarations, thus emphasizing that we are dealing with a mechanism for names and not individual declarations of such names. Note also that this kind of using-declaration can make accessible an otherwise inaccessible member. The base `BX` (and thus its members) are private to the class `DX`, except that the functions `BX::f` have been introduced in the public interface of `DX` and are therefore available to the clients of `DX`. Because using-declarations enable this, the earlier mechanism of *access declarations* is *deprecated* in C++ (meaning that future revisions of C++ may not contain the mechanism):

---

[6] This is actually not totally clear from the text of the standard, but the people who worked on that part of the text seem to agree.

```
class DX : private BX {
  public:
    BX::f;   // access declaration syntax is deprecated
             // use using BX::f instead
};
```

By now you can probably perceive the problem when a using-declaration brings in a name from a dependent class. Although we know about the name, we don't know whether it's the name of a type, a template, or something else:

```
template<typename T>
class BXT {
  public:
    typedef T Mystery;
    template<typename U>
    struct Magic;
};


template<typename T>
class DXTT : private BXT<T> {
  public:
    using typename BXT<T>::Mystery;
    Mystery* p;   // would be a syntax error if not for the typename
};
```

Again, if we want a dependent name to be brought in by a using-declaration to denote a type, we must explicitly say so by inserting the keyword typename. Strangely, the C++ standard does not provide for a similar mechanism to mark such dependent names as templates. The following snippet illustrates the problem:

```
template<typename T>
class DXTM : private BXT<T> {
  public:
    using BXT<T>::template Magic;   // ERROR: not standard
    Magic<T>* plink;                // SYNTAX ERROR: Magic is not a
};                                  //               known template
```

Most likely this is an oversight in the standard specifications and future revisions will probably make the previous construct valid.

9.3.5 ADL and Explicit Template Arguments

Consider the following example:

```
namespace N {
    class X {
        ...
    };

    template<int I> void select(X*);
}

void g (N::X* xp)
{
    select<3>(xp);   // ERROR: no ADL!
}
```

In this example, we may expect that the template `select()` is found through ADL in the call `select<3>(xp)`. However, this is not the case because a compiler cannot decide that xp is a function call argument until it has decided that `<3>` is a template argument list. Furthermore, a compiler cannot decide that `<3>` is a template argument list until it has found `select()` to be a template. Because this chicken and egg problem cannot be resolved, the expression is parsed as `(select<3>)>(xp)`, which makes no sense.

9.4 Derivation and Class Templates

Class templates can inherit or be inherited from. For many purposes, there is nothing significantly different between the template and nontemplate scenarios. However, there is one important subtlety when deriving a class template from a base class referred to by a dependent name. Let's first look at the somewhat simpler case of nondependent base classes.

9.4.1 Nondependent Base Classes

In a class template, a nondependent base class is one with a complete type that can be determined without knowing the template arguments. In other words, the name of this base is denoted using a nondependent name. For example:

```
template<typename X>
class Base {
  public:
    int basefield;
```

```
      typedef int T;
};


class D1: public Base<Base<void> > {    // not a template case really
  public:
    void f() { basefield = 3; }         // usual access to inherited member
};


template<typename T>
class D2 : public Base<double> {        // nondependent base
  public:
    void f() { basefield = 7; }         // usual access to inherited member
    T strange;            // T is Base<double>::T, not the template parameter!
};
```

Nondependent bases in templates behave very much like bases in ordinary nontemplate classes, but there is a slightly unfortunate surprise: When an unqualified name is looked up in the templated derivation, the nondependent bases are considered before the list of template parameters. This means that in the previous example, the member `strange` of the class template D2 always has the type T corresponding to Base<double>::T (in other words, int). For example, the following function is not valid C++ (assuming the previous declarations):

```
void g (D2<int*>& d2, int* p)
{
    d2.strange = p;    // ERROR: type mismatch!
}
```

This is counterintuitive and requires the writer of the derived template to be aware of names in the nondependent bases from which it derives—even when that derivation is indirect or the names are private. It would probably have been preferable to place template parameters in the scope of the entity they "templatize."

9.4.2   Dependent Base Classes

In the previous example, the base class is fully determined. It does not depend on a template parameter. This implies that a C++ compiler can look up nondependent names in those base classes as soon as the template definition is seen. An alternative—not allowed by the C++ standard—would consist in delaying the lookup of such names until the template is instantiated. The disadvantage of this alternative approach is that it also delays any error messages resulting from missing symbols until instantiation. Hence, the C++ standard specifies that a nondependent name appearing in a template is looked up as soon as it is encountered. Keeping this in mind, consider the following example:

```
template<typename T>
class DD : public Base<T> {          // dependent base
  public:
    void f() { basefield = 0; }  // (1) problem...
};


template<>    // explicit specialization
class Base<bool> {
  public:
    enum { basefield = 42 };        // (2) tricky!
};


void g (DD<bool>& d)
{
    d.f();                           // (3) oops?
}
```

At point (1) we find our reference to a nondependent name basefield: It must be looked up right away. Suppose we look it up in the template Base and bind it to the int member that we find therein. However, shortly after this we override the generic definition of Base with an explicit specialization. As it happens, this specialization changes the meaning of the basefield member to which we already committed! So, when we instantiate the definition of DD::f at point (3), we find that we too eagerly bound the nondependent name at point (1). There is no modifiable basefield in DD<bool> that was specialized at point (2), and an error message should have been issued.

To circumvent this problem, standard C++ says that nondependent names are *not* looked up in dependent base classes[7] (but they are still looked up as soon as they are encountered). So, a standard C++ compiler will emit a diagnostic at point (1). To correct the code, it suffices to make the name basefield dependent because dependent names can be looked up only at the time of instantiation, and at that time the exact base specialization that must be explored will be known. For example, at point (3), the compiler will know that the base class of DD<bool> is Base<bool> and that this has been explicitly specialized by the programmer. In this case, our preferred way to make the name dependent is as follows:

```
// Variation 1:
template<typename T>
class DD1 : public Base<T> {
  public:
    void f() { this->basefield = 0; }  // lookup delayed
};
```

---

[7] This is part of the so-called *two-phase lookup* rules that distinguish between a first phase when template definitions are first seen, and a second phase when templates are instantiated (see Section 10.3.1 on page 146).

An alternative consists in introducing a dependency using a qualified name:

```
// Variation 2:
template<typename T>
class DD2 : public Base<T> {
  public:
    void f() { Base<T>::basefield = 0; }
};
```

Care must be taken with this solution, because if the unqualified nondependent name is used to form a virtual function call, then the qualification inhibits the virtual call mechanism and the meaning of the program changes. Nonetheless, there are situations when the first variation cannot be used and this alternative is appropriate:

```
template<typename T>
class B {
  public:
    enum E { e1 = 6, e2 = 28, e3 = 496 };
    virtual void zero(E e = e1);
    virtual void one(E&);
};

template<typename T>
class D : public B<T> {
  public:
    void f() {
        typename D<T>::E e;   // this->E would not be valid syntax
        this->zero();         // D<T>::zero() would inhibit virtuality
        one(e);               // one is dependent because its argument
    }                         // is dependent
};
```

Note that the name one in the call one(e) is dependent on the template parameter simply because the type of one of the call's explicit arguments is dependent. Implicitly used default arguments with a type that depends on a template parameter do not count because the compiler cannot verify this until it already has decided the lookup—a chicken and egg problem. To avoid subtlety, we prefer to use the this-> prefix in all situations that allow it—even for nontemplate code.

    If you find that the repeated qualifications are cluttering up your code, you can bring a name from a dependent base class in the derived class once and for all:

```
// Variation 3:
template<typename T>
class DD3 : public Base<T> {
  public:
```

```
    using Base<T>::basefield;       // (1) dependent name now in scope
    void f() { basefield = 0; }     // (2) fine
};
```

The lookup at point (2) succeeds and finds the *using-declaration* of point (1). However, the using-declaration is not verified until instantiation time and our goal is achieved. There are some subtle limitations to this scheme. For example, if multiple bases are derived from, the programmer must select exactly which one contains the desired member.

9.5 Afternotes

The first compiler really to parse template definitions was developed by a company called Taligent in the mid-1990s. Before that—and even after that—most compilers treated templates as a sequence of tokens to be played back through the parser at instantiation time. Hence no parsing was done, except for a minimal amount sufficient to find the end of a template definition. Bill Gibbons was Taligent's representative to the C++ committee and was the principal advocate for making templates unambiguously parsable. The Taligent effort was not released until the compiler was acquired and completed by Hewlett-Packard (HP), to become the aC++ compiler. Among its competitive advantages, the aC++ compiler was quickly recognized for its high quality diagnostics. The fact that template diagnostics were not always delayed until instantiation time undoubtedly contributed to this perception.

Relatively early during the development of templates, Tom Pennello—a widely recognized parsing expert working for Metaware—noted some of the problems associated with angle brackets. Stroustrup also comments on that topic in [*StroustrupDnE*] and argues that humans prefer to read angle brackets rather than parentheses. However, other possibilities exist, and Pennello specifically proposed braces (for example, List{::X}) at a C++ standards meeting in 1991 (held in Dallas).[8] At that time the extent of the problem was more limited because templates nested inside other templates—so-called *member templates*—were not valid and thus the discussion of Section 9.3.3 on page 132 was largely irrelevant. As a result, the committee declined the proposal to replace the angle brackets.

The name lookup rule for nondependent names and dependent base classes that is described in Section 9.4.2 on page 136 was introduced in the C++ standard in 1993. It was described to the "general public" in Bjarne Stroustrup's [*StroustrupDnE*] in early 1994. Yet the first generally available implementation of this rule did not appear until early 1997 when HP incorporated it into their aC++ compiler, and by then large amounts of code derived class templates from dependent bases. Indeed, when the HP engineers started testing their implementation, they found that most of the programs that used templates in nontrivial ways no longer compiled.[9] In particular, all implementations of the

---

[8] Braces are not entirely without problems either. Specifically, the syntax to specialize class templates would require nontrivial adaptation.

[9] Fortunately, they found out before they released the new functionality.

STL[10] broke the rule in many hundreds—and sometimes thousands—of places. To ease the transition process for their customers, HP softened the diagnostic associated with code that assumed that nondependent names could be found in dependent base classes as follows. When a nondependent name used in the scope of a class template is not found using the standard rules, aC++ peeks inside the dependent bases. If the name is still not found, a hard error is issued and compilation fails. However, if the name is found in a dependent base, a warning is issued, and the name is marked to be treated as if it were dependent, so that lookup will be reattempted at instantiation time.

The lookup rule that causes a name in nondependent bases to hide an identically named template parameter (Section 9.4.1 on page 135) is an oversight, and it is not impossible that this will be changed in a revision of the standard. In any case, it is probably wise to avoid code with template parameter names that are also used in nondependent base classes.

Andrew Koenig first proposed ADL for operator functions only (which is why ADL is sometimes called *Koenig lookup*). The motivation was primarily esthetic: explicitly qualifying operator names with their enclosing namespace looks awkward at best (for example, instead of a+b we may need to write N::operator+(a, b)) and having to write using declarations for every operator can lead to unwieldy code. Hence, it was decided that operators would be looked up in the namespaces associated with arguments. ADL was later extended to ordinary function names to accommodate a limited kind of friend name injection and to support a two-phase lookup model for templates and their instantiations (Chapter 10). The generalized ADL rules are also called *extended Koenig lookup*.

---

[10] Ironically, the first of these implementations had been developed by HP as well.

Chapter 10

Instantiation

Template instantiation is the process that generates types and functions from generic template definitions.[1] The concept of instantiation of C++ templates is fundamental but also somewhat intricate. One of the underlying reasons for this intricacy is that the definitions of entities generated by a template are no longer limited to a single location in the source code. The location of the template, the location where the template is used, and the locations where the template arguments are defined all play a role in the meaning of the entity.

In this chapter we explain how we can organize our source code to enable proper template use. In addition, we survey the various methods that are used by the most popular C++ compilers to handle template instantiation. Although all these methods should be semantically equivalent, it is useful to understand basic principles of your compiler's instantiation strategy. Each mechanism comes with its set of little quirks when building real-life software and, conversely, each influenced the final specifications of standard C++.

10.1 On-Demand Instantiation

When a C++ compiler encounters the use of a template specialization, it will create that specialization by substituting the required arguments for the template parameters.[2] This is done automatically and requires no direction from the client code (or from the template definition for that matter). This on-demand instantiation feature sets C++ templates apart from similar facilities in other compiled languages. It is sometimes also called *implicit* or *automatic* instantiation.

---

[1] The term *instantiation* is sometimes also used to refer to the creation of objects from types. In this book, however, it always refers to *template* instantiation.

[2] The term *specialization* is used in the general sense of an entity that is a specific instance of a template (see Chapter 7). It does not refer to the *explicit specialization* mechanism described in Chapter 12.

On-demand instantiation implies that the compiler usually needs access to the full definition (in other words, not just the declaration) of the template and some of its members at the point of use. Consider the following tiny source code file:

```
template<typename T> class C;   // (1) declaration only

C<int>* p = 0;                  // (2) fine: definition of C<int> not needed

template<typename T>
class C {
  public:
    void f();                   // (3) member declaration
};                              // (4) class template definition completed

void g (C<int>& c)              // (5) use class template declaration only
{
    c.f();                      // (6) use class template definition;
}                               //     will need definition of C::f()
```

At point (1) in the source code, only the declaration of the template is available, not the definition (such a declaration is sometimes called a *forward declaration*). As is the case with ordinary classes, you do not need the definition of a class template to be in scope to declare pointers or references to this type (as was done at point (2)). For example, the type of the parameter of function g does not require the full definition of the template C. However, as soon as a component needs to know the size of a template specialization or if it accesses a member of such a specialization, the entire class template definition is required to be in scope. This explains why at point (6) in the source code, the class template definition must be seen; otherwise, the compiler cannot verify that the member exists and is accessible (not private or protected).

Here is another expression that needs the instantiation of the previous class template because the size of C<void> is needed:

```
C<void>* p = new C<void>;
```

In this case, instantiation is needed so that the compiler can determine the size of C<void>. You might observe that for this particular template, the type of the argument X substituted for T will not influence the size of the template because in any case, C<X> is an empty class. However, a compiler is not required to detect this. Furthermore, instantiation is also needed in this example to determine whether C<void> has an accessible default constructor and to ensure C<void> does not declare private operators new or delete.

The need to access a member of a class template is not always very explicitly visible in the source code. For example, C++ overload resolution requires visibility into class types for parameters of candidate functions:

```
template<typename T>
class C {
  public:
    C(int);              // a constructor that can be called with a single parameter
};                       //  may be used for implicit conversions

void candidate(C<double> const&);   // (1)
void candidate(int) {}              // (2)

int main()
{
    candidate(42);   // both previous function declarations can be called
}
```

The call `candidate(42)` will resolve to the overloaded declaration at point (2). However, the declaration at point (1) could also be instantiated to check whether it is a viable candidate for the call (it is in this case because the one-argument constructor can implicitly convert 42 to an rvalue of type `C<double>`). Note that the compiler is allowed (but not required) to perform this instantiation if it can resolve the call without it (as could be the case in this example because an implicit conversion would not be selected over an exact match). Note also that the instantiation of `C<double>` could trigger an error, which may be surprising.

10.2   Lazy Instantiation

The examples so far illustrate requirements that are not fundamentally different from the requirements when using nontemplate classes. Many uses require a class type to be *complete*. For the template case, the compiler will generate this complete definition from the class template definition.

A pertinent question now arises: How much of the template is instantiated? A vague answer is the following: Only as much as is really needed. In other words, a compiler should be "lazy" when instantiating templates. Let's look at exactly what this laziness entails.

When a class template is implicitly instantiated, each declaration of its members is instantiated as well, but the corresponding definitions are not. There are a few exceptions to this. First, if the class template contains an anonymous union, the members of that union's definition are also instantiated.[3] The other exception occurs with virtual member functions. Their definitions may or may not be instantiated as a result of instantiating a class template. Many implementations will, in fact, instantiate the definition because the internal structure that enables the virtual call mechanism requires the virtual functions actually to exist as linkable entities.

---

[3] Anonymous unions are always special in this way: Their members can be considered to be members of the enclosing class. An anonymous union is primarily a construct that says that some class members share the same storage.

Default function call arguments are considered separately when instantiating templates. Specifically, they are not instantiated unless there is a call to that function (or member function) that actually makes use of the default argument. If, on the other hand, that function is called with explicit arguments that override the default, then the default arguments are not instantiated.

Let's put together an example that illustrates all these issues:

```
// details/lazy.cpp

template <typename T>
class Safe {
};

template <int N>
class Danger {
  public:
    typedef char Block[N];   // would fail for N<=0
};

template <typename T, int N>
class Tricky {
  public:
    virtual ~Tricky() {
    }
    void no_body_here(Safe<T> = 3);
    void inclass() {
        Danger<N> no_boom_yet;
    }
    // void error() { Danger<0> boom; }
    // void unsafe(T (*p)[N]);
    T operator->();
    // virtual Safe<T> suspect();
    struct Nested {
        Danger<N> pfew;
    };
    union {   // anonymous union
        int align;
        Safe<T> anonymous;
    };
};
```

```
int main()
{
    Tricky<int, 0> ok;
}
```

First consider the previous example without the function `main()`. A standard C++ compiler normally compiles the template definitions to check the syntax and general semantic constraints. It will, however, "assume the best" when checking constraints involving template parameters. For example, the parameter N in the member typedef for `Block` could be zero or negative (which would be invalid), but it is assumed that this isn't the case. Similarly, the default argument specification (= 3) on the declaration of the member `no_body_here()` is suspicious because the template `Safe` isn't initializable with an integer, but the assumption is that the default argument won't actually be needed for the generic definition of `Safe<T>`. If it weren't commented out, the member `error()` would trigger an error while the template is compiled because the use of `Danger<0>` requires a complete definition of the class `Danger<0>`, and generating that class runs into an attempt to typedef an array with zero elements! This is the case even though the member `error()` may not be used and therefore may not be instantiated. The error is triggered during the processing of the generic template. The declaration of the member `unsafe(T (*p)[N])`, in contrast, is not a problem when N is still an unsubstituted template parameter.

Now let's analyze what happens when we add the function `main()`. It causes the compiler to substitute `int` for T and 0 for N in the template `Tricky`. Not all the member definitions will be needed, but the default constructor (implicitly declared in this case) and the destructor are definitely called, and hence their definitions must be available somehow (which is the case in our example). In practice, the definitions of virtual members should also be provided; otherwise, linker errors are likely to occur. This may have been a problem if we had uncommented the declaration of the virtual member `suspect()` for which no definition was provided. The definitions of the members `inclass()` and `struct Nested` would need the complete type `Danger<0>` (which contains an invalid typedef as we discussed earlier) but because these definitions are not used, they are not generated, and no error is triggered. However, all the member *declarations* are generated, and these could contain invalid types as the result of our substitution. For example, if we uncommented the declaration of `unsafe(T (*p)[N])`, we would again create an array type with zero elements, and this time it would be an error. Similarly, had the member `anonymous` been declared with type `Danger<N>` instead of `Safe<T>`, an error would be triggered because type `Danger<0>` cannot be completed.

Finally, we need to take note of `operator->`. Normally, this operator must return a pointer type or another class type to which `operator->` applies. This suggests that the completion of `Tricky<int, 0>` triggers an error because it declares a return type of `int` for `operator->`. However, because certain natural class template definitions[4] trigger these kinds of definitions, the language rule was made more flexible. A user-defined `operator->` must return only a type to which another (for example, builtin) `operator->` applies if that operator is actually selected by the overload resolution rules. This is true even outside templates (although it is less useful in those contexts). Hence, the declaration here triggers no error, even though `int` is substituted for the return type.

---

[4] Typical examples are so-called *smart pointer* templates (for example, the standard `std::auto_ptr<T>`). See also Chapter 20.

10.3   The C++ Instantiation Model

Template instantiation is the process of obtaining a regular class or function from a corresponding template entity by appropriately substituting the template parameters. This may sound fairly straightforward, but in practice many details need to be formally established.

10.3.1   Two-Phase Lookup

In Chapter 9 we saw that dependent names cannot be resolved when parsing templates. Instead, they are looked up again at the point of instantiation. Nondependent names, however, are looked up early so that many errors can be diagnosed when the template is first seen. This leads to the concept of *two-phase lookup*[5]: The first phase is the parsing of a template, and the second phase is its instantiation.

During the first phase, nondependent names are looked up while the template is being parsed using both the *ordinary lookup rules* and, if applicable, the rules for argument-dependent lookup (ADL). Unqualified dependent names (which are dependent because they look like the name of a function in a function call with dependent arguments) are also looked up that way, but the result of the lookup is not considered complete until an additional lookup is performed when the template is instantiated.

During the second phase, which occurs when templates are instantiated at a point called the *point of instantiation* (POI), dependent qualified names are looked up (with the template parameters replaced with the template arguments for that specific instantiation), and an additional ADL is performed for the unqualified dependent names.

10.3.2   Points of Instantiation

We have already illustrated that there are points in the source of template clients where a C++ compiler must have access to the declaration or the definition of a template entity. A *point of instantiation* (*POI*) is created when a code construct refers to a template specialization in such a way that the definition of the corresponding template needs to be instantiated to create that specialization. The POI is a point in the source where the substituted template could be inserted. For example:

```
class MyInt {
  public:
    MyInt(int i);
};

MyInt operator - (MyInt const&);

bool operator > (MyInt const&, MyInt const&);
```

---

[5] Beside *two-phase lookup*, terms such as *two-stage lookup* or *two-phase name lookup* are also used.

```
typedef MyInt Int;

template<typename T>
void f(T i)
{
    if (i>0) {
        g(-i);
    }
}
// (1)
void g(Int)
{
    // (2)
    f<Int>(42);   // point of call
    // (3)
}
// (4)
```

When a C++ compiler sees the call f<Int>(42), it knows the template f will need to be instantiated for T substituted with MyInt: A POI is created. Points (2) and (3) are very close to the point of call, but they cannot be POIs because C++ does not allow us to insert the definition of ::f<Int>(Int) there. The essential difference between point (1) and point (4) is that at point (4) the function g(Int) is visible, and hence the template-dependent call g(-i) can be resolved. However, if point (1) were the POI, then that call could not be resolved because g(Int) is not yet visible. Fortunately, C++ defines the POI for a reference to a nonclass specialization to be immediately after the nearest namespace scope declaration or definition that contains that reference. In our example, this is point (4).

You may wonder why this example involved the type MyInt rather than simple int. The answer lies in the fact that the second lookup performed at the POI is only an ADL. Because int has no associated namespace, the POI lookup would therefore not take place and would not find function g. Hence, if you were to replace the typedef for Int with

```
typedef int Int;
```

the previous example should no longer compile.[6]

For class specializations, the situation is different, as the following example illustrates:

```
template<typename T>
class S {
  public:
```

---

[6] In 2002 the C++ standardization committee was still investigating alternatives that would make the example valid with the latter typedef.

```
      T m;
};
// (5)
unsigned long h()
{
    // (6)
    return (unsigned long)sizeof(S<int>);
    // (7)
}
// (8)
```

Again, the function scope points (6) and (7) cannot be POIs because a definition of a namespace scope class S<int> cannot appear there (and templates cannot appear in function scope). If we were to follow the rule for nonclass instances, the POI would be at point (8), but then the expression sizeof(S<int>) is invalid because the size of S<int> cannot be determined until point (8) is reached. Therefore, the POI for a reference to a generated class instance is defined to be the point immediately before the nearest namespace scope declaration or definition that contains the reference to that instance. In our example, this is point (5).

When a template is actually instantiated, the need for additional instantiations may appear. Consider a short example:

```
template<typename T>
class S {
  public:
    typedef int I;
};

// (1)
template<typename T>
void f()
{
    S<char>::I var1 = 41;
    typename S<T>::I var2 = 42;
}

int main()
{
    f<double>();
}
// (2): (2a), (2b)
```

Our preceding discussion already established that the POI for f<double> is at point (2). The function template f() also refers to the class specialization S<char> with a POI that is therefore at point (1). It references S<T> too, but because this is still dependent, we cannot really instantiate it at this point. However, if we instantiate f<double> at point (2), we notice that we also need to instantiate the definition of S<double>. Such secondary or transitive POIs are defined slightly differently. For nonclass entities, the secondary POI is exactly the same as the primary POI. For class entities, the secondary POI immediately precedes (in the nearest enclosing namespace scope) the primary POI. In our example, this means that the POI of f<double> can be placed at point (2b), and just before it—at point (2a)—is the secondary POI for S<double>. Note how this differs from the POI for S<char>.

A translation unit usually contains multiple POIs for the same instance. For class template instances, only the first POI in each translation unit is retained, and the subsequent ones are ignored (they are not really considered POIs). For nonclass instances, all POIs are retained. In either case, the ODR requires that the instantiations occurring at any of the retained POIs be equivalent, but a C++ compiler does not need to verify and diagnose violations of this rule. This allows a C++ compiler to pick just one nonclass POI to perform the actual instantiation without worrying that another POI might result in a different instantiation.

In practice, most compilers delay the actual instantiation of noninline function templates to the end of the translation unit. This effectively moves the POIs of the corresponding template specializations to the end of the translation unit. The intention of the C++ language designers was for this to be a valid implementation technique, but the standard does not make this clear.

10.3.3   The Inclusion and Separation Models

Whenever a POI is encountered, the definition of the corresponding template must somehow be accessible. For class specializations this means that the class template definition must have been seen earlier in the translation unit. For nonclass POIs this is also possible, and typically nonclass template definitions are simply added to header files that are #included into the translation unit. This source model for template definitions is called the *inclusion model*, and at the time of this writing it is by far the most popular approach.

For nonclass POIs an alternative exists: The nonclass template can be declared using export and defined in another translation unit. This is known as the *separation model*. The following code excerpt illustrates this with our perennial max() template:

// Translation unit 1:
```
#include <iostream>
export template<typename T>
T const& max (T const&, T const&);

int main()
{
    std::cout << max(7, 42) << std::endl;    //(1)
}
```

```
// Translation unit 2:
export template<typename T>
T const& max (T const& a, T const& b)
{
    return a<b ? b : a;   // (2)
}
```

When compiling the first file, a compiler will notice the POI for T substituted with int created by the statement at point (1). The compilation system must then make sure that the definition in the second file is instantiated to satisfy that POI.

10.3.4   Looking Across Translation Units

Suppose the first file just shown (translation unit 1) is rewritten as follows:

```
// Translation unit 1:
#include <iostream>
export template<typename T> T const& max(T const&, T const&);

namespace N {
    class I {
      public:
        I(int i): v(i) {}
        int v;
    };

    bool operator < (I const& a, I const& b) {
        return a.v<b.v;
    }
}

int main()
{
    std::cout << max(N::I(7), N::I(42)).v << std::endl;   // (3)
}
```

The POI created at point (3) again requires the definition in the second file (translation unit 2). However, this definition uses the < operator which now refers to the overloaded operator declared in translation unit 1 and which is not visible in translation unit 2. For this to work, it is clear that the instantiation process needs to refer to two different declaration contexts.[7] The first context is the one

---

[7] A declaration context is the collection of all declarations accessible at a given point.

in which the template is defined, and the second context is the one in which type I is declared. To involve these two contexts, names in templates are therefore looked up in two phases as explained in Section 10.3.1 on page 146.

The first phase occurs when templates are parsed (in other words, when a C++ compiler first sees the template definition). At this stage, nondependent names are looked up using both the ordinary lookup rules and the ADL rules. In addition, unqualified names of functions that are dependent (because their arguments are dependent) are looked up using the ordinary lookup rules, but the result is memorized without attempting overload resolution—this is done after the second phase.

The second phase occurs at the point of instantiation. At this point, dependent qualified names are looked up using ordinary lookup rules (because argument-dependent lookup only applies to certain unqualified names). Dependent unqualified names (which were looked up using ordinary lookup rules during the first phase) are now looked up using ADL rules only, and the result of the ADL is then combined with the result of the ordinary lookup that occurred during the first phase. It is this combined set that is used to select the called function through overload resolution.

Although this two-phase lookup mechanism seems essential to enable the separation model, it is also the mechanism used with the inclusion model. However, many early implementations of the inclusion model delayed all lookups until the point of instantiation.[8]

10.3.5   Examples

A few examples illustrate more effectively the effect of what we just described.

Our first example is a simple case of the inclusion model:

```
template<typename T>
void f1(T x)
{
    g1(x);   // (1)
}


void g1(int)
{
}


int main()
{
    f1(7);   // ERROR: g1 not found!
}            // (2) POI for f1<int>(int)
```

---

[8] This results in a behavior that is close to what you'd expect from a macro expansion mechanism.

The call `f1(7)` creates a point of instantiation for `f1<int>(int)` just outside of `main()` (at point (2)). In this instantiation, the key issue is the lookup of function g1. When the definition of the template `f1` is first encountered, it is noted that the unqualified name g1 is dependent because it is the name of a function in a function call with dependent arguments (the type of the argument x depends on the template parameter T). Therefore, g1 is looked up at point (1) using ordinary lookup rules; however, no g1 is visible at this point. At point (2), the POI, the function is looked up again in associated namespaces and classes, but the only argument type is `int`, and it has no associated namespaces and classes. Therefore, g1 is never found even though ordinary lookup at the POI would have found g1.

The second example demonstrates how the separation model can lead to overload ambiguities across translation units. The example consists of three files (one of which is a header file):

```
// File common.hpp:
export template<typename T>
void f(T);

class A {
};
class B {
};

class X {
  public:
    operator A() { return A(); }
    operator B() { return B(); }
};
```

```
// File a.cpp:
#include "common.hpp"

void g(A)
{
}

int main()
{
    f<X>(X());
}
```

```
// File b.cpp:
#include "common.hpp"

void g(B)
{
}

export template<typename T>
void f(T x)
{
    g(x);
}
```

The main() function calls f<X>(X()) in file a.cpp which resolves to the exported template defined in file b.cpp. The call g(x) is therefore instantiated with an argument of type X. Function g() is looked up twice: once using ordinary lookup in file b.cpp (when the template is parsed) and once using ADL in file a.cpp (where the template is instantiated). The first lookup finds g(B), and the second lookup finds g(A). Both are viable functions through a user-defined conversion, and hence the call is really ambiguous.

Note that in file b.cpp the call g(x) does not seem ambiguous at all. It is the two-phase lookup mechanism that brings in possibly unexpected candidate functions. Extreme care should therefore be taken when writing and documenting exported templates.

10.4 Implementation Schemes

In this section we review some ways in which popular C++ implementations support the inclusion model. All these implementations rely on two classic components: a *compiler* and a *linker*. The compiler translates source code to object files, which contain machine code with symbolic annotations (cross-referencing other object files and libraries). The linker creates executable programs or libraries by combining the object files and resolving the symbolic cross-references they contain. In what follows, we assume such a model even though it is entirely possible (but not popular) to implement C++ in other ways. For example, you could imagine a C++ interpreter.

When a class template specialization is used in multiple translation units, a compiler will repeat the instantiation process in every translation unit. This poses very few problems because class definitions do not directly create low-level code. They are used only internally by a C++ implementation to verify and interpret various other expressions and declarations. In this regard, the multiple instantiations of a class definition are not materially different from the multiple inclusions of a class definition—typically through header file inclusion—in various translation units.

However, if you instantiate a (noninline) function template, the situation may be different. If you were to provide multiple definitions of an ordinary noninline function, you would violate the ODR. Assume, for example, that you compile and link a program consisting of the following two files:

```
// File a.cpp:
int main()
{
}
```

```
// File b.cpp:
int main()
{
}
```

C++ compilers will compile each module separately without any problems because indeed they are valid C++ translation units. However, your linker will most likely protest if you try to link the two together. Duplicate definitions are not allowed.

In contrast, consider the template case:

```
// File t.hpp:
// common header (inclusion model)
template<typename T>
class S {
  public:
    void f();
};
```

```
template<typename T>
void S::f()       // member definition
{
}
```

```
void helper(S<int>*);
```

```
// File a.cpp:
#include "t.hpp"
```

```
void helper(S<int>* s)
{
    s->f();       // (1) first point of instantiation of S::f
}
```

```
// File b.cpp:
#include "t.hpp"
```

```
int main()
{
    S<int> s;
    helper(&s);
    s.f();        // (2) second point of instantiation of S::f
}
```

If the linker treats instantiated members of templates just like it does ordinary functions or member functions, the compiler needs to ensure that it generates code at only one of the two POIs: at points (1) or (2), but not both. To achieve this, a compiler has to carry information from one translation unit to the other, and this is something C++ compilers were never required to do prior to the introduction of templates. In what follows, we discuss the three broad classes of solutions that are *en vogue* among C++ implementers.

Note that the same problem occurs with all linkable entities produced by template instantiation: instantiated function templates and member function templates, as well as instantiated static data members.

10.4.1 Greedy Instantiation

The first C++ compilers that popularized greedy instantiation were produced by a company called Borland. It has grown to be the most commonly used technique among the various C++ systems, and in particular it is almost universally the mechanism of choice in development environments for Microsoft Windows-based personal computers.

Greedy instantiation assumes that the linker is aware that certain entities—linkable template instantiations in particular—may in fact appear in duplicate across the various object files and libraries. The compiler will typically mark these entities in a special way. When the linker finds multiple instances, it keeps one and discards all the others. There is not much more to it than that.

In theory, greedy instantiation has some serious drawbacks:

- The compiler may be wasting time on generating and optimizing N instantiations, of which only one will be kept.

- Linkers typically do not check that two instantiations are identical because some insignificant differences in generated code can validly occur for multiple instances of one template specialization. These small differences should not cause the linker to fail. (These differences could result from tiny differences in the state of the compiler at the instantiation times.) However, this often also results in the linker not noticing more substantial differences, such as when one instantiation was compiled for maximum performance whereas the other was compiled for most convenient debugging.

- The sum of all the object files could potentially be much larger than with alternatives because the same code may be duplicated many times.

In practice, these shortcomings do not seem to have caused major problems. Perhaps this is because greedy instantiation contrasts very favorably with the alternatives in one important aspect: The traditional source-object dependency is preserved. In particular, one translation unit generates but one object file, and each object file contains compiled code for all the linkable definitions in the corresponding source file (which includes the instantiated definitions).

Finally, it may be worth noting that the linker mechanism that allows duplicate definitions of linkable entities is also typically used to handle duplicate *spilled inlined functions*[9] and *virtual function dispatch tables*.[10] If this mechanism is not available, the alternative is usually to emit these items with internal linkage, at the expense of generating larger code.

10.4.2   Queried Instantiation

The most popular implementation in this category is provided by a company called *Sun Microsystems*, starting with release 4.0 of their C++ compiler. Queried instantiation is conceptually remarkably simple and elegant and yet it is chronologically the most recent class of instantiation schemes that we review here. In this scheme, a database shared by the compilations of all translation units participating in a program is maintained. This database keeps track of which specializations have been instantiated and on what source code they depend. The generated specializations themselves are typically stored with this information in the database. Whenever a point of instantiation for a linkable entity is encountered, one of three things can happen:

1. No specialization is available: In this case, instantiation occurs, and the resulting specialization is entered in the database.

2. A specialization is available but is out of date because source changes have occurred since it was generated. Here, too, instantiation occurs, but the resulting specialization replaces the one previously stored in the database.

3. An up-to-date specialization is available in the database. Nothing needs to be done.

Although conceptually simple, this design presents a few implementation challenges:

- It is not trivial to maintain correctly the dependencies of the database contents with respect to the state of the source code. Although it is not incorrect to mistake the third case for the second, doing so increases the amount of work done by the compiler (and hence overall build time).

- It is quite common to compile multiple source files concurrently. Hence, an industrial-strength implementation needs to provide the appropriate amount of concurrency control in the database.

Despite these challenges, the scheme can be implemented quite efficiently. Furthermore, there are no obvious pathological cases that would make this solution scale poorly, in contrast, for example, with greedy instantiation, which may lead to a lot of wasted work.

The use of a database may also present some problems to the programmer, unfortunately. The origin of most of these problems lies in that fact that the traditional compilation model inherited from most C compilers no longer applies: A single translation unit no longer produces a single stand-alone object file. Assume, for example, that you wish to link your final program. This link operation needs

---

[9] When a compiler is unable to "inline" every call to a function that you marked with the keyword `inline`, a separate copy of the function is emitted in the object file. This may happen in multiple object files.

[10] Virtual function calls are usually implemented as indirect calls through a table of pointers to functions. See [*LippmanObjMod*] for a thorough study of such implementation aspects of C++.

not only the contents of each of the object files associated with your various translation units, but also the object files stored in the database. Similarly, if you create a binary library, you need to ensure that the tool that creates that library—typically a linker or an archiver—is aware of the contents of the database. More generally, any tool that operates on object files may need to be made aware of the database contents. Many of these problems can be alleviated by not storing the instantiations in the database, but instead by emitting the object code in the object file that caused the instantiation in the first place.

Libraries present yet another challenge. A number of generated specializations may be packaged in a library. When the library is added to another project, that project's database may need to be made aware of the instantiations that are already available. If not, and if the project creates some of its own points of instantiation for the specializations present in the library, duplicate instantiation may occur. A possible strategy to deal with such situations is to use the same linker technology that enables greedy instantiation: Make the linker aware of generated specializations and have it weed out duplicates (which should nonetheless occur much less frequently than with greedy instantiation). Various other subtle arrangements of sources, object files, and libraries can lead to frustrating problems such as missing instantiations because the object code containing the required instantiation was not linked in the final executable program. Such problems should not be construed as shortcomings of the queried instantiation approach but rather should be taken as a solid argument against complex and subtle software build environments.

10.4.3 Iterated Instantiation

The first compiler to support C++ templates was Cfront 3.0—a direct descendant of the compiler that Bjarne Stroustrup wrote to develop the language.[11] An inflexible constraint on Cfront was that it had to be very portable from platform to platform, and this meant that it (1) used the C language as a common target representation across all target platforms and (b) used the local target linker. In particular, this implied that the linker was not aware of templates. In fact, Cfront emitted template instantiations as ordinary C functions, and therefore it had to avoid duplicate instantiations. Although the Cfront source model was different from the standard inclusion and separation models, its instantiation strategy can be adapted to fit the inclusion model. As such, it also merits recognition as the first incarnation of iterated instantiation. The Cfront iteration can be described as follows:

1. Compile the sources without instantiating any required linkable specializations.
2. Link the object files using a *prelinker*.
3. The prelinker invokes the linker and parses its error messages to determine whether any are the result of missing instantiations. If so, the prelinker invokes the compiler on sources that contain the needed template definitions, with options to generate the missing instantiations.
4. Repeat step 3 if any definitions are generated.

---

[11] Do not let this phrase mislead you into thinking that Cfront was an abstract prototype: It was used in industrial contexts, and formed the basis of many commercial C++ compiler offerings. Release 3.0 appeared in 1991 but was plagued with bugs. Version 3.0.1 followed soon thereafter and made templates usable.

The need to iterate step 3 is prompted by the observation that the instantiation of one linkable entity may lead to the need for another such entity that was not yet instantiated. Eventually the iteration will "converge," and the linker will succeed in building a complete program.

The drawbacks of the original Cfront scheme are quite severe:

- The perceived time to link is augmented not only by the prelinker overhead but also by the cost of every required recompilation and relinking. Some users of Cfront-based systems reported link times of "a few days" compared with "about an hour" with the alternative schemes reported earlier.

- Diagnostics (errors, warnings) are delayed until link time. This is especially painful when linking becomes expensive and the developer must wait hours just to find out about a typo in a template definition.

- Special care must be taken to remember where the source containing a particular definition is located (step 1). Cfront in particular used a central repository, which had to deal with some of the challenges of the central database in the queried instantiation approach. In particular, the original Cfront implementation was not engineered to support concurrent compilations.

Despite these shortcomings, the iteration principle was refined for the two compilation systems that would later pioneer the more advanced C++ template features[12]: the Edison Design Group's (EDG) implementation and HP's aC++.[13] In what follows, we expand on the technique developed by EDG to demonstrate its C++ front-end technology.[14]

EDG's iteration enables two-way communication between the prelinker and the various compilation steps: The prelinker can direct instantiations performed for a particular translation unit through an *instantiation request* file, and the compiler can notify the prelinker about possible points of instantiation either by embedding information in the object files or by producing separate *template information* files. The instantiation request files and the template information files have names that correspond to the name of the file being compiled, but with suffixes `.ii` and `.ti` respectively. The iteration works as follows:

1. While compiling the source of a translation unit, the EDG compiler reads the corresponding `.ii` file if one exists and creates the instantiations directed therein. At the same time, it writes which points of instantiation it could have honored to the object file resulting from this compilation or to a separate `.ti` file. It also writes how this file is compiled.

---

[12] We are not unbiased. However, the first publically available implementations of such things as member templates, partial specialization, modern name lookup in templates, and the template separation model came out of these companies.

[13] HP's aC++ was grown out of technology from a company called Taligent (later absorbed by International Business Machines, or IBM). HP also added greedy instantiation to aC++ and made that the default mechanism.

[14] EDG does not sell C++ implementations to end users. Instead, they provide an essential but portable component of such an implementation to other software vendors who can then integrate this into a complete platform-specific solution. Some of EDG's customers choose to keep their portable instantiation iteration, but they can just as easily adapt it to a greedy instantiation environment (which is not portable because it depends on special linker capabilities).

2. The link step is intercepted by the prelinker, which examines the object files and corresponding
   `.ti` files that participate in the link step. For each instantiation that has not yet been generated,
   the required directive is added to a `.ii` file corresponding to a translation unit that can honor the
   directive.

3. If any `.ii` files are modified, the prelinker reinvokes the compiler (step 1) for the corresponding
   sources files, and the prelinker iteration repeats.

4. When closure has been achieved, a single actual link step is performed.

This scheme addresses the issue of concurrent builds by maintaining global information on a per-
translation-unit basis. The perceived link time can still be significantly higher than with greedy and
queried instantiation, but because no actual linking is performed, the growth is much less catas-
trophic. More important, because the prelinker maintains global consistency among the `.ii` files,
these files can be reused in the next build cycle. Specifically, after having made some changes to
the source, the programmer restarts a build of the files affected by the modifications. Each resulting
compilation immediately instantiates the specializations requested by the `.ii` files that lingered from
the previous compilation of that file and chances are good that the prelinker will not need to trigger
additional recompiles at link time.

In practice, EDG's scheme works quite well, and, although a build "from scratch" is typically
more time-consuming than the alternative schemes, subsequent build times are quite competitive.

10.5 Explicit Instantiation

It is possible to create explicitly a point of instantiation for a template specialization. The construct
that achieves this is called an *explicit instantiation directive*. Syntactically, it consists of the keyword
`template` followed by a declaration of the specialization to be instantiated. For example:

```
template<typename T>
void f(T) throw(T)
{
}


// four valid explicit instantiations:
template void f<int>(int) throw(int);
template void f<>(float) throw(float);
template void f(long) throw(long);
template void f(char);
```

Note that every instantiation directive is valid. Template arguments can be deduced (see Chapter 11),
and exception specifications can be omitted. If they are not omitted, they must match the one of the
template.

Members of class templates can also be explicitly instantiated in this way:

```
template<typename T>
class S {
  public:
    void f() {
    }
};


template void S<int>::f();


template class S<void>;
```

Furthermore, all the members of a class template specialization can be explicitly instantiated by explicitly instantiating the class template specialization.

Many early C++ compilation systems did not have automatic instantiation capabilities when they first implemented support for templates. Instead, some systems required that the function template specializations used by a program be manually instantiated in a single location. This *manual instantiation* usually involved implementation-specific #pragma directives.

The C++ standard therefore codified this practice by specifying a clean syntax for it. The standard also specifies that there can be at most one explicit instantiation of a certain template specialization in a program. Furthermore, if a template specialization is explicitly instantiated, it should not be explicitly specialized, and vice versa.

In the original context of manual instantiations, these limitations may seem harmless, but in current practice they cause some grief.

First, consider a library implementer who releases a first version of a function template:

// File toast.hpp:
```
template<typename T>
void toast(T const& x)
{
    ...
}
```

Client code is free to include this header and explicitly instantiate its template:

// Client code:
```
#include "toast.hpp"


template void toast(float);
```

Unfortunately, if the library writer decides to specialize toast<float> explicitly, the client code becomes invalid. This is even more delicate when the library is a standard library implemented by different vendors. Some may explicitly specialize some standard templates, whereas others may not (or may specialize different specializations). The client code can therefore not specify the explicit instantiation of library components in a portable manner.

At the time of this writing (2002), the C++ standardization committee appears inclined to state that if an explicit instantiation directive follows an explicit specialization for the same entity, then the directive is without effect. (The final decision in this matter is still pending and may not occur if it appears technically infeasible.)

A second challenge with the current limitations on explicit template instantiation stems from their use as a means to improve compilation times. Indeed, many C++ programmers have observed that automatic template instantiation has a nontrivial negative impact on build times. A technique to improve build times consists in manually instantiating certain template specializations in a single location and inhibiting the instantiation in all other translation units. The only portable way to ensure this inhibition is not to provide the template definition except in the translation unit where it is explicitly instantiated. For example:

// Translation unit 1:
```
template<typename T> void f(); // no definition: prevents instantiation
                               // in this translation unit

void g()
{
    f<int>();
}
```

// Translation unit 2:
```
template<typename T> void f()
{
}

template void f<int>();          // manual instantiation

void g();

int main()
{
    g();
}
```

This solution works well, but it requires control of the source code that provides the template interface. Often, this is not the case. The source code providing the template cannot be modified and always provides the definition of the templates.

One "trick" that is sometimes used is to declare a template as specialized in all translation units (which does inhibit the automatic instantiation of that specialization) except in the translation unit in which that specialization is explicitly instantiated. To illustrate this, let's modify our previous example to include a definition for the template:

```
// Translation unit 1:
template<typename T> void f()
{
}

template<> void f<int>();   // declared but not defined

void g() {
    f<int>();
}
```

```
// Translation unit 2:
template<typename T> void f()
{
}

template void f<int>();     // manual instantiation

void g();

int main()
{
    g();
}
```

Unfortunately, this assumes that the object code for a call to an explicitly specialized specialization is identical to a call to the matching generic specialization. This assumption is not correct. Several C++ compilers generate different mangled names for the two entities.[15] With these compilers, the code does not link to a complete executable program.

Some compilers provide an extension to indicate that a template specialization should not be instantiated in that translation unit. A popular (but nonstandard) syntax consists in prepending the keyword extern before an explicit instantiation directive that would otherwise trigger the instantiation. The first file in our last example can be rewritten as follows for compilers supporting that extension:

---

[15] The mangled name of a function is the name seen by the linker. It combines the plain function name with attributes of its parameters, its template arguments, and sometimes some other properties to generate a unique name that does not clash with validly overloaded functions.

```
// Translation unit 1:
template<typename T> void f()
{
}

extern template void f<int>();   // declared but not defined

void g()
{
    f<int>();
}
```

10.6 Afternotes

This chapter deals with two related but different issues: the C++ template *compilation models* and various C++ template *instantiation mechanisms*.

The compilation model determines the meaning of a template at various stages of the translation of a program. In particular, it determines what the various constructs in a template mean when it is instantiated. Name lookup is an essential ingredient of the compilation model of course. When we talk about the inclusion model and the separation model, we talk about compilation models. These models are part of the language definition.

The *instantiation mechanisms* are the external mechanisms that allow C++ implementations to create instantiations correctly. These mechanisms may be constrained by requirements of the linker and other software building tools.

However, the original (Cfront) implementation of templates transcended these two concepts. It created new translation units for the instantiation of templates using a particular convention for the organization of source files. The resulting translation unit was then compiled using what is essentially the inclusion model (although the C++ name lookup rules were substantially different back then). So although Cfront did not implement "separate compilation" of templates, it managed to create an illusion of separate compilation by creating implicit inclusions. Various later implementations provided a somewhat similar implicit inclusion mechanism by default (Sun Microsystems) or as an option (HP, EDG) to provide some amount of compatibility with existing code developed for Cfront.

An example illustrates the details of the Cfront implementation scheme:

```
// File template.hpp:
template<class T>   // Cfront doesn't know typename
void f(T);
```

```
// File template.cpp:
template<class T>    // Cfront doesn't know typename
void f(T)
{
}
```

```
// File app.hpp:
class App {
    ...
};
```

```
// File main.cpp:
#include "app.hpp"
#include "template.hpp"

int main()
{
    App a;
    f(a);
}
```

At link time, Cfront's iterated instantiation scheme then creates a new translation unit including files it expects to contain the implementation of the templates it found in header files. Cfront's convention for this is to replace the .h (or similar) suffix of header files by .c (or one of a few other suffixes like .C or .cpp). In this case, the generated translation unit becomes

```
// File main.cpp:
#include "template.hpp"
#include "template.cpp"
#include "app.hpp"

static void _dummy_(App a1)
{
    f(a1);
}
```

This translation unit is then compiled with a special option to disable the code generation of any entity defined in an included file. This prevents the inclusion of template.cpp (which was presumably already compiled to another object file) from generating duplicate definitions of any linkable entities it may contain.

The function _dummy_ is used to create references to the specializations that must be instantiated. Note also the reordering of the header files: Cfront actually includes header analysis code that causes unused headers to be omitted from the generated translation unit. Unfortunately, the technique is relatively brittle in the presence of macros with scopes that cross header boundaries.

In contrast, the standard C++ separation model involves the separate translation of two (or more) translation units, followed by an instantiation that has access to the entities of both translation units (primarily enabled by ADL across translation units). Because it is not based on inclusion, it does not impose a particular header file convention, nor do macro definitions in one translation unit pollute the other translation units. However, as we illustrated earlier in this chapter, macros aren't the only way to create surprises in C++, and the export model is exposed to other forms of "pollution."

Chapter 11

Template Argument Deduction

Explicitly specifying template arguments on every call to a function template (for example, `concat<std::string, int>(s, 3)`) can quickly lead to unwieldy code. Fortunately, a C++ compiler can often automatically determine the intended template arguments using a powerful process called *template argument deduction*.

In this chapter we explain the details of the template argument deduction process. As is often the case in C++, there are many rules that usually produce an intuitive result. A solid understanding of this chapter allows us to avoid the more surprising situations.

11.1   The Deduction Process

The deduction process compares the types of an argument of a function call with the corresponding parameterized type of a function template and attempts to conclude the correct substitution for one or more of the deduced parameters. Each argument-parameter pair is analyzed independently, and if the conclusions differ in the end, the deduction process fails. Consider the following example:

```
template<typename T>
T const& max (T const& a, T const& b)
{
    return a<b ? b : a;
}


int g = max(1, 1.0);
```

Here the first call argument is of type `int` so the parameter `T` of our original `max()` template is tentatively deduced to be `int`. The second call argument is a `double`, however, and so `T` should be `double` for this argument: This conflicts with the previous conclusion. Note that we say that "the deduction process fails," not that "the program is invalid." After all, it is possible that the deduction process would succeed for another template named `max` (function templates can be overloaded much like ordinary functions; see Section 2.4 on page 15 and Chapter 12).

If all the deduced template parameters are consistently determined, the deduction process can still fail if substituting the arguments in the rest of the function declaration results in an invalid construct. For example:

```
template<typename T>
typename T::ElementT at (T const& a, int i)
{
    return a[i];
}

void f (int* p)
{
    int x = at(p, 7);
}
```

Here `T` is concluded to be `int*` (there is only one parameter type where `T` appears, so there are obviously no analysis conflicts). However, substituting `int*` for `T` in the return type `T::ElementT` is clearly invalid C++, and the deduction process fails.[1] The error message is likely to say that no match was found for the call to `at()`. In contrast, if all the template arguments are mentioned explicitly, then there is no chance that the deduction process will succeed for another template, and the error message is more likely to say that the template arguments for `at()` are invalid. You can investigate this by comparing the diagnostic for the previous example with

```
void f (int* p)
{
    int x = at<int*>(p, 7);
}
```

on your favorite C++ implementation.

We still need to explore how argument-parameter matching proceeds. We describe it in terms of matching a type A (derived from the argument type) to a parameterized type P (derived from the parameter declaration). If the parameter is declared with a reference declarator, P is taken to be the type referenced, and A is the type of the argument. Otherwise, however, P is the declared parameter type, and A is obtained from the type of the argument by *decaying*[2] array and function types to pointer types, ignoring top-level `const` and `volatile` qualifiers. For example:

---

[1] In this case, deduction failure leads to an error. However, this falls under the SFINAE principle (see Section 8.3.1 on page 106): If there were another function for which deduction succeeds, the code could be valid.

[2] *Decay* is the term used to refer to the implicit conversion of function and array types to pointer types.

```
template<typename T> void f(T);     // P is T

template<typename T> void g(T&);    // P is also T

double x[20];

int const seven = 7;

f(x);        // nonreference parameter: T is double*
g(x);        // reference parameter:    T is double[20]
f(seven);    // nonreference parameter: T is int
g(seven);    // reference parameter:    T is int const
f(7);        // nonreference parameter: T is int
g(7);        // reference parameter:    T is int => ERROR: can't pass 7 to int&
```

For a call f(x), the array type of x decays to type double*, which is the type deduced for T. In f(seven) the const qualification is stripped and hence T is deduced to be int. In contrast, calling g(x) deduces T to be type double[20] (no decay occurs). Similarly, g(seven) has an lvalue argument of type int const, and because const and volatile qualifiers are not dropped when matching reference parameters, T is deduced to be int const. However, note that g(7) would deduce T to be int (because nonclass rvalue expressions never have const or volatile qualified types), and the call would fail because an argument 7 cannot be passed to a parameter of type int&.

The fact that no decay occurs for arguments bound to reference parameters can be surprising when the arguments are string literals. Reconsider our max() template:

```
template<typename T>
T const& max(T const& a, T const& b);
```

It would be reasonable to expect that for the expression max("Apple", "Pear") T is deduced to be char const*. However, the type of "Apple" is char const[6], and the type of "Pear" is char const[5]. No array-to-pointer decay occurs (because the deduction involves reference parameters), and therefore T would have to be both char[6] and char[5] for deduction to succeed. That is of course impossible. See Section 5.6 on page 57 for additional discussion on this topic.

11.2   Deduced Contexts

Parameterized types that are considerably more complex than T can be matched to a given argument type. Here are a few examples that are still fairly basic:

```
template<typename T>
void f1(T*);

template<typename E, int N>
void f2(E(&)[N]);
```

```
template<typename T1, typename T2, typename T3>
void f3(T1 (T2::*)(T3*));

class S {
  public:
    void f(double*);
};

void g (int*** ppp)
{
    bool b[42];
    f1(ppp);     // deduces T to be int**
    f2(b);       // deduces E to be bool and N to be 42
    f3(&S::f);   // deduces T1 = void, T2 = S, and T3 = double
}
```

Complex type declarations are built from more elementary constructs (pointer, reference, array, and function declarators; pointer-to-member declarators; template-ids; and so forth), and the matching process proceeds from the top-level construct and recurses through the composing elements. It is fair to say that most type declaration constructs can be matched in this way, and these are called *deduced contexts*. However, a few constructs are not deduced contexts:

- Qualified type names. A type name like Q<T>::X will never be used to deduce a template parameter T, for example.
- Nontype expressions that are not just a nontype parameter. A type name like S<I+1> will never be used to deduce I, for example. Neither will T be deduced by matching against a parameter of type int(&)[sizeof(S<T>)].

These limitations should come as no surprise because the deduction would, in general, not be unique (or even finite), although qualified type names are sometimes easily overlooked. A nondeduced context does not automatically imply that the program is in error or even that the parameter being analyzed cannot participate in type deduction. To illustrate this, consider the following, more intricate example:

```
// details/fppm.cpp

template <int N>
class X {
  public:
    typedef int I;
    void f(int) {
    }
};
```

```
template<int N>
void fppm(void (X<N>::*p)(typename X<N>::I));

int main()
{
    fppm(&X<33>::f);    // fine: N deduced to be 33
}
```

In the function template `fppm()`, the subconstruct X<N>::I is a nondeduced context. However, the member-class component X<N> of the pointer-to-member type is a deducible context, and when the parameter N, which is deduced from it, is plugged in the nondeduced context, a type compatible with that of the actual argument &X<33>::f is obtained. The deduction therefore succeeds on that argument-parameter pair.

Conversely, it is possible to deduce contradictions for a parameter type entirely built from deduced contexts. For example, assuming suitably declared class templates X and Y:

```
template<typename T>
void f(X<Y<T>, Y<T> >);

void g()
{
    f(X<Y<int>, Y<int> >());    // OK
    f(X<Y<int>, Y<char> >());   // ERROR: deduction fails
}
```

The problem with the second call to the function template `f()` is that the two arguments deduce different arguments for the parameter T, which is not valid. (In both cases, the function call argument is a temporary object obtained by calling the default constructor of the class template X.)

11.3 Special Deduction Situations

There are two situations in which the pair (A, P) used for deduction is not obtained from the arguments to a function call and the parameters of a function template. The first situation occurs when the address of a function template is taken. In this case, P is the parameterized type of the function template declarator, and A is the function type underlying the pointer that is initialized or assigned to. For example:

```
template<typename T>
void f(T, T);

void (*pf)(char, char) = &f;
```

In this example, P is void(T, T) and A is void(char, char). Deduction succeeds with T substituted with char, and pf is initialized to the address of the specialization f<char>.

The other special situation occurs with conversion operator templates. For example:

```
class S {
  public:
    template<typename T, int N> operator T&();
};
```

In this case, the pair (P, A) is obtained as if it involved an argument of the type to which we are attempting to convert and a parameter type that is the return type of the conversion operator. The following code illustrates one variation:

```
void f(int (&)[20]);

void g(S s)
{
    f(s);
}
```

Here we are attempting to convert S to int (&)[20]. Type A is therefore int[20] and type P is T. The deduction succeeds with T substituted with int[20].

11.4   Allowable Argument Conversions

Normally, template deduction attempts to find a substitution of the function template parameters that make the parameterized type P identical to type A. However, when this is not possible, the following differences are tolerable:

- If the original parameter was declared with a reference declarator, the substituted P type may be more const/volatile-qualified than the A type.
- If the A type is a pointer or pointer-to-member type, it may be convertible to the substituted P type by a qualification conversion (in other words, a conversion that adds const and/or volatile qualifiers).
- Unless deduction occurs for a conversion operator template, the substituted P type may be a base class type of the A type, or a pointer to a base class type of the class type for which A is a pointer type. For example:

```
template<typename T>
class B {
};

template<typename T>
class D : public B<T> {
};
```

```
template<typename T> void f(B<T>*);

void g(D<long> dl)
{
    f(&dl);   // deduction succeeds with T substituted with long
}
```

The relaxed matching requirements are considered only if an exact match was not possible. Even so, deduction succeeds only if exactly one substitution was found to fit the *A* type to the substituted *P* type with these added conversions.

11.5   Class Template Parameters

Template argument deduction applies exclusively to function and member function templates. In particular, the arguments for a class template are not deduced from the arguments to a call of one of its constructors. For example:

```
template<typename T>
class S {
  public:
    S(T b) : a(b) {
    }
  private:
    T a;
};

S x(12);  // ERROR: the class template parameter T is not deduced
          //         from the constructor call argument 12
```

11.6   Default Call Arguments

Default function call arguments can be specified in function templates just as they are in ordinary functions:

```
template<typename T>
void init (T* loc, T const& val = T())
{
    *loc = val;
}
```

In fact, as this example shows, the default function call argument can depend on a template para-meter. Such a dependent default argument is instantiated only if no explicit argument is provided—a principle that makes the following example valid:

```
class S {
  public:
    S(int, int);
};


S s(0, 0);

int main()
{
    init(&s, S(7, 42));   // T() is invalid for T = S, but the default
                          // call argument T() needs no instantiation
                          // because an explicit argument is given

}
```

Even when a default call argument is not dependent, it cannot be used to deduce template arguments. This means that the following is invalid C++:

```
template<typename T>
void f (T x = 42)
{
}

int main()
{
    f<int>(); // OK: T = int
    f();      // ERROR: cannot deduce T from default call argument
}
```

11.7   The Barton-Nackman Trick

In 1994, John J. Barton and Lee R. Nackman presented a template technique that they called *re-stricted template expansion*. The technique was motivated in part by the fact that—at the time—function templates could not be overloaded[3] and namespaces were not available in most compilers.

---

[3] It may be worthwhile to read Section 12.2 on page 183 to understand how function template overloading works in modern C++.

To illustrate this, suppose we have a class template `Array` for which we want to define the equality operator `==`. One possibility is to declare the operator as a member of the class template, but this is not good practice because the first argument (binding to the `this` pointer) is subject to conversion rules that are different from the second argument. Because operator `==` is meant to be symmetrical with respect to its arguments, it is preferable to declare it as a namespace scope function. An outline of a natural approach to its implementation may look like the following:

```
template<typename T>
class Array {
  public:
    ...
};


template<typename T>
bool operator == (Array<T> const& a, Array<T> const& b)
{
    ...
}
```

However, if function templates cannot be overloaded, this presents a problem: No other operator `==` template can be declared in that scope, and yet it is likely that such a template would be needed for other class templates. Barton and Nackman resolved this problem by defining the operator in the class as a normal friend function:

```
template<typename T>
class Array {
  public:
    ...
    friend bool operator == (Array<T> const& a,
                             Array<T> const& b) {
        return ArraysAreEqual(a, b);
    }
};
```

Suppose this version of `Array` is instantiated for type `float`. The friend operator function is then declared as a result of that instantiation, but note that this function itself is not an instantiation of a function template. It is a normal nontemplate function that gets *injected* in the global scope as a side effect of the instantiation process. Because it is a nontemplate function, it could be overloaded with other declarations of operator `==` even before overloading of function templates was added to the language. Barton and Nackman referred to this as *restricted template expansion* because it avoided the use of a template `operator==(T, T)` that applied to all types T (in other words, *unrestricted* expansion).

Because operator `== (Array<T> const&, Array<T> const&)` is defined inside a class definition, it is implicitly considered to be an `inline` function, and we therefore decided to delegate the implementation to a function template `ArraysAreEqual`, which doesn't need to be `inline` and is unlikely to conflict with another template of the same name.

The Barton-Nackman trick is no longer needed for its original purpose, but it is interesting to study it because it allows us to generate nontemplate functions along with class template instantiations. Because the functions are not generated from function templates, they do not require template argument deduction but are subject to normal overload resolution rules (see Appendix B). In theory, this could mean that additional implicit conversions may be considered when matching the friend function to a specific call site. However, this is of relatively little benefit because in standard C++ (unlike the language at the time Barton and Nackman came up with their idea), the injected friend function is not unconditionally visible in the surrounding scope: It is visible only through ADL. This means that the arguments of the function call must already have the class containing the friend function as an associated class. The friend function would not be found if the arguments were of an unrelated class type that could be converted to the class containing the friend. For example:

```cpp
class S {
};

template<typename T>
class Wrapper {
  private:
    T object;
  public:
    Wrapper(T obj) : object(obj) {   // implicit conversion from
                                     // T to Wrapper<T>
    }
    friend void f(Wrapper<T> const& a) {
    }
};

int main()
{
    S s;
    Wrapper<S> w(s);
    f(w);   // OK: Wrapper<S> is a class associated with w
    f(s);   // ERROR: Wrapper<S> is not associated with s
}
```

In this example, the call `f(w)` is valid because the function `f()` is a friend declared in `Wrapper<S>` which is a class associated with the argument `w`.[4] However, in the call `f(s)` the friend declaration

---

[4] Note that S is also a class associated with w because it is a template argument for the type of w.

of function f(Wrapper<S> const&) is not visible because the class Wrapper<S> in which it is defined is not associated with the argument s of type S. Hence, even though there is a valid implicit conversion from type S to type Wrapper<S> (through the constructor of Wrapper<S>), this conversion is never considered because the candidate function f is not found in the first place.

In conclusion, there is little advantage to define a friend function in a class template over simply defining an ordinary function template.

11.8 Afternotes

Template argument deduction for function templates was part of the original C++ design. In fact, the alternative provided by explicit template arguments did not become part of C++ until many years later.

Friend name injection was considered harmful by many C++ language experts because it made the validity of programs more sensitive to the ordering of instantiations. Bill Gibbons (who at the time was working on the Taligent compiler) was among the most vocal supporters of addressing the problem, because eliminating instantiation order dependencies enabled new and interesting C++ development environments (on which Taligent was rumored to be working). However, the Barton-Nackman trick required a form of friend name injection, and it is this particular technique that caused it to remain in the language in its current (weakened) form.

Interestingly, many people have heard of the "Barton-Nackman trick," but few correctly associate it with the technique described earlier. As a result, you may find many other techniques involving friends and templates being referred to incorrectly as the "Barton-Nackman trick" (for example, see Section 16.5 on page 299).

Chapter 12

Specialization and Overloading

So far we have studied how C++ templates allow a generic definition to be expanded into a family of related classes or functions. Although this is a powerful mechanism, there are many situations in which the generic form of an operation is far from optimal for a specific substitution of template parameters.

C++ is somewhat unique among other popular programming languages with support for generic programming because it has a rich set of features that enable the transparent replacement of a generic definition by a more specialized facility. In this chapter we study the two C++ language mechanisms that allow pragmatic deviations from pure genericness: template specialization and overloading of function templates.

12.1 When "Generic Code" Doesn't Quite Cut It

Consider the following example:

```
template<typename T>
class Array {
  private:
    T* data;
    ...
  public:
    Array(Array<T> const&);
    Array<T>& operator = (Array<T> const&);

    void exchange_with (Array<T>* b) {
        T* tmp = data;
        data = b->data;
        b->data = tmp;
    }
```

```
    T& operator[] (size_t k) {
        return data[k];
    }
    ...
};


template<typename T> inline
void exchange (T* a, T* b)
{
    T tmp(*a);
    *a = *b;
    *b = tmp;
}
```

For simple types, the generic implementation of `exchange()` works well. However, for types with expensive copy operations, the generic implementation may be much more expensive—both in terms of machine cycles and in terms of memory usage—than an implementation that is tailored to the particular, given structure. In our example, the generic implementation requires one call to the copy constructor of `Array<T>` and two calls to its copy-assignment operator. For large data structures these copies can often involve copying relatively large amounts of memory. However, the functionality of `exchange()` could presumably often be replaced just by swapping the internal `data` pointers, as is done in the member function `exchange_with()`.

12.1.1   Transparent Customization

In our previous example, the member function `exchange_with()` provides an efficient alternative to the generic `exchange()` function, but the need to use a different function is inconvenient in several ways:

1. Users of the `Array` class have to remember an extra interface and must be careful to use it when possible.
2. Generic algorithms can generally not discriminate between various possibilities. For example:
   ```
   template<typename T>
   void generic_algorithm(T* x, T* y)
   {
       ...
       exchange(x, y);    // How do we select the right algorithm?
       ...
   }
   ```

Because of these considerations, C++ templates provide ways to customize function templates and class templates transparently. For function templates, this is achieved through the overloading mechanism. For example, we can write an overloaded set of `quick_exchange()` function templates as follows:

```
template<typename T> inline
void quick_exchange(T* a, T* b)                    // (1)
{
    T tmp(*a);
    *a = *b;
    *b = tmp;
}


template<typename T> inline
void quick_exchange(Array<T>* a, Array<T>* b)   // (2)
{
    a->exchange_with(b);
}


void demo(Array<int>* p1, Array<int>* p2)
{
    int x=42, y=-7;
    quick_exchange(&x, &y);                      // uses (1)
    quick_exchange(p1, p2);                      // uses (2)
}
```

The first call to `quick_exchange()` has two arguments of type `int*` and therefore deduction succeeds only with the first template (declared at point (1)) when `T` is substituted by `int`. There is therefore no doubt regarding which function should be called. In contrast, the second call can be matched with either template: Viable functions for the call `quick_exchange(p1, p2)` are obtained both when substituting `Array<int>` for `T` in the first template and when substituting `int` in the second template. Furthermore, both substitutions result in functions with parameter types that exactly match the argument types of the second call. Ordinarily, this would lead us to conclude that the call is ambiguous, but (as we will discuss later) the C++ language considers the second template to be "more specialized" than the first. All other things being equal, overload resolution prefers the more specialized template and hence selects the template at point (2).

12.1.2   Semantic Transparency

The use of overloading as shown in the previous section is very useful in achieving transparent customization of the instantiation process, but it is important to realize that this "transparency" depends a great deal on the details of the implementation. To illustrate this, consider our `quick_exchange()` solution. Although both the generic algorithm and the one customized for `Array<T>` types end up swapping the values that are being pointed to, the side effects of the operations are very different.

This is dramatically illustrated by considering some code that compares the exchange of struct objects with the exchange of Array<T>s:

```
struct S {
    int x;
} s1, s2;

void distinguish (Array<int> a1, Array<int> a2)
{
    int* p = &a1[0];
    int* q = &s1.x;
    a1[0] = s1.x = 1;
    a2[0] = s2.x = 2;
    quick_exchange(&a1, &a2);   // *p == 1  after this (still)
    quick_exchange(&s1, &s2);   // *q == 2  after this
}
```

This example shows that a pointer p into the first Array becomes a pointer into the second array after quick_exchange() is called. However, the pointer into the non-Array s1 remains pointing into s1 even after the exchange operation: Only the values that were pointed to were exchanged. The difference is significant enough that it may confuse clients of the template implementation. The prefix quick_ is helpful in attracting attention to the fact that a shortcut may be taken to realize the desired operation. However, the original generic exchange() template can still have a useful optimization for Array<T>s:

```
template<typename T>
void exchange (Array<T>* a, Array<T>* b)
{
    T* p = &(*a)[0];
    T* q = &(*b)[0];
    for (size_t k = a->size(); k-- != 0; ) {
        exchange(p++, q++);
    }
}
```

The advantage of this version over the generic code is that no (potentially) large temporary Array<T> is needed. The exchange() template is called recursively so that good performance is achieved even for types such as Array<Array<char> >. Note also that the more specialized version of the template is not declared inline because it does a considerable amount of work of its own, whereas the original generic implementation is inline because it performs only a few operations (each of which is potentially expensive).

12.2   Overloading Function Templates

In the previous section we saw that two function templates with the same name can coexist, even though they may be instantiated so that both have identical parameter types. Here is another simple example of this:

```
// details/funcoverload.hpp

template<typename T>
int f(T)
{
    return 1;
}

template<typename T>
int f(T*)
{
    return 2;
}
```

When T is substituted by `int*` in the first template, a function is obtained that has exactly the same parameter (and return) types as the one obtained by substituting `int` for T in the second template. Not only can these templates coexist, their respective instantiations can coexist even if they have identical parameter and return types.

The following demonstrates how two such generated functions can be called using explicit template argument syntax (assuming the previous template declarations):

```
// details/funcoverload.cpp

#include <iostream>
#include "funcoverload.hpp"

int main()
{
    std::cout << f<int*>((int*)0) << std::endl;
    std::cout << f<int>((int*)0)  << std::endl;
}
```

This program has the following output:

```
1
2
```

To clarify this, let's analyze the call `f<int*>((int*)0)` in detail.[1] The syntax `f<int*>` indicates that we want to substitute the first template parameter of the template `f` with `int*` without relying on template argument deduction. In this case there is more than one template `f`, and therefore an overload set is created containing two functions generated from templates: `f<int*>(int*)` (generated from the first template) and `f<int*>(int**)` (generated from the second template). The argument to the call `(int*)0` has type `int*`. This matches only the function generated from the first template, and hence that is the function that ends up being called.

A similar analysis can be written for the second call.

12.2.1 Signatures

Two functions can coexist in a program if they have distinct signatures. We define the signature of a function as the following information[2]:

1. The unqualified name of the function (or the name of the function template from which it was generated)

2. The class or namespace scope of that name and, if the name has internal linkage, the translation unit in which the name is declared

3. The `const`, `volatile`, or `const volatile` qualification of the function (if it is a member function with such a qualifier)

4. The types of the function parameters (before template parameters are substituted if the function is generated from a function template)

5. Its return type, if the function is generated from a function template

6. The template parameters and the template arguments, if the function is generated from a function template

This means that the following templates and their instantiations could, in principle, coexist in the same program:

```
template<typename T1, typename T2>
void f1(T1, T2);

template<typename T1, typename T2>
void f1(T2, T1);

template<typename T>
long f2(T);

template<typename T>
char f2(T);
```

---

[1] Note that the expression 0 is an integer and not a null pointer constant. It becomes a null pointer constant after a special implicit conversion, but this conversion is not considered during template argument deduction.

[2] This definition is different from that given in the C++ standard, but its consequences are equivalent.

However, they cannot always be used when they're declared in the same scope because instantiating both creates an overload ambiguity. For example:

```cpp
#include <iostream>

template<typename T1, typename T2>
void f1(T1, T2)
{
    std::cout << "f1(T1, T2)\n";
}

template<typename T1, typename T2>
void f1(T2, T1)
{
    std::cout << "f1(T2, T1)\n";
}

// fine so far

int main()
{
    f1<char, char>('a', 'b');   // ERROR: ambiguous
}
```

Here, the function f1<T1 = char, T2 = char>(T1, T2) can coexist with the function f1<T1 = char, T2 = char>(T2, T1), but overload resolution will never prefer one over the other. If the templates appear in different translation units, then the two instantiations can actually exist in the same program (and, for example, a linker should not complain about duplicate definitions because the signatures of the instantiations are distinct):

```cpp
// Translation unit 1:
#include <iostream>

template<typename T1, typename T2>
void f1(T1, T2)
{
    std::cout << "f1(T1, T2)\n";
}

void g()
{
    f1<char, char>('a', 'b');
}
```

```
// Translation unit 2:
#include <iostream>

template<typename T1, typename T2>
void f1(T2, T1)
{
    std::cout << "f1(T2, T1)\n";
}

extern void g();   // defined in translation unit 1

int main()
{
    f1<char, char>('a', 'b');
    g();
}
```

This program is valid and produces the following output:

```
f1(T2, T1)
f1(T1, T2)
```

12.2.2   Partial Ordering of Overloaded Function Templates

Reconsider our earlier example:

```
#include <iostream>

template<typename T>
int f(T)
{
    return 1;
}

template<typename T>
int f(T*)
{
    return 2;
}
```

```
int main()
{
    std::cout << f<int*>((int*)0) << std::endl;
    std::cout << f<int>((int*)0)  << std::endl;
}
```

We found that after substituting the given template argument lists (`<int*>` and `<int>`), overload resolution ended up selecting the right function to call. However, a function is selected even when explicit template arguments are not provided. In this case, template argument deduction comes into play. Let's slightly modify function `main()` in the previous example to discuss this mechanism:

```
#include <iostream>

template<typename T>
int f(T)
{
    return 1;
}

template<typename T>
int f(T*)
{
    return 2;
}

int main()
{
    std::cout << f(0)        << std::endl;
    std::cout << f((int*)0) << std::endl;
}
```

Consider the first call (`f(0)`): The type of the argument is `int`, which matches the type of the parameter of the first template if we substitute `T` with `int`. However, the parameter type of the second template is always a pointer and, hence, after deduction, only an instance generated from the first template is a candidate for the call. In this case overload resolution is trivial.

The second call (`f((int*)0)`) is more interesting: Argument deduction succeeds for both templates, yielding the functions `f<int*>(int*)` and `f<int>(int*)`. From a traditional overload resolution perspective, both are equally good functions to call with an `int*` argument, which would suggest that the call is ambiguous (see Appendix B). However, in this sort of case an additional overload resolution criterion comes into play: The function generated from the "more specialized" template is selected. Here (as we see shortly), the second template is considered "more specialized" and thus the output of our example is (again):

```
1
2
```

12.2.3   Formal Ordering Rules

In our last example it may seem very intuitive that the second template is "more special" than the first because the first can accommodate just about any argument type whereas the second allows only pointer types. However, other examples are not necessarily as intuitive. In what follows, we describe the exact procedure to determine whether one function template participating in an overload set is more specialized than the other. However, note that these are *partial* ordering rules: It is possible that given two templates neither can be considered more specialized than the other. If overload resolution must select between two such templates, no decision can be made, and the program contains an ambiguity error.

Let's assume we are comparing two identically named function templates ft_1 and ft_2 that seem viable for a given function call. Function call parameters that are covered by a default argument and ellipsis parameters that are not used are ignored in what follows. We then synthesize two artificial lists of argument types (or for conversion function templates, a return type) by substituting every template parameter as follows:

1.   Replace each template type parameter with a unique "made up" type.

2.   Replace each template template parameter with a unique "made up" class template.

3.   Replace each nontype template parameter with a unique "made up" value of the appropriate type.

If template argument deduction of the second template against the first synthesized list of argument types succeeds with an exact match, but not vice versa, then the first template is said to be *more specialized* than the second. Conversely, if template argument deduction of the first template against the second synthesized list of argument types succeeds with an exact match, but not vice versa, then the second template is said to be *more specialized* than the first. Otherwise (either no deduction succeeds or both succeed), there is no ordering between the two templates.

Let's make this concrete by applying it to the two templates in our last example. From these two templates we synthesize two lists of argument types by replacing the template parameters as described earlier: (A1) and (A2*) (where A1 and A2 are unique made up types). Clearly, deduction of the first template against the second list of argument types succeeds by substituting A2* for T. However, there is no way to make T* of the second template match the nonpointer type A1 in the first list. Hence, we formally conclude that the second template is more specialized than the first.

Finally, consider a more intricate example involving multiple function parameters:

```
template<typename T>
void t(T*, T const* = 0, ...);

template<typename T>
void t(T const*, T*, T* = 0);

void example(int* p)
{
    t(p, p);
}
```

First, because the actual call does not use the ellipsis parameter for the first template and the last parameter of the second template is covered by its default argument, these parameters are ignored in the partial ordering. Note that the default argument of the first template is not used; hence the corresponding parameter participates in the ordering.

The synthesized lists of argument types are (A1*, A1 const*) and (A2 const*, A2*). Template argument deduction of (A1*, A1 const*) versus the second template actually succeeds with the substitution of T with A1 const, but the resulting match is not exact because a qualification adjustment is needed to call t<A1 const>(A1 const*, A1 const*, A1 const* = 0) with arguments of types (A1*, A1 const*). Similarly, no exact match can be found by deducing template arguments for the first template from the argument type list (A2 const*, A2*). Therefore, there is no ordering relationship between the two templates, and the call is ambiguous.

The formal ordering rules generally result in the intuitive selection of function templates. Once in a while, however, an example comes up for which the rules do not select the intuitive choice. It is therefore possible that the rules will be revised to accommodate those examples in the future.

12.2.4   Templates and Nontemplates

Function templates can be overloaded with nontemplate functions. All else being equal, the nontemplate function is preferred in selecting the actual function being called. The following example illustrates this:

```
// details/nontmpl.cpp

#include <string>
#include <iostream>

template<typename T>
std::string f(T)
{
    return "Template";
}

std::string f(int&)
{
    return "Nontemplate";
}

int main()
{
    int x = 7;
    std::cout << f(x) << std::endl;
}
```

This should output:

```
Nontemplate
```

12.3   Explicit Specialization

The ability to overload function templates, combined with the partial ordering rules to select the "best" matching function template, allows us to add more specialized templates to a generic implementation to tune code transparently for greater efficiency. However, class templates cannot be overloaded. Instead, another mechanism was chosen to enable transparent customization of class templates: *explicit specialization*. The standard term *explicit specialization* refers to a language feature that we call *full specialization* instead. It provides an implementation for a template with template parameters that are fully substituted: No template parameters remain. Class templates and function templates can be fully specialized. So can members of class templates that may be defined outside the body of a class definition (i.e., member functions, nested classes, and static data members).

In a later section, we will describe *partial specialization*. This is similar to full specialization, but instead of fully substituting the template parameters, some parameterization is left in the alternative implementation of a template. Full specializations and partial specializations are both equally "explicit" in our source code, which is why we avoid the term *explicit specialization* in our discussion. Neither full nor partial specialization introduces a totally new template or template instance. Instead, these constructs provide alternative definitions for instances that are already implicitly declared in the generic (or *unspecialized*) template. This is a relatively important conceptual observation, and it is a key difference with overloaded templates.

12.3.1   Full Class Template Specialization

A full specialization is introduced with a sequence of three tokens: `template`, `<`, and `>`.[3] In addition, the class name declarator is followed by the template arguments for which the specialization is declared. The following example illustrates this:

```
template<typename T>
class S {
  public:
    void info() {
        std::cout << "generic (S<T>::info())\n";
    }
};
```

---

[3] The same prefix is also needed to declare full function template specializations. Earlier designs of the C++ language did not include this prefix, but the addition of member templates required additional syntax to disambiguate complex specialization cases.

```
template<>
class S<void> {
  public:
    void msg() {
        std::cout << "fully specialized (S<void>::msg())\n";
    }
};
```

Note how the implementation of the full specialization does not need to be related in any way to the generic definition: This allows us to have member functions of different names (info versus msg). The connection is solely determined by the name of the class template.

The list of specified template arguments must correspond to the list of template parameters. For example, it is not valid to specify a nontype value for a template type parameter. However, template arguments for parameters with default template arguments are optional:

```
template<typename T>
class Types {
  public:
    typedef int I;
};

template<typename T, typename U = typename Types<T>::I>
class S;                         // (1)

template<>
class S<void> {                  // (2)
  public:
    void f();
};

template<> class S<char, char>; // (3)

template<> class S<char, 0>;     // ERROR: 0 cannot substitute U

int main()
{
    S<int>*      pi;   // OK: uses (1), no definition needed
    S<int>       e1;   // ERROR: uses (1), but no definition available
    S<void>*     pv;   // OK: uses (2)
    S<void,int>  sv;   // OK: uses (2), definition available
    S<void,char> e2;   // ERROR: uses (1), but no definition available
```

```
    S<char,char> e3;     // ERROR: uses (3), but no definition available
}
```

```
template<>
class S<char, char> {   // definition for (3)
};
```

As this example also shows, declarations of full specializations (and of templates) do not necessarily have to be definitions. However, when a full specialization is declared, the generic definition is never used for the given set of template arguments. Hence, if a definition is needed but none is provided, the program is in error. For class template specialization it is sometimes useful to "forward declare" types so that mutually dependent types can be constructed. A full specialization declaration is identical to a normal class declaration in this way (it is *not* a template declaration). The only differences are the syntax and the fact that the declaration must match a previous template declaration. Because it is not a template declaration, the members of a full class template specialization can be defined using the ordinary out-of-class member definition syntax (in other words, the `template<>` prefix cannot be specified):

```
template<typename T>
class S;
```

```
template<> class S<char**> {
  public:
    void print() const;
};
```

```
// the following definition cannot be preceded by template<>
void S<char**>::print() const
{
    std::cout << "pointer to pointer to char\n";
}
```

A more complex example may reinforce this notion:

```
template<typename T>
class Outside {
  public:
    template<typename U>
    class Inside {
    };
};
```

```
template<>
class Outside<void> {
    // there is no special connection between the following nested class
    // and the one defined in the generic template
    template<typename U>
    class Inside {
      private:
        static int count;
    };
};


// the following definition cannot be preceded by template<>
template<typename U>
int Outside<void>::Inside<U>::count = 1;
```

A full specialization is a replacement for the instantiation of a certain generic template, and it is not valid to have both the explicit and the generated versions of a template present in the same program. An attempt to use both in the same file is usually caught by a compiler:

```
template <typename T>
class Invalid {
};


Invalid<double> x1;      // causes the instantiation of Invalid<double>


template<>
class Invalid<double>;  // ERROR: Invalid<double> already instantiated!
```

Unfortunately, if the uses occur in different translation units, the problem may not be caught so easily. The following invalid C++ example consists of two files and compiles and links on many implementations, but it is invalid and dangerous:

```
// Translation unit 1:
template<typename T>
class Danger {
  public:
    enum { max = 10 };
};


char buffer[Danger<void>::max];   // uses generic value


extern void clear(char const*);
```

```
int main()
{
    clear(buffer);
}
```

// Translation unit 2:
```
template<typename T>
class Danger;

template<>
class Danger<void> {
  public:
    enum { max = 100 };
};

void clear(char const* buf)
{
    // mismatch in array bound!
    for (int k = 0; k<Danger<void>::max; ++k) {
        buf[k] = '\0';
    }
}
```

This example is clearly contrived to keep it short, but it illustrates that care must be taken to ensure that the declaration of the specialization is visible to all the users of the generic template. In practical terms, this means that a declaration of the specialization should normally follow the declaration of the template in its header file. When the generic implementation comes from an external source (such that the corresponding header files should not be modified), this is not necessarily practical, but it may be worth creating a header including the generic template followed by declarations of the specializations to avoid these hard-to-find errors. We find that, in general, it is better to avoid specializing templates coming from an external source unless it is clearly marked as being designed for that purpose.

12.3.2   Full Function Template Specialization

The syntax and principles behind (explicit) full function template specialization are much the same as those for full class template specialization, but overloading and argument deduction come into play.

The full specialization declaration can omit explicit template arguments when the template being specialized can be determined via argument deduction (using as argument types the parameter types provided in the declaration) and partial ordering. For example:

```
template<typename T>
int f(T)                    // (1)
{
    return 1;
}

template<typename T>
int f(T*)                   // (2)
{
    return 2;
}

template<> int f(int)     // OK: specialization of (1)
{
    return 3;
}

template<> int f(int*)   // OK: specialization of (2)
{
    return 4;
}
```

A full function template specialization cannot include default argument values. However, any default arguments that were specified for the template being specialized remain applicable to the explicit specialization:

```
template<typename T>
int f(T, T x = 42)
{
    return x;
}

template<> int f(int, int = 35)   // ERROR!
{
    return 0;
}

template<typename T>
int g(T, T x = 42)
{
    return x;
}
```

```
template<> int g(int, int y)
{
    return y/2;
}

int main()
{
    std::cout << g(0) << std::endl;    // should print 21
}
```

A full specialization is in many ways similar to a normal declaration (or rather, a normal *re*declaration). In particular, it does not declare a template, and therefore only one *definition* of a noninline full function template specialization should appear in a program. However, we must still ensure that a *declaration* of the full specialization follows the template to prevent attempts at using the function generated from the template. The declarations for template g in the previous example would therefore typically be organized in two files. The interface file might look as follows:

```
#ifndef TEMPLATE_G_HPP
#define TEMPLATE_G_HPP

// template definition should appear in header file:
template<typename T>
int g(T, T x = 42)
{
    return x;
}

// specialization declaration inhibits instantiations of the template;
// definition should not appear here to avoid multiple definition errors
template<> int g(int, int y);

#endif // TEMPLATE_G_HPP
```

The corresponding implementation file may read:

```
#include "template_g.hpp"

template<> int g(int, int y)
{
    return y/2;
}
```

Alternatively, the specialization could be made inline, in which case its definition can be (and should be) placed in the header file.

12.3.3   Full Member Specialization

Not only member templates, but also ordinary static data members and member functions of class templates, can be fully specialized. The syntax requires `template<>` prefix for every enclosing class template. If a member template is being specialized, a `template<>` must also be added to denote it is being specialized. To illustrate the implications of this, let's assume the following declarations:

```
template<typename T>
class Outer {                           // (1)
  public:
    template<typename U>
    class Inner {                       // (2)
      private:
        static int count;              // (3)
    };
    static int code;                   // (4)
    void print() const {               // (5)
        std::cout << "generic";
    }
};

template<typename T>
int Outer<T>::code = 6;                 // (6)

template<typename T> template<typename U>
int Outer<T>::Inner<U>::count = 7;     // (7)

template<>
class Outer<bool> {                     // (8)
  public:
    template<typename U>
    class Inner {                       // (9)
      private:
        static int count;              // (10)
    };
    void print() const {               // (11)
    }
};
```

The ordinary members `code` at point (4) and `print()` at point (5) of the generic `Outer` template (1) have a single enclosing class template and hence need one `template<>` prefix to specialize them fully for a specific set of template arguments:

```
template<>
int Outer<void>::code = 12;

template<>
void Outer<void>::print() const
{
    std::cout << "Outer<void>";
}
```

These definitions are used over the generic ones at points (4) and (5) for class `Outer<void>`, but other members of class `Outer<void>` are still generated from the template at point (1). Note that after these declarations it is no longer valid to provide an explicit specialization for `Outer<void>`.

Just as with full function template specializations, we need a way to declare the specialization of an ordinary member of a class template without specifying a definition (to prevent multiple definitions). Although nondefining out-of-class declarations are not allowed in C++ for member functions and static data members of ordinary classes, they *are* fine when specializing members of class templates. The previous definitions could be declared with

```
template<>
int Outer<void>::code;

template<>
void Outer<void>::print() const;
```

The attentive reader might point out that the nondefining declaration of the full specialization of `Outer<void>::code` has exactly the same syntax as that required to provide a definition to be initialized with a default constructor. This is indeed so, but such declarations are always interpreted as nondefining declarations.

Therefore, there is no way to provide a definition for the full specialization of a static data member with a type that can only be initialized using a default constructor!

```
class DefaultInitOnly {
  public:
    DefaultInitOnly() {
    }
  private:
    DefaultInitOnly(DefaultInitOnly const&);   // no copying possible
};
```

```
template<typename T>
class Statics {
  private:
    static T sm;
};
```

```
// the following is a declaration;
// no syntax exists to provide a definition
template<>
DefaultInitOnly Statics<DefaultInitOnly>::sm;
```

The member template `Outer<T>::Inner` can also be specialized for a given template argument without affecting the other members of the specific instantiation of `Outer<T>`, for which we are specializing the member template. Again, because there is one enclosing template, we will need one `template<>` prefix. This results in code like the following:

```
template<>
  template<typename X>
  class Outer<wchar_t>::Inner {
    public:
      static long count; // member type changed
  };
```

```
template<>
  template<typename X>
  long Outer<wchar_t>::Inner<X>::count;
```

The template `Outer<T>::Inner` can also be fully specialized, but only for a given instance of `Outer<T>`. We now need two `template<>` prefixes: one because of the enclosing class and one because we're fully specializing the (inner) template:

```
template<>
  template<>
  class Outer<char>::Inner<wchar_t> {
    public:
      enum { count = 1 };
  };
```

```
// the following is not valid C++:
// template<> cannot follow a template parameter list
template<typename X>
template<> class Outer<X>::Inner<void>; // ERROR!
```

Contrast this with the specialization of the member template of `Outer<bool>`. Because the latter is already fully specialized, there is no enclosing template, and we need only one `template<>` prefix:

```
template<>
class Outer<bool>::Inner<wchar_t> {
  public:
    enum { count = 2 };
};
```

12.4   Partial Class Template Specialization

Full template specialization is often useful, but sometimes it is natural to want to specialize a class template for a family of template arguments rather than just one specific set of template arguments. For example, let's assume we have a class template implementing a linked list:

```
template<typename T>
class List {            // (1)
  public:

    ...
    void append(T const&);
    inline size_t length() const;
    ...
};
```

A large project making use of this template may instantiate its members for many types. For member functions that are not expanded inline (say, `List<T>::append()`), this may cause noticeable growth in the object code. However, we may know that from a low-level point of view, the code for `List<int*>::append()` and `List<void*>::append()` is the same. In other words, we'd like to specify that all `List`s of pointers share an implementation. Although this cannot be expressed in C++, we can achieve something quite close by specifying that all `List`s of pointers should be instantiated from a different template definition:

```
template<typename T>
class List<T*> {        // (2)
  private:
    List<void*> impl;
    ...
  public:
    ...
    void append(T* p) {
        impl.append(p);
    }
```

```
        size_t length() const {
            return impl.length();
        }
        ...
};
```

In this context, the original template at point (1) is called the *primary template*, and the latter definition is called a *partial specialization* (because the template arguments for which this template definition must be used have been only partially specified). The syntax that characterizes a partial specialization is the combination of a template parameter list declaration (`template<...>`) and a set of explicitly specified template arguments on the name of the class template (`<T*>` in our example).

Our code contains a problem because `List<void*>` recursively contains a member of that same `List<void*>` type. To break the cycle, we can precede the previous partial specialization with a full specialization:

```
template<>
class List<void*> {    // (3)
    ...
    void append (void* p);
    inline size_t length() const;
    ...
};
```

This works because matching full specializations are preferred over partial specializations. As a result, all member functions of `List`s of pointers are forwarded (through easily inlineable functions) to the implementation of `List<void*>`. This is an effective way to combat so-called *code bloat* (of which C++ templates are often accused).

There exists a number of limitations on the parameter and argument lists of partial specialization declarations. Some of them are as follows:

1. The arguments of the partial specialization must match in kind (type, nontype, or template) the corresponding parameters of the primary template.
2. The parameter list of the partial specialization cannot have default arguments; the default arguments of the primary class template are used instead.
3. The nontype arguments of the partial specialization should be either nondependent values or plain nontype template parameters. They cannot be more complex dependent expressions like `2*N` (where `N` is a template parameter).
4. The list of template arguments of the partial specialization should not be identical (ignoring renaming) to the list of parameters of the primary template.

An example illustrates these limitations:

```
template<typename T, int I = 3>
class S;                          // primary template

template<typename T>
class S<int, T>;                  // ERROR: parameter kind mismatch

template<typename T = int>
class S<T, 10>;                   // ERROR: no default arguments

template<int I>
class S<int, I*2>;                // ERROR: no nontype expressions

template<typename U, int K>
class S<U, K>;                    // ERROR: no significant difference
                                  //         from primary template
```

Every partial specialization—like every full specialization—is associated with the primary template. When a template is used, the primary template is always the one that is looked up, but then the arguments are also matched against those of the associated specializations to determine which template implementation is picked. If multiple matching specializations are found, the "most specialized" one (in the sense defined for overloaded function templates) is selected; if none can be called "most specialized," the program contains an ambiguity error.

Finally, we should point out that it is entirely possible for a class template partial specialization to have more or fewer parameters than the primary template. Consider our generic template List (declared at point (1)) again. We have already discussed how to optimize the list-of-pointers case, but we may want to do the same with certain pointer-to-member types. The following code achieves this for pointer-to-member-pointers:

```
template<typename C>
class List<void* C::*> {   // (4)
  public:
      // partial specialization for any pointer-to-void* member
      // every other pointer-to-member-pointer type will use this
      typedef void* C::*ElementType;
      ...
      void append(ElementType pm);
      inline size_t length() const;
      ...
};
```

```
template<typename T, typename C>
class List<T* C::*> {        // (5)
  private:
    List<void* C::*> impl;

    ...
  public:
    // partial specialization for any pointer-to-member-pointer type
    // except pointer-to-void* member which is handled earlier;
    // note that this partial specialization has two template parameters,
    // whereas the primary template only has one parameter
    typedef T* C::*ElementType;

    ...
    void append(ElementType pm) {
        impl.append((void* C::*)pm);
    }
    inline size_t length() const {
        return impl.length();
    }
    ...
};
```

In addition to our observation regarding the number of template parameters, note that the common implementation defined at (4) to which all others are forwarded (by the declaration at point (5)) is itself a partial specialization (for the simple pointer case it is a full specialization). However, it is clear that the specialization at point (4) is more specialized than that at point (5); thus no ambiguity should occur.

12.5 Afternotes

Full template specialization was part of the C++ template mechanism from the start. Function template overloading and class template partial specialization, on the other hand, came much later. The HP aC++ compiler was the first to implement function template overloading, and EDG's C++ front end was the first to implement class template partial specialization. The partial ordering principles described in this chapter were originally invented by Steve Adamczyk and John Spicer (who are both of EDG).

The ability of template specializations to terminate an otherwise infinitely recursive template definition (such as the List<T*> example presented in Section 12.4 on page 200) was known for a long time. However, Erwin Unruh was perhaps the first to note that this could lead to the interesting notion of *template metaprogramming*: Using the template instantiation mechanism to perform nontrivial computations at compile time. We devote Chapter 17 to this topic.

You may legitimately wonder why only class templates can be partially specialized. The reasons are mostly historical. It is probably possible to define the same mechanism for function templates (see Chapter 13). In some ways the effect of overloading function templates is similar, but there are also some subtle differences. These differences are mostly related to the fact that only the primary template needs to be looked up when a use is encountered. The specializations are considered only afterward, to determine which implementation should be used. In contrast, all overloaded function templates must be brought into an overload set by looking them up, and they may come from different namespaces or classes. This increases the likelihood of unintentionally overloading a template name somewhat.

Conversely, it is also imaginable to allow a form of overloading of class templates. Here is an example:

```
// invalid overloading of class templates
template<typename T1, typename T2> class Pair;
template<int N1, int N2> class Pair;
```

However, there doesn't seem to be a pressing need for such a mechanism.

Chapter 13

Future Directions

C++ templates evolved considerably from their initial design in 1988 until the standardization of C++ in 1998 (the technical work was completed in November 1997). After that, the language definition was stable for several years, but during that time various new needs have arisen in the area of C++ templates. Some of these needs are simply a consequence of a desire for more consistency or orthogonality in the language. For example, why wouldn't default template arguments be allowed on function templates when they are allowed on class templates? Other extensions are prompted by increasingly sophisticated template programming idioms that often stretch the abilities of existing compilers.

In what follows we describe some extensions that have come up more than once among C++ language and compiler designers. Often such extensions were prompted by the designers of various advanced C++ libraries (including the C++ standard library). There is no guarantee that any of these will ever be part of standard C++. On the other hand, some of these are already provided as extensions by certain C++ implementations.

13.1   The Angle Bracket Hack

Among the most common surprises for beginning template programmers is the necessity to add some blank space between consecutive closing angle brackets. For example:

```
#include <list>
#include <vector>

typedef std::vector<std::list<int> > LineTable;    // OK

typedef std::vector<std::list<int>>  OtherTable;    // SYNTAX ERROR
```

The second typedef declaration is an error because the two closing angle brackets with no intervening blank space constitute a "right shift" (>>) operator, which makes no sense at that location in the source.

Yet detecting such an error and silently treating the >> operator as two closing angle brackets (a feature sometimes referred to as *the angle bracket hack*) is relatively simple compared with many of the other capabilities of C++ source code parsers. Indeed, many compilers are already able to recognize such situations and will accept the code with a warning.

Hence, it is likely that a future version of C++ will require the declaration of OtherTable (in the previous example) to be valid. Nevertheless, we should note that there are some subtle corners to the angle bracket hack. Indeed, there are situations when the >> operator is a valid token within a template argument list. The following example illustrates this:

```
template<int N> class Buf;


template<typename T> void strange() {}
template<int N> void strange() {}


int main()
{
    strange<Buf<16>>2> >();    // the >> token is not an error
}
```

A somewhat related issue deals with the accidental use of the digraph <:, which is equivalent to the bracket [(see Section 9.3.1 on page 129). Consider the following code extract:

```
template<typename T> class List;
class Marker;


List<::Marker>* markers; // ERROR
```

The last line of this example is treated as List[:Marker>* markers;, which makes no sense at all. However, a compiler could conceivably take into account that a template such as List can never validly be followed by a left bracket and disable the recognition of the corresponding digraph in that context.

13.2   Relaxed `typename` Rules

Some programmers and language designers find the rules for the use of typename (see Section 5.1 on page 43 and Section 9.3.2 on page 130) too strict. For example, in the following code, the occurrence of typename in typename Array<T>::ElementT is mandatory, but the one in typename Array<int>::ElementT is prohibited (an error):

```
template <typename T>
class Array {
  public:
    typedef T ElementT;
    ...
};


template <typename T>
void clear (typename Array<T>::ElementT& p);        // OK


template<>
void clear (typename Array<int>::ElementT& p);      // ERROR
```

Examples such as this can be surprising, and because it is not difficult for a C++ compiler implementation simply to ignore the extra keyword, the language designers are considering allowing the typename keyword in front of any qualified typename that is not already elaborated with one of the keywords struct, class, union, or enum. Such a decision would probably also clarify when the .template, ->template, and ::template constructs (see Section 9.3.3 on page 132) are permissible.

Ignoring extraneous uses of typename and template is relatively straightforward from an implementer's point of view. Interestingly, there are also situations when the language currently requires these keywords but when an implementation could do without them. For example, in the previous function template clear(), a compiler can know that the name Array<T>::ElementT cannot be anything but a type name (no expressions are allowed at that point), and therefore the use of typename could be made optional in that situation. The C++ standardization committee is therefore also examining changes that would reduce the number of situations when typename and template are required.

13.3   Default Function Template Arguments

When templates were originally added to the C++ language, explicit function template arguments were not a valid construct. Function template arguments always had to be deducible from the call expression. As a result, there seemed to be no compelling reason to allow default function template arguments because the default would always be overridden by the deduced value.

Since then, however, it is possible to specify explicitly function template arguments that cannot be deduced. Hence, it would be entirely natural to specify default values for those nondeducible template arguments. Consider the following example:

```
template <typename T1, typename T2 = int>
T2 count (T1 const& x);
```

```
class MyInt {
    ...
};

void test (Container const& c)
{
    int i = count(c);
    MyInt j = count<MyInt>(c);
    assert(j == i);
}
```

In this example, we have respected the constraint that if a template parameter has a default argument value, then each parameter after that must have a default template argument too. This constraint is needed for class templates; otherwise, there would be no way to specify trailing arguments in the general case. The following erroneous code illustrates this:

```
template <typename T1 = int, typename T2>
class Bad;
```

Bad<int>* b;   *// Is the given* int *a substitution for* T1 *or for* T2*?*

For function templates, however, the trailing arguments may be deduced. Hence, there is no technical difficulty in rewriting our example as follows:

```
template <typename T1 = int, typename T2>
T1 count (T2 const& x);

void test (Container const& c)
{
    int i = count(c);
    MyInt j = count<MyInt>(c);
    assert(j == i);
}
```

At the time of this writing the C++ standardization committee is considering extending function templates in this direction.

In hindsight, programmers have also noted uses that do not involve explicit template arguments. For example:

```
template <typename T = double>
void f(T const& = T());
```

```
int main()
{
    f(1);           // OK: deduce T = int
    f<long>(2);     // OK: T = long; no deduction
    f<char>();      // OK: same as f<char>('\0');
    f();            // Same as f<double>(0.0);
}
```

Here a default template argument enables a default call argument to apply without explicit template arguments.

13.4 String Literal and Floating-Point Template Arguments

Among the restrictions on nontype template arguments, perhaps the most surprising to beginning and advanced template writers alike is the inability to provide a string literal as a template argument.

The following example seems intuitive enough:

```
template <char const* msg>
class Diagnoser {
  public:
    void print();
};

int main()
{
    Diagnoser<"Surprise!">().print();
}
```

However, there are some potential problems. In standard C++, two instances of `Diagnoser` are the same type if and only if they have the same arguments. In this case the argument is a pointer value—in other words, an address. However, two identical string literals appearing in different source locations are not required to have the same address. We could thus find ourselves in the awkward situation that `Diagnoser<"X">` and `Diagnoser<"X">` are in fact two different and incompatible types! (Note that the type of "X" is `char const[2]`, but it decays to `char const*` when passed as a template argument.)

Because of these (and related) considerations, the C++ standard prohibits string literals as arguments to templates. However, some implementations do offer the facility as an extension. They enable this by using the actual string literal contents in the internal representation of the template instance. Although this is clearly feasible, some C++ language commentators feel that a nontype template parameter that can be substituted by a string literal value should be declared differently from one that can be substituted by an address. At the time of this writing, however, no such declaration syntax has received overwhelming support.

We should also note an additional technical wrinkle in this issue. Consider the following template declarations, and let's assume that the language has been extended to accept string literals as template arguments in this case:

```
template <char const* str>
class Bracket {
  public:
    static char const* address();
    static char const* bytes();
};


template <char const* str>
char const* Bracket<str>::address()
{
    return str;
}


template <char const* str>
char const* Bracket<str>::bytes()
{
    return str;
}
```

In the previous code, the two member functions are identical except for their names—a situation that is not that uncommon. Imagine that an implementation would instantiate Bracket<"X"> using a process much like macro expansion: In this case, if the two member functions are instantiated in different translation units, they may return different values. Interestingly, a test of some C++ compilers that currently provide this extension reveals that they do suffer from this surprising behavior.

A related issue is the ability to provide floating-point literals (and simple constant floating-point expressions) as template arguments. For example:

```
template <double Ratio>
class Converter {
  public:
    static double convert (double val) {
        return val*Ratio;
    }
};


typedef Converter<0.0254> InchToMeter;
```

This too is provided by some C++ implementations and presents no serious technical challenges (unlike the string literal arguments).

13.5   Relaxed Matching of Template Template Parameters

A template used to substitute a template template parameter must match that parameter's list of template parameters exactly. This can sometimes have surprising consequences, as shown in the following example:

```
#include <list>
    // declares:
    // namespace std {
    //      template <typename T,
    //                  typename Allocator = allocator<T> >
    //      class list;
    // }


template<typename T1,
         typename T2,
         template<typename> class Container>
                        // Container expects templates with only one parameter
class Relation {
  public:
    ...
  private:
    Container<T1> dom1;
    Container<T2> dom2;
};

int main()
{
    Relation<int, double, std::list> rel;
        // ERROR: std::list has more than one template parameter
    ...
}
```

This program is invalid because our template template parameter `Container` expects a template taking one parameter, whereas `std::list` has an allocator parameter in addition to its parameter that determines the element type.

However, because `std::list` has a default template argument for its allocator parameter, it would be possible to specify that `Container` matches `std::list` and that each instantiation of `Container` uses the default template argument of `std::list` (see Section 8.3.4 on page 112).

An argument in favor of the *status quo* (no match) is that the same rule applies to matching function types. However, in this case the default arguments cannot always be determined because the value of a function pointer usually isn't fixed until run time. In contrast, there are no "template pointers," and all the required information can be available at compile time.

Some C++ compilers already offer the relaxed matching rule as an extension. This issue is also related to the issue of typedef templates (discussed in the next section). Indeed, consider replacing the definition of `main()` in our previous example with:

```
template <typename T>
typedef std::list<T> MyList;

int main()
{
    Relation<int, double, MyList> rel;
}
```

The typedef template introduces a new template that now exactly matches `Container` with respect to its parameter list. Whether this strengthens or weakens the case for a relaxed matching rule is, of course, arguable.

This issue has been brought up before the C++ standardization committee, which is currently not inclined to add the relaxed matching rule.

13.6   Typedef Templates

Class templates are often combined in relatively sophisticated ways to obtain other parameterized types. When such parameterized types appear repeatedly in source code, it is natural to want a shortcut for them, just as typedefs provide a shortcut for unparameterized types.

Therefore, C++ language designers are considering a construct that may look as follows:

```
template <typename T>
typedef vector<list<T> > Table;
```

After this declaration, `Table` would be a new template that can be instantiated to become a concrete type definition. Such a template is called a *typedef template* (as opposed to a class template or a function template). For example:

```
Table<int> t;          // t has type vector<list<int> >
```

Currently, the lack of typedef templates is worked around by using member typedefs of class templates. For our example we might use:

```
template <typename T>
class Table {
  public:
```

```
        typedef vector<list<T> > Type;
};
```

Table<int>::Type t;   // t *has type* vector<list<int> >

Because typedef templates are to be full-fledged templates, they could be specialized much like class templates:

// *primary typedef template:*
```
template<typename T> typedef T Opaque;
```

// *partial specialization:*
```
template<typename T> typedef void* Opaque<T*>;
```

// *full specialization:*
```
template<> typedef bool Opaque<void>;
```

Typedef templates are not entirely straightforward. For example, it is not clear how they would participate in the deduction process:

```
void candidate(long);

template<typename T> typedef T DT;

template<typename T> void candidate(DT<T>);

int main()
{
    candidate(42);   // which candidate() should be called?
}
```

It is not clear that deduction should succeed in this case. Certainly, deduction is not possible with arbitrary typedef patterns.

13.7 Partial Specialization of Function Templates

In Chapter 12 we discussed how class templates can be partially specialized, whereas function templates are simply overloaded. The two mechanisms are somewhat different.

Partial specialization doesn't introduce a completely new template: It is an extension of an existing template (the *primary* template). When a class template is looked up, only primary templates are considered at first. If, after the selection of a primary template, it turns out that there is a partial specialization of that template with a template argument pattern that matches that of the instantiation, *its* definition (in other words, its *body*) is instantiated instead of the definition of the primary template. (Full template specializations work exactly the same way.)

In contrast, overloaded function templates are separate templates that are completely independent of one another. When selecting which template to instantiate, all the overloaded templates are considered together, and overload resolution attempts to choose one as the best fit. At first this might seem like an adequate alternative, but in practice there are a number of limitations:

- It is possible to specialize member templates of a class without changing the definition of that class. However, adding an overloaded member does require a change in the definition of a class. In many cases this is not an option because we may not own the rights to do so. Furthermore, the C++ standard does not currently allow us to add new templates to the std namespace, but it does allow us to specialize templates from that namespace.

- To overload function templates, their function parameters must differ in some material way. Consider a function template R convert(T const&) where R and T are template parameters. We may very well want to specialize this template for R = void, but this cannot be done using overloading.

- Code that is valid for a nonoverloaded function may no longer be valid when the function is overloaded. Specifically, given two function templates f(T) and g(T) (where T is a template parameter), the expression g(&f<int>) is valid only if f is not overloaded (otherwise, there is no way to decide which f is meant).

- Friend declarations refer to a specific function template or an instantiation of a specific function template. An overloaded version of a function template would not automatically have the privileges granted to the original template.

Together, this list forms a compelling argument in support of a partial specialization construct for function templates.

A natural syntax for partially specializing function templates is the generalization of the class template notation:

```
template <typename T>
T const& max (T const&, T const&);          // primary template


template <typename T>
T* const& max <T*>(T* const&, T* const&); // partial specialization
```

Some language designers worry about the interaction of this partial specialization approach with function template overloading. For example:

```
template <typename T>
void add (T& x, int i);    // a primary template

template <typename T1, typename T2>
void add (T1 a, T2 b);      // another (overloaded) primary template

template <typename T>
void add<T*> (T*&, int);  // which primary template does this specialize?
```

However, we expect such cases would be deemed errors without major impact on the utility of the feature.

At the time of this writing, this extension is under consideration by the C++ standardization committee.

13.8   The `typeof` Operator

When writing templates, it is often useful to be able to express the type of a template-dependent expression. Perhaps the poster child of this situation is the declaration of an arithmetic operator for a numeric array template in which the element types of the operands are mixed. The following example should make this clear:

```
template <typename T1, typename T2>
Array<???> operator+ (Array<T1> const& x, Array<T2> const& y);
```

Presumably, this operator is to produce an array of elements that are the result of adding corresponding elements in the arrays x and y. The type of a resulting element is thus the type of `x[0]+y[0]`. Unfortunately, C++ does not offer a reliable way to express this type in terms of T1 and T2.

Some compilers provide the `typeof` operator as an extension that addresses this issue. It is reminiscent of the `sizeof` operator in that it can take an expression and produce a compile-time entity from it, but in this case the compile-time entity can act as the name of a type. In our previous example this allows us to write:

```
template <typename T1, typename T2>
Array<typeof(T1()+T2())> operator+ (Array<T1> const& x,
                                    Array<T2> const& y);
```

This is nice, but not ideal. Indeed, it assumes that the given types can be default-initialized. We can work around this assumption by introducing a helper template as follows:

```
template <typename T>
T makeT();   // no definition needed

template <typename T1, typename T2>
Array<typeof(makeT<T1>()+makeT<T2>())>
  operator+ (Array<T1> const& x,
             Array<T2> const& y);
```

We really would prefer to use x and y in the `typeof` argument, but we cannot do so because they have not been declared at the point of the `typeof` construct. A radical solution to this problem is to introduce an alternative function declaration syntax that places the return type *after* the parameter types:

```
// operator function template:
template <typename T1, typename T2>
operator+ (Array<T1> const& x, Array<T2> const& y)
  -> Array<typeof(x[0]+y[0])>;
```

```
// regular function template:
template <typename T1, typename T2>
function exp(Array<T1> const& x, Array<T2> const& y)
  -> Array<typeof(exp(x[0], y[0]))>;
```

As the example illustrates, a new keyword (here, `function`) is necessary to enable the new syntax for nonoperator functions (for operator functions, the `operator` keyword is sufficient to guide the parsing process).

Note that `typeof` must be a compile-time operator. In particular, `typeof` will not take into account covariant return types, as the following example shows:

```
class Base {
  public:
    virtual Base* clone();
};
```

```
class Derived : public Base {
  public:
    virtual Derived* clone();   // covariant return type
};
```

```
void demo (Base* p, Base* q)
{
    typeof(p->clone()) tmp = p->clone();
                                // tmp will always have type Base*
    ...
}
```

Section 15.2.4 on page 271 shows how promotion traits are sometimes used to partially address the absence of a `typeof` operator.

13.9   Named Template Arguments

Section 16.1 on page 285 describes a technique that allows us to provide a nondefault template argument for a specific parameter without having to specify other template arguments for which a default value is available. Although it is an interesting technique, it is also clear that it results in a

fair amount of work for a relatively simple effect. Hence, providing a language mechanism to name
template arguments is a natural thought.

We should note at this point that a similar extension (sometimes called *keyword arguments*)
was proposed earlier in the C++ standardization process by Roland Hartinger (see Section 6.5.1
of [*StroustrupDnE*]). Although technically sound, the proposal was ultimately not accepted into the
language for various reasons. At this point there is no reason to believe named template arguments
will ever make it into the language.

However, for the sake of completeness, we mention one syntactic idea that has floated among
certain designers:

```
template<typename T,
         Move: typename M = defaultMove<T>,
         Copy: typename C = defaultCopy<T>,
         Swap: typename S = defaultSwap<T>,
         Init: typename I = defaultInit<T>,
         Kill: typename K = defaultKill<T> >
class Mutator {
   ...
};


void test(MatrixList ml)
{
    mySort (ml, Mutator <Matrix, Swap: matrixSwap>);
}
```

Note how the argument name (preceding a colon) is distinct from the parameter name. This allows us
to keep the practice of using short names for the parameters used in the implementation while having
a self-documenting name for the argument names. Because this can be overly verbose for some
programming styles, one can also imagine the ability to omit the argument name if it is identical to
the parameter name:

```
template<typename T,
         : typename Move = defaultMove<T>,
         : typename Copy = defaultCopy<T>,
         : typename Swap = defaultSwap<T>,
         : typename Init = defaultInit<T>,
         : typename Kill = defaultKill<T> >
class Mutator {
   ...
};
```

13.10   Static Properties

In Chapter 15 and Chapter 19 we discuss various ways to categorize types "at compile time." Such traits are useful in selecting specializations of templates based on the static properties of the type. (See, for example, our `CSMtraits` class in Section 15.3.2 on page 279, which attempts to select optimal or near-optimal policies to copy, swap, or move elements of the argument type.)

Some language designers have observed that if such "specialization selections" are commonplace, they shouldn't require elaborate user-defined code if all that is sought is a property that the implementation knows internally anyway. The language could instead provide a number of built-in type traits. The following could be a valid complete C++ program with such an extension:

```
#include <iostream>

int main()
{
    std::cout << std::type<int>::is_bit_copyable << '\n';
    std::cout << std::type<int>::is_union << '\n';
}
```

Although a separate syntax could be developed for such a construct, fitting it in a user-definable syntax may allow for a more smooth transition from the current language to a language that would include such facilities. However, some of the static properties that a C++ compiler can easily provide may not be obtainable using traditional traits techniques (for example, determining whether a type is a union), which is an argument in favor of making this a language element. Another argument is that it can significantly reduce the amount of memory and machine cycles required by a compiler to translate programs that rely on such properties.

13.11   Custom Instantiation Diagnostics

Many templates put some implicit requirements on their parameters. When the arguments of an instantiation of such a template do not fulfill the requirements, either a generic error is issued or the generated instantiation does not function correctly. In early C++ compilers, the generic errors produced during template instantiations were often exceedingly opaque (see page 75 for an example). In more recent compilers, the error messages are sufficiently clear for an experienced programmer to track down a problem quickly, but there is still a desire to improve the situation. Consider the following artificial example (meant to illustrate what happens in real template libraries):

```
template <typename T>
void clear (T const& p)
{
    *p = 0;   // assumes T is a pointerlike type
}
```

```
template <typename T>
void core (T const& p)
{
    clear(p);
}

template <typename T>
void middle (typename T::Index p)
{
    core(p);
}

template <typename T>
void shell (T const& env)
{
    typename T::Index i;
    middle<T>(i);
}

class Client {
  public:
    typedef int Index;
    ...
};

Client main_client;

int main()
{
    shell(main_client);
}
```

This example illustrates the typical layering of software development: High-level function templates like shell() rely on components like middle(), which themselves make use of basic facilities like core() and clear(). When we instantiate shell(), all the layers below it also need to be instantiated. In this example, a problem is revealed in the deepest layer: clear() is instantiated with type int (from the use of Client::Index in middle()) and attempts to dereference a value of that type, which is an error. A good generic diagnostic will include a trace of all the layers that led to the problems, but this amount of information may be unwieldy.

An alternative that has often been proposed is to insert a device in the highest level template to inhibit deeper instantiation if known requirements from lower levels are not satisfied. Various attempts have been made to implement such devices in terms of existing C++ constructs (for example, see [BCCL]), but they are not always effective. Hence, it is not surprising that language extensions have been proposed to address the issue. Such an extension could clearly build on top of the static properties facilities discussed earlier. For example, we can envision modifying the `shell()` template as follows:

```
template <typename T>
void shell (T const& env)
{
    std::instantiation_error(
            !std::type<T>::has_member_type<"Index">,
            "T must have an Index member type");
    std::instantiation_error(
            !std::type<typename T::Index>::dereferencable,
            "T::Index must be a pointer-like type");
    typename T::Index i;
    middle(i);
}
```

The `instantiation_error()` pseudo-function would presumably cause the implementation to abort the instantiation (thereby avoiding the diagnostics triggered by the instantiation of `middle()`) and cause the compiler to issue the given message.

Although this is feasible, there are some drawbacks to this approach. For example, it can quickly become cumbersome to describe all the properties of a type in this manner. Some have proposed to allow "dummy code" constructs to serve as the condition to abort instantiation. Here is one of the many proposed forms (this one introduces no new keywords):

```
template <typename T>
void shell (T const& env)
{
    template try {
        typename T::Index p;
        *p = 0;
    } catch "T::Index must be a pointer-like type";
    typename T::Index i;
    middle(i);
}
```

The idea here is that the body of a `template try` clause is tentatively instantiated without actually generating object code, and, if an error occurs, the diagnostic that follows is issued. Unfortunately, such a mechanism is hard to implement because even though the generation of code could be inhibited, there are other side effects internal to a compiler that are hard to avoid. In other words, this relatively small feature would likely require a considerable reengineering of existing compilation technology.

Most such schemes also have other limitations. For example, many C++ compilers can report diagnostics in different languages (English, German, Japanese, and so forth), but providing various translations in the source code could prove excessive. Furthermore, if the instantiation process is truly aborted and the precondition was not precisely formulated, a programmer might be much worse off than with a generic (albeit unwieldy) diagnostic.

13.12 Overloaded Class Templates

It is entirely possible to imagine that class templates could be overloaded on their template parameters. For example, one can imagine the following:

```
template <typename T1>
class Tuple {
   // singleton
   ...
};


template <typename T1, typename T2>
class Tuple {
   // pair
   ...
};


template <typename T1, typename T2, typename T3>
class Tuple {
   // three-element tuple
   ...
};
```

In the next section we discuss an application of such overloading.

The overloading isn't necessarily restricted to the number of template parameters (such overloading could be emulated using partial specialization as is done for FunctionPtr in Chapter 22). The *kind* of parameters can be varied too:

```
template <typename T1, typename T2>
class Pair {
   // pair of fields
   ...
};
```

```
template <int I1, int I2>
class Pair {
    // pair of constant integer values
    ...
};
```

Although this idea has been discussed informally by some language designers, it has not yet been formally presented to the C++ standardization committee.

13.13   List Parameters

A need that shows up sometimes is the ability to pass a list of types as a single template argument. Usually, this list is meant for one of two purposes: declaring a function with a parameterized number of parameters or defining a type structure with a parameterized list of members.

For example, we may want to define a template that computes the maximum of an arbitrary list of values. A potential declaration syntax uses the ellipsis token to denote that the last template parameter is meant to match an arbitrary number of arguments:

```
#include <iostream>

template <typename T, ... list>
T const& max (T const&, T const&, list const&);

int main()
{
    std::cout << max(1, 2, 3, 4) << std::endl;
}
```

Various possibilities can be thought of to implement such a template. Here is one that doesn't require new keywords but adds a rule to function template overloading to prefer a function template without a list parameter:

```
template <typename T> inline
T const& max (T const& a, T const& b)
{
    // our usual binary maximum:
    return a<b ? b : a;
}

template <typename T, ... list> inline
T const& max (T const& a, T const& b, list const& x)
{
    return max (a, max(b,x));
}
```

Let's go through the steps that would make this work for the call max(1, 2, 3, 4). Because there are four arguments, the binary max() function doesn't match, but the second one does match with T = int and list = int, int. This causes us to call the binary function template max() with the first argument equal to 1 and the second argument equal to the evaluation of max(2, 3, 4). Again, the binary operation doesn't match, and we call the list parameter version with T = int and list = int. This time the subexpression max(b,x) expands to max(3,4), and the recursion ends by selecting the binary template.

This works fairly well thanks to the ability of overloading function templates. There is more to it than our discussion, of course. For example, we'd have to specify precisely what list const& means in this context.

Sometimes, it may be desirable to refer to particular elements or subsets of the list. For example, we could use the subscript brackets for this purpose. The following example shows how we could construct a metaprogram to count the elements in a list using this technique:

```
template <typename T>
class ListProps {
  public:
     enum { length = 1 };
};

template <... list>
class ListProps {
  public:
     enum { length = 1+ListProps<list[1 ...]>::length };
};
```

This demonstrates that list parameters may also be useful for class templates and could be combined with the class overloading concept discussed earlier to enhance various template metaprogramming techniques.

Alternatively, the list parameter could be used to declare a list of fields:

```
template <... list>
class Collection {
     list;
};
```

A surprising number of fundamental utilities can be built on top of such a facility. For more ideas, we suggest reading *Modern C++ Design* (see [*AlexandrescuDesign*]), where the lack of this feature is replaced by extensive template- and macro-based metaprogramming.

13.14 Layout Control

A fairly common template programming challenge is to declare an array of bytes that will be sufficiently large (but not excessively so) to hold an object of an as yet unknown type T—in other words, a template parameter. One application of this is the so-called *discriminated unions* (also called *variant types* or *tagged unions*):

```
template <... list>
class D_Union {
  public:
    enum { n_bytes };
    char bytes[n_bytes];   // will eventually hold one of various types
                           // described by the template arguments

    ...
};
```

The constant n_bytes cannot always be set to sizeof(T) because T may have more strict alignment requirements than the bytes buffer. Various heuristics exist to take this alignment into account, but they are often complicated or make somewhat arbitrary assumptions.

For such an application, what is really desired is the ability to express the alignment requirement of a type as a constant expression and, conversely, the ability to impose an alignment on a type, a field, or a variable. Many C and C++ compilers already support an __alignof__ operator, which returns the alignment of a given type or expression. This is almost identical to the sizeof operator except that the alignment is returned instead of the size of the given type. Many compilers also provide #pragma directives or similar devices to set the alignment of an entity. A possible approach may be to introduce an alignof keyword that can be used both in expressions (to obtain the alignment) and in declarations (to set the alignment).

```
template <typename T>
class Alignment {
  public:
    enum { max = alignof(T) };
};


template <... list>
class Alignment {
  public:
    enum { max = alignof(list[0]) > Alignment<list[1 ...]>::max
                    ? alignof(list[0])
                    : Alignment<list[1 ...]>::max };
};
```

// a set of Size templates could similarly be designed
// to determine the largest size among a given list of types

```
template <... list>
class Variant {
  public:
    char buffer[Size<list>::max] alignof(Alignment<list>::max);
    ...
};
```

13.15 Initializer Deduction

It is often said that "programmers are lazy," and sometimes this refers to our desire to keep program-matic notation compact. Consider, in that respect, the following declaration:

```
std::map<std::string, std::list<int> >* dict
  = new std::map<std::string, std::list<int> >;
```

This is verbose, and in practice we would (and most likely should) introduce a typedef synonym for the type. However, there is something redundant in this declaration: We specify the type of dict, but it is also implicit in the type of its initializer. Wouldn't it be considerably more elegant to be able to write an equivalent declaration with only one type specification? For example:

```
dcl dict = new std::map<std::string, std::list<int> >;
```

In this last declaration, the type of a variable is deduced from the type of the initializer. A keyword (dcl in the example, but var, let, and even auto have been proposed as alternatives) is needed to make the declaration distinguishable from an ordinary assignment.

So far, this isn't a template-only issue. In fact, it appears such a construct was accepted by a very early version of the Cfront compiler (in 1982, before templates came on the scene). However, it is the verbosity of many template-based types that increases the demand for this feature.

One could also imagine partial deduction in which only the arguments of a template must be deduced:

```
std::list<> index = create_index();
```

Another variant of this is to deduce the template arguments from the constructor arguments. For example:

```
template <typename T>
class Complex {
  public:
    Complex(T const& re, T const& im);
    ...
};

Complex<> z(1.0, 3.0);   // deduces T = double
```

Precise specifications for this kind of deduction are made more complicated by the possibility of overloaded constructors, including constructor templates. Suppose, for example, that our `Complex` template contains a constructor template in addition to a normal copy constructor:

```
template <typename T>
class Complex {
  public:
    Complex(Complex<T> const&);

    template <typename T2> Complex(Complex<T2> const&);
    ...
};


Complex<double> j(0.0, 1.0);
Complex<> z = j;    // Which constructor was intended?
```

In the latter initialization, it is probable that the regular copy constructor was intended; hence z should have the same type as j. However, making it an implicit rule to ignore constructor templates may be overly bold.

13.16   Function Expressions

Chapter 22 illustrates that it is often convenient to pass small functions (or functors) as parameters to other functions. We also mention in Chapter 18 that expression template techniques can be used to build small functors concisely without the overhead of explicit declarations (see Section 18.3 on page 340).

For example, we may want to call a particular member function on each element of a standard vector to initialize it:

```
class BigValue {
  public:
    void init();
  ...
};

class Init {
  public:
    void operator() (BigValue& v) const {
        v.init();
    }
};
```

```
void compute (std::vector<BigValue>& vec)
{
    std::for_each (vec.begin(), vec.end(),
                    Init());
    ...
}
```

The need to define a separate class `Init` for this purpose is unwieldy. Instead, we can imagine that we may write (unnamed) function bodies as part of an expression:

```
class BigValue {
  public:
    void init();
  ...
};

void compute (std::vector<BigValue>& vec)
{
    std::for_each (vec.begin(), vec.end(),
                    $(BigValue&) { $1.init(); });
    ...
}
```

The idea here is that we can introduce a *function expression* with a special token $ followed by parameter types in parentheses and a brace-enclosed body. Within such a construct, we can refer to the parameters with the special notation $n, where n is a constant indicating the number of the parameter.

This form is closely related to so-called *lambda expressions* (or *lambda functions*) and *closures* in other programming languages. However, other solutions are possible. For example, a solution might use anonymous inner classes, as seen in Java:

```
class BigValue {
  public:
    void init();
  ...
};

void compute (std::vector<BigValue>& vec)
{
    std::for_each (vec.begin(), vec.end(),
                    class {
                      public:
```

```
                              void operator() (BigValue& v) const {
                                  v.init();
                              }
                          };
                      );

         ...
     }
```

Although these sorts of constructs regularly come up among language designers, concrete proposals
are rare. This is probably a consequence of the fact that designing such an extension is a considerable
task that amounts to much more than our examples may suggest. Among the issues to be tackled
are the specification of the return type and the rules that determine what entities are available within
the body of a function expression. For example, can local variables in the surrounding function
be accessed? Function expressions could also conceivably be templates in which the types of the
parameters would be deduced from the use of the function expression. Such an approach may make
the previous example even more concise (by allowing us to omit the parameter list altogether), but it
brings with it new challenges for the template argument deduction system.

It is not at all clear that C++ will ever include a concept like function expressions. However,
the *Lambda Library* of Jaakko Järvi and Gary Powell (see [*LambdaLib*]) goes a long way toward
providing the desired functionality, albeit at a considerable price in compiler resources.

13.17 Afternotes

It seems perhaps premature to talk about extending the language when C++ compilers are only
barely becoming mostly compliant to the 1998 standard (C++98). However, it is in part because this
compliance is being achieved that we (the C++ programmers community) are gaining insight into
the true limitations of C++ (and templates in particular).

To meet the new needs of C++ programmers, the C++ standards committee (often referred to as
ISO WG21/ANSI J16, or just WG21/J16) started examining a road to a new standard: C++0x. After
a preliminary presentation at its April 2001 meeting in Copenhagen, WG21/J16 started examining
concrete library extension proposals.

Indeed, the intention is to attempt as much as possible to confine extensions to the C++ standard
library. However, it is well understood that some of these extensions may require work in the core
language. We expect that many of these required modifications will relate to C++ templates, just as
the introduction of STL in the C++ standard library stimulated template technology in the 1990s.

Finally, C++0x is also expected to address some "embarrassments" in C++98. It is hoped that doing so will improve the accessibility of C++. Some of the extensions in that direction were discussed
in this chapter.

Part III

Templates and Design

Programs are generally constructed using designs that map relatively well on the mechanisms offered by a chosen programming language. Because templates are a whole new language mechanism, it is not surprising to find that they call for new design elements. We explore these elements in this part of the book.

Templates are different from more traditional language constructs in that they allow us to parameterize the types and constants of our code. When combined with (1) partial specialization and (2) recursive instantiation, this leads to a surprising amount of expressive power. In the following chapters, this is illustrated by a large number of design techniques:

- Generic programming
- Traits
- Policy classes
- Metaprogramming
- Expression templates

Our presentation aims not only at listing the various known design elements, but also at conveying the principles that inspire such designs so that new techniques may be created.

Chapter 14

The Polymorphic Power of Templates

Polymorphism is the ability to associate different specific behaviors with a single generic notation.[1] Polymorphism is also a cornerstone of the object-oriented programming paradigm, which in C++ is supported mainly through class inheritance and virtual functions. Because these mechanisms are (at least in part) handled at run time, we talk about *dynamic polymorphism*. This is usually what is thought of when talking about plain polymorphism in C++. However, templates also allow us to associate different specific behaviors with a single generic notation, but this association is generally handled at compile time, which we refer to as *static polymorphism*. In this chapter we review the two forms of polymorphism and discuss which form is appropriate in which situations.

14.1   Dynamic Polymorphism

Historically, C++ started with supporting polymorphism only through the use of inheritance combined with virtual functions.[2] The art of polymorphic design in this context consists of identifying a common set of capabilities among related object types and declaring them as virtual function interfaces in a common base class.

The poster child for this design approach is an application that manages geometric shapes and allows them to be rendered in some way (for example, on a screen). In such an application we might identify a so-called *abstract base class* (*ABC*) GeoObj, which declares the common operations and properties applicable to geometric objects. Each concrete class for specific geometric objects then derives from GeoObj (see Figure 14.1):

---

[1] *Polymorphism* literally refers to the condition of having many forms or shapes (from the Greek *polumorphos*).

[2] Strictly speaking, macros can also be thought of as an early form of static polymorphism. However, they are left out of consideration because they are mostly orthogonal to the other language mechanisms.

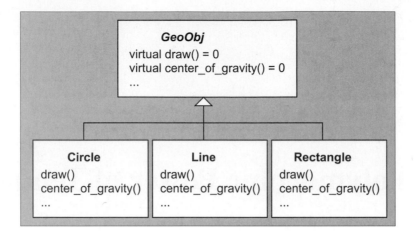

Figure 14.1. Polymorphism implemented via inheritance

```
// poly/dynahier.hpp

#include "coord.hpp"

// common abstract base class GeoObj for geometric objects
class GeoObj {
  public:
    // draw geometric object:
    virtual void draw() const = 0;
    // return center of gravity of geometric object:
    virtual Coord center_of_gravity() const = 0;
    ...
};

// concrete geometric object class Circle
// - derived from GeoObj
class Circle : public GeoObj {
  public:
    virtual void draw() const;
    virtual Coord center_of_gravity() const;
    ...
};
```

```cpp
// concrete geometric object class Line
// - derived from GeoObj
class Line : public GeoObj {
  public:
    virtual void draw() const;
    virtual Coord center_of_gravity() const;
    ...
};
...
```

After creating concrete objects, client code can manipulate these objects through references or pointers to the base class, which enables the virtual function dispatch mechanism. Calling a virtual member function through a pointer or reference to a base class subobject results in an invocation of the appropriate member of the specific concrete object to which was referred.

In our example, the concrete code can be sketched as follows:

```cpp
// poly/dynapoly.cpp

#include "dynahier.hpp"
#include <vector>

// draw any GeoObj
void myDraw (GeoObj const& obj)
{
    obj.draw();              // call draw() according to type of object
}


// process distance of center of gravity between two GeoObjs
Coord distance (GeoObj const& x1, GeoObj const& x2)
{
    Coord c = x1.center_of_gravity() - x2.center_of_gravity();
    return c.abs();          // return coordinates as absolute values
}


// draw heterogeneous collection of GeoObjs
void drawElems (std::vector<GeoObj*> const& elems)
{
    for (unsigned i=0; i<elems.size(); ++i) {
        elems[i]->draw();   // call draw() according to type of element
    }
}
```

```
int main()
{
    Line l;
    Circle c, c1, c2;

    myDraw(l);              // myDraw(GeoObj&) => Line::draw()
    myDraw(c);              // myDraw(GeoObj&) => Circle::draw()

    distance(c1,c2);        // distance(GeoObj&,GeoObj&)
    distance(l,c);          // distance(GeoObj&,GeoObj&)

    std::vector<GeoObj*> coll;    // heterogeneous collection
    coll.push_back(&l);           // insert line
    coll.push_back(&c);           // insert circle
    drawElems(coll);              // draw different kinds of GeoObjs
}
```

The key polymorphic interface elements are the functions `draw()` and `center_of_gravity()`. Both are virtual member functions. Our example demonstrates their use in the functions `mydraw()`, `distance()`, and `drawElems()`. The latter functions are expressed using the common base type `GeoObj`. As a consequence it cannot be determined at compile time which version of `draw()` or `center_of_gravity()` has to be used. However, at run time, the complete dynamic type of the objects for which the virtual functions are invoked is accessed to dispatch the function calls. Hence, depending on the actual type of a geometric object, the appropriate operation is done: If `mydraw()` is called for a `Line` object, the expression `obj.draw()` calls `Line::draw()`, whereas for a `Circle` object the function `Circle::draw()` is called. Similarly, with `distance()` the member functions `center_of_gravity()` appropriate for the argument objects are called.

Perhaps the most compelling feature of this dynamic polymorphism is the ability to handle heterogeneous collections of objects. `drawElems()` illustrates this concept: The simple expression

```
elems[i]->draw()
```

results in invocations of different member functions, depending on the type of the element being iterated over.

14.2   Static Polymorphism

Templates can also be used to implement polymorphism. However, they don't rely on the factoring of common behavior in base classes. Instead, the commonality is implicit in that the different "shapes" of an application must support operations using common syntax (that is, the relevant functions must have the same names). Concrete classes are defined independently from each other (see Figure 14.2). The polymorphic power is then enabled when templates are instantiated with the concrete classes.

Circle	Line	Rectangle
draw()	draw()	draw()
center_of_gravity()	center_of_gravity()	center_of_gravity()
...	...	...

Figure 14.2. Polymorphism implemented via templates

For example, the function `myDraw()` in the previous section

```
void myDraw (GeoObj const& obj)      // GeoObj is abstract base class
{
    obj.draw();
}
```

could conceivably be rewritten as follows:

```
template <typename GeoObj>
void myDraw (GeoObj const& obj)      // GeoObj is template parameter
{
    obj.draw();
}
```

Comparing the two implementations of `myDraw()`, we may conclude that the main difference is the specification of `GeoObj` as a template parameter instead of a common base class. There are, however, more fundamental differences under the hood. For example, using dynamic polymorphism we had only one `myDraw()` function at run time, whereas with the template we have distinct functions, such as `myDraw<Line>()` and `myDraw<Circle>()`.

We may attempt to recode the complete example of the previous section using static polymorphism. First, instead of a hierarchy of geometric classes, we have several individual geometric classes:

```
// poly/statichier.hpp

#include "coord.hpp"


// concrete geometric object class Circle
// - not derived from any class
```

```
class Circle {
  public:
    void draw() const;
    Coord center_of_gravity() const;
    ...
};
```

```
// concrete geometric object class Line
// - not derived from any class
class Line {
  public:
    void draw() const;
    Coord center_of_gravity() const;
    ...
};
...
```

Now, the application of these classes looks as follows:

```
// poly/staticpoly.cpp

#include "statichier.hpp"
#include <vector>

// draw any GeoObj
template <typename GeoObj>
void myDraw (GeoObj const& obj)
{
    obj.draw();      // call draw() according to type of object
}

// process distance of center of gravity between two GeoObjs
template <typename GeoObj1, typename GeoObj2>
Coord distance (GeoObj1 const& x1, GeoObj2 const& x2)
{
    Coord c = x1.center_of_gravity() - x2.center_of_gravity();
    return c.abs();   // return coordinates as absolute values
}
```

```
// draw homogeneous collection of GeoObjs
template <typename GeoObj>
void drawElems (std::vector<GeoObj> const& elems)
{
    for (unsigned i=0; i<elems.size(); ++i) {
        elems[i].draw();      // call draw() according to type of element
    }
}

int main()
{
    Line l;
    Circle c, c1, c2;

    myDraw(l);            // myDraw<Line>(GeoObj&) => Line::draw()
    myDraw(c);            // myDraw<Circle>(GeoObj&) => Circle::draw()

    distance(c1,c2);  // distance<Circle,Circle>(GeoObj1&,GeoObj2&)
    distance(l,c);    // distance<Line,Circle>(GeoObj1&,GeoObj2&)

    // std::vector<GeoObj*> coll;   // ERROR: no heterogeneous
                                    //           collection possible
    std::vector<Line> coll;    // OK: homogeneous collection possible
    coll.push_back(l);         // insert line
    drawElems(coll);           // draw all lines
}
```

As with `myDraw()`, GeoObj can no longer be used as a concrete parameter type for `distance()`. Instead, we provide for two template parameters GeoObj1 and GeoObj2. By using two different template parameters, different combinations of geometric object types can be accepted for the distance computation:

```
distance(l,c);     // distance<Line,Circle>(GeoObj1&,GeoObj2&)
```

However, heterogeneous collections can no longer be handled transparently. This is where the *static* part of *static polymorphism* imposes its constraint: All types must be determined at compile time. Instead, we can easily introduce different collections for different geometric object types. There is no longer a requirement that the collection be limited to pointers, which can have significant advantages in terms of performance and type safety.

14.3   Dynamic versus Static Polymorphism

Let's categorize and compare both forms of polymorphism.

Terminology

Dynamic and static polymorphism provide support for different C++ programming idioms[3]:

- Polymorphism implemented via inheritance is *bounded* and *dynamic*:
  - *Bounded* means that the interfaces of the types participating in the polymorphic behavior are predetermined by the design of the common base class (other terms for this concept are *invasive* or *intrusive*).
  - *Dynamic* means that the binding of the interfaces is done at run time (dynamically).
- Polymorphism implemented via templates is *unbounded* and *static*:
  - *Unbounded* means that the interfaces of the types participating in the polymorphic behavior are not predetermined (other terms for this concept are *noninvasive* or *nonintrusive*).
  - *Static* means that the binding of the interfaces is done at compile time (statically).

So, strictly speaking, in C++ parlance, *dynamic polymorphism* and *static polymorphism* are shortcuts for *bounded dynamic polymorphism* and *unbounded static polymorphism*. In other languages other combinations exist (for example, Smalltalk provides unbounded dynamic polymorphism). However, in the context of C++, the more concise terms *dynamic polymorphism* and *static polymorphism* do not cause confusion.

Strengths and Weaknesses

Dynamic polymorphism in C++ exhibits the following strengths:

- Heterogeneous collections are handled elegantly.
- The executable code size is potentially smaller (because only one polymorphic function is needed, whereas distinct template instances must be generated to handle different types).
- Code can be entirely compiled; hence no implementation source must be published (distributing template libraries usually requires distribution of the source code of the template implementations).

In contrast, the following can be said about static polymorphism in C++:

- Collections of built-in types are easily implemented. More generally, the interface commonality need not be expressed through a common base class.
- Generated code is potentially faster (because no indirection through pointers is needed *a priori* and nonvirtual functions can be inlined much more often).
- Concrete types that provide only partial interfaces can still be used if only that part ends up being exercised by the application.

---

[3] For a detailed discussion of polymorphism terminology, see also Sections 6.5 to 6.7 of [*CzarneckiEisenecker-GenProg*].

Static polymorphism is often regarded as more *type safe* than dynamic polymorphism because all the bindings are checked at compile time. For example, there is little danger of inserting an object of the wrong type in a container instantiated from a template. However, in a container expecting pointers to a common base class, there is a possibility that these pointers unintentionally end up pointing to complete objects of different types.

In practice, template instantiations can also cause some grief when different semantic assumptions hide behind identical-looking interfaces. For example, surprises can occur when a template that assumes an associative operator + is instantiated for a type that is not associative with respect to that operator. In practice, this kind of semantic mismatch occurs less often with inheritance-based hierarchies, presumably because the interface specification is more explicitly specified.

Combining Both Forms

Of course, you could combine both forms of polymorphism. For example, you could derive different kinds of geometric objects from a common base class to be able to handle heterogeneous collections of geometric objects. However, you can still use templates to write code for a certain kind of geometric object.

The combination of inheritance and templates is further described in Chapter 16. We will see (among other things) how the virtuality of a member function can be parameterized and how an additional amount of flexibility is afforded to static polymorphism using the inheritance-based *curiously recurring template pattern* (or *CRTP*).

14.4   New Forms of Design Patterns

The new form of static polymorphism leads to new ways of implementing design patterns. Take, for example, the *bridge pattern*, which plays a major role in C++ programs. One goal of using

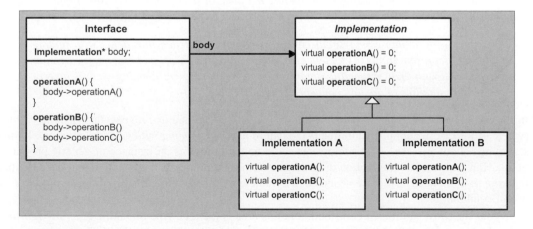

Figure 14.3. Bridge pattern implemented using inheritance

the bridge pattern is to switch between different implementations of an interface. According to [*DesignPatternsGoV*] this is usually done by using a pointer to refer to the actual implementation and delegating all calls to this class (see Figure 14.3).

However, if the type of the implementation is known at compile time, you could use the approach via templates instead (see Figure 14.4). This leads to more type safety, avoids pointers, and should be faster.

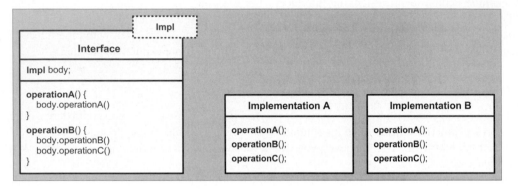

Figure 14.4. Bridge pattern implemented using templates

14.5   Generic Programming

Static polymorphism leads to the concept of *generic programming*. However, there is no one universally agreed-on definition of *generic programming* (just as there is no one agreed-on definition of *object-oriented programming*). According to [*CzarneckiEiseneckerGenProg*], definitions go from *programming with generic parameters* to *finding the most abstract representation of efficient algorithms*. The book summarizes:

> *Generic programming is a subdiscipline of computer science that deals with finding abstract representations of efficient algorithms, data structures, and other software concepts, and with their systematic organization.... Generic programming focuses on representing families of domain concepts.* (pages 169 and 170)

In the context of C++, generic programming is sometimes defined as *programming with templates* (whereas object-oriented programming is thought of as *programming with virtual functions*). In this sense, just about any use of C++ templates could be thought of as an instance of generic programming. However, practitioners often think of generic programming as having an additional essential ingredient: Templates have to be designed in a framework for the purpose of enabling a multitude of useful combinations.

By far the most significant contribution in this area is the STL (the *Standard Template Library*, which later was adapted and incorporated into the C++ standard library). The STL is a framework that provides a number of useful operations, called *algorithms*, for a number of linear data structures for collections of objects, called *containers*. Both algorithms and containers are templates. However, the key is that the algorithms are *not* member functions of the containers. Instead, the algorithms are written in a *generic* way so that they can be used by any container (and linear collection of elements). To do this, the designers of STL identified an abstract concept of *iterators* that can be provided for any kind of linear collection. Essentially, the collection-specific aspects of container operations have been factored out into the iterators' functionality.

As a consequence, implementing an operation such as computing the maximum value in a sequence can be done without knowing the details of how values are stored in that sequence:

```cpp
template <class Iterator>
Iterator max_element (Iterator beg,      // refers to start of collection
                      Iterator end)      // refers to end of collection
{
      // use only certain Iterator operations to traverse all elements
      // of the collection to find the element with the maximum value
      // and return its position as Iterator

      ...
}
```

Instead of providing all useful operations such as `max_element()` by every linear container, the container has to provide only an iterator type to traverse the sequence of values it contains and member functions to create such iterators:

```cpp
namespace std {
    template <class T, ... >
    class vector {
      public:
        typedef ...  const_iterator;       // implementation-specific iterator
        ...                                //  type for constant vectors
        const_iterator begin() const;      // iterator for start of collection
        const_iterator end() const;        // iterator for end of collection
        ...
    };

    template <class T, ... >
    class list {
      public:
        typedef ...  const_iterator;       // implementation-specific iterator
        ...                                //  type for constant lists
        const_iterator begin() const;      // iterator for start of collection
        const_iterator end() const;        // iterator for end of collection
        ...
    };
}
```

Now, you can find the maximum of any collection by calling the *generic* `max_element()` operation with the beginning and end of the collection as arguments (special handling of empty collections is omitted):

```
// poly/printmax.cpp

#include <vector>
#include <list>
#include <algorithm>
#include <iostream>
#include "MyClass.hpp"

template <typename T>
void print_max (T const& coll)
{
    // declare local iterator of collection
    typename T::const_iterator pos;

    // compute position of maximum value
    pos = std::max_element(coll.begin(),coll.end());

    // print value of maximum element of coll (if any):
    if (pos != coll.end()) {
        std::cout << *pos << std::endl;
    }
    else {
        std::cout << "empty" << std::endl;
    }
}

int main()
{
    std::vector<MyClass> c1;
    std::list<MyClass>   c2;
    ...
    print_max (c1);
    print_max (c2);
}
```

By parameterizing its operations in terms of these iterators, the STL avoids an explosion in the number of operation definitions. Instead of implementing each operation for every container, you implement the algorithm once so that it can be used for every container. The *generic glue* is the iterators that are provided by the containers and that are used by the algorithms. This works because iterators have a certain interface that is provided by the containers and used by the algorithms. This interface is usually called a *concept*, which denotes a set of constraints that a template has to fulfill to fit into this framework.

In principle, functionality such as an STL-like approach could be implemented with dynamic polymorphism. In practice, however, it would be of limited use because the iterator concept is too lightweight compared with the virtual function call mechanism. Adding an interface layer based on virtual functions would most likely slow down our operations by an order of magnitude (or more).

Generic programming is practical exactly because it relies on static polymorphism, which resolves interfaces at compile time. On the other hand, the requirement that the interfaces be resolved at compile time also calls for new design principles that are different in many ways from object-oriented design principles. Many of the most important of these *generic design principles* are described in the remainder of this book.

14.6   Afternotes

Container types were a primary motivation for the introduction of templates into the C++ programming language. Prior to templates, polymorphic hierarchies were a popular approach to containers. A popular example was the National Institutes of Health Class Library (NIHCL), which to a large extent translated the container class hierarchy of Smalltalk (see Figure 14.5).

Much like the C++ standard library, the NIHCL supported a rich variety of containers as well as iterators. However, the implementation followed the Smalltalk style of dynamic polymorphism: Iterators used the abstract base class Collection to operate on different types of collections:

```
Bag c1;
Set c2;
...
Iterator i1(c1);
Iterator i2(c2);
...
```

Unfortunately, the price of this approach was high both in terms of running time and memory usage. Running time was typically orders of magnitude worse than equivalent code using the C++ standard library because most operations ended up requiring a virtual call (whereas in the C++ standard library many operations are inlined, and no virtual functions are involved in iterator and container interfaces). Furthermore, because (unlike Smalltalk) the interfaces were bounded, built-in types had to be wrapped in larger polymorphic classes (such wrappers were provided by the NIHCL), which in turn could lead to dramatic increases in storage requirements.

Some sought solace in macros, but even in today's age of templates many projects still make suboptimal choices in their approach to polymorphism. Clearly there are many situations when

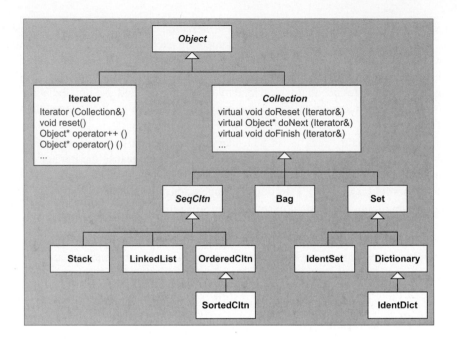

Figure 14.5. Class hierarchy of the NIHCL

dynamic polymorphism is the "right choice." Heterogeneous iterations are an example. However, in the same vein, many programming tasks are naturally and efficiently solved using templates, and homogeneous containers are an example of this.

Static polymorphism lends itself well to code very fundamental computing structures. In contrast, the need to choose a common base type implies that a dynamic polymorphic library will normally have to make domain-specific choices. It's no surprise then that the STL part of the C++ standard library never included polymorphic containers, but it contains a rich set of containers and iterators that use static polymorphism (as demonstrated in Section 14.5 on page 241).

Medium and large C++ programs typically need to handle both kinds of polymorphism discussed in this chapter. In some situations it may even be necessary to combine them very intimately. In many cases the optimal design choices are clear in light of our discussion, but spending some time thinking about long-term, potential evolutions almost always pay off.

Chapter 15

Traits and Policy Classes

Templates enable us to parameterize classes and functions for various types. It could be tempting to introduce as many template parameters as possible to enable the customization of every aspect of a type or algorithm. In this way, our "templatized" components could be instantiated to meet the exact needs of client code. However, from a practical point of view it is rarely desirable to introduce dozens of template parameters for maximal parameterization. Having to specify all the corresponding arguments in the client code is overly tedious.

Fortunately, it turns out that most of the extra parameters we would introduce have reasonable default values. In some cases the extra parameters are entirely determined by a few *main* parameters, and we'll see that such extra parameters can be omitted altogether. Other parameters can be given default values that depend on the main parameters and will meet the needs of most situations, but the default values must occasionally be overridden (for special applications). Yet other parameters are unrelated to the main parameters: In a sense they are themselves main parameters, except for the fact that there exist default values that almost always fit the bill.

Policy classes and *traits* (or *traits templates*) are C++ programming devices that greatly facilitate the management of the sort of extra parameters that come up in the design of industrial-strength templates. In this chapter we show a number of situations in which they prove useful and demonstrate various techniques that will enable you to write robust and powerful devices of your own.

15.1   An Example: Accumulating a Sequence

Computing the sum of a sequence of values is a fairly common computational task. However, this seemingly simple problem provides us with an excellent example to introduce various levels at which policy classes and traits can help.

15.1.1   Fixed Traits

Let's first assume that the values of the sum we want to compute are stored in an array, and we are given a pointer to the first element to be accumulated and a pointer one past the last element to be accumulated. Because this book is about templates, we wish to write a template that will work for many types. The following may seem straightforward by now[1]:

```
// traits/accum1.hpp

#ifndef ACCUM_HPP
#define ACCUM_HPP

template <typename T>
inline
T accum (T const* beg, T const* end)
{
    T total = T();   // assume T() actually creates a zero value
    while (beg != end) {
        total += *beg;
        ++beg;
    }
    return total;
}

#endif // ACCUM_HPP
```

The only slightly subtle decision here is how to create a *zero value* of the correct type to start our summation. We use the expression T() here, which normally should work for built-in numeric types like int and float (see Section 5.5 on page 56).

To motivate our first traits template, consider the following code that makes use of our accum():

```
// traits/accum1.cpp

#include "accum1.hpp"
#include <iostream>

int main()
{
```

---

[1] Most examples in this section use ordinary pointers for the sake of simplicity. Clearly, an industrial-strength interface may prefer to use iterator parameters following the conventions of the C++ standard library (see [*JosuttisStdLib*]). We revisit this aspect of our example later.

```
// create array of 5 integer values
int num[] = { 1, 2, 3, 4, 5 };

// print average value
std::cout << "the average value of the integer values is "
          << accum(&num[0], &num[5]) / 5
          << '\n';

// create array of character values
char name[] = "templates";
int length = sizeof(name)-1;

// (try to) print average character value
std::cout << "the average value of the characters in \""
          << name << "\" is "
          << accum(&name[0], &name[length]) / length
          << '\n';
}
```

In the first half of the program we use `accum()` to sum five integer values:

```
int num[] = { 1, 2, 3, 4, 5 };
...
accum(&num[0], &num[5])
```

The average integer value is then obtained by simply dividing the resulting sum by the number of values in the array.

The second half of the program attempts to do the same for all letters in the word `templates` (provided the characters from a to z form a contiguous sequence in the actual character set, which is true for ASCII but not for EBCDIC[2]). The result should presumably lie between the value of a and the value of z. On most platforms today, these values are determined by the ASCII codes: a is encoded as 97 and z is encoded as 122. Hence, we may expect a result between 97 and 122. However, on our platform the output of the program is as follows:

```
the average value of the integer values is 3
the average value of the characters in "templates" is -5
```

The problem here is that our template was instantiated for the type `char`, which turns out to be too small a range for the accumulation of even relatively small values. Clearly, we could resolve this

---

[2] EBCDIC is an abbreviation of Extended Binary-Coded Decimal Interchange Code, which is an IBM character set that is widely used on large IBM computers.

by introducing an additional template parameter `AccT` that describes the type used for the variable `total` (and hence the return type). However, this would put an extra burden on all users of our template: They would need to specify an extra type in every invocation of our template. In our example we may, therefore, need to write the following:

```
accum<int>(&name[0],&name[length])
```

This is not an excessive constraint, but it can be avoided.

An alternative approach to the extra parameter is to create an association between each type `T` for which `accum()` is called and the corresponding type that should be used to hold the accumulated value. This association could be considered characteristic of the type `T`, and therefore the type in which the sum is computed is sometimes called a *trait* of `T`. As is turns out, our association can be encoded as specializations of a template:

```
// traits/accumtraits2.hpp

template<typename T>
class AccumulationTraits;

template<>
class AccumulationTraits<char> {
  public:
    typedef int AccT;
};

template<>
class AccumulationTraits<short> {
  public:
    typedef int AccT;
};

template<>
class AccumulationTraits<int> {
  public:
    typedef long AccT;
};

template<>
class AccumulationTraits<unsigned int> {
  public:
    typedef unsigned long AccT;
};
```

```
template<>
class AccumulationTraits<float> {
  public:
    typedef double AccT;
};
```

The template `AccumulationTraits` is called a *traits template* because it holds a trait of its parameter type. (In general, there could be more than one trait and more than one parameter.) We chose not to provide a generic definition of this template because there isn't a great way to select a good accumulation type when we don't know what the type is. However, an argument could be made that T itself is often a good candidate for such a type (although clearly not in our earlier example).

With this in mind, we can rewrite our `accum()` template as follows:

```
// traits/accum2.hpp

#ifndef ACCUM_HPP
#define ACCUM_HPP

#include "accumtraits2.hpp"

template <typename T>
inline
typename AccumulationTraits<T>::AccT accum (T const* beg,
                                            T const* end)
{
    // return type is traits of the element type
    typedef typename AccumulationTraits<T>::AccT AccT;

    AccT total = AccT();   // assume AccT() actually creates a zero value
    while (beg != end) {
        total += *beg;
        ++beg;
    }
    return total;
}

#endif // ACCUM_HPP
```

The output of our sample program then becomes what we expect:

```
the average value of the integer values is 3
the average value of the characters in "templates" is 108
```

Overall, the changes aren't very dramatic considering that we have added a very useful mechanism to customize our algorithm. Furthermore, if new types arise for use with accum(), an appropriate AccT can be associated with it simply by declaring an additional explicit specialization of the AccumulationTraits template. Note that this can be done for any type: fundamental types, types that are declared in other libraries, and so forth.

15.1.2 Value Traits

So far, we have seen that traits represent additional type information related to a given "main" type. In this section we show that this extra information need not be limited to types. Constants and other classes of values can be associated with a type as well.

Our original accum() template uses the default constructor of the return value to initialize the result variable with what is hoped to be a zero-like value:

```
AccT total = AccT();   // assume AccT() actually creates a zero value
...
return total;
```

Clearly, there is no guarantee that this produces a good value to start the accumulation loop. Type AccT may not even have a default constructor.

Again, traits can come to the rescue. For our example, we can add a new *value trait* to our AccumulationTraits:

```
// traits/accumtraits3.hpp

template<typename T>
class AccumulationTraits;

template<>
class AccumulationTraits<char> {
  public:
    typedef int AccT;
    static AccT const zero = 0;
};

template<>
class AccumulationTraits<short> {
  public:
    typedef int AccT;
    static AccT const zero = 0;
};
```

```
template<>
class AccumulationTraits<int> {
  public:
    typedef long AccT;
    static AccT const zero = 0;
};
...
```

In this case, our new trait is a constant that can be evaluated at compile time. Thus, `accum()` becomes:

// traits/accum3.hpp

```
#ifndef ACCUM_HPP
#define ACCUM_HPP

#include "accumtraits3.hpp"

template <typename T>
inline
typename AccumulationTraits<T>::AccT accum (T const* beg,
                                            T const* end)
{
    // return type is traits of the element type
    typedef typename AccumulationTraits<T>::AccT AccT;

    AccT total = AccumulationTraits<T>::zero;
    while (beg != end) {
        total += *beg;
        ++beg;
    }
    return total;
}

#endif // ACCUM_HPP
```

In this code, the initialization of the accumulation variable remains straightforward:

```
AccT total = AccumulationTraits<T>::zero;
```

A drawback of this formulation is that C++ allows us to initialize only a static constant data member inside its class if it has an integral or enumeration type. This excludes our own classes, of course, and floating-point types as well. The following specialization is, therefore, an error:

```
...
template<>
class AccumulationTraits<float> {
public:
    typedef double AccT;
    static double const zero = 0.0;   // ERROR: not an integral type
};
```

The straightforward alternative is not to define the value trait in its class:

```
...
template<>
class AccumulationTraits<float> {
public:
    typedef double AccT;
    static double const zero;
};
```

The initializer then goes in a source file and looks something like the following:

```
...
double const AccumulationTraits<float>::zero = 0.0;
```

Although this works, it has the disadvantage of being more opaque to compilers. While processing client files, compilers are typically unaware of definitions in other files. In this case, for example, a compiler would not be able to take advantage of the fact that the value `zero` is really `0.0`.

Consequently, we prefer to implement value traits, which are not guaranteed to have integral values as inline member functions.[3] For example, we could rewrite `AccumulationTraits` as follows:

```
// traits/accumtraits4.hpp

template<typename T>
class AccumulationTraits;

template<>
class AccumulationTraits<char> {
  public:
    typedef int AccT;
    static AccT zero() {
        return 0;
```

---

[3] Most modern C++ compilers can "see through" calls of simple inline functions.

```
        }
};

template<>
class AccumulationTraits<short> {
  public:
    typedef int AccT;
    static AccT zero() {
        return 0;
    }
};

template<>
class AccumulationTraits<int> {
  public:
    typedef long AccT;
    static AccT zero() {
        return 0;
    }
};

template<>
class AccumulationTraits<unsigned int> {
  public:
    typedef unsigned long AccT;
    static AccT zero() {
        return 0;
    }
};

template<>
class AccumulationTraits<float> {
  public:
    typedef double AccT;
    static AccT zero() {
        return 0;
    }
};
...
```

For the application code, the only difference is the use of function call syntax (instead of the slightly more concise access to a static data member):

```
AccT total = AccumulationTraits<T>::zero();
```

Clearly, traits can be more than just extra *types*. In our example, they can be a mechanism to provide all the necessary information that `accum()` needs about the element type for which it is called. This is the key of the traits concept: Traits provide an avenue to *configure* concrete elements (mostly types) for generic computations.

15.1.3 Parameterized Traits

The use of traits in `accum()` in the previous sections is called *fixed*, because once the decoupled trait is defined, it cannot be overridden in the algorithm. There may be cases when such overriding is desirable. For example, we may happen to know that a set of `float` values can safely be summed into a variable of the same type, and doing so may buy us some efficiency.

In principle, the solution consists of adding a template parameter but with a default value determined by our traits template. In this way, many users can omit the extra template argument, but those with more exceptional needs can override the preset accumulation type. The only bee in our bonnet for this particular case is that function templates cannot have default template arguments.[4]

For now, let's circumvent the problem by formulating our algorithm as a class. This also illustrates the fact that traits can be used in class templates at least as easily as in function templates. The drawback in our application is that class templates cannot have their template arguments deduced. They must be provided explicitly. Hence, we need the form

```
Accum<char>::accum(&name[0], &name[length])
```

to use our revised accumulation template:

```
// traits/accum5.hpp

#ifndef ACCUM_HPP
#define ACCUM_HPP

#include "accumtraits4.hpp"

template <typename T,
          typename AT = AccumulationTraits<T> >
class Accum {
  public:
```

---

[4] This is almost certainly going to change in a revision of the C++ standard, and compiler vendors are likely to provide the feature even before this revised standard is published (see Section 13.3 on page 207).

```
    static typename AT::AccT accum (T const* beg, T const* end) {
        typename AT::AccT total = AT::zero();
        while (beg != end) {
            total += *beg;
            ++beg;
        }
        return total;
    }
};
```

`#endif` *// ACCUM_HPP*

Presumably, most users of this template would never have to provide the second template argument explicitly because it can be configured to an appropriate default for every type used as a first argument.

As is often the case, we can introduce convenience functions to simplify the interface:

```
template <typename T>
inline
typename AccumulationTraits<T>::AccT accum (T const* beg,
                                            T const* end)
{
    return Accum<T>::accum(beg, end);
}


template <typename Traits, typename T>
inline
typename Traits::AccT accum (T const* beg, T const* end)
{
    return Accum<T, Traits>::accum(beg, end);
}
```

15.1.4   Policies and Policy Classes

So far we have equated *accumulation* with *summation*. Clearly we can imagine other kinds of accumulations. For example, we could multiply the sequence of given values. Or, if the values were strings, we could concatenate them. Even finding the maximum value in a sequence could be formulated as an accumulation problem. In all these alternatives, the only `accum()` operation that needs to change is `total += *beg`. This operation can be called a *policy* of our accumulation process. A policy class, then, is a class that provides an interface to apply one or more policies in an algorithm.[5]

Here is an example of how we could introduce such an interface in our `Accum` class template:

```
// traits/accum6.hpp

#ifndef ACCUM_HPP
#define ACCUM_HPP

#include "accumtraits4.hpp"
#include "sumpolicy1.hpp"

template <typename T,
          typename Policy = SumPolicy,
          typename Traits = AccumulationTraits<T> >
class Accum {
  public:
    typedef typename Traits::AccT AccT;
    static AccT accum (T const* beg, T const* end) {
        AccT total = Traits::zero();
        while (beg != end) {
            Policy::accumulate(total, *beg);
            ++beg;
        }
        return total;
    }
};

#endif // ACCUM_HPP
```

With this a `SumPolicy` could be written as follows:

```
// traits/sumpolicy1.hpp

#ifndef SUMPOLICY_HPP
#define SUMPOLICY_HPP

class SumPolicy {
  public:
```

---

[5] We could generalize this to a *policy parameter*, which could be a class (as discussed) or a pointer to a function.

```
        template<typename T1, typename T2>
        static void accumulate (T1& total, T2 const & value) {
            total += value;
        }
    };
```

#endif // *SUMPOLICY_HPP*

In this example we chose to make our policy an ordinary class (that is, not a template) with a static member function template (which is implicitly inline). We discuss an alternative option later.

By specifying a different policy to accumulate values we can compute different things. Consider, for example, the following program, which intends to determine the product of some values:

```
// traits/accum7.cpp

#include "accum6.hpp"
#include <iostream>

class MultPolicy {
  public:
    template<typename T1, typename T2>
    static void accumulate (T1& total, T2 const& value) {
        total *= value;
    }
};

int main()
{
    // create array of 5 integer values
    int num[] = { 1, 2, 3, 4, 5 };

    // print product of all values
    std::cout << "the product of the integer values is "
              << Accum<int,MultPolicy>::accum(&num[0], &num[5])
              << '\n';
}
```

However, the output of this program isn't what we would like:

```
the product of the integer values is 0
```

The problem here is caused by our choice of initial value: Although 0 works well for summation, it does not work for multiplication (a zero initial value forces a zero result for accumulated multiplications). This illustrates that different traits and policies may interact, underscoring the importance of careful template design.

In this case we may recognize that the initialization of an accumulation loop is a part of the accumulation policy. This policy may or may not make use of the trait `zero()`. Other alternatives are not to be forgotten: Not everything must be solved with traits and policies. For example, the `accumulate()` function of the C++ standard library takes the initial value as a third (function call) argument.

15.1.5   Traits and Policies: What's the Difference?

A reasonable case can be made in support of the fact that policies are just a special case of traits. Conversely, it could be claimed that traits just encode a policy.

The *New Shorter Oxford English Dictionary* (see [*NewShorterOED*]) has this to say:

- **trait** *n. . . . a distinctive feature characterizing a thing*
- **policy** *n. . . . any course of action adopted as advantageous or expedient*

Based on this, we tend to limit the use of the term *policy classes* to classes that encode an action of some sort that is largely orthogonal with respect to any other template argument with which it is combined. This is in agreement with Andrei Alexandrescu's statement in his book *Modern C++ Design* (see page 8 of [*AlexandrescuDesign*])[6]:

> *Policies have much in common with traits but differ in that they put less emphasis on type and more on behavior.*

Nathan Myers, who introduced the traits technique, proposed the following more open-ended definition (see [*MyersTraits*]):

> *Traits class: A class used in place of template parameters. As a class, it aggregates useful types and constants; as a template, it provides an avenue for that "extra level of indirection" that solves all software problems.*

In general, we therefore tend to use the following (slightly fuzzy) definitions:

- **Traits** represent natural additional properties of a template parameter.
- **Policies** represent configurable behavior for generic functions and types (often with some commonly used defaults).

To elaborate further on the possible distinctions between the two concepts, we list the following observations about traits:

- Traits can be useful as *fixed traits* (that is, without being passed through template parameters).

---

[6] Alexandrescu has been the main voice in the world of policy classes, and he has developed a rich set of techniques based on them.

- Traits parameters usually have very natural default values (which are rarely overridden, or simply cannot be overridden).
- Traits parameters tend to depend tightly on one or more main parameters.
- Traits mostly combine types and constants rather than member functions.
- Traits tend to be collected in traits *templates*.

For policy classes, we make the following observations:

- Policy classes don't contribute much if they aren't passed as template parameters.
- Policy parameters need not have default values and are often specified explicitly (although many generic components are configured with commonly used default policies).
- Policy parameters are mostly orthogonal to other parameters of a template.
- Policy classes mostly combine member functions.
- Policies can be collected in plain classes or in class templates.

However, there is certainly an indistinct line between both terms. For example, the character traits of the C++ standard library also define functional behavior such as comparing, moving, and finding characters. And by replacing these traits you can define string classes that behave in a case-insensitive manner (see Section 11.2.14 in [*JosuttisStdLib*]) while keeping the same character type. Thus, although they are called *traits*, they have some properties associated with policies.

15.1.6 Member Templates versus Template Template Parameters

To implement an accumulation policy we chose to express SumPolicy and MultPolicy as ordinary classes with a member template. An alternative consists of designing the policy class interface using class templates, which are then used as template template arguments. For example, we could rewrite SumPolicy as a template:

```
// traits/sumpolicy2.hpp

#ifndef SUMPOLICY_HPP
#define SUMPOLICY_HPP

template <typename T1, typename T2>
class SumPolicy {
  public:
    static void accumulate (T1& total, T2 const & value) {
        total += value;
    }
};

#endif // SUMPOLICY_HPP
```

The interface of `Accum` can then be adapted to use a template template parameter:

```
// traits/accum8.hpp

#ifndef ACCUM_HPP
#define ACCUM_HPP

#include "accumtraits4.hpp"
#include "sumpolicy2.hpp"

template <typename T,
          template<typename,typename> class Policy = SumPolicy,
          typename Traits = AccumulationTraits<T> >
class Accum {
  public:
    typedef typename Traits::AccT AccT;
    static AccT accum (T const* beg, T const* end) {
        AccT total = Traits::zero();
        while (beg != end) {
            Policy<AccT,T>::accumulate(total, *beg);
            ++beg;
        }
        return total;
    }
};

#endif // ACCUM_HPP
```

The same transformation can be applied to the traits parameter. (Other variations on this theme are possible: For example, instead of explicitly passing the `AccT` type to the policy type, it may be advantageous to pass the accumulation trait and have the policy determine the type of its result from a traits parameter.)

The major advantage of accessing policy classes through template template parameters is that it makes it easier to have a policy class carry with it some state information (that is, static data members) with a type that depends on the template parameters. (In our first approach the static data members would have to be embedded in a member class template.)

However, a downside of the template template parameter approach is that policy classes must now be written as templates, with the exact set of template parameters defined by our interface. This, unfortunately, disallows any additional template parameters in our policies. For example, we may want to add a Boolean nontype template parameter to `SumPolicy` that selects whether summation should happen with the += operator or whether + only should be used. In the program using a member template we can simply rewrite SumPolicy as a template:

```
// traits/sumpolicy3.hpp

#ifndef SUMPOLICY_HPP
#define SUMPOLICY_HPP

template<bool use_compound_op = true>
class SumPolicy {
  public:
    template<typename T1, typename T2>
    static void accumulate (T1& total, T2 const & value) {
      total += value;
    }
};

template<>
class SumPolicy<false> {
  public:
    template<typename T1, typename T2>
    static void accumulate (T1& total, T2 const & value) {
      total = total + value;
    }
};

#endif // SUMPOLICY_HPP
```

With implementation of Accum using template template parameters such an adaptation is no longer possible.

15.1.7   Combining Multiple Policies and/or Traits

As our development has shown, traits and policies don't entirely do away with having multiple template parameters. However, they do reduce their number to something manageable. An interesting question, then, is how to order such multiple parameters.

A simple strategy is to order the parameters according to the increasing likelihood of their default value to be selected. Typically, this would mean that the traits parameters follow the policy parameters because the latter are more often overridden in client code. (The observant reader may have noticed this strategy in our development.)

If we are willing to add a significant amount of complexity to our code, an alternative exists that essentially allows us to specify the nondefault arguments in any order. Refer to Section 16.1 on page 285 for details. Chapter 13 also discusses potential future template features that could simplify the resolution of this aspect of template design.

15.1.8   Accumulation with General Iterators

Before we end this introduction to traits and policies, it is instructive to look at one version of accum() that adds the capability to handle generalized iterators (rather than just pointers), as expected from an industrial-strength generic component. Interestingly, this still allows us to call accum() with pointers because the C++ standard library provides so-called *iterator traits*. (Traits are everywhere!) Thus, we could have defined our initial version of accum() as follows (ignoring our later refinements):

```
// traits/accum0.hpp

#ifndef ACCUM_HPP
#define ACCUM_HPP

#include <iterator>

template <typename Iter>
inline
typename std::iterator_traits<Iter>::value_type
accum (Iter start, Iter end)
{
    typedef typename std::iterator_traits<Iter>::value_type VT;

    VT total = VT();   // assume VT() actually creates a zero value
    while (start != end) {
        total += *start;
        ++start;
    }
    return total;
}

#endif // ACCUM_HPP
```

The iterator_traits structure encapsulates all the relevant properties of iterator. Because a partial specialization for pointers exists, these traits are conveniently used with any ordinary pointer types. Here is how a standard library implementation may implement this support:

```
namespace std {
    template <typename T>
    struct iterator_traits<T*> {
        typedef T                        value_type;
        typedef ptrdiff_t                difference_type;
        typedef random_access_iterator_tag iterator_category;
        typedef T*                       pointer;
        typedef T&                       reference;
    };
}
```

However, there is no type for the accumulation of values to which an iterator refers; hence we still need to design our own `AccumulationTraits`.

15.2 Type Functions

The initial traits example demonstrates that you can define behavior that depends on types. This is different from what you usually implement in programs. In C and C++, functions more exactly can be called *value functions*: They take some values as parameters and return another value as a result. Now, what we have with templates are *type functions*: a function that takes some type arguments and produces a type or constant as a result.

A very useful built-in type function is `sizeof`, which returns a constant describing the size (in bytes) of the given type argument. Class templates can also serve as type functions. The parameters of the type function are the template parameters, and the result is extracted as a member type or member constant. For example, the `sizeof` operator could be given the following interface:

```
// traits/sizeof.cpp

#include <stddef.h>
#include <iostream>

template <typename T>
class TypeSize {
  public:
    static size_t const value = sizeof(T);
};

int main()
{
    std::cout << "TypeSize<int>::value = "
              << TypeSize<int>::value << std::endl;
}
```

In what follows we develop a few more general-purpose type functions that can be used as traits classes in this way.

15.2.1 Determining Element Types

For another example, assume that we have a number of container templates such as vector<T>, list<T>, and stack<T>. We want a type function that, given such a container type, produces the element type. This can be achieved using partial specialization:

```
// traits/elementtype.cpp

#include <vector>
#include <list>
#include <stack>
#include <iostream>
#include <typeinfo>

template <typename T>
class ElementT;                           // primary template

template <typename T>
class ElementT<std::vector<T> > {    // partial specialization
  public:
    typedef T Type;
};

template <typename T>
class ElementT<std::list<T> > {      // partial specialization
  public:
    typedef T Type;
};

template <typename T>
class ElementT<std::stack<T> > {     // partial specialization
  public:
    typedef T Type;
};

template <typename T>
void print_element_type (T const & c)
{
```

```
        std::cout << "Container of "
                  << typeid(typename ElementT<T>::Type).name()
                  << " elements.\n";
}

int main()
{
    std::stack<bool> s;
    print_element_type(s);
}
```

The use of partial specialization allows us to implement this without requiring the container types to know about the type function. In many cases, however, the type function is designed along with the applicable types and the implementation can be simplified. For example, if the container types define a member type value_type (as the standard containers do), we can write the following:

```
template <typename C>
class ElementT {
  public:
    typedef typename C::value_type Type;
};
```

This can be the default implementation, and it does not exclude specializations for container types that do not have an appropriate member type value_type defined. Nonetheless, it is usually advisable to provide type definitions for template type parameters so that they can be accessed more easily in generic code. The following sketches the idea:

```
template <typename T1, typename T2, ... >
class X {
  public:
    typedef T1 ... ;
    typedef T2 ... ;

    ...
};
```

How is a type function useful? It allows us to parameterize a template in terms of a container type, without also requiring parameters for the element type and other characteristics. For example, instead of

```
template <typename T, typename C>
T sum_of_elements (C const& c);
```

which requires syntax like sum_of_elements<int>(list) to specify the element type explicitly, we can declare

```
template<typename C>
typename ElementT<C>::Type sum_of_elements (C const& c);
```

where the element type is determined from the type function.

Note that the traits can be implemented as an extension to the existing types. Thus, you can define these type functions even for fundamental types and types of closed libraries.

In this case, the type `ElementT` is called a traits class because it is used to access a trait of the given container type C (in general, more than one trait can be collected in such a class). Thus, traits classes are not limited to describing characteristics of container parameters but of any kind of "main parameters."

15.2.2 Determining Class Types

With the following type function we can determine whether a type is a class type:

```
// traits/isclasst.hpp

template<typename T>
class IsClassT {
  private:
    typedef char One;
    typedef struct { char a[2]; } Two;
    template<typename C> static One test(int C::*);
    template<typename C> static Two test(...);
  public:
    enum { Yes = sizeof(IsClassT<T>::test<T>(0)) == 1 };
    enum { No = !Yes };
};
```

This template uses the SFINAE (substitution-failure-is-not-an-error) principle of Section 8.3.1 on page 106. The key to exploit SFINAE is to find a type construct that is invalid for class types but not for other types, or vice versa. For class types we can rely on the observation that the pointer-to-member type construct `int C::*` is valid only if C is a class type.

The following program uses this type function to test whether certain types and objects are class types:

```
// traits/isclasst.cpp

#include <iostream>
#include "isclasst.hpp"

class MyClass {
};
```

```
struct MyStruct {
};

union MyUnion {
};

void myfunc()
{
}

enum E { e1 } e;

// check by passing type as template argument
template <typename T>
void check()
{
    if (IsClassT<T>::Yes) {
        std::cout << " IsClassT " << std::endl;
    }
    else {
        std::cout << " !IsClassT " << std::endl;
    }
}

// check by passing type as function call argument
template <typename T>
void checkT (T)
{
    check<T>();
}

int main()
{
    std::cout << "int:    ";
    check<int>();

    std::cout << "MyClass: ";
    check<MyClass>();
```

```
        std::cout << "MyStruct:";
        MyStruct s;
        checkT(s);

        std::cout << "MyUnion: ";
        check<MyUnion>();

        std::cout << "enum:    ";
        checkT(e);

        std::cout << "myfunc():";
        checkT(myfunc);
    }
```

The program has the following output:

```
    int:       !IsClassT
    MyClass:   IsClassT
    MyStruct:  IsClassT
    MyUnion:   IsClassT
    enum:      !IsClassT
    myfunc():  !IsClassT
```

15.2.3   References and Qualifiers

Consider the following function template definition:

```
// traits/apply1.hpp

template <typename T>
void apply (T& arg, void (*func)(T))
{
    func(arg);
}
```

Consider also the following code that attempts to use it:

```
// traits/apply1.cpp

#include <iostream>
#include "apply1.hpp"
```

```
void incr (int& a)
{
    ++a;
}

void print (int a)
{
    std::cout << a << std::endl;
}

int main()
{
    int x = 7;
    apply (x, print);
    apply (x, incr);
}
```

The call

```
apply (x, print)
```

is fine. With T substituted by int, the parameter types of apply() arc int& and void(*)(int), which corresponds to the types of the arguments. The call

```
apply (x, incr)
```

is less straightforward. Matching the second parameter requires T to be substituted with int&, and this implies that the first parameter type is int& &, which ordinarily is not a legal C++ type. Indeed, the original C++ standard ruled this an invalid substitution, but because of examples like this, a later *technical corrigendum* (a set of small corrections of the standard; see [*Standard02*]) made T& with T substituted by int& equivalent to int&.[7]

For C++ compilers that do not implement the newer reference substitution rule, we can create a type function that applies the "reference operator" if and only if the given type is not already a reference. We can also provide the opposite operation: Strip the reference operator (if and only if the type is indeed a reference). And while we are at it, we can also add or strip const qualifiers.[8] All this is achieved using partial specialization of the following generic definition:

---

[7] Note that we still cannot write int& &. This is similar to the fact that T const allows T to be substituted with int const, but an explicit int const const is not valid.

[8] The handling of volatile and const volatile qualifiers is omitted for brevity, but they can be handled similarly.

```
// traits/typeop1.hpp

template <typename T>
class TypeOp {              // primary template
  public:
    typedef T         ArgT;
    typedef T         BareT;
    typedef T const   ConstT;
    typedef T &       RefT;
    typedef T &       RefBareT;
    typedef T const & RefConstT;
};
```

First, a partial specialization to catch const types:

```
// traits/typeop2.hpp

template <typename T>
class TypeOp <T const> {   // partial specialization for const types
  public:
    typedef T const   ArgT;
    typedef T         BareT;
    typedef T const   ConstT;
    typedef T const & RefT;
    typedef T &       RefBareT;
    typedef T const & RefConstT;
};
```

The partial specialization to catch reference types also catches reference-to-const types. Hence, it applies the TypeOp device recursively to obtain the bare type when necessary. In contrast, C++ allows us to apply the const qualifier to a template parameter that is substituted with a type that is already const. Hence, we need not worry about stripping the const qualifier when we are going to reapply it anyway:

```
// traits/typeop3.hpp

template <typename T>
class TypeOp <T&> {              // partial specialization for references
  public:
    typedef T &                      ArgT;
    typedef typename TypeOp<T>::BareT BareT;
    typedef T const                  ConstT;
```

```
        typedef T &                                    RefT;
        typedef typename TypeOp<T>::BareT & RefBareT;
        typedef T const &                       RefConstT;
};
```

References to void types are not allowed. It is sometimes useful to treat such types as plain void however. The following specialization takes care of this:

```
// traits/typeop4.hpp

template<>
class TypeOp <void> {        // full specialization for void
  public:
    typedef void        ArgT;
    typedef void        BareT;
    typedef void const ConstT;
    typedef void        RefT;
    typedef void        RefBareT;
    typedef void        RefConstT;
};
```

With this in place, we can rewrite the apply template as follows:

```
template <typename T>
void apply (typename TypeOp<T>::RefT arg, void (*func)(T))
{
    func(arg);
}
```

and our example program will work as intended.

Remember that T can no longer be deduced from the first argument because it now appears in a name qualifier. So T is deduced from the second argument only, and T is used to create the type of the first parameter.

15.2.4   Promotion Traits

So far we have studied and developed type functions of a single type: Given one type, other related types or constants were defined. In general, however, we can develop type functions that depend on multiple arguments. One example that is very useful when writing operator templates are so-called *promotion traits*. To motivate the idea, let's write a function template that allows us to add two Array containers:

```
template<typename T>
Array<T> operator+ (Array<T> const&, Array<T> const&);
```

This would be nice, but because the language allows us to add a char value to an int value, we really would prefer to allow such mixed-type operations with arrays too. We are then faced with determining what the return type of the resulting template should be:

```
template<typename T1, typename T2>
Array<???> operator+ (Array<T1> const&, Array<T2> const&);
```

A promotion traits template allows us to fill in the question marks in the previous declaration as follows:

```
template<typename T1, typename T2>
Array<typename Promotion<T1, T2>::ResultT>
operator+ (Array<T1> const&, Array<T2> const&);
```

or, alternatively, as follows:

```
template<typename T1, typename T2>
typename Promotion<Array<T1>, Array<T2> >::ResultT
operator+ (Array<T1> const&, Array<T2> const&);
```

The idea is to provide a large number of specializations of the template Promotion to create a type function that matches our needs. Another application of promotion traits was motivated by the introduction of the max() template, when we want to specify that the maximum of two values of different type should have the "the more powerful type" (see Section 2.3 on page 13).

There is no really reliable generic definition for this template, so it may be best to leave the primary class template undefined:

```
template<typename T1, typename T2>
class Promotion;
```

Another option would be to assume that if one of the types is larger than the other, we should promote to that larger type. This can by done by a special template IfThenElse that takes a Boolean nontype template parameter to select one of two type parameters:

```
// traits/ifthenelse.hpp

#ifndef IFTHENELSE_HPP
#define IFTHENELSE_HPP

// primary template: yield second or third argument depending on first argument
template<bool C, typename Ta, typename Tb>
class IfThenElse;
```

```
// partial specialization: true yields second argument
template<typename Ta, typename Tb>
class IfThenElse<true, Ta, Tb> {
  public:
    typedef Ta ResultT;
};

// partial specialization: false yields third argument
template<typename Ta, typename Tb>
class IfThenElse<false, Ta, Tb> {
  public:
    typedef Tb ResultT;
};

#endif // IFTHENELSE_HPP
```

With this in place, we can create a three-way selection between T1, T2, and void, depending on the sizes of the types that need promotion:

```
// traits/promote1.hpp

// primary template for type promotion
template<typename T1, typename T2>
class Promotion {
  public:
    typedef typename
            IfThenElse<(sizeof(T1)>sizeof(T2)),
                       T1,
                       typename IfThenElse<(sizeof(T1)<sizeof(T2)),
                                           T2,
                                           void
                                          >::ResultT
                      >::ResultT ResultT;
};
```

The size-based heuristic used in the primary template works sometimes, but it requires checking. If it selects the wrong type, an appropriate specialization must be written to override the selection. On the other hand, if the two types are identical, we can safely make it to be the promoted type. A partial specialization takes care of this:

```
// traits/promote2.hpp
```

```
// partial specialization for two identical types
template<typename T>
class Promotion<T,T> {
  public:
    typedef T ResultT;
};
```

Many specializations are needed to record the promotion of fundamental types. A macro can reduce the amount of source code somewhat:

```
// traits/promote3.hpp
```

```
#define MK_PROMOTION(T1,T2,Tr)                 \
    template<> class Promotion<T1, T2> {       \
      public:                                  \
        typedef Tr ResultT;                    \
    };                                         \
                                               \
    template<> class Promotion<T2, T1> {       \
      public:                                  \
        typedef Tr ResultT;                    \
    };
```

The promotions are then added as follows:

```
// traits/promote4.hpp
```

```
MK_PROMOTION(bool, char, int)
MK_PROMOTION(bool, unsigned char, int)
MK_PROMOTION(bool, signed char, int)
...
```

This approach is relatively straightforward, but requires the several dozen possible combinations to be enumerated. Various alternative techniques exist. For example, the IsFundaT and IsEnumT templates (see Chapter 19) could be adapted to define the promotion type for integral and floating-point types. Promotion would then need to be specialized only for the resulting fundamental types (and user-defined types, as shown in a moment).

Once Promotion is defined for fundamental types (and enumeration types if desired), other promotion rules can often be expressed through partial specialization. For our Array example:

```
// traits/promotearray.hpp

template<typename T1, typename T2>
class Promotion<Array<T1>, Array<T2> > {
  public:
    typedef Array<typename Promotion<T1,T2>::ResultT> ResultT;
};

template<typename T>
class Promotion<Array<T>, Array<T> > {
  public:
    typedef Array<typename Promotion<T,T>::ResultT> ResultT;
};
```

This last partial specialization deserves some special attention. At first it may seem that the earlier partial specialization for identical types (Promotion<T,T>) already takes care of this case. Unfortunately, the partial specialization Promotion<Array<T1>, Array<T2> > is neither more nor less specialized than the partial specialization Promotion<T,T> (see also Section 12.4 on page 200).[9] To avoid template selection ambiguity, the last partial specialization was added. It is more specialized than either of the previous two partial specializations.

More specializations and partial specializations of the Promotion template can be added as more types are added for which a concept promotion makes sense.

15.3 Policy Traits

So far, our examples of traits templates have been used to determine properties of template parameters: what sort of type they represent, to which type they should promote in mixed-type operations, and so forth. Such traits are called *property traits*.

In contrast, some traits define how some types should be treated. We call them *policy traits*. This is reminiscent of the previously discussed concept of policy classes (and we already pointed out that the distinction between traits and policies is not entirely clear), but policy traits tend to be more unique properties associated with a template parameter (whereas policy classes are usually independent of other template parameters).

Although property traits can often be implemented as type functions, policy traits usually encapsulate the policy in member functions. As a first illustration, let's look at a type function that defines a policy for passing read-only parameters.

---

[9] To see this, try to find a substitution of T that makes the latter become the former, or substitutions for T1 and T2 that make the former become the latter.

15.3.1   Read-only Parameter Types

In C and C++, function call arguments are passed "by value" by default. This means that the values of the arguments computed by the caller are copied to locations controlled by the callee. Most programmers know that this can be costly for large structures and that for such structures it is appropriate to pass the arguments "by reference-to-const" (or "by pointer-to-const" in C). For smaller structures, the picture is not always clear, and the best mechanism from a performance point of view depends on the exact architecture for which the code is being written. This is not so critical in most cases, but sometimes even the small structures must be handled with care.

With templates, of course, things get a little more delicate: We don't know a priori how large the type substituted for the template parameter will be. Furthermore, the decision doesn't depend just on size: A small structure may come with an expensive copy constructor that would still justify passing read-only parameters "by reference-to-const."

As hinted at earlier, this problem is conveniently handled using a policy traits template that is a type function: The function maps an intended argument type T onto the optimal parameter type T or T const&. As a first approximation, the primary template can use "by value" passing for types no larger than two pointers and "by reference-to-const" for everything else:

```
template<typename T>
class RParam {
  public:
    typedef typename IfThenElse<sizeof(T)<=2*sizeof(void*),
                                T,
                                T const&>::ResultT Type;
};
```

On the other hand, container types for which sizeof returns a small value may involve expensive copy constructors. So we may need many specializations and partial specializations, such as the following:

```
template<typename T>
class RParam<Array<T> > {
  public:
    typedef Array<T> const& Type;
};
```

Because such types are common in C++, it may be safer to mark nonclass types "by value" in the primary template and then selectively add the class types when performance considerations dictate it (the primary template uses IsClassT<> from page 266 to identify class types):

```
// traits/rparam.hpp

#ifndef RPARAM_HPP
#define RPARAM_HPP
```

```cpp
#include "ifthenelse.hpp"
#include "isclasst.hpp"

template<typename T>
class RParam {
  public:
    typedef typename IfThenElse<IsClassT<T>::No,
                                T,
                                T const&>::ResultT Type;
};
```

#endif // *RPARAM_HPP*

Either way, the policy can now be centralized in the traits template definition, and clients can exploit it to good effect. For example, let's suppose we have two classes, with one class specifying that calling by value is better for read-only arguments:

```cpp
// traits/rparamcls.hpp

#include <iostream>
#include "rparam.hpp"

class MyClass1 {
  public:
    MyClass1 () {
    }
    MyClass1 (MyClass1 const&) {
        std::cout << "MyClass1 copy constructor called\n";
    }
};

class MyClass2 {
  public:
    MyClass2 () {
    }
    MyClass2 (MyClass2 const&) {
        std::cout << "MyClass2 copy constructor called\n";
    }
};
```

```
// pass MyClass2 objects with RParam<> by value
template<>
class RParam<MyClass2> {
  public:
    typedef MyClass2 Type;
};
```

Now, you can declare functions that use RParam<> for read-only arguments and call these functions:

```
// traits/rparam1.cpp

#include "rparam.hpp"
#include "rparamcls.hpp"

// function that allows parameter passing by value or by reference
template <typename T1, typename T2>
void foo (typename RParam<T1>::Type p1,
          typename RParam<T2>::Type p2)
{
    ...
}

int main()
{
    MyClass1 mc1;
    MyClass2 mc2;
    foo<MyClass1,MyClass2>(mc1,mc2);
}
```

There are unfortunately some significant downsides to using RParam. First, the function declaration is significantly messier. Second, and perhaps more objectionable, is the fact that a function like foo() cannot be called with argument deduction because the template parameter appears only in the qualifiers of the function parameters. Call sites must therefore specify explicit template arguments.

An unwieldy workaround for this option is the use of an inline wrapper function template, but it assumes the inline function will be elided by the compiler. For example:

```
// traits/rparam2.cpp

#include "rparam.hpp"
#include "rparamcls.hpp"
```

```
// function that allows parameter passing by value or by reference
template <typename T1, typename T2>
void foo_core (typename RParam<T1>::Type p1,
               typename RParam<T2>::Type p2)
{
    ...
}


// wrapper to avoid explicit template parameter passing
template <typename T1, typename T2>
inline
void foo (T1 const & p1, T2 const & p2)
{
    foo_core<T1,T2>(p1,p2);
}


int main()
{
    MyClass1 mc1;
    MyClass2 mc2;
    foo(mc1,mc2);   // same as foo_core<MyClass1,MyClass2>(mc1,mc2)
}
```

15.3.2 Copying, Swapping, and Moving

To continue the theme of performance, we can introduce a policy traits template to select the best operation to copy, swap, or move elements of a certain type.

Presumably, copying is covered by the copy constructor and the copy-assignment operator. This is definitely true for a single element, but it is not impossible that copying a large number of items of a given type can be done significantly more efficiently than by repeatedly invoking the constructor or assignment operations of that type.

Similarly, certain types can be swapped or moved much more efficiently than a generic sequence of the classic form:

```
T tmp(a);
a = b;
b = tmp;
```

Container types typically fall in this category. In fact, it occasionally happens that copying is not allowed, whereas swapping or moving is fine. In the chapter on utilities, we develop a so-called *smart pointer* with this property (see Chapter 20).

Hence, it can be useful to centralize decisions in this area in a convenient traits template. For the generic definition, we will distinguish class types from nonclass types because we need not worry about user-defined copy constructors and copy assignments for the latter. This time we use inheritance to select between two traits implementations:

```
// traits/csmtraits.hpp

template <typename T>
class CSMtraits : public BitOrClassCSM<T, IsClassT<T>::No > {
};
```

The implementation is thus completely delegated to specializations of `BitOrClassCSM<>` ("CSM" stands for "copy, swap, move"). The second template parameter indicates whether bitwise copying can be used safely to implement the various operations. The generic definition conservatively assumes that class types can not be bitwise-copied safely, but if a certain class type is known to be a *plain old data type* (or *POD*), the `CSMtraits` class is easily specialized for better performance:

```
template<>
class CSMtraits<MyPODType>
  : public BitOrClassCSM<MyPODType, true> {
};
```

The `BitOrClassCSM` template consists, by default, of two partial specializations. The primary template and the safe partial specialization that doesn't copy bitwise is as follows:

```
// traits/csm1.hpp

#include <new>
#include <cassert>
#include <stddef.h>
#include "rparam.hpp"

// primary template
template<typename T, bool Bitwise>
class BitOrClassCSM;

// partial specialization for safe copying of objects
template<typename T>
class BitOrClassCSM<T, false> {
  public:
    static void copy (typename RParam<T>::Type src, T* dst) {
        // copy one item onto another one
```

```
        *dst = src;
    }

    static void copy_n (T const* src, T* dst, size_t n) {
        // copy n items onto n other ones
        for (size_t k = 0; k<n; ++k) {
            dst[k] = src[k];
        }
    }

    static void copy_init (typename RParam<T>::Type src,
                           void* dst) {
        // copy an item onto uninitialized storage
        ::new(dst) T(src);
    }

    static void copy_init_n (T const* src, void* dst, size_t n) {
        // copy n items onto uninitialized storage
        for (size_t k = 0; k<n; ++k) {
            ::new((void*)((T*)dst+k)) T(src[k]);
        }
    }

    static void swap (T* a, T* b) {
        // swap two items
        T tmp(*a);
        *a = *b;
        *b = tmp;
    }

    static void swap_n (T* a, T* b, size_t n) {
        // swap n items
        for (size_t k = 0; k<n; ++k) {
            T tmp(a[k]);
            a[k] = b[k];
            b[k] = tmp;
        }
    }
```

```
static void move (T* src, T* dst) {
    // move one item onto another
    assert(src != dst);
    *dst = *src;
    src->~T();
}

static void move_n (T* src, T* dst, size_t n) {
    // move n items onto n other ones
    assert(src != dst);
    for (size_t k = 0; k<n; ++k) {
        dst[k] = src[k];
        src[k].~T();
    }
}

static void move_init (T* src, void* dst) {
    // move an item onto uninitialized storage
    assert(src != dst);
    ::new(dst) T(*src);
    src->~T();
}

static void move_init_n (T const* src, void* dst, size_t n) {
    // move n items onto uninitialized storage
    assert(src != dst);
    for (size_t k = 0; k<n; ++k) {
        ::new((void*)((T*)dst+k)) T(src[k]);
        src[k].~T();
    }
}
};
```

The term *move* here means that a value is transferred from one place to another, and hence the original value no longer exists (or, more precisely, the original location may have been destroyed). The *copy* operation, on the other hand, guarantees that both the source and destination locations have valid and identical values. This should not be confused with the distinction between memcpy() and memmove(), which is made in the standard C library: In that case, *move* implies that the source and destination areas may overlap, whereas for *copy* they do not. In our implementation of the CSM traits, we always assume that the sources and destinations do not overlap. In an industrial-strength library, a *shift* operation should probably be added to express the policy for shifting objects within a contiguous area of memory (the operation enabled by `memmove()`). We omit it for the sake of simplicity.

The member functions of our policy traits template are all static. This is almost always the case, because the member functions are meant to apply to objects of the parameter type rather than objects of the traits class type.

The other partial specialization implements the traits for bitwise types that can be copied:

```
// traits/csm2.hpp
```

```cpp
#include <cstring>
#include <cassert>
#include <stddef.h>
#include "csm1.hpp"


// partial specialization for fast bitwise copying of objects
template <typename T>
class BitOrClassCSM<T,true> : public BitOrClassCSM<T,false> {
  public:
    static void copy_n (T const* src, T* dst, size_t n) {
        // copy n items onto n other ones
        std::memcpy((void*)dst, (void*)src, n*sizeof(T));
    }

    static void copy_init_n (T const* src, void* dst, size_t n) {
        // copy n items onto uninitialized storage
        std::memcpy(dst, (void*)src, n*sizeof(T));
    }

    static void move_n (T* src, T* dst, size_t n) {
        // move n items onto n other ones
        assert(src != dst);
        std::memcpy((void*)dst, (void*)src, n*sizeof(T));
    }

    static void move_init_n (T const* src, void* dst, size_t n) {
        // move n items onto uninitialized storage
        assert(src != dst);
        std::memcpy(dst, (void*)src, n*sizeof(T));
    }
};
```

We used another level of inheritance to simplify the implementation of the traits for bitwise types that can be copied. This is certainly not the only possible implementation. In fact, for particular platforms it may be desirable to introduce some inline assembly (for example, to take advantage of hardware swap operations).

15.4   Afternotes

Nathan Myers was the first to formalize the idea of traits parameters. He originally presented them to the C++ standardization committee as a vehicle to define how character types should be treated in standard library components (for example, input and output streams). At that time he called them *baggage templates* and noted that they contained traits. However, some C++ committee members did not like the term *baggage*, and the name *traits* was promoted instead. The latter term has been widely used since then.

Client code usually does not deal with traits at all: The default traits classes satisfy the most common needs, and because they are default template arguments, they need not appear in the client source at all. This argues in favor of long descriptive names for the default traits templates. When client code does adapt the behavior of a template by providing a custom traits argument, it is good practice to typedef the resulting specializations to a name that is appropriate for the custom behavior. In this case the traits class can be given a long descriptive name without sacrificing too much source estate.

Our discussion has presented traits templates as being class templates exclusively. Strictly speaking, this does not need to be the case. If only a single policy trait needs to be provided, it could be passed as an ordinary function template. For example:

```
template <typename T, void (*Policy)(T const&, T const&)>
class X;
```

However, the original goal of traits was to reduce the baggage of secondary template arguments, which is not achieved if only a single trait is encapsulated in a template parameter. This justifies Myers's preference for the term *baggage* as a collection of traits. We revisit the problem of providing an ordering criterion in Chapter 22.

The standard library defines a class template `std::char_traits`, which is used as a policy traits parameter. To adapt algorithms easily to the kind of STL iterators for which they are used, a very simple `std::iterator_traits` property traits template is provided (and used in standard library interfaces). The template `std::numeric_limits` can also be useful as a property traits template, but it is not visibly used in the standard library proper. The class templates `std::unary_function` and `std::binary_function` fall in the same category and are very simple type functions: They only typedef their arguments to member names that make sense for functors (also known as *function objects*, see Chapter 22). Lastly, memory allocation for the standard container types is handled using a policy traits class. The template `std::allocator` is provided as the standard item for this purpose.

Policy classes have apparently been developed by many programmers and a few authors. Andrei Alexandrescu made the term *policy classes* popular, and his book *Modern C++ Design* covers them in more detail than our brief section (see [*AlexandrescuDesign*]).

Chapter 16

Templates and Inheritance

A priori, there might be no reason to think that templates and inheritance interact in interesting ways. If anything, we know from Chapter 9 that deriving from dependent base classes forces us to deal carefully with unqualified names. However, it turns out that some interesting techniques make use of so-called *parameterized inheritance*. In this chapter we describe a few of these techniques.

16.1   Named Template Arguments

Various template techniques sometimes cause a class template to end up with many different template type parameters. However, many of these parameters often have reasonable default values. A natural way to define such a class template may look as follows:

```
template<typename Policy1 = DefaultPolicy1,
         typename Policy2 = DefaultPolicy2,
         typename Policy3 = DefaultPolicy3,
         typename Policy4 = DefaultPolicy4>
class BreadSlicer {
    ...
};
```

Presumably, such a template can often be used with the default template argument values using the syntax BreadSlicer<>. However, if a nondefault argument must be specified, all preceding arguments must be specified too (even though they may have the default value).

Clearly, it would be attractive to be able to use a construct akin to `BreadSlicer<Policy3 = Custom>` rather than `BreadSlicer<DefaultPolicy1, DefaultPolicy2, Custom>` as is the case right now. In what follows we develop a technique to enable almost exactly that.[1]

Our technique consists of placing the default type values in a base class and overriding some of them through derivation. Instead of directly specifying the type arguments, we provide them through helper classes. For example, we could write `BreadSlicer<Policy3_is<Custom> >`. Because each template argument can describe any of the policies, the defaults cannot be different. In other words, at a high level every template parameter is equivalent:

```
template <typename PolicySetter1 = DefaultPolicyArgs,
          typename PolicySetter2 = DefaultPolicyArgs,
          typename PolicySetter3 = DefaultPolicyArgs,
          typename PolicySetter4 = DefaultPolicyArgs>
class BreadSlicer {
    typedef PolicySelector<PolicySetter1, PolicySetter2,
                           PolicySetter3, PolicySetter4>
            Policies;
    // use Policies::P1, Policies::P2, ... to refer to the various policies
    ...
};
```

The remaining challenge is to write the `PolicySelector` template. It has to merge the different template arguments into a single type that overrides default typedef members with whichever non-defaults were specified. This merging can be achieved using inheritance:

```
// PolicySelector<A,B,C,D> creates A,B,C,D as base classes
// Discriminator<> allows having even the same base class more than once

template<typename Base, int D>
class Discriminator : public Base {
};

template <typename Setter1, typename Setter2,
          typename Setter3, typename Setter4>
class PolicySelector : public Discriminator<Setter1,1>,
                       public Discriminator<Setter2,2>,
                       public Discriminator<Setter3,3>,
                       public Discriminator<Setter4,4> {
};
```

---

[1] Note that a similar language extension for function call arguments was proposed (and rejected) earlier in the C++ standardization process (see Section 13.9 on page 216 for details).

Note the use of an intermediate `Discriminator` template. It is needed to allow the various `Setter` types to be identical. (You cannot have multiple direct base classes of the same type. Indirect base classes, on the other hand, can have types that are identical to those of other bases.)

As announced earlier, we're collecting the defaults in a base class:

```
// name default policies as P1, P2, P3, P4
class DefaultPolicies {
  public:
    typedef DefaultPolicy1 P1;
    typedef DefaultPolicy2 P2;
    typedef DefaultPolicy3 P3;
    typedef DefaultPolicy4 P4;
};
```

However, we must be careful to avoid ambiguities if we end up inheriting multiple times from this base class. Therefore, we ensure that the base class is inherited virtually:

```
// class to define a use of the default policy values
// avoids ambiguities if we derive from DefaultPolicies more than once
class DefaultPolicyArgs : virtual public DefaultPolicies {
};
```

Finally, we also need some templates to override the default policy values:

```
template <typename Policy>
class Policy1_is : virtual public DefaultPolicies {
  public:
    typedef Policy P1;   // overriding typedef
};

template <typename Policy>
class Policy2_is : virtual public DefaultPolicies {
  public:
    typedef Policy P2;   // overriding typedef
};

template <typename Policy>
class Policy3_is : virtual public DefaultPolicies {
  public:
    typedef Policy P3;   // overriding typedef
};
```

```
template <typename Policy>
class Policy4_is : virtual public DefaultPolicies {
  public:
    typedef Policy P4;   // overriding typedef
};
```

With all this in place, our desired objective is achieved. Now let's look at what we have by example. Let's instantiate a `BreadSlicer<>` as follows:

```
BreadSlicer<Policy3_is<CustomPolicy> > bc;
```

For this `BreadSlicer<>` the type `Policies` is defined as

```
PolicySelector<Policy3_is<CustomPolicy>,
               DefaultPolicyArgs,
               DefaultPolicyArgs,
               DefaultPolicyArgs>
```

With the help of the `Discriminator<>` class templates this results in a hierarchy, in which all template arguments are base classes (see Figure 16.1). The important point is that these base classes

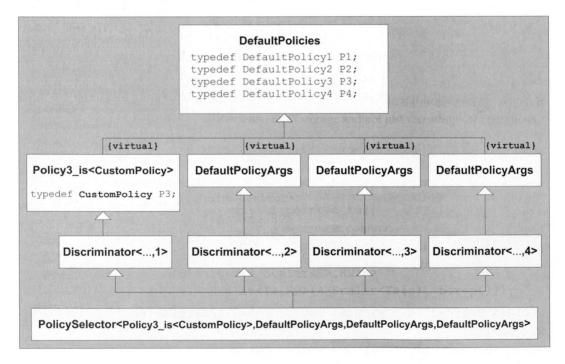

Figure 16.1. Resulting type hierarchy of `BreadSlicer<>::Policies`

all have the same virtual base class `DefaultPolicies`, which defines the default types for P1, P2, P3, and P4. However, P3 is redefined in one of the derived classes—namely, in `Policy3_is<>`. According to the so-called *domination rule* this definition hides the definition of the base class. Thus, this is *not* an ambiguity.[2]

Inside the template `BreadSlicer` you can refer to the four policies by using qualified names such as `Policies::P3`. For example:

```
template <... >
class BreadSlicer {
    ...
  public:
    void print () {
        Policies::P3::doPrint();
    }
    ...
};
```

In `inherit/namedtmpl.cpp` you can find the entire example.

We developed the technique for four template type parameters, but it obviously scales to any reasonable number of such parameters. Note that we never actually instantiate objects of the helper class that contain virtual bases. Hence, the fact that they are virtual bases is not a performance or memory consumption issue.

16.2   The Empty Base Class Optimization (EBCO)

C++ classes are often "empty," which means that their internal representation does not require any bits of memory at run time. This is the case typically for classes that contain only type members, nonvirtual function members, and static data members. Nonstatic data members, virtual functions, and virtual base classes, on the other hand, do require some memory at run time.

Even empty classes, however, have nonzero size. Try the following program if you'd like to verify this:

```
// inherit/empty.cpp

#include <iostream>

class EmptyClass {
};
```

---

[2] You can find the domination rule in Section 10.2/6 in the C++ Standard (see [*Standard98*]) and a discussion about it in Section 10.1.1 of [*EllisStroustrupARM*].

```
int main()
{
    std::cout << "sizeof(EmptyClass): " << sizeof(EmptyClass)
              << '\n';
}
```

For many platforms, this program will print 1 as size of `EmptyClass`. A few systems impose more strict alignment requirements on class types and may print another small integer (typically, 4).

16.2.1   Layout Principles

The designers of C++ had various reasons to avoid zero-size classes. For example, an array of zero-size classes would presumably have size zero too, but then the usual properties of pointer arithmetic would not apply anymore. For example, let's assume `ZeroSizedT` is a zero-size type:

```
ZeroSizedT z[10];
...
&z[i] - &z[j]        // compute distance between pointers/addresses
```

Normally, the difference in the previous example is obtained by dividing the number of bytes between the two addresses by the size of the type to which it is pointing, but when that size is zero this is clearly not satisfactory.

However, even though there are no zero-size types in C++, the C++ standard does specify that when an empty class is used as a base class, no space needs to be allocated for it *provided that it does not cause it to be allocated to the same address as another object or subobject of the same type.* Let's look at some examples to clarify what this so-called *empty base class optimization* (or *EBCO*) means in practice. Consider the following program:

```
// inherit/ebco1.cpp

#include <iostream>

class Empty {
    typedef int Int;    // typedef members don't make a class nonempty
};

class EmptyToo : public Empty {
};

class EmptyThree : public EmptyToo {
};
```

```
int main()
{
    std::cout << "sizeof(Empty):      " << sizeof(Empty)
              << '\n';
    std::cout << "sizeof(EmptyToo):   " << sizeof(EmptyToo)
              << '\n';
    std::cout << "sizeof(EmptyThree): " << sizeof(EmptyThree)
              << '\n';
}
```

If your compiler implements the empty base optimization, it will print the same size for every class, but none of these classes has size zero (see Figure 16.2). This means that within class EmptyToo, the class Empty is not given any space. Note also that an empty class with optimized empty bases (and no other bases) is also empty. This explains why class EmptyThree can also have the same size as class Empty. If your compiler does not implement the empty base optimization, it will print different sizes (see Figure 16.3).

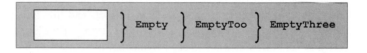

Figure 16.2. Layout of EmptyThree by a compiler that implements the EBCO

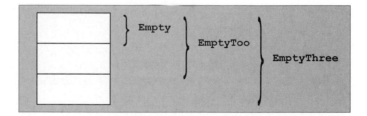

Figure 16.3. Layout of EmptyThree by a compiler that does not implement the EBCO

Consider an example that runs into a constraint of empty base optimization:

```
// inherit/ebco2.cpp

#include <iostream>

class Empty {
    typedef int Int;    // typedef members don't make a class nonempty
};
```

```
class EmptyToo : public Empty {
};

class NonEmpty : public Empty, public EmptyToo {
};

int main()
{
    std::cout << "sizeof(Empty):    " << sizeof(Empty) << '\n';
    std::cout << "sizeof(EmptyToo): " << sizeof(EmptyToo) << '\n';
    std::cout << "sizeof(NonEmpty): " << sizeof(NonEmpty) << '\n';
}
```

It may come as a surprise that class NonEmpty is not an empty class. After all, it does not have any members and neither do its base classes. However, the base classes Empty and EmptyToo of NonEmpty cannot be allocated to the same address because this would cause the base class Empty of EmptyToo to end up at the same address as the base class Empty of class NonEmpty. In other words, two subobjects of the same type would end up at the same offset, and this is not permitted by the object layout rules of C++. It may be conceivable to decide that one of the Empty base subobjects is placed at offset "0 bytes" and the other at offset "1 byte," but the complete NonEmpty object still cannot have a size of one byte because in an array of two NonEmpty objects, an Empty subobject of the first element cannot end up at the same address as an Empty subobject of the second element (see Figure 16.4).

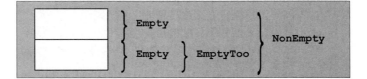

Figure 16.4. Layout of NonEmpty *by a compiler that implements the EBCO*

The rationale for the constraint on empty base optimization stems from the fact that it is desirable to be able to compare whether two pointers point to the same object. Because pointers are nearly always internally represented as just addresses, we must ensure that two different addresses (that is, pointer values) correspond to two different objects.

The constraint may not seem very significant. However, in practice, it is often encountered because many classes tend to inherit from a small set of empty classes that define some common typedefs. When two subobjects of such classes are used in the same complete object, the optimization is inhibited.

16.2.2 Members as Base Classes

The empty base class optimization has no equivalent for data members because (among other things) it would create some problems with the representation of pointers to members. As a result, it is sometimes desirable to implement as a (private) base class what would at first sight be thought of as a member variable. However, this is not without its challenges.

The problem is most interesting in the context of templates because template parameters are often substituted with empty class types, but in general one cannot rely on this rule. If nothing is known about a template type parameter, empty base optimization cannot easily be exploited. Indeed, consider the following trivial example:

```
template <typename T1, typename T2>
class MyClass {
  private:
    T1 a;
    T2 b;
    ...
};
```

It is entirely possible that one or both template parameters are substituted by an empty class type. If this is the case, then the representation of MyClass<T1,T2> may be suboptimal and may waste a word of memory for every instance of a MyClass<T1,T2>.

This can be avoided by making the template arguments base classes instead:

```
template <typename T1, typename T2>
class MyClass : private T1, private T2 {
};
```

However, this straightforward alternative has its own set of problems. It doesn't work when T1 or T2 is substituted with a nonclass type or with a union type. It also doesn't work when the two parameters are substituted with the same type (although this can be addressed fairly easily by adding another layer of inheritance; see page 287 or page 449). However, even if we satisfactorily addressed these problems, a very serious problem persists: Adding a base class can fundamentally modify the interface of the given class. For our MyClass class, this may not seem very significant because there are very few interface elements to affect, but as we see later in this chapter, inheriting from a template parameter can affect whether a member function is virtual. Clearly, this approach to exploiting EBCO is fraught with all kinds of trouble.

A more practical tool can be devised for the common case when a template parameter is known to be substituted by class types only and when another member of the class template is available. The main idea is to "merge" the potentially empty type parameter with the other member using EBCO. For example, instead of writing

```
template <typename CustomClass>
class Optimizable {
  private:
    CustomClass info;        // might be empty
    void*        storage;
    ...
};
```

a template implementer would use the following:

```
template <typename CustomClass>
class Optimizable {
  private:
    BaseMemberPair<CustomClass, void*> info_and_storage;
    ...
};
```

Even without seeing the implementation of the template BaseMemberPair, it is clear that its use makes the implementation of Optimizable more verbose. However, various template library implementers have reported that the performance gains (for the clients of their libraries) do justify the added complexity.

The implementation of BaseMemberPair can be fairly compact:

```
// inherit/basememberpair.hpp

#ifndef BASE_MEMBER_PAIR_HPP
#define BASE_MEMBER_PAIR_HPP

template <typename Base, typename Member>
class BaseMemberPair : private Base {
  private:
    Member member;
  public:
    // constructor
    BaseMemberPair (Base const & b, Member const & m)
     : Base(b), member(m) {
    }

    // access base class data via first()
    Base const& first() const {
        return (Base const&)*this;
    }
```

```
    Base& first() {
        return (Base&)*this;
    }

    // access member data via second()
    Member const& second() const {
        return this->member;
    }
    Member& second() {
        return this->member;
    }
};


#endif // BASE_MEMBER_PAIR_HPP
```

An implementation needs to use the member functions `first()` and `second()` to access the encapsulated (and possibly storage-optimized) data members.

16.3   The Curiously Recurring Template Pattern (CRTP)

This oddly named pattern refers to a general class of techniques that consists of passing a derived class as a template argument to one of its own base classes. In its simplest form, C++ code for such a pattern looks as follows:

```
template <typename Derived>
class CuriousBase {
    ...
};


class Curious : public CuriousBase<Curious> {
    ...
};
```

Our first outline of CRTP shows a nondependent base class: The class `Curious` is not a template and is therefore immune to some of the name visibility issues of dependent base classes. However, this is not an intrinsic characteristic of CRTP. Indeed, we could just as well have used the following alternative outline:

```
template <typename Derived>
class CuriousBase {
    ...
};


template <typename T>
class CuriousTemplate : public CuriousBase<CuriousTemplate<T> > {
    ...
};
```

From this outline, however, it is not a far stretch to propose yet another alternative formulation, this time involving a template template parameter:

```
template <template<typename> class Derived>
class MoreCuriousBase {
    ...
};


template <typename T>
class MoreCurious : public MoreCuriousBase<MoreCurious> {
    ...
};
```

A simple application of CRTP consists of keeping track of how many objects of a certain class type were created. This is easily achieved by incrementing an integral static data member in every constructor and decrementing it in the destructor. However, having to provide such code in every class is tedious. Instead, we can write the following template:

```
// inherit/objectcounter.hpp

#include <stddef.h>

template <typename CountedType>
class ObjectCounter {
  private:
    static size_t count;       // number of existing objects

  protected:
    // default constructor
    ObjectCounter() {
        ++count;
    }
```

```cpp
    // copy constructor
    ObjectCounter (ObjectCounter<CountedType> const&) {
        ++count;
    }

    // destructor
    ~ObjectCounter() {
        --count;
    }

  public:
    // return number of existing objects:
    static size_t live() {
        return count;
    }
};

// initialize counter with zero
template <typename CountedType>
size_t ObjectCounter<CountedType>::count = 0;
```

If we want to count the number of live (that is, not yet destroyed) objects for a certain class type, it suffices to derive the class from the ObjectCounter template. For example, we can define and use a counted string class along the following lines:

```cpp
// inherit/testcounter.cpp

#include "objectcounter.hpp"
#include <iostream>

template <typename CharT>
class MyString : public ObjectCounter<MyString<CharT> > {
  ...
};

int main()
{
    MyString<char> s1, s2;
    MyString<wchar_t> ws;
```

```
    std::cout << "number of MyString<char>:      "
              << MyString<char>::live() << std::endl;
    std::cout << "number of MyString<wchar_t>: "
              << ws.live() << std::endl;
}
```

In general, CRTP is useful to factor out implementations of interfaces that can only be member functions (for example, constructor, destructors, and subscript operators).

16.4   Parameterized Virtuality

C++ allows us to parameterize directly three kinds of entities through templates: types, constants ("nontypes"), and templates. However, indirectly, it also allows us to parameterize other attributes such as the virtuality of a member function. A simple example shows this rather surprising technique:

```
// inherit/virtual.cpp

#include <iostream>

class NotVirtual {
};

class Virtual {
  public:
    virtual void foo() {
    }
};

template <typename VBase>
class Base : private VBase {
  public:
    // the virtuality of foo() depends on its declaration
    // (if any) in the base class VBase
    void foo() {
        std::cout << "Base::foo()" << '\n';
    }
};
```

```
template <typename V>
class Derived : public Base<V> {
  public:
    void foo() {
        std::cout << "Derived::foo()" << '\n';
    }
};

int main()
{
    Base<NotVirtual>* p1 = new Derived<NotVirtual>;
    p1->foo();   // calls Base::foo()

    Base<Virtual>* p2 = new Derived<Virtual>;
    p2->foo();   // calls Derived::foo()
}
```

This technique can provide a tool to design a class template that is usable both to instantiate concrete classes and to extend using inheritance. However, it is rarely sufficient just to sprinkle virtuality on some member functions to obtain a class that makes a good base class for more specialized functionality. This sort of development method requires more fundamental design decisions. It is therefore usually more practical to design two different tools (class or class template hierarchies) rather than trying to integrate them all into one template hierarchy.

16.5   Afternotes

Named template arguments are used to simplify certain class templates in the Boost library. Boost uses metaprogramming to create a type with properties similar to our `PolicySelector` (but without using virtual inheritance). The simpler alternative presented here was developed by one of us (Vandevoorde).

CRTPs have been in use since at least 1991. However, James Coplien was first to describe them formally as a class of so-called *patterns* (see [*CoplienCRTP*]). Since then, many applications of CRTP have been published. The phrase *parameterized inheritance* is sometimes wrongly equated with CRTP. As we have shown, CRTP does not require the derivation to be parameterized at all, and many forms of parameterized inheritance do not conform to CRTP. CRTP is also sometimes confused with the Barton-Nackman trick (see Section 11.7 on page 174) because Barton and Nackman frequently used CRTP in combination with friend name injection (and the latter is an important component of the Barton-Nackman trick). Our `ObjectCounter` example is almost identical to a technique developed by Scott Meyers in [*MeyersCounting*].

Bill Gibbons was the main sponsor behind the introduction of EBCO into the C++ programming language. Nathan Myers made it popular and proposed a template similar to our `BaseMemberPair` to take better advantage of it. The Boost library contains a considerably more sophisticated template, called `compressed_pair`, that resolves some of the problems we reported for the `MyClass` template in this chapter. `boost::compressed_pair` can also be used instead of our `BaseMemberPair`.

Chapter 17

Metaprograms

Metaprogramming consists of "programming a program." In other words, we lay out code that the programming system executes to generate new code that implements the functionality we really want. Usually the term *metaprogramming* implies a reflexive attribute: The metaprogramming component is part of the program for which it generates a bit of code/program.

Why would metaprogramming be desirable? As with most other programming techniques, the goal is to achieve more functionality with less effort, where effort can be measured as code size, maintenance cost, and so forth. What characterizes metaprogramming is that some user-defined computation happens at translation time. The underlying motivation is often performance (things computed at translation time can frequently be optimized away) or interface simplicity (a metaprogram is generally shorter than what it expands to) or both.

Metaprogramming often relies on the concepts of traits and type functions as developed in Chapter 15. We therefore recommend getting familiar with that chapter prior to delving into this one.

17.1 A First Example of a Metaprogram

In 1994 during a meeting of the C++ standardization committee, Erwin Unruh discovered that templates can be used to compute something at compile time. He wrote a program that produced prime numbers. The intriguing part of this exercise, however, was that the production of the prime numbers was performed by the compiler during the compilation process and not at run time. Specifically, the compiler produced a sequence of error messages with all prime numbers from two up to a certain configurable value. Although this program wasn't strictly portable (error messages aren't standardized), the program did show that the template instantiation mechanism is a primitive recursive language that can perform nontrivial computations at compile time. This sort of compile-time computation that occurs through template instantiation is commonly called *template metaprogramming*.

As an introduction to the details of metaprogramming we start with a simple exercise (we will show Erwin's prime number program later on page 318). The following program shows how to compute at compile time the power of three for a given value:

```
// meta/pow3.hpp

#ifndef POW3_HPP
#define POW3_HPP

// primary template to compute 3 to the Nth
template<int N>
class Pow3 {
  public:
    enum { result = 3 * Pow3<N-1>::result };
};

// full specialization to end the recursion
template<>
class Pow3<0> {
  public:
    enum { result = 1 };
};

#endif // POW3_HPP
```

The driving force behind template metaprogramming is recursive template instantiation.[1] In our program to compute 3^N, recursive template instantiation is driven by the following two rules:

1. $3^N = 3 * 3^{N-1}$

2. $3^0 = 1$

The first template implements the general recursive rule:

```
template<int N>
class Pow3 {
  public:
    enum { result = 3 * Pow3<N-1>::result };
};
```

When instantiated over a positive integer N, the template Pow3<> needs to compute the value for its enumeration value `result`. This value is simply three times the corresponding value in the same template instantiated over N-1.

The second template is a specialization that ends the recursion. It establishes the `result` of Pow3<0>:

---

[1] We saw an example of a recursive template in Section 12.4 on page 200. It could be considered a simple case of metaprogramming.

```
template<>
class Pow3<0> {
  public:
    enum { result = 1 };
};
```

Let's study the details of what happens when we use this template to compute 3^7 by instantiating Pow3<7>:

```
// meta/pow3.cpp

#include <iostream>
#include "pow3.hpp"

int main()
{
    std::cout << "Pow3<7>::result = " << Pow3<7>::result
              << '\n';
}
```

First, the compiler instantiates Pow3<7>. Its result is

```
3 * Pow3<6>::result
```

Thus, this requires the instantiation of the same template for 6. Similarly, the result of Pow3<6> instantiates Pow3<5>, Pow3<4>, and so forth. The recursion stops when Pow3<> is instantiated over zero which yields one as its result.

The Pow3<> template (including its specialization) is called a *template metaprogram*. It describes a bit of computation that is evaluated at translation time as part of the template instantiation process. It is relatively simple and may not look very useful at first, but there are situations when such a tool comes in very handy.

17.2   Enumeration Values versus Static Constants

In old C++ compilers, enumeration values were the only available possibility to have "true constants" (so-called *constant-expressions*) inside class declarations. However, this has changed during the standardization of C++, which introduced the concept of in-class static constant initializers. A brief example illustrates the construct:

```
struct TrueConstants {
    enum { Three = 3 };
    static int const Four = 4;
};
```

In this example, Four is a "true constant"—just as is Three.

With this, our Pow3 metaprogram may also look as follows:

```
// meta/pow3b.hpp

#ifndef POW3_HPP
#define POW3_HPP

// primary template to compute 3 to the Nth
template<int N>
class Pow3 {
  public:
    static int const result = 3 * Pow3<N-1>::result;
};

// full specialization to end the recursion
template<>
class Pow3<0> {
  public:
    static int const result = 1;
};

#endif // POW3_HPP
```

The only difference is the use of static constant members instead of enumeration values. However, there is a drawback with this version: Static constant members are lvalues. So, if you have a declaration such as

```
void foo(int const&);
```

and you pass it the result of a metaprogram

```
foo(Pow3<7>::result);
```

a compiler must pass the address of Pow3<7>::result, which forces the compiler to instantiate and allocate the definition for the static member. As a result, the computation is no longer limited to a pure "compile-time" effect.

Enumeration values aren't lvalues (that is, they don't have an address). So, when you pass them "by reference," no static memory is used. It's almost exactly as if you passed the computed value as a literal. These considerations motivate us to use enumeration values in all metaprograms throughout this book.

17.3   A Second Example: Computing the Square Root

Let's look at a slightly more complicated example: a metaprogram that computes the square root of a given value N. The metaprogram looks as follows (explanation of the technique follows):

```cpp
// meta/sqrt1.hpp

#ifndef SQRT_HPP
#define SQRT_HPP

// primary template to compute sqrt(N)
template <int N, int LO=1, int HI=N>
class Sqrt {
  public:
    // compute the midpoint, rounded up
    enum { mid = (LO+HI+1)/2 };

    // search a not too large value in a halved interval
    enum { result = (N<mid*mid) ? Sqrt<N,LO,mid-1>::result
                                : Sqrt<N,mid,HI>::result };
};

// partial specialization for the case when LO equals HI
template<int N, int M>
class Sqrt<N,M,M> {
  public:
    enum { result = M };
};

#endif // SQRT_HPP
```

The first template is the general recursive computation that is invoked with the template parameter N (the value for which to compute the square root) and two other optional parameters. These optional parameters represent the minimum and maximum values the result can have. If the template is called with only one argument, we know that the square root is at least one and at most the value itself.

Our recursion then proceeds using a binary search technique (often called *method of bisection* in this context). Inside the template, we compute whether result is in the first or the second half of the range between LO and HI. This case differentiation is done using the conditional operator ?:. If mid^2 is greater than N, we continue the search in the first half. If mid^2 is less than or equal to N, we use the same template for the second half again.

The specialization that ends the recursive process is invoked when LO and HI have the same value M, which is our final result.

Again, let's look at the details of a simple program that uses this metaprogram:

```
// meta/sqrt1.cpp

#include <iostream>
#include "sqrt1.hpp"

int main()
{
    std::cout << "Sqrt<16>::result = " << Sqrt<16>::result
              << '\n';
    std::cout << "Sqrt<25>::result = " << Sqrt<25>::result
              << '\n';
    std::cout << "Sqrt<42>::result = " << Sqrt<42>::result
              << '\n';
    std::cout << "Sqrt<1>::result =  " << Sqrt<1>::result
              << '\n';
}
```

The expression

```
    Sqrt<16>::result
```

is expanded to

```
    Sqrt<16,1,16>::result
```

Inside the template, the metaprogram computes Sqrt<16,1,16>::result as follows:

```
    mid = (1+16+1)/2
        = 9
    result = (16<9*9) ? Sqrt<16,1,8>::result
                      : Sqrt<16,9,16>::result
           = (16<81)  ? Sqrt<16,1,8>::result
                      : Sqrt<16,9,16>::result
           = Sqrt<16,1,8>::result
```

Thus, the result is computed as Sqrt<16,1,8>::result, which is expanded as follows:

```
    mid = (1+8+1)/2
        = 5
    result = (16<5*5) ? Sqrt<16,1,4>::result
                      : Sqrt<16,5,8>::result
           = (16<25)  ? Sqrt<16,1,4>::result
                      : Sqrt<16,5,8>::result
           = Sqrt<16,1,4>::result
```

And similarly Sqrt<16,1,4>::result is decomposed as follows:

```
mid = (1+4+1)/2
    = 3
result = (16<3*3) ? Sqrt<16,1,2>::result
                  : Sqrt<16,3,4>::result
       = (16<9) ? Sqrt<16,1,2>::result
                : Sqrt<16,3,4>::result
       = Sqrt<16,3,4>::result
```

Finally, Sqrt<16,3,4>::result results in the following:

```
mid = (3+4+1)/2
    = 4
result = (16<4*4) ? Sqrt<16,3,3>::result
                  : Sqrt<16,4,4>::result
       = (16<16) ? Sqrt<16,3,3>::result
                 : Sqrt<16,4,4>::result
       = Sqrt<16,4,4>::result
```

and Sqrt<16,4,4>::result ends the recursive process because it matches the explicit specialization that catches equal high and low bounds. The final result is therefore as follows:

```
result = 4
```

Tracking All Instantiations

In the preceding example, we followed the significant instantiations that compute the square root of 16. However, when a compiler evaluates the expression

```
(16<=8*8) ? Sqrt<16,1,8>::result
          : Sqrt<16,9,16>::result
```

it not only instantiates the templates in the positive branch, but also those in the negative branch (Sqrt<16,9,16>). Furthermore, because the code attempts to access a member of the resulting class type using the :: operator, all the members inside that class type are also instantiated. This means that the full instantiation of Sqrt<16,9,16> results in the full instantiation of Sqrt<16,9,12> and Sqrt<16,13,16>. When the whole process is examined in detail, we find that dozens of instantiations end up being generated. The total number is almost twice the value of N.

This is unfortunate because template instantiation is a fairly expensive process for most compilers, particularly with respect to memory consumption. Fortunately, there are techniques to reduce this explosion in the number of instantiations. We use specializations to select the result of a computation instead of using the condition operator ?:. To illustrate this, we rewrite our Sqrt metaprogram as follows:

```
// meta/sqrt2.hpp

#include "ifthenelse.hpp"

// primary template for main recursive step
template<int N, int LO=1, int HI=N>
class Sqrt {
  public:
    // compute the midpoint, rounded up
    enum { mid = (LO+HI+1)/2 };

    // search a not too large value in a halved interval
    typedef typename IfThenElse<(N<mid*mid),
                                Sqrt<N,LO,mid-1>,
                                Sqrt<N,mid,HI> >::ResultT
            SubT;
    enum { result = SubT::result };
};

// partial specialization for end of recursion criterion
template<int N, int S>
class Sqrt<N, S, S> {
  public:
    enum { result = S };
};
```

The key change here is the use of the `IfThenElse` template, which was introduced in Section 15.2.4 on page 272:

```
// meta/ifthenelse.hpp

#ifndef IFTHENELSE_HPP
#define IFTHENELSE_HPP

// primary template: yield second or third argument depending on first argument
template<bool C, typename Ta, typename Tb>
class IfThenElse;

// partial specialization: true yields second argument
template<typename Ta, typename Tb>
class IfThenElse<true, Ta, Tb> {
```

```
  public:
    typedef Ta ResultT;
};
```

```
// partial specialization: false yields third argument
template<typename Ta, typename Tb>
class IfThenElse<false, Ta, Tb> {
  public:
    typedef Tb ResultT;
};
```

#endif *// IFTHENELSE_HPP*

Remember, the `IfThenElse` template is a device that selects between two types based on a given Boolean constant. If the constant is true, the first type is `typedefc`d to `ResultT`; otherwise, `ResultT` stands for the second type. At this point it is important to remember that defining a typedef for a class template instance does not cause a C++ compiler to instantiate the body of that instance. Therefore, when we write

```
typedef typename IfThenElse<(N<mid*mid),
                            Sqrt<N,LO,mid-1>,
                            Sqrt<N,mid,HI> >::ResultT
        SubT;
```

neither `Sqrt<N,LO,mid-1>` nor `Sqrt<N,mid,HI>` is fully instantiated. Whichever of these two types ends up being a synonym for `SubT` is fully instantiated when looking up `SubT::result`. In contrast to our first approach, this strategy leads to a number of instantiations that is proportional to $log_2(N)$: a very significant reduction in the cost of metaprogramming when N gets moderately large.

17.4 Using Induction Variables

You may argue that the way the metaprogram is written in the previous example looks rather complicated. And you may wonder whether you have learned something *you* can use whenever you have a problem to solve by a metaprogram. So, let's look for a more "naive" and maybe "more iterative" implementation of a metaprogram that computes the square root.

A "naive iterative algorithm" can be formulated as follows: To compute the square root of a given value N, we write a loop in which a variable I iterates from one to N until its square is equal to or greater than N. This value I is our square root of N. If we formulate this problem in ordinary C++, it looks as follows:

```
int I;
for (I=1; I*I<N; ++I) {
    ;
}
```
// I now contains the square root of N

However, as a metaprogram we have to formulate this loop in a recursive way, and we need an end criterion to end the recursion. As a result, an implementation of this loop as a metaprogram looks as follows:

// meta/sqrt3.hpp

```
#ifndef SQRT_HPP
#define SQRT_HPP
```

// primary template to compute sqrt(N) via iteration
```
template <int N, int I=1>
class Sqrt {
  public:
    enum { result = (I*I<N) ? Sqrt<N,I+1>::result
                            : I };
};
```

// partial specialization to end the iteration
```
template<int N>
class Sqrt<N,N> {
  public:
    enum { result = N };
};
```

```
#endif // SQRT_HPP
```

We loop by "iterating" I over Sqrt<N,I>. As long as I*I<N yields true, we use the result of the next iteration Sqrt<N,I+1>::result as result. Otherwise I is our result.

For example, if we evaluate Sqrt<16> this gets expanded to Sqrt<16,1>. Thus, we start an iteration with one as a value of the so-called *induction variable* I. Now, as long as I^2 (that is I*I) is less than N, we use the next iteration value by computing Sqrt<N,I+1>::result. When I^2 is equal to or greater than N we know that I is the result.

You may wonder why we need a template specialization to end the recursion because the first template always, sooner or later, finds I as the result, which seems to end the recursion. Again, this is the effect of the instantiation of both branches of operator ?:, which was discussed in the previous section. Thus, the compiler computes the result of Sqrt<4> by instantiating as follows:

- Step 1:
  ```
  result = (1*1<4) ? Sqrt<4,2>::result
                   : 1
  ```

- Step 2:
  ```
  result = (1*1<4) ? (2*2<4) ? Sqrt<4,3>::result
                             : 2
                   : 1
  ```

- Step 3:
  ```
  result = (1*1<4) ? (2*2<4) ? (3*3<4) ? Sqrt<4,4>::result
                                       : 3
                             : 2
                   : 1
  ```

- Step 4:
  ```
  result = (1*1<4) ? (2*2<4) ? (3*3<4) ? 4
                                       : 3
                             : 2
                   : 1
  ```

Although we find the result in step 2, the compiler instantiates until we find a step that ends the recursion with a specialization. Without the specialization, the compiler would continue to instantiate until internal compiler limits are reached.

Again, the application of the IfThenElse template solves the problem:

```
// meta/sqrt4.hpp

#ifndef SQRT_HPP
#define SQRT_HPP

#include "ifthenelse.hpp"

// template to yield template argument as result
template<int N>
class Value {
  public:
    enum { result = N };
};

// template to compute sqrt(N) via iteration
template <int N, int I=1>
class Sqrt {
  public:
```

```
        // instantiate next step or result type as branch
        typedef typename IfThenElse<(I*I<N),
                                     Sqrt<N,I+1>,
                                     Value<I>
                             >::ResultT
                SubT;

        // use the result of branch type
        enum { result = SubT::result };
    };


#endif // SQRT_HPP
```

Instead of the end criterion we use a `Value<>` template that returns the value of the template argument as `result`.

This time, using `IfThenElse<>` leads to a number of instantiations that is proportional to $sqrt(N)$ instead of N. This is a very significant reduction in the cost of metaprogramming. And for compilers with template instantiation limits, this means that you can evaluate the square root of much larger values. If your compiler supports up to 64 nested instantiations, for example, you can process the square root of up to 4096 (instead of up to 64).

The output of the "iterative" Sqrt templates is as follows:

```
Sqrt<16>::result = 4
Sqrt<25>::result = 5
Sqrt<42>::result = 7
Sqrt<1>::result =  1
```

Note that this implementation produces the integer square root rounded up for simplicity (the square root of 42 is produced as 7 instead of 6).

17.5   Computational Completeness

The Pow3<> and Sqrt<> examples show that a template metaprogram can contain:
- State variables: the template parameters
- Loop constructs: through recursion
- Path selection: by using conditional expressions or specializations
- Integer arithmetic

If there are no limits to the amount of recursive instantiations and the amount of state variables that are allowed, it can be shown that this is sufficient to compute anything that is computable. However, it may not be convenient to do so using templates. Furthermore, template instantiation typically requires substantial compiler resources, and extensive recursive instantiation quickly slows down a compiler or even exhausts the resources available. The C++ standard recommends but does not mandate that 17 levels of recursive instantiations be allowed as a minimum. Intensive template metaprogramming easily exhausts such a limit.

Hence, in practice, template metaprograms should be used sparingly. There are a few situations, however, when they are irreplaceable as a tool to implement convenient templates. In particular, they can sometimes be hidden in the innards of more conventional templates to squeeze more performance out of critical algorithm implementations.

17.6 Recursive Instantiation versus Recursive Template Arguments

Consider the following recursive template:

```
template<typename T, typename U>
struct Doublify {};

template<int N>
struct Trouble {
    typedef Doublify<typename Trouble<N-1>::LongType,
                        typename Trouble<N-1>::LongType> LongType;
};

template<>
struct Trouble<0> {
    typedef double LongType;
};


Trouble<10>::LongType ouch;
```

The use of `Trouble<10>::LongType` not only triggers the recursive instantiation of `Trouble<9>`, `Trouble<8>`, ..., `Trouble<0>`, but it also instantiates `Doublify` over increasingly complex types. Indeed, Table 17.1 illustrates how quickly it grows.

As can be seen from Table 17.1, the complexity of the type description of the expression `Trouble<N>::LongType` grows exponentially with N. In general, such a situation stresses a C++ compiler even more than recursive instantiations that do not involve recursive template arguments. One of the problems here is that a compiler keeps a representation of the mangled name for the type. This mangled name encodes the exact template specialization in some way, and early C++ implementations used an encoding that is roughly proportional to the length of the template-id. These compilers then used well over 10,000 characters for `Trouble<10>::LongType`.

Newer C++ implementations take into account the fact that nested template-ids are fairly common in modern C++ programs and use clever compression techniques to reduce considerably the growth

Typedef Name	Underlying Type
Trouble<0>::LongType	double
Trouble<1>::LongType	Doublify<double,double>
Trouble<2>::LongType	Doublify<Doublify<double,double>, Doublify<double,double> >

Trouble<3>::LongType	Doublify<Doublify<Doublify<double,double>,
	                              Doublify<double,double> >,
	                 <Doublify<double,double>,
	                              Doublify<double,double> > >

Table 17.1. Growth of `Trouble<N>::LongType`

in name encoding (for example, a few hundred characters for `Trouble<10>::LongType`). Still, all other things being equal, it is probably preferable to organize recursive instantiation in such a way that template arguments need not also be nested recursively.

17.7 Using Metaprograms to Unroll Loops

One of the first practical applications of metaprogramming was the unrolling of loops for numeric computations, which is shown here as a complete example.

Numeric applications often have to process *n*-dimensional arrays or mathematical vectors. One typical operation is the computation of the so-called *dot product*. The dot product of two mathematical vectors a and b is the sum of all products of corresponding elements in both vectors (for the sake of simplicity, we do not consider complex arithmetic in our example). For example, if each vector has three elements, the result is

```
a[0]*b[0] + a[1]*b[1] + a[2]*b[2]
```

A mathematical library typically provides a function to compute such a dot product. Consider the following straightforward implementation:

```
// meta/loop1.hpp

#ifndef LOOP1_HPP
#define LOOP1_HPP

template <typename T>
inline T dot_product (int dim, T* a, T* b)
{
    T result = T();
    for (int i=0; i<dim; ++i) {
        result += a[i]*b[i];
    }
    return result;
```

```
}

#endif // LOOP1_HPP
```

When we call this function as follows

```
// meta/loop1.cpp

#include <iostream>
#include "loop1.hpp"

int main()
{
    int a[3] = { 1, 2, 3};
    int b[3] = { 5, 6, 7};

    std::cout << "dot_product(3,a,b) = " << dot_product(3,a,b)
              << '\n';
    std::cout << "dot_product(3,a,a) = " << dot_product(3,a,a)
              << '\n';
}
```

we get the following result:

```
dot_product(3,a,b) = 38
dot_product(3,a,a) = 14
```

This is correct, but it takes too long for high-performance applications. Even declaring the function inline is often not sufficient to attain optimal performance.

The problem is that compilers usually optimize loops for many iterations, which is counterproductive in this case. Simply expanding the loop to

```
a[0]*b[0] + a[1]*b[1] + a[2]*b[2]
```

would be a lot better.

Of course, this performance doesn't matter if we compute only some dot products from time to time. But, if we use this library component to perform millions of dot product computations, the differences become significant.

Alternatively, we could implement the computation directly instead of calling dot_product(), or we could provide special functions for dot product computations with only a few dimensions, but this is tedious. Template metaprogramming solves this issue for us: We "program" to unroll the loops. Here is the metaprogram:

```
// meta/loop2.hpp

#ifndef LOOP2_HPP
#define LOOP2_HPP

// primary template
template <int DIM, typename T>
class DotProduct {
  public:
    static T result (T* a, T* b) {
        return *a * *b  +  DotProduct<DIM-1,T>::result(a+1,b+1);
    }
};

// partial specialization as end criteria
template <typename T>
class DotProduct<1,T> {
  public:
    static T result (T* a, T* b) {
        return *a * *b;
    }
};

// convenience function
template <int DIM, typename T>
inline T dot_product (T* a, T* b)
{
    return DotProduct<DIM,T>::result(a,b);
}

#endif // LOOP2_HPP
```

Now, by changing your application program only slightly, you can get the same result:

```
// meta/loop2.cpp

#include <iostream>
#include "loop2.hpp"
```

```
int main()
{
    int a[3] = { 1, 2, 3};
    int b[3] = { 5, 6, 7};

    std::cout << "dot_product<3>(a,b) = " << dot_product<3>(a,b)
              << '\n';
    std::cout << "dot_product<3>(a,a) = " << dot_product<3>(a,a)
              << '\n';
}
```

Instead of writing

```
dot_product(3,a,b)
```

we write

```
dot_product<3>(a,b)
```

This expression instantiates a convenience function template that translates the call into

```
DotProduct<3,int>::result(a,b)
```

And this is the start of the metaprogram.

Inside the metaprogram the `result` is the product of the first elements of a and b plus the `result` of the dot product of the remaining dimensions of the vectors starting with their next elements:

```
template <int DIM, typename T>
class DotProduct {
  public:
    static T result (T* a, T* b) {
        return *a * *b + DotProduct<DIM-1,T>::result(a+1,b+1);
    }
};
```

The end criterion is the case of a one-dimensional vector:

```
template <typename T>
class DotProduct<1,T> {
  public:
    static T result (T* a, T* b) {
        return *a * *b;
    }
};
```

Thus, for

```
dot_product<3>(a,b)
```

the instantiation process computes the following:

```
DotProduct<3,int>::result(a,b)
= *a * *b + DotProduct<2,int>::result(a+1,b+1)
= *a * *b + (*(a+1) * *(b+1) + DotProduct<1,int>::result(a+2,b+2))
= *a * *b + (*(a+1) * *(b+1) + *(a+2) * *(b+2))
```

Note that this way of programming requires that the number of dimensions is known at compile time, which is often (but not always) the case.

Libraries, such as Blitz++ (see [*Blitz++*]), the MTL library (see [*MTL*]), and POOMA (see [*POOMA*]), use these kinds of metaprograms to provide fast routines for numeric linear algebra. Such metaprograms often do a better job than optimizers because they can integrate higher-level knowledge into the computations.[2] The industrial-strength implementation of such libraries involves many more details than the template-related issues we present here. Indeed, reckless unrolling does not always lead to optimal running times. However, these additional engineering considerations fall outside the scope of our text.

17.8 Afternotes

As mentioned earlier, the earliest documented example of a metaprogram was by Erwin Unruh, then representing Siemens on the C++ standardization committee. He noted the computational completeness of the template instantiation process and demonstrated his point by developing the first metaprogram. He used the Metaware compiler and coaxed it into issuing error messages that would contain successive prime numbers. Here is the code that was circulated at a C++ committee meeting in 1994 (modified so that it now compiles on standard conforming compilers)[3]:

```
// meta/unruh.cpp

// prime number computation by Erwin Unruh

template <int p, int i>
class is_prime {
  public:
    enum { prim = (p==2) || (p%i) && is_prime<(i>2?p:0),i-1>::prim
         };
};
```

----

[2] In some situations metaprograms significantly outperform their Fortran counterparts, even though Fortran optimizers are usually highly tuned for these sorts of applications.

[3] Thanks to Erwin Unruh for providing the code for this book. You can find the original example at [*Unruh-PrimeOrig*].

```
template<>
class is_prime<0,0> {
  public:
    enum {prim=1};
};

template<>
class is_prime<0,1> {
  public:
    enum {prim=1};
};

template <int i>
class D {
  public:
    D(void*);
};

template <int i>
class Prime_print {        // primary template for loop to print prime numbers
  public:
    Prime_print<i-1> a;
    enum { prim = is_prime<i,i-1>::prim
         };
    void f() {
        D<i> d = prim ? 1 : 0;
        a.f();
    }
};

template<>
class Prime_print<1> {    // full specialization to end the loop
  public:
    enum {prim=0};
    void f() {
        D<1> d = prim ? 1 : 0;
    };
};
```

```
#ifndef LAST
#define LAST 18
#endif

int main()
{
    Prime_print<LAST> a;
    a.f();
}
```

If you compile this program, the compiler will print error messages when in `Prime_print::f()` the initialization of d fails. This happens when the initial value is 1 because there is only a constructor for `void*`, and only 0 has a valid conversion to `void*`. For example, on one compiler we get (among other messages) the following errors:

```
unruh.cpp:36: conversion from 'int' to non-scalar type 'D<17>' requested
unruh.cpp:36: conversion from 'int' to non-scalar type 'D<13>' requested
unruh.cpp:36: conversion from 'int' to non-scalar type 'D<11>' requested
unruh.cpp:36: conversion from 'int' to non-scalar type 'D<7>' requested
unruh.cpp:36: conversion from 'int' to non-scalar type 'D<5>' requested
unruh.cpp:36: conversion from 'int' to non-scalar type 'D<3>' requested
unruh.cpp:36: conversion from 'int' to non-scalar type 'D<2>' requested
```

The concept of C++ template metaprogramming as a serious programming tool was first made popular (and somewhat formalized) by Todd Veldhuizen in his paper *Using C++ Template Metaprograms* (see [*VeldhuizenMeta95*]). Todd's work on Blitz++ (a numeric array library for C++, see [*Blitz++*]) also introduced many refinements and extensions to metaprogramming (and to expression template techniques, introduced in the next chapter).

Chapter 18

Expression Templates

In this chapter we explore a template programming technique called *expression templates*. It was originally invented in support of numeric array classes, and that is also the context in which we introduce it here.

A numeric array class supports numeric operations on whole array objects. For example, it is possible to add two arrays, and the result contains elements that are the sums of the corresponding values in the argument arrays. Similarly, a whole array can be multiplied by a scalar, meaning that each element of the array is scaled. Naturally, it is desirable to keep the operator notation that is so familiar for built-in scalar types:

```
Array<double> x(1000), y(1000);
...
x = 1.2*x + x*y;
```

For the serious number cruncher it is crucial that such expressions be evaluated as efficiently as can be expected from the platform on which the code is run. Achieving this with the compact operator notation of this example is no trivial task, but expression templates will come to our rescue.

Expression templates are reminiscent of template metaprogramming. In part this is due to the fact that expression templates rely on sometimes deeply nested template instantiations, which are not unlike the recursive instantiations encountered in template metaprograms. The fact that both techniques were originally developed to support high-performance (see our example using templates to unroll loops on page 314) array operations probably also contributes to a sense that they are related. Certainly the techniques are complementary. For example, metaprogramming is convenient for small fixed-size arrays whereas expression templates are very effective for operations on medium-to-large arrays sized at run time.

18.1   Temporaries and Split Loops

To motivate expression templates, let's start with a straightforward (or maybe "naive") approach to implement templates that enable numeric array operations. A basic array template might look as follows (SArray stands for *simple array*):

```
// exprtmpl/sarray1.hpp

#include <stddef.h>
#include <cassert>

template<typename T>
class SArray {
  public:
    // create array with initial size
    explicit SArray (size_t s)
     : storage(new T[s]), storage_size(s) {
        init();
    }

    // copy constructor
    SArray (SArray<T> const& orig)
     : storage(new T[orig.size()]), storage_size(orig.size()) {
        copy(orig);
    }

    // destructor: free memory
    ~SArray() {
        delete[] storage;
    }

    // assignment operator
    SArray<T>& operator= (SArray<T> const& orig) {
        if (&orig!=this) {
            copy(orig);
        }
        return *this;
    }
```

```cpp
    // return size
    size_t size() const {
        return storage_size;
    }

    // index operator for constants and variables
    T operator[] (size_t idx) const {
        return storage[idx];
    }
    T& operator[] (size_t idx) {
        return storage[idx];
    }

  protected:
    // init values with default constructor
    void init() {
        for (size_t idx = 0; idx<size(); ++idx) {
            storage[idx] = T();
        }
    }
    // copy values of another array
    void copy (SArray<T> const& orig) {
        assert(size()==orig.size());
        for (size_t idx = 0; idx<size(); ++idx) {
            storage[idx] = orig.storage[idx];
        }
    }

  private:
    T*      storage;        // storage of the elements
    size_t storage_size;    // number of elements
};
```

The numeric operators can be coded as follows:

```
// exprtmpl/sarrayops1.hpp
```

// *addition of two* SArrays
```
template<typename T>
SArray<T> operator+ (SArray<T> const& a, SArray<T> const& b)
{
    SArray<T> result(a.size());
    for (size_t k = 0; k<a.size(); ++k) {
        result[k] = a[k]+b[k];
    }
    return result;
}
```

// *multiplication of two* SArrays
```
template<typename T>
SArray<T> operator* (SArray<T> const& a, SArray<T> const& b)
{
    SArray<T> result(a.size());
    for (size_t k = 0; k<a.size(); ++k) {
        result[k] = a[k]*b[k];
    }
    return result;
}
```

// *multiplication of scalar and* SArray
```
template<typename T>
SArray<T> operator* (T const& s, SArray<T> const& a)
{
    SArray<T> result(a.size());
    for (size_t k = 0; k<a.size(); ++k) {
        result[k] = s*a[k];
    }
    return result;
}
```

// *multiplication of* SArray *and scalar*
// *addition of scalar and* SArray
// *addition of* SArray *and scalar*
...

Many other versions of these and other operators can be written, but these suffice to allow our example expression:

```
// exprtmpl/sarray1.cpp

#include "sarray1.hpp"
#include "sarrayops1.hpp"

int main()
{
    SArray<double> x(1000), y(1000);
    ...
    x = 1.2*x + x*y;
}
```

This implementation turns out to be very inefficient for two reasons:

1. Every application of an operator (except assignment) creates at least one temporary array (that is, at least three temporary arrays of size 1,000 each in our example, assuming a compiler performs all the allowable temporary copy eliminations).

2. Every application of an operator requires additional traversals of the argument and result arrays (approximately 6,000 `doubles` are read, and approximately 4,000 `doubles` are written in our example, assuming only three temporary `SArray` objects are generated).

What happens concretely is a sequence of loops that operates with temporaries:

```
tmp1 = 1.2*x;        // loop of 1,000 operations
                     //  plus creation and destruction of tmp1
tmp2 = x*y           // loop of 1,000 operations
                     //  plus creation and destruction of tmp2
tmp3 = tmp1+tmp2;    // loop of 1,000 operations
                     //  plus creation and destruction of tmp3
x = tmp3;            // 1,000 read operations and 1,000 write operations
```

The creation of unneeded temporaries often dominates the time needed for operations on small arrays unless special fast allocators are used. For truly large arrays, temporaries are totally unacceptable because there is no storage to hold them. (Challenging numeric simulations often try to use all the available memory for more realistic results. If the memory is used to hold unneeded temporaries instead, the quality of the simulation will suffer.)

Early implementations of numeric array libraries faced this problem and encouraged users to use computed assignments (such as +=, *=, and so forth) instead. The advantage of these assignments is that both the argument and the destination are provided by the caller, and hence no temporaries are needed. For example, we could add `SArray` members as follows:

```
// exprtmpl/sarrayops2.hpp

// additive assignment of SArray
template<class T>
SArray<T>& SArray<T>::operator+= (SArray<T> const& b)
{
    for (size_t k = 0; k<size(); ++k) {
        (*this)[k] += b[k];
    }
    return *this;
}


// multiplicative assignment of SArray
template<class T>
SArray<T>& SArray<T>::operator*= (SArray<T> const& b)
{
    for (size_t k = 0; k<size(); ++k) {
        (*this)[k] *= b[k];
    }
    return *this;
}


// multiplicative assignment of scalar
template<class T>
SArray<T>& SArray<T>::operator*= (T const& s)
{
    for (size_t k = 0; k<size(); ++k) {
        (*this)[k] *= s;
    }
    return *this;
}
```

With operators such as these, our example computation could be rewritten as

```
// exprtmpl/sarray2.cpp

#include "sarray2.hpp"
#include "sarrayops1.hpp"
#include "sarrayops2.hpp"
```

```
int main()
{
    SArray<double> x(1000), y(1000);
    ...
    // process x = 1.2*x + x*y
    SArray<double> tmp(x);
    tmp *= y;
    x *= 1.2;
    x += tmp;
}
```

Clearly, the technique using computed assignments still falls short:

- The notation has become clumsy.
- We are still left with an unneeded temporary `tmp`.
- The loop is split over multiple operations, requiring a total of approximately 6,000 `double` elements to be read from memory and 4,000 `doubles` to be written to memory.

What we really want is *one* "ideal loop" that processes the whole expression for each index:

```
int main()
{
    SArray<double> x(1000), y(1000);
    ...
    for (int idx = 0; idx<x.size(); ++idx) {
        x[idx] = 1.2*x[idx] + x[idx]*y[idx];
    }
}
```

Now we need no temporary array and we have only two memory reads (`x[idx]` and `y[idx]`) and one memory write (`x[k]`) per iteration. As a result, the manual loop requires only approximately 2,000 memory reads and 1,000 memory writes.

Given that on modern, high-performance computer architectures memory bandwidth is the limiting factor for the speed of these sorts of array operations, it is not surprising that in practice the performance of the simple operator overloading approaches shown here is one or two orders of magnitude slower than the manually coded loop. However, we would like to get this performance without the cumbersome and error-prone effort of writing these loops by hand or using a clumsy notation.

18.2   Encoding Expressions in Template Arguments

The key to resolving our problem is not to attempt to evaluate part of an expression until the whole expression has been seen (in our example, until the assignment operator is invoked). Thus, before the evaluation we must record which operations are being applied to which objects. The operations are determined at compile time and can therefore be encoded in template arguments.

For our example expression

```
1.2*x + x*y;
```

this means that the result of `1.2*x` is not a new array but an object that represents *each value of* x *multiplied by* `1.2`. Similarly, `x*y` must yield *each element of* x *multiplied by each corresponding element of* y. Finally, when we need the values of the resulting array, we do the computation that we stored for later evaluation.

Let's look at a concrete implementation. With this implementation we transform the written expression

```
1.2*x + x*y;
```

into an object with the following type:

```
A_Add< A_Mult<A_Scalar<double>,Array<double> >,
       A_Mult<Array<double>,Array<double> > >
```

We combine a new fundamental `Array` class template with class templates `A_Scalar`, `A_Add`, and `A_Mult`. You may recognize a prefix representation for the syntax tree corresponding to this expression (see Figure 18.1). This nested template-id represents the operations involved and the types of the objects to which the operations should be applied. `A_Scalar` is presented later but is essentially just a placeholder for a scalar in an array expression.

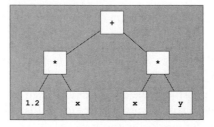

Figure 18.1. Tree representation of expression `1.2*x+x*y`

18.2.1   Operands of the Expression Templates

To complete the representation of the expression, we must store references to the arguments in each of the `A_Add` and `A_Mult` objects and record the value of the scalar in the `A_Scalar` object (or a reference thereto). Here are possible definitions for the corresponding operands:

```
// exprtmpl/exprops1.hpp

#include <stddef.h>
```

```
#include <cassert>
```

```
// include helper class traits template to select whether to refer to an
// "expression template node" either "by value" or "by reference."
#include "exprops1a.hpp"
```

```
// class for objects that represent the addition of two operands
template <typename T, typename OP1, typename OP2>
class A_Add {
  private:
    typename A_Traits<OP1>::ExprRef op1;      // first operand
    typename A_Traits<OP2>::ExprRef op2;      // second operand

  public:
    // constructor initializes references to operands
    A_Add (OP1 const& a, OP2 const& b)
     : op1(a), op2(b) {
    }

    // compute sum when value requested
    T operator[] (size_t idx) const {
        return op1[idx] + op2[idx];
    }

    // size is maximum size
    size_t size() const {
        assert (op1.size()==0 || op2.size()==0
                || op1.size()==op2.size());
        return op1.size()!=0 ? op1.size() : op2.size();
    }
};
```

```
// class for objects that represent the multiplication of two operands
template <typename T, typename OP1, typename OP2>
class A_Mult {
  private:
    typename A_Traits<OP1>::ExprRef op1;      // first operand
    typename A_Traits<OP2>::ExprRef op2;      // second operand
```

```cpp
  public:
    // constructor initializes references to operands
    A_Mult (OP1 const& a, OP2 const& b)
      : op1(a), op2(b) {
    }

    // compute product when value requested
    T operator[] (size_t idx) const {
        return op1[idx] * op2[idx];
    }

    // size is maximum size
    size_t size() const {
        assert (op1.size()==0 || op2.size()==0
                || op1.size()==op2.size());
        return op1.size()!=0 ? op1.size() : op2.size();
    }
};
```

As you can see, we added subscripting and size-querying operations that allow us to compute the size and the values of the elements for the array resulting from the operations represented by the subtree of "nodes" rooted at the given object.

For operations involving arrays only, the size of the result is the size of either operand. However, for operations involving both an array and a scalar, the size of the result is the size of the array operand. To distinguish array operands from scalar operands, we define a size of zero for scalars. The A_Scalar template is therefore defined as follows:

```cpp
// exprtmpl/exprscalar.hpp

// class for objects that represent scalars
template <typename T>
class A_Scalar {
  private:
    T const& s;    // value of the scalar

  public:
    // constructor initializes value
    A_Scalar (T const& v)
      : s(v) {
    }
```

```
// for index operations the scalar is the value of each element
T operator[] (size_t) const {
    return s;
}

// scalars have zero as size
size_t size() const {
    return 0;
    };
};
```

Note that scalars also provide an index operator. Inside the expression, they represent an array with the same scalar value for each index.

You probably saw that the operator classes used a helper class `A_Traits` to define the members for the operands:

```
typename A_Traits<OP1>::ExprRef op1;    // first operand
typename A_Traits<OP2>::ExprRef op2;    // second operand
```

This is necessary because of the following: In general, we can declare them to be references because most temporary nodes are bound in the top-level expression and therefore live until the end of the evaluation of that complete expression. The one exception are the `A_Scalar` nodes. They are bound within the operator functions and might not live until the end of the evaluation of the complete expression. Thus, to avoid that the members refer to scalars that don't exist anymore, for scalars the operands have to get copied "by value." In other words, we need members that are

- constant references in general:
```
OP1 const& op1;    // refer to first operand by reference
OP2 const& op2;    // refer to second operand by reference
```
- but ordinary values for scalars:
```
OP1 op1;           // refer to first operand by value
OP2 op2;           // refer to second operand by value
```

This is a perfect application of traits classes. The traits class defines a type to be a constant reference in general, but an ordinary value for scalars:

```
// exprtmpl/exprops1a.hpp

/* helper traits class to select how to refer to an ''expression template node''
 * - in general: by reference
 * - for scalars: by value
 */

template <typename T> class A_Scalar;
```

```
// primary template
template <typename T>
class A_Traits {
  public:
    typedef T const& ExprRef;        // type to refer to is constant reference
};

// partial specialization for scalars
template <typename T>
class A_Traits<A_Scalar<T> > {
  public:
    typedef A_Scalar<T> ExprRef;    // type to refer to is ordinary value
};
```

Note that since A_Scalar objects refer to scalars in the top-level expression, those scalars can use reference types.

18.2.2   The **Array** Type

With our ability to encode expressions using lightweight expression templates, we must now create an Array type that controls actual storage and that knows about the expression templates. However, it is also useful for engineering purposes to keep as similar as possible the interface for a real array with storage and one for a representation of an expression that results in an array. To this end, we declare the Array template as follows:

```
template <typename T, typename Rep = SArray<T> >
class Array;
```

The type Rep can be SArray if Array is a real array of storage,[1] or it can be the nested template-id such as A_Add or A_Mult that encodes an expression. Either way we are handling Array instantiations, which considerably simplify our later dealings. In fact, even the definition of the Array template needs no specializations to distinguish the two cases, although some of the members cannot be instantiated for types like A_Mult substituted for Rep.

Here is the definition. The functionality is limited roughly to what was provided by our SArray template, although once the code is understood, it is not hard to add to that functionality:

---

[1] It is convenient to reuse the previously developed SArray here, but in an industrial-strength library, a special-purpose implementation may be preferable because we won't use all the features of SArray.

```
// exprtmpl/exprarray.hpp

#include <stddef.h>
#include <cassert>
#include "sarray1.hpp"

template <typename T, typename Rep = SArray<T> >
class Array {
  private:
    Rep expr_rep;      // (access to) the data of the array

  public:
    // create array with initial size
    explicit Array (size_t s)
     : expr_rep(s) {
    }

    // create array from possible representation
    Array (Rep const& rb)
     : expr_rep(rb) {
    }

    // assignment operator for same type
    Array& operator= (Array const& b) {
        assert(size()==b.size());
        for (size_t idx = 0; idx<b.size(); ++idx) {
            expr_rep[idx] = b[idx];
        }
        return *this;
    }

    // assignment operator for arrays of different type
    template<typename T2, typename Rep2>
    Array& operator= (Array<T2, Rep2> const& b) {
        assert(size()==b.size());
        for (size_t idx = 0; idx<b.size(); ++idx) {
            expr_rep[idx] = b[idx];
        }
        return *this;
    }
```

```
// size is size of represented data
size_t size() const {
    return expr_rep.size();
}

// index operator for constants and variables
T operator[] (size_t idx) const {
    assert(idx<size());
    return expr_rep[idx];
}
T& operator[] (size_t idx) {
    assert(idx<size());
    return expr_rep[idx];
}

// return what the array currently represents
Rep const& rep() const {
    return expr_rep;
}
Rep& rep() {
    return expr_rep;
}
};
```

As you can see, many operations are simply forwarded to the underlying Rep object. However, when copying another array, we must take into account the possibility that the other array is really built on an expression template. Thus, we parameterize these copy operations in terms of the underlying Rep representation.

18.2.3   The Operators

We have most of the machinery in place to have efficient numeric operators for our numeric Array template, except the operators themselves. As implied earlier, these operators only assemble the expression template objects—they don't actually evaluate the resulting arrays.

For each ordinary binary operator we must implement three versions: array-array, array-scalar, and scalar-array. To be able to compute our initial value, we need, for example, the following operators:

```
// exprtmpl/exprops2.hpp
```

// addition of two `Arrays`
```
template <typename T, typename R1, typename R2>
Array<T,A_Add<T,R1,R2> >
operator+ (Array<T,R1> const& a, Array<T,R2> const& b) {
    return Array<T,A_Add<T,R1,R2> >
            (A_Add<T,R1,R2>(a.rep(),b.rep()));
}
```

// multiplication of two `Arrays`
```
template <typename T, typename R1, typename R2>
Array<T, A_Mult<T,R1,R2> >
operator* (Array<T,R1> const& a, Array<T,R2> const& b) {
    return Array<T,A_Mult<T,R1,R2> >
            (A_Mult<T,R1,R2>(a.rep(), b.rep()));
}
```

// multiplication of scalar and `Array`
```
template <typename T, typename R2>
Array<T, A_Mult<T,A_Scalar<T>,R2> >
operator* (T const& s, Array<T,R2> const& b) {
    return Array<T,A_Mult<T,A_Scalar<T>,R2> >
            (A_Mult<T,A_Scalar<T>,R2>(A_Scalar<T>(s), b.rep()));
}
```

// multiplication of `Array` *and scalar*
// addition of scalar and `Array`
// addition of `Array` *and scalar*

...

The declaration of these operators is somewhat cumbersome (as can be seen from these examples), but the functions really don't do much. For example, the plus operator for two arrays first creates an `A_Add<>` object that represents the operator and the operands

```
A_Add<T,R1,R2>(a.rep(),b.rep())
```

and wraps this object in an `Array` object so that we can use the result as any other object that represents data of an array:

```
return Array<T,A_Add<T,R1,R2> > (... );
```

For scalar multiplication, we use the `A_Scalar` template to create the `A_Mult` object

```
A_Mult<T,A_Scalar<T>,R2>(A_Scalar<T>(s), b.rep())
```

and wrap again:

```
return Array<T,A_Mult<T,A_Scalar<T>,R2> > (... );
```

Other nonmember binary operators are so similar that macros can be used to cover most operators with relatively little source code. Another (smaller) macro could be used for nonmember unary operators.

18.2.4   Review

On first discovery of the expression template idea, the interaction of the various declarations and definitions can be daunting. Hence, a top-down review of what happens with our example code may help crystallize understanding. The code we will analyze is the following (you can find it as part of `meta/exprmain.cpp`):

```
int main()
{
    Array<double> x(1000), y(1000);
    ...
    x = 1.2*x + x*y;
}
```

Because the Rep argument is omitted in the definition of x and y, it is set to the default, which is `SArray<double>`. So, x and y are arrays with "real" storage and not just recordings of operations.

When parsing the expression

```
1.2*x + x*y
```

the compiler first applies the leftmost * operation, which is a scalar-array operator. Overload resolution thus selects the scalar-array form of `operator*`:

```
template <typename T, typename R2>
Array<T, A_Mult<T,A_Scalar<T>,R2> >
operator* (T const& s, Array<T,R2> const& b) {
    return Array<T,A_Mult<T,A_Scalar<T>,R2> >
            (A_Mult<T,A_Scalar<T>,R2>(A_Scalar<T>(s), b.rep()));
}
```

The operand types are double and Array<double, SArray<double> >. Thus, the type of the result is

```
Array<double, A_Mult<double, A_Scalar<double>, SArray<double> > >
```

The result value is constructed to reference an `A_Scalar<double>` object constructed from the double value `1.2` and the `SArray<double>` representation of the object x.

Next, the second multiplication is evaluated: It is an array-array operation x*y. This time we use the appropriate `operator*`:

```
template <typename T, typename R1, typename R2>
Array<T, A_Mult<T,R1,R2> >
operator* (Array<T,R1> const& a, Array<T,R2> const& b) {
    return Array<T,A_Mult<T,R1,R2> >
            (A_Mult<T,R1,R2>(a.rep(), b.rep()));
}
```

The operand types are both `Array<double, SArray<double> >`, so the result type is

```
Array<double, A_Mult<double, SArray<double>, SArray<double> > >
```

This time the wrapped `A_Mult` object refers to two `SArray<double>` representations: the one of x and the one of y.

Finally, the + operation is evaluated. It is again an array-array operation, and the operand types are the result types that we just deduced. So, we invoke the array-array operator +:

```
template <typename T, typename R1, typename R2>
Array<T,A_Add<T,R1,R2> >
operator+ (Array<T,R1> const& a, Array<T,R2> const& b) {
    return Array<T,A_Add<T,R1,R2> >
            (A_Add<T,R1,R2>(a.rep(),b.rep()));
}
```

T is substituted with `double` whereas R1 is substituted with

```
A_Mult<double, A_Scalar<double>, SArray<double> >
```

and R2 is substituted with

```
A_Mult<double, SArray<double>, SArray<double> >
```

Hence, the type of the expression to the right of the assignment token is

```
Array<double,
      A_Add<double,
            A_Mult<double, A_Scalar<double>, SArray<double> >,
            A_Mult<double, SArray<double>, SArray<double> > > >
```

This type is matched to the assignment operator template of the `Array` template:

```
template <typename T, typename Rep = SArray<T> >
class Array {
  public:
    ...
```

```
// assignment operator for arrays of different type
template<typename T2, typename Rep2>
Array& operator= (Array<T2, Rep2> const& b) {
    assert(size()==b.size());
    for (size_t idx = 0; idx<b.size(); ++idx) {
        expr_rep[idx] = b[idx];
    }
    return *this;
}
...
};
```

The assignment operator computes each element of the destination x by applying the subscript operator to the representation of the right side, the type of which is

```
A_Add<double,
        A_Mult<double, A_Scalar<double>, SArray<double> >,
        A_Mult<double, SArray<double>, SArray<double> > > >
```

Carefully tracing this subscript operator shows that for a given subscript idx, it computes

```
(1.2*x[idx]) + (x[idx]*y[idx])
```

which is exactly what we want.

18.2.5   Expression Templates Assignments

It is not possible to instantiate write operations for an array with a Rep argument that is built on our example A_Mult and A_Add expression templates. (Indeed, it makes no sense to write a+b = c.) However, it is entirely reasonable to write other expression templates for which assignment to the result is possible. For example, indexing with an array of integral values would intuitively correspond to subset selection. In other words, the expression

```
x[y] = 2*x[y];
```

should mean the same as

```
for (size_t idx = 0; idx<y.size(); ++idx) {
    x[y[idx]] = 2*x[y[idx]];
}
```

Enabling this implies that an array built on an expression template behaves like an lvalue (that is, is "writable"). The expression template component for this is not fundamentally different from, say, A_Mult, except that both const and non-const versions of the subscript operators are provided and they return lvalues (references):

```
// exprtmpl/exprops3.hpp

template<typename T, typename A1, typename A2>
class A_Subscript {
  public:
    // constructor initializes references to operands
    A_Subscript (A1 const& a, A2 const& b)
     : a1(a), a2(b) {
    }

    // process subscription when value requested
    T operator[] (size_t idx) const {
        return a1[a2[idx]];
    }
    T& operator[] (size_t idx) {
        return a1[a2[idx]];
    }

    // size is size of inner array
    size_t size() const {
        return a2.size();
    }
  private:
    A1 const& a1;       // reference to first operand
    A2 const& a2;       // reference to second operand
};
```

The extended subscript operator with subset semantics that was suggested earlier would require that additional subscript operators be added to the Array template. One of these operators could be defined as follows (a corresponding const version would presumably also be needed):

```
// exprtmpl/exprops4.hpp

template<typename T, typename R>
  template<typename T2, typename R2> inline
Array<T, A_Subscript<T, R, R2> >
Array<T, R>::operator[](Array<T2, R2> const& b) {
    return Array<T, A_Subscript<T, R, R2> >
           (A_Subscript<T, R, R2>(*this, b));
}
```

18.3 Performance and Limitations of Expression Templates

To justify the complexity of the expression template idea, we have already invoked greatly enhanced performance on arraywise operations. As you trace what happens with the expression templates, you'll find that many small inline functions call each other and that many small expression template objects are allocated on the call stack. The optimizer must perform complete inlining and elimination of the small objects to produce code that performs as well as manually coded loops. The latter feat is still rare among C++ compilers at the time of this writing.

The expression templates technique does not resolve all the problematic situations involving numeric operations on arrays. For example, it does not work for matrix-vector multiplications of the form

```
x = A*x;
```

where x is a column vector of size n and A is an n-by-n matrix. The problem here is that a temporary must be used because each element of the result can depend on each element of the original x. Unfortunately, the expression template loop updates the first element of x right away and then uses that newly computed element to compute the second element, which is wrong. The slightly different expression

```
x = A*y;
```

on the other hand, does not need a temporary if x and y aren't aliases for each other, which implies that a solution would have to know the relationship of the operands at run time. This in turn suggests creating a run-time structure that represents the expression tree instead of encoding the tree in the type of the expression template. This approach was pioneered by the NewMat library of Robert Davies (see [*NewMat*]). It was known long before expression templates were developed.

Expression templates aren't limited to numeric computations either. An intriguing application, for example, is Jaakko Järvi and Gary Powell's *Lambda Library* (see [*LambdaLib*]). This library uses standard library function objects as expression objects. For example, it allows us to write the following:

```
void lambda_demo (std::vector<long*> & ones) {
    std::sort(ones.begin(), ones.end(), *_1 > *_2);
}
```

This short code excerpt sorts an array in increasing order of the value of what its elements *refer to*. Without the Lambda library, we'd have to define a simple (but cumbersome) special-purpose functor type. Instead, we can now use simple inline syntax to express the operations we want to apply. In our example, _1 and _2 are placeholders provided by the Lambda library. They correspond to elementary expression objects that are also functors. They can then be used to construct more complex expressions using the techniques developed in this chapter.

18.4   Afternotes

Expression templates were developed independently by Todd Veldhuizen and David Vandevoorde (Todd coined the term) at a time when member templates were not yet part of the C++ programming language (and it seemed at the time that they would never be added to C++). This caused some problems in implementing the assignment operator: It could not be parameterized for the expression template. One technique to work around this consisted of introducing in the expression templates a conversion operator to a `Copier` class parameterized with the expression template but inheriting from a base class that was parameterized only in the element type. This base class then provided a (virtual) `copy_to` interface to which the assignment operator could refer. Here is a sketch of the mechanism (with the template names used in this chapter):

```cpp
template<typename T>
class CopierInterface {
  public:
    virtual void copy_to(Array<T, SArray<T> >&) const;
};


template<typename T, typename X>
class Copier : public CopierInterface<T> {
  public:
    Copier(X const &x): expr(x) {}
    virtual void copy_to(Array<T, SArray<T> >&) const {
        // implementation of assignment loop
        ...
    }
  private:
    X const &expr;
};


template<typename T, typename Rep = SArray<T> >
class Array {
  public:
    // delegated assignment operator
    Array<T, Rep>& operator=(CopierInterface<T> const &b) {
        b.copy_to(rep);
    };
    ...
};
```

```
template<typename T, typename A1, typename A2>
class A_mult {
  public:
    operator Copier<T, A_Mult<T, A1, A2> >();
    ...
};
```

This adds another level of complexity and some additional run-time cost to expression templates, but even so the resulting performance benefits were impressive at the time.

The C++ standard library contains a class template `valarray` that was meant to be used for applications that would justify the techniques used for the `Array` template developed in this chapter. A precursor of `valarray` had been designed with the intention that compilers aiming at the market for scientific computation would recognize the array type and use highly optimized internal code for their operations. Such compilers would have "understood" the types in some sense. However, this never happened (in part because the market in question is relatively small and in part because the problem grew in complexity as `valarray` became a template). Some time after the expression template technique was discovered, one of us (Vandevoorde) submitted to the C++ committee a proposal that turned `valarray` essentially into the `Array` template we developed (with many bells and whistles inspired by the existing `valarray` functionality). The proposal was the first time that the concept of the `Rep` parameter was documented. Prior to this, the arrays with actual storage and the expression template pseudo-arrays were different templates. When client code introduced a function `foo()` accepting an array—for example,

```
double foo(Array<double> const&);
```

calling `foo(1.2*x)` forced the conversion for the expression template to an array with actual storage, even when the operations applied to that argument did not require a temporary. With expresssion templates embedded in the `Rep` argument it is possible instead to declare

```
template<typename Rep>
double foo(Array<double, Rep> const&);
```

and no conversion happens unless one is actually needed.

The `valarray` proposal came late in the C++ standardization process and practically rewrote all the text regarding `valarray` in the standard. It was rejected as a result, and instead, a few tweaks were added to the existing text to allow implementations based on expression templates. However, the exploitation of this allowance remains much more cumbersome than what was discussed here. At the time of this writing, no such implementation is known, and standard `valarrays` are, generally speaking, quite inefficient at performing the operations for which they were designed.

Finally, it is worth observing here that many of the pioneering techniques presented in this chapter, as well as what later became known as the STL,[2] were all originally implemented on the same compiler: version 4 of the Borland C++ compiler. This was perhaps the first compiler that made template programming widely available to the C++ programming community.

---

[2] The STL or *standard template library* revolutionized the world of C++ libraries and was later made part of the C++ standard library (see [*JosuttisStdLib*]).

Part IV

Advanced Applications

Templates can be used to develop elaborate libraries of elements that connect in seamless ways. Non-template libraries can often do such things too. However, when it comes to small, fairly simple utilities that make everyday programming easier, traditional procedural or object-oriented libraries are not always viable because the overhead needed to invoke the simple functionality is disproportionate to the facility offered. The C preprocessor allows some of these "simple needs" to be addressed, but often it is not quite adequate for the tasks at hand.

In this part we explore some small stand-alone utilities for which templates are an ideal means of implementation:

- A framework for type classification
- Smart Pointers
- Tuples
- Functors

Our goal is to demonstrate the techniques discussed earlier. We combine them and modify them to create genuinely useful software components. However, our main topic is still *C++ Templates* and not (for example) the development of a complete C++ library. We hope the code we present is a useful tutorial and source of inspiration for C++ library writers, but we don't claim that it is the best choice for off-the-shelf components.

Chapter 19

Type Classification

It is sometimes useful to be able to know whether a template parameter is a built-in type, a pointer type, or a class type, and so forth. In the following sections we develop a general-purpose type template that allows us to determine various properties of a given type. As a result we will be able to write code like the following:

```
if (TypeT<T>::IsPtrT) {
    ...
}
else if (TypeT<T>::IsClassT) {
    ...
}
```

Furthermore, expressions such as `TypeT<T>::IsPtrT` will be Boolean constants that are valid non-type template arguments. In turn, this allows the construction of more sophisticated and more powerful templates that specialize their behavior on the properties of their type arguments.

19.1   Determining Fundamental Types

To start, let's develop a template to determine whether a type is a fundamental type. By default, we assume a type is not fundamental, and we specialize the template for the fundamental cases:

```
// types/type1.hpp

// primary template: in general T is no fundamental type
template <typename T>
class IsFundaT {
  public:
    enum { Yes = 0, No = 1};
};
```

```
// macro to specialize for fundamental types
#define MK_FUNDA_TYPE(T)                      \
    template<> class IsFundaT<T> {           \
      public:                                \
        enum { Yes = 1, No = 0 };            \
    };

MK_FUNDA_TYPE(void)

MK_FUNDA_TYPE(bool)
MK_FUNDA_TYPE(char)
MK_FUNDA_TYPE(signed char)
MK_FUNDA_TYPE(unsigned char)
MK_FUNDA_TYPE(wchar_t)

MK_FUNDA_TYPE(signed short)
MK_FUNDA_TYPE(unsigned short)
MK_FUNDA_TYPE(signed int)
MK_FUNDA_TYPE(unsigned int)
MK_FUNDA_TYPE(signed long)
MK_FUNDA_TYPE(unsigned long)
#if LONGLONG_EXISTS
  MK_FUNDA_TYPE(signed long long)
  MK_FUNDA_TYPE(unsigned long long)
#endif   // LONGLONG_EXISTS

MK_FUNDA_TYPE(float)
MK_FUNDA_TYPE(double)
MK_FUNDA_TYPE(long double)

#undef MK_FUNDA_TYPE
```

The primary template defines the general case. That is, in general, IsFundaT<T>::Yes will yield 0 (or false):

```
template <typename T>
class IsFundaT {
  public:
    enum { Yes = 0, No = 1};
};
```

For each fundamental type a specialization is defined so that IsFundaT<*T*>::Yes will yield 1 (or true). This is done by defining a macro that expands the necessary code. For example,

```
MK_FUNDA_TYPE(bool)
```

expands to the following:

```
template<> class IsFundaT<bool> {
  public:
    enum { Yes = 1, No = 0 };
};
```

The following program demonstrates a possible use of this template:

```
// types/type1test.cpp

#include <iostream>
#include "type1.hpp"

template <typename T>
void test (T const& t)
{
    if (IsFundaT<T>::Yes) {
        std::cout << "T is fundamental type" << std::endl;
    }
    else {
        std::cout << "T is no fundamental type" << std::endl;
    }
}

class MyType {
};

int main()
{
    test(7);
    test(MyType());
}
```

It has the following output:

```
T is fundamental type
T is no fundamental type
```

In the same way, we can define type functions IsIntegralT and IsFloatingT to identify which of these types are integral scalar types and which are floating-point scalar types.

19.2   Determining Compound Types

Compound types are types constructed from other types. Simple compound types include plain types, pointer types, reference types, and even array types. They are constructed from a single base type. Class types and function types are also compound types, but their composition can involve multiple types (for parameters or members). Simple compound types can be classified using partial specialization. We start with a generic definition of a traits class describing compound types other than class types and enumeration types (the latter are treated separately):

```
// types/type2.hpp

template<typename T>
class CompoundT {              // primary template
  public:
    enum { IsPtrT = 0, IsRefT = 0, IsArrayT = 0,
           IsFuncT = 0, IsPtrMemT = 0 };
    typedef T BaseT;
    typedef T BottomT;
    typedef CompoundT<void> ClassT;
};
```

The member type BaseT is a synonym for the immediate type on which the template parameter type T builds. BottomT, on the other hand, refers to the ultimate nonpointer, nonreference, and nonarray type on which T is built. For example, if T is int**, then BaseT would be int*, and BottomT would be int. For pointer-to-member types, BaseT is the type of the member, and ClassT is the class to which the member belongs. For example, if T is a pointer-to-member function of type int(X::*)(), then BaseT is the function type int(), and ClassT is X. If T is not a pointer-to-member type, the ClassT is CompoundT<void> (an arbitrary choice; you might prefer a nonclass).

Partial specializations for pointers and references are fairly straightforward:

```
// types/type3.hpp

template<typename T>
class CompoundT<T&> {          // partial specialization for references
  public:
    enum { IsPtrT = 0, IsRefT = 1, IsArrayT = 0,
           IsFuncT = 0, IsPtrMemT = 0 };
    typedef T BaseT;
    typedef typename CompoundT<T>::BottomT BottomT;
    typedef CompoundT<void> ClassT;
};
```

```
template<typename T>
class CompoundT<T*> {          // partial specialization for pointers
  public:
    enum { IsPtrT = 1, IsRefT = 0, IsArrayT = 0,
           IsFuncT = 0, IsPtrMemT = 0 };
    typedef T BaseT;
    typedef typename CompoundT<T>::BottomT BottomT;
    typedef CompoundT<void> ClassT;
};
```

Arrays and pointers to members can be treated using the same technique, but it may come as a surprise that the partial specializations involve more template parameters than the primary template:

```
// types/type4.hpp

#include <stddef.h>

template<typename T, size_t N>
class CompoundT <T[N]> {     // partial specialization for arrays
  public:
    enum { IsPtrT = 0, IsRefT = 0, IsArrayT = 1,
           IsFuncT = 0, IsPtrMemT = 0 };
    typedef T BaseT;
    typedef typename CompoundT<T>::BottomT BottomT;
    typedef CompoundT<void> ClassT;
};

template<typename T>
class CompoundT <T[]> {       // partial specialization for empty arrays
  public:
    enum { IsPtrT = 0, IsRefT = 0, IsArrayT = 1,
           IsFuncT = 0, IsPtrMemT = 0 };
    typedef T BaseT;
    typedef typename CompoundT<T>::BottomT BottomT;
    typedef CompoundT<void> ClassT;
};

template<typename T, typename C>
class CompoundT <T C::*> {   // partial specialization for pointer-to-members
```

```
  public:
    enum { IsPtrT = 0, IsRefT = 0, IsArrayT = 0,
           IsFuncT = 0, IsPtrMemT = 1 };
    typedef T BaseT;
    typedef typename CompoundT<T>::BottomT BottomT;
    typedef C ClassT;
};
```

The watchful reader may have noted that the definition of the `BottomT` member requires the recursive instantiation of the `CompoundT` template for various types T. The recursion ends when T is no longer a compound type; hence the generic template definition is used (or when T is a function type, as we see later on).

Function types are harder to recognize. In the next section we use fairly advanced template techniques to recognize function types.

19.3   Identifying Function Types

The problem with function types is that because of the arbitrary number of parameters, there isn't a finite syntactic construct using template parameters that describes them all. One approach to resolve this problem is to provide partial specializations for functions with a template argument list that is shorter than a chosen limit. The first few such partial specializations can be defined as follows:

```
// types/type5.hpp

template<typename R>
class CompoundT<R()> {
  public:
    enum { IsPtrT = 0, IsRefT = 0, IsArrayT = 0,
           IsFuncT = 1, IsPtrMemT = 0 };
    typedef R BaseT();
    typedef R BottomT();
    typedef CompoundT<void> ClassT;
};

template<typename R, typename P1>
class CompoundT<R(P1)> {
  public:
    enum { IsPtrT = 0, IsRefT = 0, IsArrayT = 0,
           IsFuncT = 1, IsPtrMemT = 0 };
    typedef R BaseT(P1);
```

```
        typedef R BottomT(P1);
        typedef CompoundT<void> ClassT;
    };


    template<typename R, typename P1>
    class CompoundT<R(P1, ...)> {
      public:
        enum { IsPtrT = 0, IsRefT = 0, IsArrayT = 0,
               IsFuncT = 1, IsPtrMemT = 0 };
        typedef R BaseT(P1);
        typedef R BottomT(P1);
        typedef CompoundT<void> ClassT;
    };
    ...
```

This approach has the advantage that we can create typedef members for each parameter type.

A more general technique uses the SFINAE (substitution-failure-is-not-an-error) principle of Section 8.3.1 on page 106: An overloaded function template can be followed by explicit template arguments that are invalid for some of the templates. This can be combined with the approach used for the classification of enumeration types using overload resolution. The key to exploit SFINAE is to find a type construct that is invalid for function types but not for other types, or vice versa. Because we are already able to recognize various type categories, we can also exclude them from consideration. Therefore, one construct that is useful is the array type. Its elements cannot be void, references, or functions. This inspires the following code:

```
    template<typename T>
    class IsFunctionT {
      private:
        typedef char One;
        typedef struct { char a[2]; } Two;
        template<typename U> static One test(...);
        template<typename U> static Two test(U (*)[1]);
      public:
        enum { Yes = sizeof(IsFunctionT<T>::test<T>(0)) == 1 };
        enum { No = !Yes };
    };
```

With this template definition, IsFunctionT<T>::Yes is nonzero only for types that cannot be types of array elements. The only shortcoming of this observation is that this is not only the case for function types, but it is also the case for reference types and for void types. Fortunately, this is

easily remedied by providing partial specialization for reference types and explicit specializations
for void types:

```
template<typename T>
class IsFunctionT<T&> {
  public:
    enum { Yes = 0 };
    enum { No = !Yes };
};


template<>
class IsFunctionT<void> {
  public:
    enum { Yes = 0 };
    enum { No = !Yes };
};


template<>
class IsFunctionT<void const> {
  public:
    enum { Yes = 0 };
    enum { No = !Yes };
};
...
```

Various alternatives exist. For example, a function type F is also unique in that a reference F&
implicitly converts to F* without a user-defined conversion.

These considerations allow us to rewrite the primary CompoundT template as follows:

```
// types/type6.hpp

template<typename T>
class IsFunctionT {
  private:
    typedef char One;
    typedef struct { char a[2]; } Two;
    template<typename U> static One test(...);
    template<typename U> static Two test(U (*)[1]);
  public:
    enum { Yes = sizeof(IsFunctionT<T>::test<T>(0)) == 1 };
    enum { No = !Yes };
};
```

```
template<typename T>
class IsFunctionT<T&> {
  public:
    enum { Yes = 0 };
    enum { No = !Yes };
};


template<>
class IsFunctionT<void> {
  public:
    enum { Yes = 0 };
    enum { No = !Yes };
};


template<>
class IsFunctionT<void const> {
  public:
    enum { Yes = 0 };
    enum { No = !Yes };
};


// same for void volatile and void const volatile
...


template<typename T>
class CompoundT {                   // primary template
  public:
    enum { IsPtrT = 0, IsRefT = 0, IsArrayT = 0,
           IsFuncT = IsFunctionT<T>::Yes,
           IsPtrMemT = 0 };
    typedef T BaseT;
    typedef T BottomT;
    typedef CompoundT<void> ClassT;
};
```

This implementation of the primary template does not exclude the specializations proposed earlier, so that for a limited number of parameters the return types and the parameter types can be accessed.

An interesting historical alternative relies on the fact that at some time in the history of C++,

```
template<class T>
struct X {
    long aligner;
    T m;
};
```

could declare a member function `X::m()` instead of a nonstatic data member `X::m` (this is no longer true in standard C++). On all implementations of that time, `X<T>` would not be larger than the following `X0` type when `T` was a function type (because nonvirtual member functions don't increase the size of a class in practice):

```
struct X0 {
    long aligner;
};
```

On the other hand, `X<T>` would be larger than `X0` if `T` were an object type (the member `aligner` was required because, for example, an empty class typically has the same size as a class with just a `char` member).

With all this in place, we can now classify all types, except class types and enumeration types. If a type is not a fundamental type and not one of the types recognized using the `CompoundT` template, it must be an enumeration or a class type. In the following section, we rely on overload resolution to distinguish between the two.

19.4   Enumeration Classification with Overload Resolution

Overload resolution is the process that selects among various functions with the same name based on the types of their arguments. As shown shortly, we can determine the outcome of a case of overload resolution without actually evaluating a function call. This is useful to test whether a particular implicit conversion exists. The implicit conversion that interests us particularly is the conversion from an enumeration type to an integral type: It allows us to identify enumeration types.

Explanations follow the complete implementation of this technique:

```
// types/type7.hpp

struct SizeOverOne { char c[2]; };

template<typename T,
         bool convert_possible = !CompoundT<T>::IsFuncT &&
                                 !CompoundT<T>::IsArrayT>
```

```
class ConsumeUDC {
  public:
    operator T() const;
};

// conversion to function and array types is not possible
template <typename T>
class ConsumeUDC<T, false> {
};

// conversion to void type is not possible
template <bool convert_possible>
class ConsumeUDC<void, convert_possible> {
};

char enum_check(bool);
char enum_check(char);
char enum_check(signed char);
char enum_check(unsigned char);
char enum_check(wchar_t);

char enum_check(signed short);
char enum_check(unsigned short);
char enum_check(signed int);
char enum_check(unsigned int);
char enum_check(signed long);
char enum_check(unsigned long);
#if LONGLONG_EXISTS
  char enum_check(signed long long);
  char enum_check(unsigned long long);
#endif  // LONGLONG_EXISTS

// avoid accidental conversions from float to int
char enum_check(float);
char enum_check(double);
char enum_check(long double);

SizeOverOne enum_check(...);      // catch all
```

```
template<typename T>
class IsEnumT {
  public:
    enum { Yes = IsFundaT<T>::No &&
                 !CompoundT<T>::IsRefT &&
                 !CompoundT<T>::IsPtrT &&
                 !CompoundT<T>::IsPtrMemT &&
                 sizeof(enum_check(ConsumeUDC<T>()))==1 };
    enum { No = !Yes };
};
```

At the heart of our device is a sizeof expression applied to a function call. It results in the size of the return type of the selected function. Hence, overload selection rules are applied to resolve the call to enum_check(), but no definition of the function is needed because the function is not actually called. In this case, enum_check() returns a char, which has size 1 if the argument is convertible to an integral type. All other types are covered by an ellipsis function, but passing an argument "by ellipsis" is the least desirable from an overload resolution point of view. The return type of the ellipsis version of enum_check() was created specifically to ensure it has a size larger than one byte.[1]

The argument for the call to enum_check() must be created carefully. First, note that we don't actually know how a T can be constructed. Perhaps a special constructor must be called? To resolve this problem, we can declare a function that returns a T and create an argument by calling that function instead. Because we are in a sizeof expression, we don't actually need to define the function. Perhaps more subtle is the fact that overload resolution could select an enum_check() declaration for an integral type if the argument has a class type T, but that class type defines a *user-defined conversion* (sometimes also called *UDC*) function to an integral type. This problem is solved by actually forcing a user-defined conversion to T using the ConsumeUDC template. The conversion operator also takes care of creating the argument of type T. The expression for the call to enum_check() is thus analyzed as follows (see Appendix B for a detailed overview of overload resolution):

- The original argument is a temporary ConsumeUDC<T> object.
- If T is a fundamental integral type, the conversion operator is relied on to create a match with an enum_check() that takes type T as its argument.
- If T is an enumeration type, the conversion operator is relied on to enable conversion to T, and type promotion is invoked to match an enum_check() that takes an integral type (typically, enum_check(int)).

---

[1] A type like double would almost surely work in practice, but in theory such a type may have size "one byte." An array type cannot be used as a return type, so we encapsulated one in a structure.

- If T is a class type with a conversion operator to an integral type, the conversion operator cannot be considered because only one user-defined conversion can be invoked for a match and we would first have to use another such conversion from ConsumeUDC<T> to T.
- No other type T could be made to match an integral type, so the ellipsis version of enum_check() is selected.

Finally, because we want to identify only enumeration types and not fundamental or pointer types, we use the IsFundaT and CompoundT types developed earlier to exclude those from the set of types that cause IsEnumT<T>::Yes to be nonzero.

19.5   Determining Class Types

With all the classification templates described in the previous section, only class types (classes, structs, and unions) remain to be recognized. One approach is to use the SFINAE principle as demonstrated in Section 15.2.2 on page 266.

Another approach is to proceed by elimination: If a type is not a fundamental type, not an enumeration type, and not a compound type, it must be a class type. The following straightforward template implements this idea:

```
// types/type8.hpp

template<typename T>
class IsClassT {
  public:
    enum { Yes = IsFundaT<T>::No &&
                 IsEnumT<T>::No &&
                 !CompoundT<T>::IsPtrT &&
                 !CompoundT<T>::IsRefT &&
                 !CompoundT<T>::IsArrayT &&
                 !CompoundT<T>::IsPtrMemT &&
                 !CompoundT<T>::IsFuncT };
    enum { No = !Yes };
};
```

19.6   Putting It All Together

Now that we are able to classify any type according to its kind, it is convenient to group all the classifying templates in a single general-purpose template. The following relatively small header file does just that:

```
// types/typet.hpp

#ifndef TYPET_HPP
#define TYPET_HPP

// define IsFundaT<>
#include "type1.hpp"

// define primary template CompoundT<> (first version)
//#include "type2.hpp"

// define primary template CompoundT<> (second version)
#include "type6.hpp"

// define CompoundT<> specializations
#include "type3.hpp"
#include "type4.hpp"
#include "type5.hpp"

// define IsEnumT<>
#include "type7.hpp"

// define IsClassT<>
#include "type8.hpp"

// define template that handles all in one style
template <typename T>
class TypeT {
  public:
    enum { IsFundaT  = IsFundaT<T>::Yes,
           IsPtrT    = CompoundT<T>::IsPtrT,
           IsRefT    = CompoundT<T>::IsRefT,
           IsArrayT  = CompoundT<T>::IsArrayT,
           IsFuncT   = CompoundT<T>::IsFuncT,
           IsPtrMemT = CompoundT<T>::IsPtrMemT,
           IsEnumT   = IsEnumT<T>::Yes,
           IsClassT  = IsClassT<T>::Yes };
};

#endif // TYPET_HPP
```

The following program shows an application of all these classification templates:

```cpp
// types/types.cpp

#include "typet.hpp"
#include <iostream>

class MyClass {
};

void myfunc()
{
}

enum E { e1 };

// check by passing type as template argument
template <typename T>
void check()
{
    if (TypeT<T>::IsFundaT) {
        std::cout << " IsFundaT ";
    }
    if (TypeT<T>::IsPtrT) {
        std::cout << " IsPtrT ";
    }
    if (TypeT<T>::IsRefT) {
        std::cout << " IsRefT ";
    }
    if (TypeT<T>::IsArrayT) {
        std::cout << " IsArrayT ";
    }
    if (TypeT<T>::IsFuncT) {
        std::cout << " IsFuncT ";
    }
    if (TypeT<T>::IsPtrMemT) {
        std::cout << " IsPtrMemT ";
    }
    if (TypeT<T>::IsEnumT) {
        std::cout << " IsEnumT ";
    }
```

```
    if (TypeT<T>::IsClassT) {
        std::cout << " IsClassT ";
    }
    std::cout << std::endl;
}

// check by passing type as function call argument
template <typename T>
void checkT (T)
{
    check<T>();

    // for pointer types check type of what they refer to
    if (TypeT<T>::IsPtrT || TypeT<T>::IsPtrMemT) {
        check<typename CompoundT<T>::BaseT>();
    }
}

int main()
{
    std::cout << "int:" << std::endl;
    check<int>();

    std::cout << "int&:" << std::endl;
    check<int&>();

    std::cout << "char[42]:" << std::endl;
    check<char[42]>();

    std::cout << "MyClass:" << std::endl;
    check<MyClass>();

    std::cout << "ptr to enum:" << std::endl;
    E* ptr = 0;
    checkT(ptr);

    std::cout << "42:" << std::endl;
    checkT(42);
```

```
        std::cout << "myfunc():" << std::endl;
        checkT(myfunc);

        std::cout << "memptr to array:" << std::endl;
        char (MyClass::* memptr) [] = 0;
        checkT(memptr);
    }
```

The program has the following output:

```
int:
 IsFundaT
int&:
 IsRefT
char[42]:
 IsArrayT
MyClass:
 IsClassT
ptr to enum:
 IsPtrT
 IsEnumT
42:
 IsFundaT
myfunc():
 IsPtrT
 IsFuncT
memptr to array:
 IsPtrMemT
 IsArrayT
```

19.7   Afternotes

The ability for a program to inspect its own high-level properties (such as its type structures) is sometimes called *reflection*. Our framework therefore implements a form of *compile-time reflection*, which turns out to be a powerful ally to *metaprogramming* (see Chapter 17).

The idea of storing properties of types as members of template specializations dates back to at least the mid-1990s. Among the earlier serious applications of type classification templates was the __type_traits utility in the STL implementation distributed by SGI (then known as *Silicon Graphics*). The SGI template was meant to represent some properties of its template argument (for example, whether it was a POD type or whether its destructor was trivial). This information was then used to optimize certain STL algorithms for the given type. An interesting feature of the SGI solution was that some SGI compilers recognized the `__type_traits` specializations and provided information about the arguments that could not be derived using standard techniques. (The generic implementation of the `__type_traits` template was safe to use, albeit suboptimal.)

The use of the SFINAE principle for type classification purposes had been noted when the SFINAE principle was clarified during the standardization effort. However, it was never formally documented, and as a result much effort was later spent trying to recreate some of the techniques described in this chapter. One of the notable early contributions was by Andrei Alexandrescu who made popular the use of the `sizeof` operator to determine the outcome of overload resolution.

Finally, we should note that a rather complete type classification template has been incorporated in the Boost library (see [*BoostTypeTraits*]). In turn, this implementation is the basis of an effort to add such a facility to the standard library. See also Section 13.10 on page 218 for a related language extension.

Chapter 20

Smart Pointers

Memory is a resource that is normally explicitly managed in C++ programs. This management involves the acquisition and disposal of blocks of raw memory.

One of the more delicate issues in managing dynamically allocated memory is the decision of when to deallocate it. Among the various tools to simplify this aspect of programming are so-called *smart pointer* templates. In C++, smart pointers are classes that behave somewhat like ordinary pointers (in that they provide the dereferencing operators -> and *) but in addition encapsulate some memory or resource management policy.

In this chapter we develop smart pointer templates that encapsulate two different *ownership* models—exclusive and shared:

- Exclusive ownership can be enforced with little overhead, compared with handling raw pointers. Smart pointers that enforce such a policy are useful to deal with exceptions thrown while manipulating dynamically allocated objects.

- Shared ownership can sometimes lead to excessively complicated object lifetime situations. In such cases, it may be advisable to move the burden of the lifetime decisions from the programmer to the program.

The term *smart pointer* implies that *objects* are being pointed to. Alternatives for *function* pointers are subject to different issues, some of which are discussed in Chapter 22.

20.1 Holders and Trules

This section introduces two smart pointer types: a *holder* type to hold an object exclusively and a so-called *trule* to enable the transfer of ownership from one holder to another.

20.1.1   Protecting Against Exceptions

Exceptions were introduced in C++ to improve the reliability of C++ programs. They allow regular and exceptional execution paths to be more cleanly separated. Yet shortly after exceptions were introduced, various C++ programming authors and columnists started observing that a naive use of exceptions leads to trouble, and particularly to memory leaks. The following example shows but one of the many troublesome situations that could arise:

```
void do_something()
{
    Something* ptr = new Something;

    // perform some computation with *ptr
    ptr->perform();
    ...

    delete ptr;
}
```

This function creates an object with new, performs some operations with this object, and destroys the object at the end of the function with delete. Unfortunately, if something goes wrong after the creation but before the deletion of the object and an exception gets thrown, the object is not deallocated and the program leaks memory. Other problems may arise because the destructor is not called (for example, buffers may not be written out to disk, network connections may not be released, on-screen windows may not be closed, and so forth). This particular case can be handled fairly easily using an explicit exception handler:

```
void do_something()
{
    Something* ptr = 0;
    try {
        ptr = new Something;

        // perform some computation with *ptr
        ptr->perform();
        ...
    }
    catch (...) {
        delete ptr;
        throw;   // rethrow the exception that was caught
    }
    delete ptr;
}
```

This is manageable, but already we find that the exceptional path is starting to dominate the regular path, and the deletion of the object has to be done in two different places: once in the regular path and once in the exceptional path. This avenue quickly grows worse. Consider what happens if we need to create two objects in a single function:

```
void do_two_things()
{
    Something* first = new Something;
    first->perform();

    Something* second = new Something;
    second->perform();

    delete second;
    delete first;
}
```

Using an explicit exception handler, there are various ways to make this exception-safe, but none seems very appealing. Here is one option:

```
void do_two_things()
{
    Something* first = 0;
    Something* second = 0;
    try {
        first = new Something;
        first->perform();
        second = new Something;
        second->perform();
    }
    catch (...) {
        delete first;
        delete second;
        throw;   // rethrow the exception that was caught
    }
    delete second;
    delete first;
}
```

Here we made the assumption that the `delete` operations will not themselves trigger exceptions.[1] In this example, the exception handling code is a very large part of the routine, but more important, it could be argued that it is the most subtle part of it. The need for exception safety has also significantly changed the structure of the regular path of our routine—perhaps more so than you may feel comfortable with.

20.1.2 Holders

Fortunately, it is not very hard to write a small class template that essentially encapsulates the policy in the second example. The idea is to write a class that behaves most like a pointer, but which destroys the object to which it points if it is itself destroyed or if another pointer is assigned to it. Such a class could be called a *holder* because it is meant to hold an object safely while we perform various computations. Here is how we could do this:

```cpp
// pointers/holder.hpp

template <typename T>
class Holder {
  private:
    T* ptr;      // refers to the object it holds (if any)

  public:
    // default constructor: let the holder refer to nothing
    Holder() : ptr(0) {
    }

    // constructor for a pointer: let the holder refer to where the pointer refers
    explicit Holder (T* p) : ptr(p) {
    }

    // destructor: releases the object to which it refers (if any)
    ~Holder() {
        delete ptr;
    }

    // assignment of new pointer
    Holder<T>& operator= (T* p) {
```

---

[1] This is a reasonable assumption. Destructors that throw exceptions should generally be avoided because destructors are automatically called when an exception is thrown, and throwing another exception while this happens results in immediate program termination.

```
                delete ptr;
                ptr = p;
                return *this;
        }

        // pointer operators
        T& operator* () const {
                return *ptr;
        }

        T* operator-> () const {
                return ptr;
        }

        // get referenced object (if any)
        T* get() const {
                return ptr;
        }

        // release ownership of referenced object
        void release() {
                ptr = 0;
        }

        // exchange ownership with other holder
        void exchange_with (Holder<T>& h) {
                std::swap(ptr,h.ptr);
        }

        // exchange ownership with other pointer
        void exchange_with (T*& p) {
                std::swap(ptr,p);
        }

    private:
        // no copying and copy assignment allowed
        Holder (Holder<T> const&);
        Holder<T>& operator= (Holder<T> const&);
};
```

Semantically, the holder takes ownership of the object to which `ptr` refers. This object has to be created with `new`, because `delete` is used whenever the object owned by the holder has to be destroyed.[2] The `release()` member removes control over the held object from the holder. However, the plain assignment operator is smart enough to destroy and deallocate any object held because another object will be held instead and the assignment operator does not return a holder or pointer for the original object. We added two `exchange_with()` members that allow us to replace conveniently the object being held without destroying it.

Our example with two allocations can be rewritten as follows:

```
void do_two_things()
{
    Holder<Something> first(new Something);
    first->perform();

    Holder<Something> second(new Something);
    second->perform();
}
```

This is much cleaner. Not only is the code exception-safe because of the work done by the `Holder` destructors, but the deletion is also automatically done when the function terminates through its regular path (at which point the objects indeed were to be destroyed).

Note that you can't use the assignment-like syntax for initialization:

```
Holder<Something> first = new Something;   // ERROR
```

This is because the constructor is declared as `explicit` and there is a minor difference between

```
X x;
Y y(x);      // explicit conversion
```

and

```
X x;
Y y = x;    // implicit conversion
```

The former creates a new object of type `Y` by using an explicit conversion from type `X`, whereas the latter creates a new object of type `Y` by using an implicit conversion, but in our case implicit conversions are inhibited by the keyword `explicit`.

20.1.3   Holders as Members

We can also avoid resource leaks by using holders within a class. When a member has a holder type instead of an ordinary pointer type, we often no longer need to deal explicitly with that member in the destructor because the object to which it refers gets deleted with the deletion of the holder

---

[2] A template parameter defining a deallocation policy could be added to improve flexibility in this area.

member. In addition, a holder helps to avoid resource leaks that are caused by exceptions that are
thrown during the initialization of an object. Note that destructors are called only for those objects
that are completely constructed. So, if an exception occurs inside a constructor, destructors are called
only for member objects with a constructor that finished normally. Without holders, this may result
in a resource leak if, for example, a first successful allocation was followed by an unsuccessful one.
For example:

```
// pointers/refmem1.hpp

class RefMembers {
  private:
    MemType* ptr1;           // referenced members
    MemType* ptr2;
  public:
    // default constructor
    // - will cause resource leak if second new throws
    RefMembers ()
      : ptr1(new MemType), ptr2(new MemType) {
    }

    // copy constructor
    // - might cause resource leak if second new throws
    RefMembers (RefMembers const& x)
      : ptr1(new MemType(*x.ptr1)), ptr2(new MemType(*x.ptr2)) {
    }

    // assignment operator
    const RefMembers& operator= (RefMembers const& x) {
        *ptr1 = *x.ptr1;
        *ptr2 = *x.ptr2;
        return *this;
    }

    ~RefMembers () {
        delete ptr1;
        delete ptr2;
    }
    ...
};
```

By using holders instead of ordinary pointer members, we easily avoid these potential resource leaks:

```
// pointers/refmem2.hpp

#include "holder.hpp"

class RefMembers {
  private:
    Holder<MemType> ptr1;           // referenced members
    Holder<MemType> ptr2;
  public:
    // default constructor
    // - no resource leak possible
    RefMembers ()
      : ptr1(new MemType), ptr2(new MemType) {
    }

    // copy constructor
    // - no resource leak possible
    RefMembers (RefMembers const& x)
      : ptr1(new MemType(*x.ptr1)), ptr2(new MemType(*x.ptr2)) {
    }

    // assignment operator
    const RefMembers& operator= (RefMembers const& x) {
        *ptr1 = *x.ptr1;
        *ptr2 = *x.ptr2;
        return *this;
    }

    // no destructor necessary
    // (default destructor lets ptr1 and ptr2 delete their objects)
    ...
};
```

Note that although we can now omit a user-defined destructor, we still have to program the copy constructor and the assignment operator.

20.1.4   Resource Acquisition Is Initialization

The general idea supported by holders is a pattern called *resource acquisition is initialization* or just *RAII*, which was introduced in [*StroustrupDnE*]. By introducing template parameters for deallocation policies, we can replace all code that matches the following outline:

```
void do_something()
{
    // acquire resources
    RES1* res1 = acquire_resource_1();
    RES2* res2 = acquire_resource_2();
    ...

    // release resources
    release_resource_2(res);
    release_resource_1(res);
}
```

with

```
void do_something()
{
    // acquire resources
    Holder<RES1,... > res1(acquire_resource_1());
    Holder<RES2,... > res2(acquire_resource_2());
    ...
}
```

This can be done by something similar to our uses of Holder, with the added advantage that the code is exception-safe.

20.1.5   **Holder** Limitations

Not every problem is resolved with our implementation of the Holder template. Consider the following example:

```
Something* load_something()
{
    Something* result = new Something;

    read_something(result);

    return result;
}
```

In this example, two things make the code more complicated:

1. Inside the function, `read_something()`, which is a function that expects an ordinary pointer as its argument, is called.
2. `load_something()` returns an ordinary pointer.

Now, using a holder, the code becomes exception-safe but more complicated:

```
Something* load_something()
{
    Holder<Something> result(new Something);

    read_something(result.get_pointer());

    Something* ret = result.get_pointer();
    result.release();
    return ret;
}
```

Presumably, the function `read_something()` is not aware of the `Holder` type; hence we must extract the real pointer using the member function `get_pointer()`. By using this member function, the holder keeps control over the object, and the recipient of the result of the function call should understand that it does not own the object whose pointer it gets—the holder does.

If no `get_pointer()` member function is provided, we can also use the user-defined indirection operator *, followed by the built-in address-of operator &. Yet another alternative is to call operator -> explicitly. The following example illustrates this:

```
read_something(&*result);
read_something(result.operator->());
```

You'll probably agree that the latter is a particularly ugly alternative. However, it may be appropriate to attract the attention to the fact that something relatively dangerous is being done.

Another issue in the example code is that we must call `release()` to cancel the ownership of the object being referred to. This prevents that object from being destroyed when the function is done; hence it can be returned to the caller. Note that we must store the return value in a temporary variable before releasing it:

```
Something* ret = result.get_pointer();
result.release();
return ret;
```

To avoid this, we can enable statements such as

```
return result.release();
```

by modifying `release()` so that it returns the object previously owned:

```
template <typename T>
class Holder {
    ...
    T* release() {
        T* ret = ptr;
        ptr = 0;
        return ret;
    }
    ...
};
```

This leads to an important observation: Smart pointers are not *that* smart, but used with a simple consistent policy they do make life much simpler.

20.1.6 Copying Holders

You probably noticed that in our implementation of the `Holder` template we disabled copying of holders by making the copy constructor and the copy-assignment operator private. Indeed, the purpose of copying is usually to obtain a second object that is essentially identical to the original. For a holder this would mean that the copy also thinks it controls when the object gets deallocated, and chaos ensues because both holders are inclined to deallocate the controlled object. Thus, copying is not an appropriate operation for holders. Instead, we can conceive of *transfer* as being the natural counterpart of copying in this case.

A transfer operation is fairly easily achieved using a release operation followed by initialization or assignment, as shown in the following:

```
Holder<Something> h1(new Something);
Holder<Something> h2(h1.release());
```

Note again that the syntax

```
Holder<X> h = p;
```

will not work because it implies an implicit conversion whereas the constructor is declared as `explicit`:

```
Holder<Something> h2 = h1.release();   // ERROR
```

20.1.7 Copying Holders Across Function Calls

The explicit transfer works well, but the situation is a little more subtle when the transfer is across a function call. For the case of passing a holder from a caller to a callee, we can always pass by reference instead of passing by value. Using the "release followed by initialization" approach can lead to problems when more than one argument is passed:

```
MyClass x;
```

```
callee(h1.release(),x);   // passing x may throw!
```

If the compiler chooses first to cause `h1.release()` to be evaluated, then the subsequent copying of x (assuming it is passed by value) may trigger an exception, whereas no component is in charge of releasing the object that used to be owned by holder `h1`. Hence, a holder should always be passed by reference.

Unfortunately, it is in general not convenient to *return* a holder by reference because this requires the holder to have a lifetime that exceeds the function call, which in turn makes it unclear when and how the holder will deallocate the object under its control. You can build an argument that it is fine to call `release()` on a holder just prior to returning the encapsulated pointer. This is essentially what we did with `load_something()` earlier. Consider the following situation:

```
Something* creator()
{
    Holder<Something> h(new Something);
    MyClass x;   // for illustration purposes
    return h.release();
}
```

We must be aware here that the destruction of x could cause an exception to be thrown after h has released the object it owned and before that object was placed under the control of another entity. If so, we would again have a resource leak. (Allowing exceptions to escape from destructors is rarely a good idea: It makes it easy for an exception to be thrown while the call stack is being unwound for a previous exception, and this leads to immediate termination of the program. The latter situation can be guarded against, but it makes for harder to understand—and therefore more brittle—code.)

20.1.8   Trules

To solve such problems let's introduce a helper class template dedicated to transferring holders. We call this class template a *trule*, which is a term derived from the contraction of *transfer capsule*. Here is its definition:

```
// pointers/trule.hpp

#ifndef TRULE_HPP
#define TRULE_HPP

template <typename T>
class Holder;

template <typename T>
class Trule {
```

```
private:
    T* ptr;        // objects to which the trule refers (if any)

public:
    // constructor to ensure that a trule is used only as a return type
    // to transfer holders from callee to caller!
    Trule (Holder<T>& h) {
        ptr = h.get();
        h.release();
    }

    // copy constructor
    Trule (Trule<T> const& t) {
        ptr = t.ptr;
        const_cast<Trule<T>&>(t).ptr = 0;
    }

    // destructor
    ~Trule() {
        delete ptr;
    }

private:
    Trule(Trule<T>&);                        // discourage use of lvalue trules
    Trule<T>& operator= (Trule<T>&); // discourage copy assignment
    friend class Holder<T>;
};


#endif // TRULE_HPP
```

Clearly, something ugly is going on in the copy constructor. Because transfer capsules are meant as the return type of functions that wish to transfer holders, they always occur as temporary objects (rvalues); hence they can be bound only to reference-to-const types. However, the transfer cannot just be a copy and must remove the ownership, by nulling the encapsulated pointer, from the original Trule. The latter operation is intrinsically non-const. This state of affairs is ugly, but it is in fact legal to cast away constness in these cases because the original object was not declared const. Hence, we must be careful to declare the return type of a function transferring a holder as Trule<T> and not Trule<T> const.

Note that no such code is used for converting a holder into a trule: The holder must be a modifiable lvalue. This is why we use a separate type for the transfer capsule instead of merging this
functionality into the `Holder` class template.

To discourage the use of `Trule` as anything but a return type for transferring holders, a copy
constructor taking a reference to a non-`const` object and a similar copy-assignment operator were
declared private. This prevents us from doing much with lvalue `Trule`s, but it is only a very partial
measure. The goal of a trule is to help the responsible software engineer, not to thwart the mad
scientist.

The `Trule` template is not complete until it is recognized by the `Holder` template:

```
// pointers/holder2extr.hpp

template <typename T>
class Holder {
  // previously defined members
  ...

  public:
    Holder (Trule<T> const& t) {
        ptr = t.ptr;
        const_cast<Trule<T>&>(t).ptr = 0;
    }

    Holder<T>& operator= (Trule<T> const& t) {
        delete ptr;
        ptr = t.ptr;
        const_cast<Trule<T>&>(t).ptr = 0;
        return *this;
    }
};
```

To illustrate this refined Holder/Trule pair, we can rewrite our `load_something()` example and
invent a caller for it:

```
// pointers/truletest.cpp

#include "holder2.hpp"
#include "trule.hpp"

class Something {
};
```

```
void read_something (Something* x)
{
}

Trule<Something> load_something()
{
    Holder<Something> result(new Something);
    read_something(result.get());
    return result;
}

int main()
{
    Holder<Something> ptr(load_something());

    ...
}
```

To conclude, we have created a pair of class templates that are almost as convenient to use as plain pointers with the added benefit of managing the deallocation of objects necessary when the stack gets unwound as the result of an exception being thrown.

20.2   Reference Counting

The Holder template (and its Trule helper) works well to hold allocated structures temporarily so that they will be deallocated if an exception causes the local stack frame to be unwound. However, memory leaks can also occur in other contexts, and in particular when many objects are interconnected in complex structures.

A general rule about the management of dynamically allocated objects is easily stated: If nothing in an application points to a dynamically allocated object, that object should be destroyed and its storage should be made available for reuse. It is therefore not surprising that programmers everywhere have been looking for ways to automate such a policy. The challenge is to determine that nothing is pointing to an object.

One idea that has been implemented many times over is so-called *reference counting*: For each object that is pointed to, keep a count of the number of pointers to it, and when that count drops to zero, delete the object. For this to be feasible in C++, we need to adhere to some convention. Specifically, because it is not practical to track how ordinary pointers to an object are created, copied, and destroyed, it is common to require that the only "pointers" to a reference-counted object are a specific kind of smart pointer. In this section we discuss the implementation of such a *reference-counting smart pointer*. This pointer is a template whose main parameter is the type of the object to which it points:

```
template <typename T ... >
class CountingPtr {
  public:
    // a constructor that starts a new count for the object
    // pointed to by T:
    explicit CountingPtr (T*);

    // copying increases the count:
    CountingPtr (CountingPtr<T... > const&);

    // destruction decreases the count:
    inline ~CountingPtr();

    // assignment decreases the count for the object previously
    // pointed to and increases it for the new object pointed to
    // (but beware of self-assignment):
    CountingPtr<T... >& operator= (CountingPtr<T... > const&);

    // the operators that make this a smart pointer:
    inline T& operator* ();
    inline T* operator-> ();
    ...
};
```

The parameter T is the only parameter that is truly needed to build a functional counting pointer template. Indeed, a good case can be made in favor of keeping a basic template like this as simple and reliable as possible. Nonetheless, we choose to use CountingPtr to demonstrate *policy* parameters (a concept described in detail in Chapter 15).

The comments in the code explain the general approach to reference counting: Every construction, destruction, and assignment of a CountingPtr may potentially change the reference counts (when one of the counts drops to zero, the object pointed to is deleted).

20.2.1   Where Is the Counter?

Because our idea is to count the number of pointers to an object, it would be entirely logical to place the counter in the object. Unfortunately, this is not viable when the type of the object pointed to has been designed without reference counting in mind.

If no counter is available in a reference-counted object, the counter must be allocated in a separate storage area that is at least as long-lived as the object pointed to; in other words, it must be dynamically allocated. Using the plain ::operator new that comes with your C++ compiler is likely to result in disappointing performance. Indeed, ::operator new must be able to allocate quasi-arbitrary object sizes without excessive storage overhead, and this requires some computational compromises. Instead, for counting pointers it is more common to use a special-purpose allocator.

A less common alternative to the separate allocation of a counter is to use a special-purpose allocator for the reference-counted object. Indeed, such an allocator could allocate some extra storage to keep the counter.

Instead of prescribing where the counter is located, we leave the location of the counter as a template parameter. In effect, this parameter is our *counter policy* (see Chapter 15). This policy's interface could consist simply of a function returning an integer type and one that allocates that integer if necessary. However, there are good reasons to provide a slightly higher level interface.

20.2.2 Concurrent Counter Access

In an environment with only one thread of execution, managing the counter is straightforward. Incrementing, decrementing, and testing for equality with zero are basic operations. However, in multithreaded environments a counter can be shared by smart pointers operating in different threads of execution. In this case we may need to add smart pointers to the counter itself so that, for example, simultaneous increment operations from two threads are appropriately sequenced. In practice this requires a form of (implicit or explicit) *locking*.

Rather than specifying how this locking is done, we specify for the counter an interface that is of a sufficiently high level to introduce locking operations. Specifically, we require that a counter be a class with the following interface:

```
class CounterPolicy {
  public:
      // the following four special members (constructors, destructor, and
      // copy assignment) need not be declared explicitly in some cases,
      // but they must be accessible
      CounterPolicy();
      CounterPolicy(CounterPolicy const&);
      ~CounterPolicy();
      CounterPolicy& operator=(CounterPolicy const&);

      // assume T is the type of object pointed to
      void init(T*);          // initialization to one, possibly allocation
      void dispose(T*);       // possibly involves deallocation of the counter
      void increment(T*);     // atomic increment by one
      void decrement(T*);     // atomic decrement by one
      bool is_zero(T*);       // check for zero

      ...
};
```

The type T used in this interface is presumably provided as a template parameter. It is used only by policies that use the object pointed to to store the counter.

Locking the counter protects concurrent access only to the counter and not to the CountingPtr itself. Hence, if multiple smart pointers to a unique object are shared among different threads of execution, an application may need to introduce additional locks to sequence the CountingPtr operations correctly. The smart pointer itself, however, cannot be held responsible for locking at that level.

20.2.3   Destruction and Deallocation

When no counting pointers are pointing to an object, our policy is to dispose of that object. In C++ this can often be achieved using the standard delete operator. However, this is not always the case. Sometimes objects must be deallocated using different functions, such as the standard C function free(). Furthermore, if the object pointed to is really an array, the disposal may need to use operator delete[].

Because we anticipate that there are sufficient cases when the disposal of the object will be nonstandard, it is worthwhile to introduce a separate *object policy* for it. Its interface is very simple:

```
class ObjectPolicy {
  public:
      // the following four special members (constructors, destructor, and
      // copy assignment) need not be declared explicitly in some cases,
      // but they must be accessible
      ObjectPolicy();
      ObjectPolicy(CounterPolicy const&);
      ~ObjectPolicy();
      ObjectPolicy& operator=(ObjectPolicy const&);

      // assume T is the type of object pointed to
      void dispose (T*);
};
```

It is possible to enrich this policy for other operations that may involve the object pointed to (for example, the operator* and operator-> dereferencing operators). One popular option is to incorporate some checking against dereferencing our smart pointer when it is not actually pointing to any object. On the other hand it is also entirely possible to add a specific policy parameter for this sort of checking. In the interest of brevity we do not pursue this option, but it is not hard to implement if you are comfortable with the remainder of this section.

For most objects counted by CountingPtrs, we can use the following simple object policy:

```
// pointers/stdobjpolicy.hpp

class StandardObjectPolicy {
  public:
    template<typename T> void dispose (T* object) {
        delete object;
    }
};
```

Clearly, this does not work for arrays allocated with operator new[]. A replacement policy for this case is trivial, fortunately:

```
// pointers/stdarraypolicy.hpp

class StandardArrayPolicy {
  public:
    template<typename T> void dispose (T* array) {
        delete[] array;
    }
};
```

Note that in both cases we chose to implement dispose() as a member template. We could also have parameterized the policy class instead. A discussion of such alternatives can be found in Section 15.1.6 on page 259.

20.2.4   The CountingPtr Template

Now that we have decided our policy interfaces, we are ready to implement the CountingPtr interface itself:

```
// pointers/countingptr.hpp

template<typename T,
         typename CounterPolicy = SimpleReferenceCount,
         typename ObjectPolicy = StandardObjectPolicy>
class CountingPtr : private CounterPolicy, private ObjectPolicy {
  private:
    // shortcuts:
    typedef CounterPolicy CP;
    typedef ObjectPolicy  OP;

    T* object_pointed_to;       // the object referred to (or NULL if none)
```

```
public:
    // default constructor (no explicit initialization):
    CountingPtr() {
        this->object_pointed_to = NULL;
    }

    // a converting constructor (from a built-in pointer):
    explicit CountingPtr (T* p) {
        this->init(p);              // init with ordinary pointer
    }

    // copy constructor:
    CountingPtr (CountingPtr<T,CP,OP> const& cp)
      : CP((CP const&)cp),          // copy policies
        OP((OP const&)cp) {
        this->attach(cp);           // copy pointer and increment counter
    }

    // destructor:
    ~CountingPtr() {
        this->detach();             // decrement counter
                                    //  (and dispose counter if last owner)
    }

    // assignment of a built-in pointer
    CountingPtr<T,CP,OP>& operator= (T* p) {
        // no counting pointer should point to *p yet:
        assert(p != this->object_pointed_to);
        this->detach();             // decrement counter
                                    //  (and dispose counter if last owner)
        this->init(p);              // init with ordinary pointer
        return *this;
    }

    // copy assignment (beware of self-assignment):
    CountingPtr<T,CP,OP>&
    operator= (CountingPtr<T,CP,OP> const& cp) {
        if (this->object_pointed_to != cp.object_pointed_to) {
            this->detach();         // decrement counter
```

```
                                   // (and dispose counter if last owner)
            CP::operator=((CP const&)cp);   // assign policies
            OP::operator=((OP const&)cp);
            this->attach(cp);   // copy pointer and increment counter
        }
        return *this;
    }

    // the operators that make this a smart pointer:
    T* operator-> () const {
        return this->object_pointed_to;
    }

    T& operator* () const {
        return *this->object_pointed_to;
    }

    // additional interfaces will be added later
    ...

  private:
    // helpers:
    // - init with ordinary pointer (if any)
    void init (T* p) {
        if (p != NULL) {
            CounterPolicy::init(p);
        }
        this->object_pointed_to = p;
    }

    // - copy pointer and increment counter (if any)
    void attach (CountingPtr<T,CP,OP> const& cp) {
        this->object_pointed_to = cp.object_pointed_to;
        if (cp.object_pointed_to != NULL) {
            CounterPolicy::increment(cp.object_pointed_to);
        }
    }

    // - decrement counter (and dispose counter if last owner)
```

```
        void detach() {
            if (this->object_pointed_to != NULL) {
                CounterPolicy::decrement(this->object_pointed_to);
                if (CounterPolicy::is_zero(this->object_pointed_to)) {
                    // dispose counter, if necessary:
                    CounterPolicy::dispose(this->object_pointed_to);
                    // use object policy to dispose the object pointed to:
                    ObjectPolicy::dispose(this->object_pointed_to);
                }
            }
        }
};
```

There is relatively little complexity in this template, except perhaps for the fact that the copy-assignment operation must be careful with the self-assignment case. Indeed, in most cases the assignment operator can just detach the counting pointer from the object to which it used to point, thereby possibly decreasing the associated counter to zero and disposing of the object. However, if this happens when the counting pointer is assigned to itself, this disposal is premature (and incorrect).

Note also that we must explicitly check for the null pointer case because a null pointer does not have an associated counter. An alternative to our approach is to leave the checking to the policy classes. In fact, a possible policy could be not to allow null CountingPtrs at all. When such a policy is applicable, it results in slightly improved performance.

We use inheritance to include the policies. This ensures that if the policies are empty classes, they do not need to take up storage (provided our compiler implements the empty base class optimization, see Section 16.2 on page 289). We could use the BaseMemberPair template introduced in Section 16.2.2 on page 294 to avoid having the members of the policy classes be visible in the smart pointer class. In this example we chose to avoid making the source code more complicated for the sake of keeping the discussion simpler.

Because there is more than one default template argument, it could be beneficial to use the technique of Section 16.1 on page 285 to override the defaults conveniently and selectively. Again, we did not do so here for the sake of brevity.

20.2.5   A Simple Noninvasive Counter

Although we have completed the design of our CountingPtr, we haven't actually finished *implementing* the design. There is no code yet for a counter policy. Let's first look at a policy for a counter that is *not* stored in the object pointed to—that is, a *noninvasive* (or *nonintrusive*) counter policy.

The main issue with our counter is its allocation. Indeed, the counter may need to be shared by many CountingPtrs; hence it must be given a lifetime that lasts until the last smart pointer is destroyed. Usually this is done using a special-purpose allocator specialized for the allocation of small objects of a fixed size. However, because the design of such allocators is not particularly pertinent to the topic of C++ templates, we forgo the in-depth discussion of an industrial-strength allocator.[3] Instead, let's assume the existence of functions `alloc_counter()` and `dealloc_counter()` that manage storage of type `size_t`. With these assumptions, we can write our simple counter as follows:

```
// pointers/simplerefcount.hpp

#include <stddef.h>   // for the definition of size_t
#include "allocator.hpp"

class SimpleReferenceCount {
  private:
    size_t* counter;      // the allocated counter
  public:
    SimpleReferenceCount () {
        counter = NULL;
    }

    // default copy constructor and copy-assignment operator
    // are fine in that they just copy the shared counter

  public:
    // allocate the counter and initialize its value to one:
    template<typename T> void init (T*) {
        counter = alloc_counter();
        *counter = 1;
    }

    // dispose of the counter:
    template<typename T> void dispose (T*) {
        dealloc_counter(counter);
    }

    // increment by one:
    template<typename T> void increment (T*) {
        ++*counter;
    }
```

---

[3] Allocators can be parameterized in all sorts of ways (for example, to select policies with reference to concurrent access), but we do not think this significantly adds to our understanding of templates and their applications.

```
// decrement by one:
template<typename T> void decrement (T*) {
    --*counter;
}


// test for zero:
template<typename T> bool is_zero (T*) {
    return *counter == 0;
}
};
```

Because this policy is nonempty (it stores a pointer to the counter), it increases the size of a CountingPtr. The size can be reduced by storing the pointer to the object alongside the counter instead of placing it directly in the smart pointer class. Doing so requires a change in our policy design and decreases the performance of accessing the object by requiring an additional level of indirection.

Note also that this particular policy doesn't make use of the counted object itself. In other words, the parameter passed to its member functions is never used. In the following section we see an alternative policy that does make use of this parameter.

20.2.6   A Simple Invasive Counter Template

An *invasive* (or *intrusive*) counter policy is one that places the counter in the type of the managed objects themselves (or perhaps in some storage controlled by these managed objects). This normally needs to be designed at the time the object type is designed; hence the solution is likely to be very specific to that type. However, for illustrative purposes we develop a more generic invasive policy.

To select the location of the counter in the referenced object let's use a nontype pointer-to-member parameter. Because the counter is allocated as part of the object, the implementation of this policy is in some ways simpler than our noninvasive example, but the pointer-to-member syntax is a little less common:

```
// pointers/memberrefcount.hpp

template<typename ObjectT,            // the class type containing the counter
         typename CountT,             // the type of the counter
         CountT ObjectT::*CountP>     // the location of the counter
class MemberReferenceCount
{
  public:
    // the default constructor and destructor are fine

    // initialize the counter to one:
```

```
        void init (ObjectT* object) {
            object->*CountP = 1;
        }

        // no action is needed to dispose of the counter:
        void dispose (ObjectT*) {
        }

        // increment by one:
        void increment (ObjectT* object) {
            ++object->*CountP;
        }

        // decrement by one:
        void decrement (ObjectT* object) {
            --object->*CountP;
        }

        // test for zero:
        template<typename T> bool is_zero (ObjectT* object) {
            return object->*CountP == 0;
        }
};
```

This policy allows a class implementer to provide a reference-counting pointer type quickly for the class. The outline of the design of such a class could be as follows:

```
class ManagedType {
  private:
    size_t ref_count;
  public:
    typedef CountingPtr<ManagedType,
                        MemberReferenceCount
                          <ManagedType,
                           size_t,
                           &ManagedType::ref_count> >
            Ptr;
    ...
};
```

With this approach, `ManagedType::Ptr` is a convenient way to refer to the smart pointer type that should be used to access a `ManagedType` object.

20.2.7   Constness

In C++ the types X const* and X* const are distinct. The former indicates that the element pointed to should not be modified, whereas the latter indicates that the pointer itself cannot be modified. The same duality exists with our reference counting pointer: X const* corresponds to CountingPtr<X const> whereas X* const corresponds to CountingPtr<X> const. In other words, the constness of the object pointed to is a property of the template argument. Let's look at some of the public member functions of CountingPtr to see how they are affected by this observation.

The dereferencing operators do not modify the pointer, which is why they are const member functions. However, they do provide access to the object pointed to. Because the constness of this object is captured by the template parameter T, T can be used without added qualification in the return type of these operators.

An int* cannot be initialized by an int const* because this would create a way to modify an object through an entity that wasn't meant to provide that kind of mutable access. In the same vein, we must ensure that a CountingPtr<int> cannot be initialized by a CountingPtr<int const> or even by an int const*. Again, using the plain (not const-qualified) template parameter T achieves the desired effect. This may seem straightforward, but smart pointer implementations that declare a constructor or assignment operator accepting a T const* are quite common (and presumably erroneous).

The assignment operators are subject to the same observations as the constructors. Naturally, such operators are never const themselves.

20.2.8   Implicit Conversions

Built-in pointers are subject to several implicit conversions:
- Conversion to void*
- Conversion to a pointer to a base subobject of the object pointed to
- Conversion to bool (false if the pointer is null, true otherwise)

We may want to emulate these in our CountingPtr template, but doing so is not trivial, as we shall see. In addition, some programmers like their smart pointers to have a conversion to a corresponding built-in pointer type (for example, some like CountingPtr<int const> to be convertible to int const*).

Unfortunately, enabling implicit conversions to built-in pointer types creates a loophole in the assumption that *all* the pointers to a reference-counted object are CountingPtrs. We therefore choose not to provide such a conversion. Therefore, a CountingPtr<X> cannot implicitly be converted to void* or to X*.

Other drawbacks to implicit conversions to built-in pointer types include (assume cp is a counting pointer):
- delete cp; and ::delete cp; become valid
- All sorts of meaningless pointer arithmetic goes undiagnosed (for example, cp[n], cp2 - cp1, and so forth)

On the other hand, implicit conversions to other CountingPtr specializations can make perfect sense. For example, we can imagine an implicit conversion to CountingPtr<void> (the latter can be a useful opaque pointer type, just like void*). There is a limitation, however: An invasive counter policy cannot accommodate such a conversion because the void type doesn't contain a counter. Similarly, a base class may not be compatible with an invasive counter policy either.

Nonetheless, we can add such implicit conversions to our CountingPtr template. Instantiation errors occur when attempting conversions that are not compatible with a given counter policy. The implicit conversions might look as follows:

```cpp
template<typename T,
         typename CounterPolicy = SimpleReferenceCount,
         typename ObjectPolicy = StandardObjectPolicy>
class CountingPtr : private CounterPolicy, private ObjectPolicy {
  private:
    // Shortcuts:
    typedef CounterPolicy CP;
    typedef ObjectPolicy  OP;

    ...

  public:
    // add a converting constructor and make sure it can access
    // the private components of other instantiations:
    template<typename T2, typename CP2, typename OP2>
    friend class CountingPtr;

    template<typename S>      // S could be void or a base of T
    CountingPtr(CountingPtr<S, OP, CP> const& cp)
      : OP((OP const&)cp),
        CP((CP const&)cp),
        object_pointed_to(cp.object_pointed_to) {
        if (cp.object_pointed_to != NULL) {
            CP::increment(cp.object_pointed_to);
        }
    }
};
```

Note that in this case a converting constructor more easily enabled the desired implicit conversions than a conversion operator. In particular, we must make sure that the reference count is correctly copied.

The conversion to bool may seem straightforward. We can just add a user-defined conversion operator to CountingPtr:

```
template<typename T,
         typename CounterPolicy = SimpleReferenceCount,
         typename ObjectPolicy = StandardObjectPolicy>
class CountingPtr : private CounterPolicy, private ObjectPolicy {
  ...
  public:
    operator bool() const {
        return this->object_pointed_to != (T*)0;
    }
};
```

This works, but it also allows surprising and unintentional operations on `CountingPtr`s. For example, with this conversion in place, we can add two `CountingPtr`s! This is sufficiently serious that we prefer not to provide that operator.

The conversion to `bool` is mostly useful to support constructs of the form

```
if (cp) ...
```

or

```
while (!cp) ...
```

Therefore, this problem has traditionally been worked around by providing a conversion to `void*` (which in turn is implicitly converted to `bool` in just the right places).[4] This approach has its own drawbacks in general, but it has them especially for a smart pointer for which we already decided not to provide an implicit conversion to `void*`.

A simple (but often overlooked) solution to this problem is to define a conversion to a pointer-to-member type instead of to a built-in type. Indeed, pointer-to-member types also support implicit conversion to `bool`, but unlike regular pointers they're not valid types for operator `delete` or for pointer arithmetic. The following addition to our `CountingPtr` template illustrates how to apply this technique:

```
template<typename T,
         typename CounterPolicy = SimpleReferenceCount,
         typename ObjectPolicy = StandardObjectPolicy>
class CountingPtr : private CounterPolicy, private ObjectPolicy {
  ...
  private:
    struct BoolConversionSupport {
        int dummy;
    };
  public:
```

---

[4] For example, this is done in the standard C++ stream classes.

```
    operator int BoolConversionSupport::*() const {
        return this->object_pointed_to
                    ? &BoolConversionSupport::dummy
                    : 0;
    }
  ...
};
```

Note that this does *not* increase the size of a `CountingPtr` because no data members are added. By using a private nested class we avoid potential conflicts with client code.

20.2.9   Comparisons

We conclude our discussion of counting pointers with the development of various comparison operators for such pointers. Built-in pointers support both equality operators (== and !=) and ordering operators (<, <=, and so forth).

For built-in pointers, ordering operators are guaranteed to work only on two pointers that point to the same array, but this is not a useful scenario for counting pointers. Counting pointers always point to a single object or to the head of an array. Thus, we don't discuss these operators in the text that follows. (However, the operators could be implemented for `CountingPtr` along the same lines as the equality operators if an ordering was needed among `CountingPtrs`.)

Here are the details of operator == (operator != is similar):

```
template<typename T,
         typename CounterPolicy = SimpleReferenceCount,
         typename ObjectPolicy = StandardObjectPolicy>
class CountingPtr : private CounterPolicy, private ObjectPolicy {
    ...
  public:
    friend bool operator==(CountingPtr<T,CP,OP> const& cp,
                           T const* p) {
        return cp.operator->() == p;
    }
    friend bool operator==(T const* p,
                           CountingPtr<T,CP,OP> const& cp) {
        return p == cp.operator->();
    }
};

template <typename T1, typename T2,
          typename CP, typename OP>
```

```
inline
bool operator== (CountingPtr<T1,CP,OP> const& cp1,
                 CountingPtr<T2,CP,OP> const& cp2)
{
    return cp1.operator->() == cp2.operator->();
}
```

The out-of-class operator is a template, which allows us to compare counting pointers to different types. Its implementation allows us to demonstrate that it *is* possible to extract the built-in pointer encapsulated by `CountingPtr`. The explicit `operator->` invocation that this requires is unusual enough to draw our attention that something potentially unsafe is going on.

Two other operators are provided as nontemplate operators. Because these operators still must depend on template parameters, they must be implemented as in-class friend definitions. Because they are nontemplates, the ordinary implicit conversions apply to their arguments. This includes the implicit conversion of zero to a null pointer value.

20.3   Afternotes

Smart pointer templates are probably the second-most obvious application of templates after container templates; however, the details are far from obvious, as this chapter illustrates. Indeed, many authors cover the topic in some detail. Good material supplementing our discussion can be found in [*MeyersMoreEffective*], which offers a more basic discussion, and in [*AlexandrescuDesign*], which describes a complete, policy-based design of a family of smart pointers.

The C++ standard library contains a smart pointer template `auto_ptr`. It is intended for the same use as our `Holder/Trule` pair of templates, but avoids the use of a second template by exploiting a controversial piece of the C++ overloading rules in the context of variable initialization.[5]

Other smart pointers were proposed for inclusion in the C++ standard library, but the C++ standardization committee decided not to support them.

The Boost project offers a library containing a variety of smart pointer classes to meet a variety of needs (see [*BoostSmartPtr*]).

---

[5] An explanation of the mechanisms involved is well beyond the scope of this text (and not really related to templates). The controversy arises because one of the mechanisms on which `auto_ptr` relies is considered by some to be a defect in the C++ standard. See [*JosuttisAutoPtr*] for additional discussion on this topic.

Chapter 21

Tuples

Throughout this book we often use homogeneous containers and array-like types to illustrate the power of templates. Such homogeneous structures extend the concept of a C/C++ array and are pervasive in most applications. C++ (and C) also has a nonhomogeneous containment facility: the class (or struct). Tuples are class templates that similarly allow us to aggregate objects of differing types. We start with the *duo*—an entity analogous to the standard `std::pair` template—but we also show how it can be nested to assemble an arbitrary number of members, thereby forming trios, quartets, and so forth.[1]

21.1   Duos

A duo is the assembly of two objects into a single type. This is similar to the `std::pair` class template in the standard library, but because we will add slightly different functionality to this very basic utility, we opted for a name other than `pair` to avoid confusion with the standard item. At its very simplest, we can define Duo as follows:

```
template <typename T1, typename T2>
struct Duo {
    T1 v1;    // value of first field
    T2 v2;    // value of second field
};
```

This can, for example, be useful as a return type for a function that may return an invalid result:

---

[1] The number is not entirely arbitrary because there exists an implementation-dependent limit on the depth of template nesting.

```
Duo<bool,X> result = foo();
if (result.v1) {
```
      // result is valid; value is in `result.v2`
```
    ...
}
```

Many other applications are possible.

The benefit of Duo as defined here is not insignificant, but it is rather small. After all, it would not be that much work to define a structure with two fields, and doing so allows us to choose meaningful names for these fields. However, we can extend the basic facility in a few ways to add to the convenience. First, we can add constructors:

```
template <typename T1, typename T2>
class Duo {
  public:
    T1 v1;    // value of first field
    T2 v2;    // value of second field

    // constructors
    Duo() : v1(), v2() {
    }
    Duo (T1 const& a, T2 const& b)
     : v1(a), v2(b) {
    }
};
```

Note that we used an initializer list for the default constructor so that the members get zero initialized for built-in types (see Section 5.5 on page 56).

To avoid the need for explicit type parameters, we can further add a function so that the field types can be deduced:

```
template <typename T1, typename T2>
inline
Duo<T1,T2> make_duo (T1 const& a, T2 const& b)
{
    return Duo<T1,T2>(a,b);
}
```

Now the creation and initialization of a Duo becomes more convenient. Instead of

```
Duo<bool,int> result;
result.v1 = true;
result.v2 = 42;
return result;
```

we can write

```
return make_duo(true,42);
```

Good C++ compilers can optimize this well enough so that this generates code equivalent to

```
return Duo<bool,int>(true,42);
```

Another refinement is to provide access to the field types, so that adapter templates can be built on top of Duo:

```
template <typename T1, typename T2>
class Duo {
  public:
    typedef T1 Type1;    // type of first field
    typedef T2 Type2;    // type of second field
    enum { N = 2 };      // number of fields

    T1 v1;               // value of first field
    T2 v2;               // value of second field

    // constructors
    Duo() : v1(), v2() {
    }
    Duo (T1 const& a, T2 const& b)
      : v1(a), v2(b) {
    }
};
```

At this stage we're rather close to the implementation of std::pair with the following differences:

- We use different names.
- We provide a member N for the number of fields.
- We have no member template initialization to allow implicit type conversions during construction.
- We don't provide comparison operators.

A more powerful and cleaner implementation might look as follows:

```
// tuples/duo1.hpp

#ifndef DUO_HPP
#define DUO_HPP

template <typename T1, typename T2>
class Duo {
  public:
```

```cpp
    typedef T1 Type1;   // type of first field
    typedef T2 Type2;   // type of second field
    enum { N = 2 };     // number of fields

  private:
    T1 value1;          // value of first field
    T2 value2;          // value of second field

  public:
    // constructors
    Duo() : value1(), value2() {
    }
    Duo (T1 const & a, T2 const & b)
     : value1(a), value2(b) {
    }

    // for implicit type conversion during construction
    template <typename U1, typename U2>
    Duo (Duo<U1,U2> const & d)
     : value1(d.v1()), value2(d.v2()) {
    }

    // for implicit type conversion during assignments
    template <typename U1, typename U2>
    Duo<T1, T2>& operator = (Duo<U1,U2> const & d) {
        value1 = d.value1;
        value2 = d.value2;
        return *this;
    }

    // field access
    T1& v1() {
        return value1;
    }
    T1 const& v1() const {
        return value1;
    }
```

```cpp
    T2& v2() {
        return value2;
    }
    T2 const& v2() const {
        return value2;
    }
};

// comparison operators (allow mixed types):
template <typename T1, typename T2,
          typename U1, typename U2>
inline
bool operator == (Duo<T1,T2> const& d1, Duo<U1,U2> const& d2)
{
    return d1.v1()==d2.v1() && d1.v2()==d2.v2();
}

template <typename T1, typename T2,
          typename U1, typename U2>
inline
bool operator != (Duo<T1,T2> const& d1, Duo<U1,U2> const& d2)
{
    return !(d1==d2);
}

// convenience function for creation and initialization
template <typename T1, typename T2>
inline
Duo<T1,T2> make_duo (T1 const & a, T2 const & b)
{
    return Duo<T1,T2>(a,b);
}

#endif // DUO_HPP
```

We made the following changes:

- We made the data members private and added access functions.
- With the explicit initialization of both members in the default constructor

```
template <typename T1, typename T2>
class Duo {
    ...
    Duo() : value1(), value2() {
    }
    ...
}
```

  we made sure that values of built-in types are zero initialized (see Section 5.5 on page 56).
- We provided member templates so that construction and initialization are possible with mixed types.
- We provided comparison operators == and !=. Note that we introduced separate sets of template parameters for both sides of a comparison to allow for comparisons of mixed types.

All the member templates are used to enable mixed type operations. That is, we can initialize, assign, and compare a Duo for which an implicit type conversion is necessary to perform the task. For example:

```
// tuples/duo1.cpp

#include "duo1.hpp"

Duo<float,int> foo ()
{
    return make_duo(42,42);
}

int main()
{
    if (foo() == make_duo(42,42.0)) {
        ...
    }
}
```

In this program, in `foo()` there is a conversion from the return type of `make_duo()`, `Duo<int,int>` to the return type of `foo()`, `Duo<float,int>`. Similarly, the return value of `foo()` is compared with the return value of `make_duo(42, 42.0)`, which is a `Duo<int,double>`.

It would not be difficult to add `Trio` and other templates to collect larger numbers of values. However, a more structured alternative can be obtained by nesting Duo objects. This idea is developed in the following sections.

21.2   Recursive Duos

Consider the following object definition:

```
Duo<int, Duo<char, Duo<bool, double> > > q4;
```

The type of q4 is a so-called *recursive duo*. It is a type instantiated from the Duo template, and the second type argument is itself a Duo as well. We could also use recursion of the first parameter, but in the remainder of this discussion, *recursive duo* refers only to Duos with a second template argument that is instantiated from the Duo template.

21.2.1   Number of Fields

It's relatively straightforward to count that q4 collects four values of types `int`, `char`, `bool`, and `double` respectively. To facilitate the formal counting of the number of fields, we can further partially specialize the Duo template:

```
// tuples/duo2.hpp

template <typename A, typename B, typename C>
class Duo<A, Duo<B,C> > {
  public:
    typedef A        T1;           // type of first field
    typedef Duo<B,C> T2;           // type of second field
    enum { N = Duo<B,C>::N + 1 };  // number of fields

  private:
    T1 value1;                     // value of first field
    T2 value2;                     // value of second field

  public:
    // the other public members are unchanged

    ...
};
```

For completeness, let's provide a partial specialization of Duo so that it can degenerate into a nonhomogeneous container holding just one field:

```
// tuples/duo6.hpp
```

// partial specialization for Duo<> *with only one field*
```cpp
template <typename A>
struct Duo<A,void> {
  public:
    typedef A     T1;    // type of first field
    typedef void T2;    // type of second field
    enum { N = 1 };     // number of fields

  private:
    T1 value1;          // value of first field

  public:
    // constructors
    Duo() : value1() {
    }
    Duo (T1 const & a)
     : value1(a) {
    }

    // field access
    T1& v1() {
        return value1;
    }
    T1 const& v1() const {
        return value1;
    }

    void v2() {
    }
    void v2() const {
    }
    ...
};
```

Note that the v2() members aren't really meaningful in the partial specialization, but occasionally it is useful to have them for orthogonality.

21.2.2 Type of Fields

A recursive duo is not really handy compared with, say, a Trio or Quartet class that we could
write. For example, to access the third value of the q4 object in the previous code, we'd have to use
an expression like

```
q4.v2().v2().v1()
```

This is hardly compact or intuitive. Fortunately, it is possible to write recursive templates that efficiently retrieve the values and types of fields in a recursive duo.

Let's first look at the code for a type function DuoT to retrieve the *n*th type of a recursive duo
(you can find the code in tuples/duo3.hpp). The generic definition

```
// primary template for type of Nth field of (duo) T
template <int N, typename T>
class DuoT {
  public:
    typedef void ResultT;      // in general, the result type is void
};
```

ensures that the result type is void for non-Duos. Fairly simple partial specializations take care of
retrieving the types from nonrecursive Duos:

```
// specialization for 1st field of a plain duo
template <typename A, typename B>
class DuoT <1, Duo<A,B> > {
  public:
    typedef A ResultT;
};


// specialization for 2nd field of a plain duo
template <typename A, typename B>
class DuoT<2, Duo<A,B> > {
  public:
    typedef B ResultT;
};
```

With this in place, the *n*th type of a recursive duo, in general, is the (*n*−1)th type of the second field:

```
// specialization for Nth field of a recursive duo
template <int N, typename A, typename B, typename C>
class DuoT<N, Duo<A, Duo<B,C> > > {
  public:
    typedef typename DuoT<N-1, Duo<B,C> >::ResultT ResultT;
};
```

However, the request for the first type of a recursive duo ends the recursion:

```
// specialization for 1st field of a recursive duo
template <typename A, typename B, typename C>
class DuoT<1, Duo<A, Duo<B,C> > > {
  public:
    typedef A ResultT;
};
```

Note that the case for the second type of the recursive duo also needs a partial specialization to avoid ambiguity with the nonrecursive case:

```
// specialization for 2nd field of a recursive duo
template<typename A, typename B, typename C>
class DuoT<2, Duo<A, Duo<B, C> > > {
  public:
    typedef B ResultT;
};
```

This is certainly not the only way to implement the DuoT template. The interested reader could, for example, try to leverage the IfThenElse template (see Section 15.2.4 on page 272) to achieve an equivalent effect.

21.2.3   Value of Fields

Extracting the nth value (as an lvalue) from a recursive duo is only slightly more complex than extracting the corresponding type. The interface we intend to achieve is the form val<N>(*duo*). However, we need a helper class template DuoValue to implement it because only class templates can be partially specialized, and partial specialization allows us to recur to the desired value more efficiently. Here is how the val() functions delegate their task:

```
// tuples/duo5.hpp

#include "typeop.hpp"


// return Nth value of variable duo
template <int N, typename A, typename B>
inline
typename TypeOp<typename DuoT<N, Duo<A, B> >::ResultT>::RefT
val(Duo<A, B>& d)
{
    return DuoValue<N, Duo<A, B> >::get(d);
}
```

```
// return Nth value of constant duo
template <int N, typename A, typename B>
inline
typename TypeOp<typename DuoT<N, Duo<A, B> >::ResultT>::RefConstT
val(Duo<A, B> const& d)
{
    return DuoValue<N, Duo<A, B> >::get(d);
}
```

The DuoT template already proves itself useful to declare the return type of the val() functions. We also used the TypeOp type function developed in Section 15.2.3 on page 269 to create a reference type reliably, even if the field type is itself already a reference.

The following complete implementation of DuoValue clearly parallels our previous discussion of DuoT (the role of each element of the implementation is discussed next):

```
// tuples/duo4.hpp

#include "typeop.hpp"

// primary template for value of Nth field of (duo) T
template <int N, typename T>
class DuoValue {
  public:
    static void get(T&) {          // in general, we have no value
    }
    static void get(T const&) {
    }
};

// specialization for 1st field of a plain duo
template <typename A, typename B>
class DuoValue<1, Duo<A, B> > {
  public:
    static A& get(Duo<A, B> &d) {
        return d.v1();
    }
    static A const& get(Duo<A, B> const &d) {
        return d.v1();
    }
};
```

```
// specialization for 2nd field of a plain duo
template <typename A, typename B>
class DuoValue<2, Duo<A, B> > {
  public:
    static B& get(Duo<A, B> &d) {
        return d.v2();
    }
    static B const& get(Duo<A, B> const &d) {
        return d.v2();
    }
};
```

```
// specialization for Nth field of recursive duo
template <int N, typename A, typename B, typename C>
struct DuoValue<N, Duo<A, Duo<B,C> > > {
    static
    typename TypeOp<typename DuoT<N-1, Duo<B,C> >::ResultT>::RefT
    get(Duo<A, Duo<B,C> > &d) {
        return DuoValue<N-1, Duo<B,C> >::get(d.v2());
    }

    static typename TypeOp<typename DuoT<N-1, Duo<B,C>
                          >::ResultT>::RefConstT
    get(Duo<A, Duo<B,C> > const &d) {
        return DuoValue<N-1, Duo<B,C> >::get(d.v2());
    }
};
```

```
// specialization for 1st field of recursive duo
template <typename A, typename B, typename C>
class DuoValue<1, Duo<A, Duo<B,C> > > {
  public:
    static A& get(Duo<A, Duo<B,C> > &d) {
        return d.v1();
    }
    static A const& get(Duo<A, Duo<B,C> > const &d) {
        return d.v1();
    }
};
```

```
// specialization for 2nd field of recursive duo
template <typename A, typename B, typename C>
class DuoValue<2, Duo<A, Duo<B,C> > > {
  public:
    static B& get(Duo<A, Duo<B,C> > &d) {
        return d.v2().v1();
    }
    static B const& get(Duo<A, Duo<B,C> > const &d) {
        return d.v2().v1();
    }
};
```

As with DuoT, we provide a generic definition of DuoValue that maps to functions that return void. Because function templates can return void expressions, this makes the application of val() to nonduos or out-of-range values of N valid (although useless, but it can simplify the implementation of certain templates):

```
// primary template for value of Nth field of (duo) T
template <int N, typename T>
class DuoValue {
  public:
    static void get(T&) {          // in general, we have no value
    }
    static void get(T const&) {
    }
};
```

As before, we first specialize for nonrecursive duos:

```
// specialization for 1st field of a plain duo
template <typename A, typename B>
class DuoValue<1, Duo<A, B> > {
  public:
    static A& get(Duo<A, B> &d) {
        return d.v1();
    }
    static A const& get(Duo<A, B> const& d) {
        return d.v1();
    }
};
...
```

Then we specialize for recursive duos (again DuoT comes in handy):

```
template <int N, typename A, typename B, typename C>
class DuoValue<N, Duo<A, Duo<B, C> > > {
  public:
    static
    typename TypeOp<typename DuoT<N-1, Duo<B, C> >::ResultT>::RefT
    get(Duo<A, Duo<B, C> > &d) {
        return DuoValue<N-1, Duo<B, C> >::get(d.v2());
    }
    ...
};

// specialization for 1st field of recursive duo
template <typename A, typename B, typename C>
class DuoValue<1, Duo<A, Duo<B, C> > > {
  public:
    static A& get(Duo<A, Duo<B, C> > &d) {
        return d.v1();
    }
    ...
};

// specialization for 2nd field of recursive duo
template <typename A, typename B, typename C>
class DuoValue<2, Duo<A, Duo<B, C> > > {
  public:
    static B& get(Duo<A, Duo<B, C> > &d) {
        return d.v2().v1();
    }
    ...
};
```

The following program shows how to use duos:

```
// tuples/duo5.cpp

#include "duo1.hpp"
#include "duo2.hpp"
#include "duo3.hpp"
#include "duo4.hpp"
#include "duo5.hpp"
#include <iostream>

int main()
{
    // create and use simple duo
    Duo<bool,int> d;
    std::cout << d.v1() << std::endl;
    std::cout << val<1>(d) << std::endl;

    // create and use triple
    Duo<bool,Duo<int,float> > t;

    val<1>(t) = true;
    val<2>(t) = 42;
    val<3>(t) = 0.2;

    std::cout << val<1>(t) << std::endl;
    std::cout << val<2>(t) << std::endl;
    std::cout << val<3>(t) << std::endl;
}
```

The call of

```
    val<3>(t)
```

ends up in the call of

```
    t.v2().v2()
```

Because the recursion is unwrapped at compile time during the template instantiation process and the functions are simple inline accessors, these facilities end up being quite efficient. A good compiler reduces this to the same code as a simple structure field access.

However, it is still cumbersome to declare and construct recursive Duo objects. The next section addresses this challenge.

21.3   Tuple Construction

The nested structure of recursive duos makes it convenient to apply template metaprogramming techniques to them. However, for a human programmer it is more pleasing to have a flat interface to this structure. To obtain this, we can define a recursive `Tuple` template with many parameters and have it be a derivation from a recursive duo type of appropriate size. We show the code here for tuples up to five fields, but it is not significantly harder to provide for a dozen fields or so. You can find the code in `tuples/tuple1.hpp`.

To allow for tuples of varying sizes, we have unused type parameters that default to a null type, `NullT`, which we define as a placeholder for that purpose. We use `NullT` rather than `void` because we will create parameters of that type (`void` cannot be a parameter type):

```
// type that represents unused type parameters
class NullT {
};
```

`Tuple` is defined as a template that derives from a `Duo` having one more type parameter with `NullT` defined:

```
// in general, Tuple<> is built from Tuple<> with one more NullT
template<typename P1,
         typename P2 = NullT,
         typename P3 = NullT,
         typename P4 = NullT,
         typename P5 = NullT>
class Tuple
  : public Duo<P1, typename Tuple<P2,P3,P4,P5,NullT>::BaseT> {
  public:
    typedef Duo<P1, typename Tuple<P2,P3,P4,P5,NullT>::BaseT>
            BaseT;

    // constructors:
    Tuple() {}
    Tuple(TypeOp<P1>::RefConstT a1,
        TypeOp<P2>::RefConstT a2,
        TypeOp<P3>::RefConstT a3 = NullT(),
        TypeOp<P4>::RefConstT a4 = NullT(),
        TypeOp<P5>::RefConstT a5 = NullT())
      : BaseT(a1, Tuple<P2,P3,P4,P5,NullT>(a2,a3,a4,a5)) {
    }
};
```

Note the shifting pattern when passing the parameters to the recursive step. Because we derive from a base type that defines member types T1 and T2, we used template parameter names of the form P*n* instead of the usual T*n*.[2]

We need a partial specialization to end this recursion with the derivation from a nonrecursive duo:

```
// specialization to end deriving recursion
template <typename P1, typename P2>
class Tuple<P1,P2,NullT,NullT,NullT> : public Duo<P1,P2> {
  public:
    typedef Duo<P1,P2> BaseT;
    Tuple() {}
    Tuple(TypeOp<P1>::RefConstT a1,
          TypeOp<P2>::RefConstT a2,
          TypeOp<NullT>::RefConstT = NullT(),
          TypeOp<NullT>::RefConstT = NullT(),
          TypeOp<NullT>::RefConstT = NullT())
      : BaseT(a1, a2) {
    }
};
```

A declaration such as

```
Tuple<bool,int,float,double> t4(true,42,13,1.95583);
```

ends up in the hierarchy shown in Figure 21.1.

The other specialization takes care of the case when the tuple is really a singleton:

```
// specialization for singletons
template <typename P1>
class Tuple<P1,NullT,NullT,NullT,NullT> : public Duo<P1,void> {
  public:
    typedef Duo<P1,void> BaseT;
    Tuple() {}
    Tuple(TypeOp<P1>::RefConstT a1,
          TypeOp<NullT>::RefConstT = NullT(),
          TypeOp<NullT>::RefConstT = NullT(),
```

---

[2] A very curious lookup rule in C++ prefers names inherited from nondependent base classes over template parameter names. This should not be a problem in this case because the base class is dependent, but some compilers still get this wrong at the time of this writing.

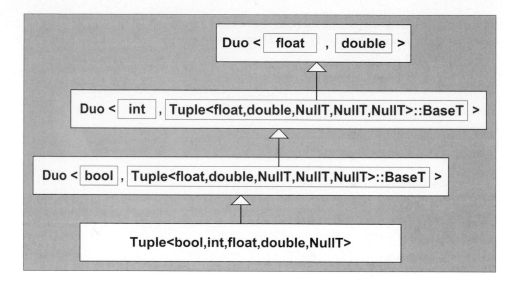

Figure 21.1. Type of Tuple<bool,int,float,double>

```
        TypeOp<NullT>::RefConstT = NullT(),
        TypeOp<NullT>::RefConstT = NullT())
    : BaseT(a1) {
    }
};
```

Finally, it is natural to desire functions like make_duo() in Section 21.1 on page 396 to deduce the template parameters automatically. Unfortunately, a different function template declaration is needed for each tuple size that must be supported because function templates cannot have default template arguments,[3] nor are their default function call arguments considered in the template parameter deduction process. The functions are defined as follows:

```
// convenience function for 1 argument
template <typename T1>
inline
Tuple<T1> make_tuple(T1 const &a1)
{
    return Tuple<T1>(a1);
}
```

---

[3] A revision of the C++ standard will most likely remove this limitation (see Section 13.3 on page 207).

```
// convenience function for 2 arguments
template <typename T1, typename T2>
inline
Tuple<T1,T2> make_tuple(T1 const &a1, T2 const &a2)
{
    return Tuple<T1,T2>(a1,a2);
}

// convenience function for 3 arguments
template <typename T1, typename T2, typename T3>
inline
Tuple<T1,T2,T3> make_tuple(T1 const &a1, T2 const &a2,
                           T3 const &a3)
{
    return Tuple<T1,T2,T3>(a1,a2,a3);
}

// convenience function for 4 arguments
template <typename T1, typename T2, typename T3, typename T4>
inline
Tuple<T1,T2,T3,T4> make_tuple(T1 const &a1, T2 const &a2,
                              T3 const &a3, T4 const &a4)
{
    return Tuple<T1,T2,T3,T4>(a1,a2,a3,a4);
}

// convenience function for 5 arguments
template <typename T1, typename T2, typename T3,
          typename T4, typename T5>
inline
Tuple<T1,T2,T3,T4,T5> make_tuple(T1 const &a1, T2 const &a2,
                                 T3 const &a3, T4 const &a4,
                                 T5 const &a5)
{
    return Tuple<T1,T2,T3,T4,T5>(a1,a2,a3,a4,a5);
}
```

The following program shows how to use Tuples:

```
// tuples/tuple1.cpp

#include "tuple1.hpp"
#include <iostream>

int main()
{
    // create and use tuple with only one field
    Tuple<int> t1;
    val<1>(t1) += 42;
    std::cout << t1.v1() << std::endl;

    // create and use duo
    Tuple<bool,int> t2;
    std::cout << val<1>(t2) << ", ";
    std::cout << t2.v1() << std::endl;

    // create and use triple
    Tuple<bool,int,double> t3;

    val<1>(t3) = true;
    val<2>(t3) = 42;
    val<3>(t3) = 0.2;

    std::cout << val<1>(t3) << ", ";
    std::cout << val<2>(t3) << ", ";
    std::cout << val<3>(t3) << std::endl;

    t3 = make_tuple(false, 23, 13.13);

    std::cout << val<1>(t3) << ", ";
    std::cout << val<2>(t3) << ", ";
    std::cout << val<3>(t3) << std::endl;

    // create and use quadruple
    Tuple<bool,int,float,double> t4(true,42,13,1.95583);
    std::cout << val<4>(t4) << std::endl;
    std::cout << t4.v2().v2().v2() << std::endl;
}
```

An industrial-strength implementation would complete the code we presented so far with various extensions. For example, we could define assignment operator templates to facilitate tuple conversions; otherwise, the types have to match exactly:

```
Tuple<bool,int,float> t3;

t3 = make_tuple(false, 23, 13.13);   // ERROR: 13.13 has type double
```

21.4   Afternotes

Tuple construction is one of those template applications that appears to have been independently attempted by many programmers. The details of these attempts vary widely, but many are based on the idea of a recursive pair structure (such as our recursive duos). One interesting alternative was developed by Andrei Alexandrescu in [*AlexandrescuDesign*]. He cleanly separates the list of types from the list of fields in the tuple. This leads to the concept of a *type list* that has various applications of its own (one of which is the construction of a tuple with the encapsulated types).

Section 13.13 on page 222 discusses the concept of *template list parameters*, which are a language extension that makes the implementation of tuples almost trivial.

Chapter 22

Function Objects and Callbacks

A *function object* (also called a *functor*) is any object that can be called using the *function call syntax*. In the C programming language, three kinds of entities can lead to syntax that looks like a function call: functions, function-like macros, and pointers to functions. Because functions and macros are not objects, this implies that only pointers to functions are available as functors in C. In C++, additional possibilities are added: The *function call operator* can be overloaded for class types, a concept of references to functions exists, and member functions and pointer-to-member functions have a call syntax of their own. Not all of these concepts are equally useful, but the combination of the concept of a functor with the compile-time parameterization offered by templates leads to powerful programming techniques.

Besides developing functor types, this chapter also delves into some usage idioms for functors. Nearly all uses end up being a form of *callback*: The client of a library wants that library to call back some function of the client code. The classic example is a sorting routine that needs a function to compare two elements in the set being sorted. The comparison routine is passed as a functor in this case. Traditionally, the term *callback* has been reserved for functors that are passed as function call arguments (as opposed to, for example, template arguments), and we maintain this tradition.

The terms *function object* and *functor* are unfortunately a little fuzzy in the sense that different members of the C++ programming community may give slightly different meanings to these terms. A common variation of the definition we have given is to include only objects of class types in the functor or function object concept; function pointers are then excluded. In addition, it is not uncommon to read or hear discussions referring to the class *type* of a function object as a "function object." In other words, the phrase "class of function objects so and so ..." is shortened to "function objects so and so ...." Although we sometimes handle this terminology somewhat sloppily in our own daily work, we have made it a point to stick to our initial definitions in this chapter.

Before digging into the use of templates to implement useful functors, we discuss some properties of function calls that motivate some of the advantages of template-based functors.

22.1   Direct, Indirect, and Inline Calls

Typically, when a C or C++ compiler encounters the definition of a noninline function, it generates and stores machine code for that function in an object file. It also creates a name associated with the machine code; in C, this name is typically the function name itself, but in C++ the name is usually extended with an encoding of the parameter types to allow for unique names even when a function is overloaded (the resulting name is usually called a *mangled name*, although the term *decorated name* is also used). Similarly, when the compiler encounters a call site like

```
f();
```

it generates machine code for a call to a function of that type. For most machine languages, the call instruction itself necessitates the starting address of the routine. This address can be part of the instruction (in which case the instruction is called a *direct call*), or it may reside somewhere in memory or in a machine register (*indirect call*). Almost all modern computer architectures provide both types of routine calling instructions, but (for reasons that are beyond the scope of this book) direct calls are executed more efficiently than indirect calls. In fact, as computer architectures get more sophisticated, it appears that the performance gap between direct calls and indirect calls increases. Hence, compilers generally attempt to generate a direct call instruction when possible.

In general, a compiler does not know at which address a function is located (the function could, for example, be in another translation unit). However, if the compiler knows the name of the function, it generates a direct call instruction with a dummy address. In addition, it generates an entry in the generated object file directing the linker to update that instruction to point to the address of a function with the given name. Because the linker sees the object files created from all the translation units, it knows the call sites as well as the definition sites and hence is able to patch up all the direct call sites.[1]

Unfortunately, when the name of the function is not available, an indirect call must be used. This is usually the case for calls through pointers to functions:

```
void foo (void (*pf)())
{
    pf();   // indirect call through pointer to function pf
}
```

In this example it is, in general, not possible for a compiler to know to which function the parameter `pf` points (after all, it is most likely different for a different invocation of `foo()`). Hence, the technique of having the linker match names does not work. The call destination is not known until the code is actually executed.

Although a modern computer can often execute a direct call instruction about as quickly as other common instructions (for example, an instruction to add two integers), function calls can still be a serious performance impediment. The following example shows this:

---

[1] The linker performs a similar role for accesses to namespace scope variables, for example.

```cpp
int f1(int const & r)
{
    return ++(int&)r;    // not reasonable, but legal
}

int f2(int const & r)
{
    return r;
}

int f3()
{
    return 42;
}

int foo()
{
    int param = 0;
    int answer = 0;
    answer = f1(param);
    f2(param);
    f3();
    return answer + param;
}
```

Function f1() takes a const int reference argument. Ordinarily, this means that the function does not modify the object that is passed by reference. However, if the object passed in is a modifiable value, a C++ program can legally cast away the const property and change the value of the object anyway. (You could argue that this is not reasonable; however, it is standard C++.) Function f1() does exactly this. Because of this possibility, a compiler that optimizes generated code on a per-function basis (and most compilers do) has to assume that every function that takes references or pointers to objects may modify those objects. Note that in general a compiler sees only the *declaration* of a function because the *definition* (the *implementation*) is in another translation unit.

In the code example, most compilers therefore assume that f2() can modify param too (even though it does not). In fact, the compiler cannot even assume that f3() does not modify the local variable param. Indeed, the functions f1() and f2() had an opportunity to store the address of param in a globally accessible pointer. From the limited perspective of the compiler, it is therefore not impossible for f3() to use such a globally accessible pointer to modify param. The net effect is that ordinary function calls confuse most compilers regarding what happened to various objects, forcing them often to store their intermediate values in main memory instead of keeping them in fast registers and preventing many optimizations that involve the movement of machine code (the function call often forms a *barrier* for code motion).

Advanced C++ compilation systems exist that are capable of tracking many instances of such potential *aliasing* (in the scope of f1(), the expression r is an alias for the object named param in the scope of foo()). However, this ability comes at a price: compilation speed, resource usage, and code reliability. Projects that otherwise build in minutes sometimes take hours or even days to be compiled (provided the necessary gigabytes of memory are available to the compiler). Furthermore, such compilation systems are typically much more complex and are therefore more often prone to generating wrong code. Even when a superoptimizing compiler generates correct code, the source code may contain unintended violations of subtle C and C++ aliasing rules.[2] Some of these violations are fairly harmless with ordinary optimizers, but superoptimizers may turn them into true bugs.

However, ordinary optimizers can be helped tremendously by the process of inlining. Suppose f1(), f2(), and f3() are declared inline. The compiler can then transform the code of foo() to something essentially equivalent to

```
int foo'()
{
    int param = 0;
    int answer = 0;
    answer = ++(int&)param;
    return answer + param;
}
```

which a very ordinary optimizer can turn into

```
int foo''()
{
    return 2;
}
```

This illustrates that the benefit of inlining lies not only in the avoidance of executing machine code for a calling sequence but also (and often more important) in making visible to an optimizer what happens to the variables passed to the function.

What does this have to do with templates? Well, as we see later, it is sometimes possible using template-based callbacks to generate code that involves direct or even inline calls when more traditional callbacks would result in indirect calls. The savings in running time can be considerable.

---

[2] For example, accessing an unsigned int through a pointer to a regular (signed) int is such an error.

22.2   Pointers and References to Functions

Consider the following fairly trivial definition of a function foo():

```
extern "C++" void foo() throw()
{
}
```

The type of this function ought to be "function with C++ linkage that takes no arguments, returns no value, and does not throw any exceptions." For historical reasons, the formal definition of the C++ language does not actually make the exception specification part of a function type.[3] However, that may change in the future. It is a good idea to make sure that when you create code in which function types must match, the exception specifications also match. *Name linkage* (usually for "C" and "C++") is properly a part of the type system, but some C++ implementations are a little lax in enforcing it. Specifically, they allow a pointer to a function with C linkage to be assigned to a pointer to a function with C++ linkage and vice versa. This is a consequence of the fact that, on most platforms, calling conventions for C and C++ functions are identical as far as the common subset of parameter and return types is concerned.

In most contexts, the expression foo undergoes an implicit conversion to a pointer to the function foo(). Note that foo itself does not denote the pointer, just as the expression ia after the declaration

```
int ia[10];
```

does not denote a pointer to the array (or to the first element of the array). The implicit conversion from a function (or array) to a pointer is often called *decay*. To illustrate this, we can write the following complete C++ program:

```
// functors/funcptr.cpp

#include <iostream>
#include <typeinfo>

void foo()
{
    std::cout << "foo() called" << std::endl;
}


typedef void FooT();   // FooT is a function type,
                       // the same type as that of function foo()
```

---

[3] The historical origin of this is not clear, and the C++ standard is somewhat inconsistent in this area.

```
int main()
{
    foo();                  // direct call

    // print types of foo and FooT
    std::cout << "Types of foo:  " << typeid(foo).name()
              << '\n';
    std::cout << "Types of FooT: " << typeid(FooT).name()
              << '\n';

    FooT* pf = foo;   // implicit conversion (decay)
    pf();                   // indirect call through pointer
    (*pf)();                // equivalent to pf()

    // print type of pf
    std::cout << "Types of pf:   " << typeid(pf).name()
              << '\n';

    FooT& rf = foo;   // no implicit conversion
    rf();                   // indirect call through reference

    // print type of rf
    std::cout << "Types of rf:   " << typeid(rf).name()
              << '\n';
}
```

This example shows various uses of function types, including some unusual ones.

The example uses the `typeid` operator, which returns a static type `std::type_info`, for which `name()` shows the types of some expressions (see Section 5.6 on page 58). No type decay occurs when `typeid` is applied to a function type.

Here is the output produced by one of our C++ implementations:

```
foo() called
Types of foo:  void ()
Types of FooT: void ()
foo() called
foo() called
Types of pf:   FooT *
foo() called
Types of rf:   void ()
```

As you can see, this implementation keeps typedef names in the string returned by name() (for example, FooT * instead of its expanded form void (*)()), but this is certainly not a language requirement.

This example also shows that references to functions exist as a language concept, but pointers to functions are almost always used instead (and to avoid confusion, it is probably best to keep with this use). Observe that the expression foo is in fact a so-called *lvalue* because it can be bound to a reference to a non-const type. However, it is not possible to modify that lvalue.

Note that the name of a pointer to a function (like pf) or the name of a reference to a function (like rf) can be used in a function call exactly like the name of a function itself. Hence, *a pointer to a function is a functor*—an object that can be used in place of a function name in function call syntax. On the other hand, because a reference is not an object, a reference to a function is not a functor. Recall from our discussion of direct and indirect calls that behind these identical notations can be considerably different performance characteristics.

22.3   Pointer-to-Member Functions

To understand why a distinction is made between pointers to ordinary functions and pointers to member functions, it is useful to study the typical C++ implementation of a call to a member function. Such a call could take the form p->mf() or a close variation of this syntax. Here, p is a pointer to an object or to a subobject. It is passed in some form as a hidden parameter to mf(), where it is known as the this pointer.

The member function mf() may have been defined for the subobject pointed to by p, or it may be inherited by the subobject. For example:

```
class B1 {
  private:
    int b1;
  public:
    void mf1();
};

void B1::mf1()
{
    std::cout << "b1 = " << b1 << std::endl;
}
```

As a member function, mf1() expects to be called for an object of type B1. Thus, this refers to an object of type B1.

Let's add some more code to this:

```
class B2 {
  private:
    int b2;
  public:
    void mf2();
};

void B2::mf2()
{
    std::cout << "b2 = " << b2 << std::endl;
}
```

The member mf2() similarly expects the hidden parameter this to point to a B2 subobject.

Now let's derive a class from both B1 and B2:

```
class D: public B1, public B2 {
  private:
    int d;
};
```

With this declaration, an object of type D can behave as an object of type B1 or an object of type B2. For this to work, a D object contains both a B1 subobject and a B2 subobject. On nearly all 32-bit implementations we know of today, a D object will be organized as shown in Figure 22.1. That is, if the size of the int members is 4 bytes, member b1 has the address of this, member b2 has the address of this plus 4 bytes, and member d has the address of this plus 8 bytes. Note how the B1 subobject shares its origin with the origin of the D subobject, but the B2 subobject does not.

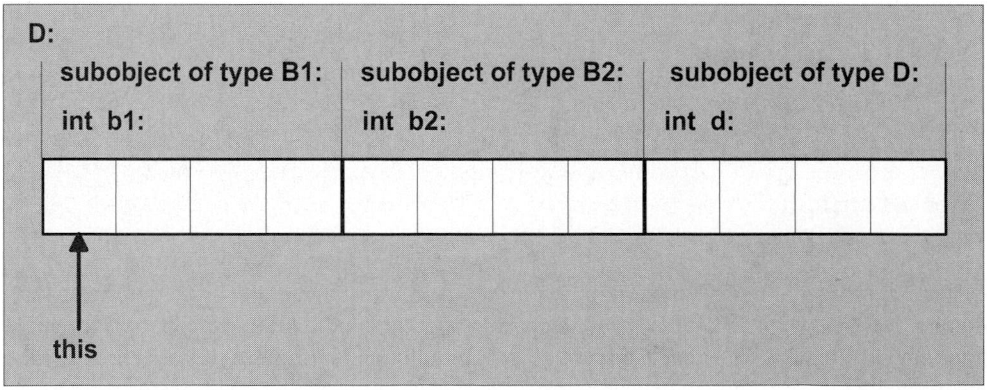

Figure 22.1. Typical organization of type D

Consider now the following elementary member function calls:

```
int main()
{
    D obj;
    obj.mf1();
    obj.mf2();
}
```

The call `obj.mf2()` requires the address of the subobject of type B2 in `obj` to be passed to `mf2()`. Assuming the typical implementation described, this is the address of `obj` plus 4 bytes. It is not at all hard for a C++ compiler to generate code to perform this adjustment. Note that for the call to `mf1()`, this adjustment should not be done because the address of `obj` is also the address of the subobject of type B1 within `obj`.

However, with pointer-to-member functions the compiler does not know what adjustment is needed. To see this, replace the previous `main()` routine with the following:

```
void call_memfun (D obj, void (D::*pmf)())
{
    (obj.*pmf)();
}

int main()
{
    D obj;
    call_memfun(obj, &D::mf1);
    call_memfun(obj, &D::mf2);
}
```

To make the situation even more opaque to a C++ compiler, the `call_memfun()` and `main()` may be placed in different translation units.

The conclusion is that in addition to the address of the function, a pointer to a member function also needs to track the `this` pointer adjustment needed for a particular member function. This adjustment may change when a pointer-to-member function is casted. With our example:

```
void (D::*pmf_a)()  = &D::mf2;                       // adjustment of +4 recorded
void (B2::*pmf_b)() = (void (B2::*)())pmf_a;         // adjustment changed to 0
```

The main purpose of this discussion is to illustrate the intrinsic difference between a pointer to a member function and a pointer to a function. However, the outline is not sufficient when it comes to virtual functions, and in practice many implementations use a three-word structure for pointers to member functions:

1. The address of the member function, or NULL if it is a virtual function
2. The required `this` adjustment
3. A virtual function index

The details are beyond the scope of this book. If you're curious about this topic, a good introduction can be found in Stan Lippman's *Inside the C++ Object Model* (see [*LippmanObjMod*]). There you will also find that pointers to data members are typically not pointers at all, but the offsets needed to get from `this` to a given field (a single word of storage is sufficient for their representation).

Finally, note how "getting to a member function through a pointer-to-member function" is really a binary operation involving not only the *pointer* but also the *object* to which the pointer is applied. Hence, special pointer-to-member dereferencing operators `.*` and `->*` were introduced into the language:

```
(obj.*pmf)(... )        // call member function, to which pmf refers, for obj
(ptr->*pmf)(... )       // call member function, to which pmf refers, for object,
                        // to which ptr refers
```

In contrast, "getting to an ordinary function through a pointer" is a unary operation:

```
(*ptr)()
```

The dereferencing operator can be left out because it is implicit in the function call operator. The previous expression is therefore usually written as

```
ptr()
```

There is no such implicit form for pointers to member functions.[4]

22.4   Class Type Functors

Although pointers to functions are functors directly available in the language, there are many situations in which it is advantageous to use a class type object with an overloaded function call operator. Doing so can lead to added flexibility, added performance, or both.

22.4.1   A First Example of Class Type Functors

Here is a very simple example of a class type functor:

```
// functors/functor1.cpp

#include <iostream>

// class for function objects that return constant value
class ConstantIntFunctor {
  private:
```

---

[4] There is also no implicit decay of a member function name such as `MyType::print` to a pointer to that member. The ampersand is always required (for example, `&MyType::print`). For ordinary functions, the implicit decay of `f` to `&f` is well known.

```cpp
    int value;      // value to return on "function call"
  public:
    // constructor: initialize value to return
    ConstantIntFunctor (int c) : value(c) {
    }

    // "function call"
    int operator() () const {
        return value;
    }
};

// client function that uses the function object
void client (ConstantIntFunctor const& cif)
{
    std::cout << "calling back functor yields " << cif() << '\n';
}

int main()
{
    ConstantIntFunctor seven(7);
    ConstantIntFunctor fortytwo(42);
    client(seven);
    client(fortytwo);
}
```

ConstantIntFunctor is a class type from which functors can be generated. That is, if you create an object with

```cpp
    ConstantIntFunctor seven(7);    // create function object
```

the expression

```cpp
    seven();                                // call operator () for function object
```

is a call of operator () for the object seven rather than a call of function seven(). We achieve the same effect (indirectly) when passing the function objects seven and fortytwo through parameter cif to client().

This example illustrates what is in practice perhaps the most important advantage of class type functors over pointers to functions: the ability to associate some state (data) with the function. This is a fundamental improvement in capabilities for callback mechanisms. We can have multiple "instances" of a function with behavior that is (in a sense) parameterized.

22.4.2   Type of Class Type Functors

There is more to class type functors than the addition of state information, however. In fact, if a class type functor does not encapsulate any state, its behavior is entirely subsumed by its type, and it is sufficient to pass the type as a template argument to customize a library component's behavior.

A classic illustration of this special case includes container classes that maintain their elements in some sorted order. The sorting criterion becomes a template argument, and because it is part of the container's type, accidental mixing of containers with different sorting criteria (for example, in an assignment) is caught by the type system.

The set and map containers of the C++ standard library are parameterized this way. For example, if we define two different sets using the same element type, Person, but different sorting criteria, a comparison of the sets results in a compile-time error:

```
#include <set>

class Person {
  ...
};

class PersonSortCriterion {
  public:
    bool operator() (Person const& p1, Person const& p2) const {
        // returns whether p1 is ''less than'' p2
      ...
    }
};

void foo()
{
    std::set<Person, std::less<Person> > c0, c1; // sort with operator <
    std::set<Person, std::greater<Person> > c2;  // sort with operator >
    std::set<Person, PersonSortCriterion> c3;    // sort with user-
    ...                                          // defined criterion
    c0 = c1;          // OK: identical types
    c1 = c2;          // ERROR: different types
    ...
    if (c1 == c3) {   // ERROR: different types
      ...
    }
}
```

For all three declarations of a `set`, the element type and the sorting criterion are passed as template arguments. The standard function object type template `std::less` is defined to return the result of operator < as a result of a "function call." The following simplified implementation of `std::less` clarifies the idea[5]:

```
namespace std {
    template <typename T>
    class less {
      public:
        bool operator() (T const& x, T const& y) const {
            return x < y;
        }
    };
}
```

The `std::greater` template is similar.

Because all three sorting criteria have different types, the resulting sets also have different types. Therefore, any attempt to assign or to compare two of these sets fails at compile time (the comparison operator requires the same type). This may seem straightforward, but prior to templates, the sorting criterion might have been maintained as a function pointer field of the container. Any mismatch would likely not have been detected until run time (and perhaps not without much frustrating detective work).

22.5 Specifying Functors

Our previous example of the standard `set` class shows only one way to handle the selection of functors. A number of different approaches are discussed in this section.

22.5.1 Functors as Template Type Arguments

One way to pass a functor is to make its type a template argument. A type by itself is not a functor, however, so the client function or class must create a functor object with the given type. This, of course, is possible only for class type functors, and it rules out function pointer types. A function pointer type does not by itself specify any behavior. Along the same lines of thought, this is not an appropriate mechanism to pass a class type functor that encapsulates some state information (because no particular state is encapsulated by the type alone; a specific object of that type is needed).

Here is an outline of a function template that takes a functor class type as a sorting criterion:

---

[5] The exact implementation differs because it is derived from a class `std::binary_function`. See Section 8.2.4 of [*JosuttisStdLib*] for details.

```
template <typename FO>
void my_sort (... )
{
    FO cmp;                     // create function object
    ...
    if (cmp(x,y)) {   // use function object to compare two values
        ...
    }
    ...
}


// call function with functor
my_sort<std::less<... > > (... );
```

With this approach, the selection of the comparison code has become a compile-time affair. And because the comparison can be "inlined," a good optimizing compiler should be able to produce code that is essentially equivalent to replacing the functor calls by direct applications of the resulting operations. To be entirely perfect, an optimizer must also be able to elide the storage used by the `cmp` functor object. In practice, however, only a few compilers are capable of such features.

22.5.2   Functors as Function Call Arguments

Another way to pass functors is to pass them as function call arguments. This allows the caller to construct the function object (possibly using a nontrivial constructor) at run time.

The efficiency argument is essentially similar to that of having just a functor type parameter, except that we must now copy a functor object as it is passed into the routine. This cost is usually low and can in fact be reduced to zero if the functor object has no data members (which is often the case). Indeed, consider this variation of our `my_sort` example:

```
template <typename F>
void my_sort (... , F cmp)
{
    ...
    if (cmp(x,y)) {   // use function object to compare two values
        ...
    }
    ...
}


// call function with functor
my_sort (... , std::less<... >());
```

Within the `my_sort()` function, we are dealing with a copy `cmp` of the value passed in. When this value is an empty class object, there is no state to distinguish a locally constructed functor object from a copy passed in. Therefore, instead of actually passing the "empty functor" as a function call argument, the compiler could just use it for overload resolution and then elide the parameter/argument altogether. Inside the instantiated function, a dummy local object can then serve as the functor.

This almost works, except that the copy constructor of the "empty functor" must also be free of side effects. In practice this means that any functor with a user-defined copy constructor should not be optimized this way.

As written, the advantage of this functor specification technique is that it is also possible to pass an ordinary function pointer as an argument. For example:

```
bool my_criterion () (T const& x, T const& y);
```

```
// call function with function object
my_sort (... , my_criterion);
```

Many programmers also prefer the function call syntax over the syntax involving a template type argument.

22.5.3   Combining Function Call Parameters and Template Type Parameters

It is possible to combine the two previous forms of passing functors to functions and classes by defining default function call arguments:

```
template <typename F>
void my_sort (... , F cmp = F())
{
    ...
    if (cmp(x,y)) {   // use function object to compare two values
        ...
    }
    ...
}
```

```
bool my_criterion () (T const& x, T const& y);
```

```
// call function with functor passed as template argument
my_sort<std::less<... > > (... );
```

```
// call function with functor passed as value argument
my_sort (... , std::less<... >());
```

// call function with function pointer passed as value argument
```
my_sort (... , my_criterion);
```

The ordered collection classes of the C++ standard library are defined in this way: The sorting criterion can be passed as a constructor argument at run time:

```
class RuntimeCmp {
    ...
};
```

// pass sorting criterion as a compile-time template argument
// (uses default constructor of sorting criterion)
```
set<int,RuntimeCmp> c1;
```

// pass sorting criterion as a run-time constructor argument
```
set<int,RuntimeCmp> c2(RuntimeCmp(... ));
```

For details, see pages 178 and 197 of [*JosuttisStdLib*].

22.5.4   Functors as Nontype Template Arguments

Functors can also be provided through nontype template arguments. However, as mentioned in Section 4.3 on page 40 and Section 8.3.3 on page 109, a class type functor (and, in general, a class type object) is never a valid nontype template argument. For example, the following is invalid:

```
class MyCriterion {
  public:
    bool operator() (SomeType const&, SomeType const&) const;
};
```

```
template <MyCriterion F>      // ERROR: MyCriterion is a class type
void my_sort (... );
```

However, it is possible to have a pointer or reference to a class type object as a nontype argument. This might inspire us to write the following:

```
class MyCriterion {
  public:
    virtual bool operator() (SomeType const&,
                             SomeType const&) const = 0;
};
```

```
class LessThan : public MyCriterion {
  public:
```

```
              virtual bool operator() (SomeType const&,
                                        SomeType const&) const;
};


template<MyCriterion& F>
void sort (... );


LessThan order;


sort<order> (... );              // ERROR: requires derived-to-base
                                 //          conversion
sort<(MyCriterion&)order> (... );  // ERROR: reference nontype argument
                                 //          must be simple name
                                 //          (without a cast)
```

Our idea in the previous example is to capture the interface of the sorting criterion in an abstract base class type and use that type for the nontype template parameter. In an ideal world, we could then just plug in derived classes (such as `LessThan`) to request a specific implementation of the base class interface (`MyCriterion`). Unfortunately, C++ does not permit such an approach: Nontype arguments with reference or pointer types must match the parameter type exactly. An implicit derived-to-base conversion is not considered, and making the conversion explicit also invalidates the argument.

In light of our previous examples, we conclude that class type functors are not conveniently passed as nontype template arguments. In contrast, pointers (and references) to functions can be valid nontype template arguments. The following section explores some of the possibilities offered by this concept.

22.5.5   Function Pointer Encapsulation

Suppose we have a framework that expects functors like the sorting criteria of the examples in the previous sections. Furthermore, we may have some functions from an older (nontemplate) library that we'd like to act as such a functor.

To solve this problem, we can simply wrap the function call. For example:

```
class CriterionWrapper {
  public:
    bool operator() (... ) {
        return wrapped_function(... );
    }
};
```

Here, *wrapped_function*() is a legacy function that we like to fit in our more general functor framework.

Often, the need to integrate legacy functions in a framework of class type functors is not an isolated event. Therefore, it can be convenient to define a template that concisely integrates such functions:

```
template<int (*FP)()>
class FunctionReturningIntWrapper {
  public:
    int operator() () {
        return FP();
    }
};
```

Here is a complete example:

```
// functors/funcwrap.cpp

#include <vector>
#include <iostream>
#include <cstdlib>

// wrapper for function pointers to function objects
template<int (*FP)()>
class FunctionReturningIntWrapper {
  public:
    int operator() () {
        return FP();
    }
};

// example function to wrap
int random_int()
{
    return std::rand();   // call standard C function
}

// client that uses function object type as template parameter
template <typename FO>
void initialize (std::vector<int>& coll)
{
    FO fo;  // create function object
    for (std::vector<int>::size_type i=0; i<coll.size(); ++i) {
        coll[i] = fo();  // call function for function object
    }
}
```

```
int main()
{
    // create vector with 10 elements
    std::vector<int> v(10);

    // (re)initialize values with wrapped function
    initialize<FunctionReturningIntWrapper<random_int> >(v);

    // output elements
    for (std::vector<int>::size_type i=0; i<v.size(); ++i) {
        std::cout << "coll[" << i << "]: " << v[i] << std::endl;
    }
}
```

The expression

```
FunctionReturningIntWrapper<random_int>
```

inside the call of `initialize()` wraps the function pointer `random_int` so that it can be passed as a template type parameter.

Note that we can't pass a function pointer with C linkage to this template. For example,

```
initialize<FunctionReturningIntWrapper<std::rand> >(v);
```

may not work because the `std::rand()` function comes from the C standard library (and may therefore have C linkage[6]). Instead, we can introduce a typedef for a function pointer type with the appropriate linkage:

```
// type for function pointer with C linkage
extern "C" typedef int (*C_int_FP)();

// wrapper for function pointers to function objects
template<C_int_FP FP>
class FunctionReturningIntWrapper {
  public:
    int operator() () {
        return FP();
    }
};
```

---

[6] In many implementations, functions from the C standard library have C linkage, but a C++ implementation is allowed to provide these functions with C++ linkage instead. Whether the example call is valid therefore depends on the particular implementation being used.

It may be worthwhile to reemphasize at this point that templates correspond to a compile-time mechanism. This means that the compiler knows which value is substituted for the nontype parameter FP of the template `FunctionReturningIntWrapper`. Because of this, most C++ implementations should be able to convert what at first may look like an indirect call to a direct call. Indeed, if the function were inline and its definition visible at the point of the functor invocation, it would be reasonable to expect the call to be inline.

22.6   Introspection

In the context of programming, the term *introspection* refers to the ability of a program to inspect itself. For example, in Chapter 15 we designed templates that can inspect a type and determine what kind of type it is. For functors, it is often useful to be able to tell, for example, how many arguments the functor accepts, the return type of the functor, or the *n*th parameter type of the functor type.

Introspection is not easily achieved for an arbitrary functor. For example, how would we write a type function that evaluates to the type of the second parameter in a functor like the following?

```
class SuperFunc {
  public:
    void operator() (int, char**);
};
```

Some C++ compilers provide a special type function known as `typeof`. It evaluates to the type of its argument expression (but doesn't actually evaluate the expression, much like the `sizeof` operator). With such an operator, the previous problem can be solved to a large extent, albeit not easily. The `typeof` concept is discussed in Section 13.8 on page 215.

Alternatively, we can develop a functor framework that requires participating functors to provide some extra information to enable some level of introspection. This is the approach we use in the remainder of this chapter.

22.6.1   Analyzing a Functor Type

In our framework, we handle only class type functors[7] and require them to provide the following information:

- The number of parameters of the functor (as a member enumerator constant `NumParams`)
- The type of each parameter (through member typedefs `Param1T`, `Param2T`, `Param3T`, ...)
- The return type of the functor (through a member typedef `ReturnT`)

For example, we could rewrite our `PersonSortCriterion` as follows to fit this framework:

---

[7] To reduce the strength of this constraint, we also develop a tool to encapsulate function pointers in the framework.

```
class PersonSortCriterion {
  public:
    enum { NumParams = 2 };
    typedef bool ReturnT;
    typedef Person const& Param1T;
    typedef Person const& Param2T;
    bool operator() (Person const& p1, Person const& p2) const {
        // returns whether p1 is "less than" p2
        ...
    }
};
```

These conventions are sufficient for our purposes. They allow us to write templates to create new functors from existing ones (for example, through composition).

There are other properties of a functor that can be worth representing in this manner. For example, we could decide to encode the fact that a functor has no side effects and use this information to optimize certain generic templates. Such functors are sometimes called *pure functors*. It would also be useful to enable introspection of this property to enforce the need for a pure functor at compile time. For example, usually a sorting criterion should be pure[8]; otherwise, the results of the sorting operation could be meaningless.

22.6.2   Accessing Parameter Types

A functor can have an arbitrary number of parameters. With our conventions it is relatively straightforward to access, say, the eighth parameter type: Param8T. However, when dealing with templates it is always useful to plan for maximum flexibility. In this case, how do we write a type function that produces the Nth parameter type given the functor type and a constant N? We can do this by writing partial specializations of the following class template:

```
template<typename FunctorType, int N>
class FunctorParam;
```

We can provide partial specializations for values of N from one to some reasonably large number (say 20; functors rarely have more than 20 parameters). Each of these partial specializations can then define a member typedef Type that reflects the corresponding parameter type.

This presents one difficulty: To what should FunctorParam<F, N>::Type evaluate when N is larger than the number of parameters of the functor F? One possibility is to let such situations result in a compilation error. Although this is easily accomplished, it makes the FunctorParam type function much less useful than it could be. A second possibility is to default to type void. The disadvantage

---

[8] At least to a large extent. Some caching and logging side effects can be tolerated to the extent that they don't affect the value returned by the functor.

of this approach is that there are some unfortunate restrictions on type void; for example, a function cannot have a parameter type of type void, nor can we create references to void. Therefore, we opt for a third possibility: a private member class type. Objects of such a type are not easily constructed, but there are few syntactic constraints on their use. Here is an implementation of this idea:

```
// functors/functorparam1.hpp

#include "ifthenelse.hpp"

template <typename F, int N>
class UsedFunctorParam;

template <typename F, int N>
class FunctorParam {
  private:
    class Unused {
      private:
        class Private {};
      public:
        typedef Private Type;
    };
  public:
    typedef typename IfThenElse<F::NumParams>=N,
                                UsedFunctorParam<F,N>,
                                Unused>::ResultT::Type
          Type;
};

template <typename F>
class UsedFunctorParam<F, 1> {
  public:
    typedef typename F::Param1T Type;
};
```

The IfThenElse template was introduced in Section 15.2.4 on page 272. Note that we introduced a helper template UsedFunctorParam, and it is this template that needs to be partially specialized for specific values of N. A concise way to do this is to use a macro:

```
// functors/functorparam2.hpp

#define FunctorParamSpec(N)                            \
        template<typename F>                           \
        class UsedFunctorParam<F, N> {                 \
          public:                                      \
            typedef typename F::Param##N##T Type;      \
        }

...

FunctorParamSpec(2);
FunctorParamSpec(3);

...

FunctorParamSpec(20);


#undef FunctorParamSpec
```

22.6.3 Encapsulating Function Pointers

Requiring that functor types support some introspection in the form of member typedefs excludes the use of function pointers in our framework. As discussed earlier, we can mitigate this limitation by encapsulating the function pointer. Let's develop a small tool that enables us to encapsulate functions with as many as two parameters (a larger number of parameters are handled in the same way, but let's keep the number small in the interest of clarity). We cover only the case of functions with C++ linkage; C linkage can be done in a similar way.

The solution presented here has two main components: a class template `FunctionPtr` with instances that are functor types encapsulating a function pointer, and an overloaded function template `func_ptr()` that takes a function pointer and returns a corresponding functor that fits our framework. The class template is parameterized with the return type and the parameter types:

```
template<typename RT, typename P1 = void, typename P2 = void>
class FunctionPtr;
```

Substituting a parameter with type `void` amounts to saying that the parameter isn't actually available. Hence, our template is able to handle multiple numbers of functor call arguments.

Because we need to encapsulate a function pointer, we need a tool to create the type of the function pointer from the parameter types. This is achieved through partial specialization as follows:

```
// functors/functionptrt.hpp

// primary template handles maximum number of parameters:
template<typename RT, typename P1 = void,
                      typename P2 = void,
```

```
                                  typename P3 = void>
class FunctionPtrT {
  public:
    enum { NumParams = 3 };
    typedef RT (*Type)(P1,P2,P3);
};


// partial specialization for two parameters:
template<typename RT, typename P1,
                        typename P2>
class FunctionPtrT<RT, P1, P2, void> {
  public:
    enum { NumParams = 2 };
    typedef RT (*Type)(P1,P2);
};


// partial specialization for one parameter:
template<typename RT, typename P1>
class FunctionPtrT<RT, P1, void, void> {
  public:
    enum { NumParams = 1 };
    typedef RT (*Type)(P1);
};


// partial specialization for no parameters:
template<typename RT>
class FunctionPtrT<RT, void, void, void> {
  public:
    enum { NumParams = 0 };
    typedef RT (*Type)();
};
```

Notice how we used the same template to "count" the number of parameters.

The functor type we are developing passes its parameters to the function pointer it encapsulates. Passing a function call argument can have side effects: If the corresponding parameter has a class type (and not a *reference* to a class type), its copy constructor is invoked. To avoid this extra cost, it is useful to have a type function that leaves its argument type unchanged, except if it is a class type, in which case a reference to the corresponding const class type is produced. With the TypeT template developed in Chapter 15 and our IfThenElse utility template, this is achieved fairly concisely:

// functors/forwardparam.hpp

```cpp
#ifndef FORWARD_HPP
#define FORWARD_HPP

#include "ifthenelse.hpp"
#include "typet.hpp"
#include "typeop.hpp"
```

```cpp
// ForwardParamT<T>::Type is
// - constant reference for class types
// - plain type for almost all other types
// - a dummy type (Unused) for type void
template<typename T>
class ForwardParamT {
  public:
    typedef typename IfThenElse<TypeT<T>::IsClassT,
                                typename TypeOp<T>::RefConstT,
                                typename TypeOp<T>::ArgT
                               >::ResultT
            Type;
};

template<>
class ForwardParamT<void> {
  private:
    class Unused {};
  public:
    typedef Unused Type;
};
```

```cpp
#endif // FORWARD_HPP
```

Note the similarity of this template with the `RParam` template developed in Section 15.3.1 on page 276. The difference is that we need to map the type `void` (which, as mentioned earlier, is used to denote an unused parameter type) to a type that can validly appear as a parameter type.

We are now ready to define the `FunctionPtr` template. Because we don't know *a priori* how many parameters it will take, we overload the function call operator for every number of parameters (up to three in our case):

```cpp
// functors/functionptr.hpp

#include "forwardparam.hpp"
#include "functionptrt.hpp"

template<typename RT, typename P1 = void,
                      typename P2 = void,
                      typename P3 = void>
class FunctionPtr {
  private:
    typedef typename FunctionPtrT<RT,P1,P2,P3>::Type FuncPtr;
    // the encapsulated pointer:
    FuncPtr fptr;
  public:
    // to fit in our framework:
    enum { NumParams = FunctionPtrT<RT,P1,P2,P3>::NumParams };
    typedef RT ReturnT;
    typedef P1 Param1T;
    typedef P2 Param2T;
    typedef P3 Param3T;

    // constructor:
    FunctionPtr(FuncPtr ptr)
     : fptr(ptr) {
    }

    // ``function calls'':
    RT operator()() {
        return fptr();
    }
    RT operator()(typename ForwardParamT<P1>::Type a1) {
        return fptr(a1);
    }
    RT operator()(typename ForwardParamT<P1>::Type a1,
                  typename ForwardParamT<P2>::Type a2) {
        return fptr(a1, a2);
    }
    RT operator()(typename ForwardParamT<P1>::Type a1,
                  typename ForwardParamT<P2>::Type a2,
```

```
                        typename ForwardParamT<P3>::Type a3) {
            return fptr(a1, a2, a3);
        }
};
```

This class template works well, but using it directly can be cumbersome. A few (inline) function templates allow us to exploit the template argument deduction mechanism to alleviate this burden:

```
// functors/funcptr.hpp

#include "functionptr.hpp"

template<typename RT> inline
FunctionPtr<RT> func_ptr (RT (*fp)())
{
    return FunctionPtr<RT>(fp);
}

template<typename RT, typename P1> inline
FunctionPtr<RT,P1> func_ptr (RT (*fp)(P1))
{
    return FunctionPtr<RT,P1>(fp);
}

template<typename RT, typename P1, typename P2> inline
FunctionPtr<RT,P1,P2> func_ptr (RT (*fp)(P1,P2))
{
    return FunctionPtr<RT,P1,P2>(fp);
}

template<typename RT, typename P1, typename P2, typename P3> inline
FunctionPtr<RT,P1,P2,P3> func_ptr (RT (*fp)(P1,P2,P3))
{
    return FunctionPtr<RT,P1,P2,P3>(fp);
}
```

All there is left to do is to try the advanced template tool we just developed with the following little demonstration program:

```
// functors/functordemo.cpp

#include <iostream>
#include <string>
#include <typeinfo>
#include "funcptr.hpp"

double seven()
{
    return 7.0;
}

std::string more()
{
    return std::string("more");
}

template <typename FunctorT>
void demo (FunctorT func)
{
    std::cout << "Functor returns type "
              << typeid(typename FunctorT::ReturnT).name() << '\n'
              << "Functor returns value "
              << func() << '\n';
}

int main()
{
    demo(func_ptr(seven));
    demo(func_ptr(more));
}
```

22.7 Function Object Composition

Let's assume we have the following two simple mathematical functors in our framework:

```
// functors/math1.hpp

#include <cmath>
#include <cstdlib>

class Abs {
  public:
    // "function call":
    double operator() (double v) const {
        return std::abs(v);
    }
};

class Sine {
  public:
    // "function call":
    double operator() (double a) const {
        return std::sin(a);
    }
};
```

However, the functor we really want is the one that computes the absolute value of the sine of a given angle. Writing the new functor is not hard:

```
class AbsSine {
  public:
    double operator() (double a) {
        return std::abs(std::sin(a));
    }
};
```

Nevertheless, it is inconvenient to write new declarations for every new combination of functors. Instead, we may prefer to write a functor utility that *composes* two other functors. In this section we develop some templates that enable us to do this. Along the way, we introduce various concepts that prove useful in the remainder of this chapter.

22.7.1   Simple Composition

Let's start with a first cut at an implementation of a composition tool:

```
// functors/compose1.hpp

template <typename FO1, typename FO2>
class Composer {
  private:
    FO1 fo1;   // first/inner function object to call
    FO2 fo2;   // second/outer function object to call
  public:
    // constructor: initialize function objects
    Composer (FO1 f1, FO2 f2)
     : fo1(f1), fo2(f2) {
    }

    // "function call": nested call of function objects
    double operator() (double v) {
        return fo2(fo1(v));
    }
};
```

Note that when describing the composition of two functions, the function that is *applied* first is listed first. This means that the notation Composer<Abs, Sine> corresponds to the function $sin(abs(x))$ (note the reversal of order). To test our little template, we can use the following program:

```
// functors/compose1.cpp

#include <iostream>
#include "math1.hpp"
#include "compose1.hpp"

template<typename FO>
void print_values (FO fo)
{
    for (int i=-2; i<3; ++i) {
        std::cout << "f(" << i*0.1
                  << ") = " << fo(i*0.1)
                  << "\n";
    }
}
```

```
int main()
{
    // print sin(abs(-0.5))
    std::cout << Composer<Abs,Sine>(Abs(),Sine())(-0.5) << "\n\n";

    // print abs() of some values
    print_values(Abs());
    std::cout << '\n';

    // print sin() of some values
    print_values(Sine());
    std::cout << '\n';

    // print sin(abs()) of some values
    print_values(Composer<Abs, Sine>(Abs(), Sine()));
    std::cout << '\n';

    // print abs(sin()) of some values
    print_values(Composer<Sine, Abs>(Sine(), Abs()));
}
```

This demonstrates the general principle, but there is room for various improvements.

A usability improvement is achieved by introducing a small inline helper function so that the template arguments for Composer may be deduced (by now, this is a rather common technique):

```
// functors/composeconv.hpp

template <typename FO1, typename FO2>
inline
Composer<FO1,FO2> compose (FO1 f1, FO2 f2) {
    return Composer<FO1,FO2> (f1, f2);
}
```

With this in place, our sample program can now be rewritten as follows:

```
// functors/compose2.cpp

#include <iostream>
#include "math1.hpp"
#include "compose1.hpp"
#include "composeconv.hpp"
```

```
template<typename FO>
void print_values (FO fo)
{
    for (int i=-2; i<3; ++i) {
        std::cout << "f(" << i*0.1
                  << ") = " << fo(i*0.1)
                  << "\n";
    }
}

int main()
{
    // print sin(abs(-0.5))
    std::cout << compose(Abs(),Sine())(0.5) << "\n\n";

    // print abs() of some values
    print_values(Abs());
    std::cout << '\n';

    // print sin() of some values
    print_values(Sine());
    std::cout << '\n';

    // print sin(abs()) of some values
    print_values(compose(Abs(),Sine()));
    std::cout << '\n';

    // print abs(sin()) of some values
    print_values(compose(Sine(),Abs()));
}
```

Instead of

```
Composer<Abs, Sine>(Abs(), Sine())
```

we can now use the more concise

```
compose(Abs(), Sine())
```

The next refinement is driven by a desire to optimize the Composer class template itself. More specifically, we want to avoid having to allocate any space for the members functors first and second if these functors are themselves empty classes (that is, when they are *stateless*), which is a common special case. This may seem to be a modest savings in storage, but remember that empty classes can undergo a special optimization when passed as function call parameters. The standard technique for our purpose is the *empty base class optimization* (see Section 16.2 on page 289), which turns the members into base classes:

```
// functors/compose3.hpp

template <typename FO1, typename FO2>
class Composer : private FO1, private FO2 {
  public:
    // constructor: initialize function objects
    Composer(FO1 f1, FO2 f2)
      : FO1(f1), FO2(f2) {
    }

    // "function call": nested call of function objects
    double operator() (double v) {
        return FO2::operator()(FO1::operator()(v));
    }
};
```

This approach, however, is not really commendable. It prevents us from composing a function with itself. Indeed, the call of

```
// print sin(sin()) of some values
print_values(compose(Sine(),Sine())); // ERROR: duplicate base class name
```

leads to the instantiation of Composer such that it derives twice from class Sine, which is invalid.

This duplicate base problem can be easily avoided by adding an additional level of inheritance:

```
// functors/compose4.hpp

template <typename C, int N>
class BaseMem : public C {
  public:
    BaseMem(C& c) : C(c) { }
    BaseMem(C const& c) : C(c) { }
};

template <typename FO1, typename FO2>
class Composer : private BaseMem<FO1,1>,
                 private BaseMem<FO2,2> {
  public:
```

```
// constructor: initialize function objects
Composer(FO1 f1, FO2 f2)
  : BaseMem<FO1,1>(f1), BaseMem<FO2,2>(f2) {
}

// "function call": nested call of function objects
double operator() (double v) {
    return BaseMem<FO2,2>::operator()
              (BaseMem<FO1,1>::operator()(v));
}
};
```

Clearly, the latter implementation is messier than the original, but this may be an acceptable cost if it helps an optimizer realize that the resulting functor is "empty."

Interestingly, the function call operator can be declared virtual. Doing so in a functor that participates in a composition makes the function call operator of the resulting Composer object virtual too. This can lead to some strange results. We will therefore assume that the function call operator is nonvirtual in the remainder of this section.

22.7.2   Mixed Type Composition

A more crucial improvement to the simple Composer template is to allow for more flexibility in the types involved. With the previous implementation, we allow only functors that take a double value and return another double value. Life would be more elegant if we could compose any matching type of functor. For example, we should be able to compose a functor that takes an int and returns a bool with one that takes a bool and returns a double. This is a situation in which our decision to require member typedefs in functor types comes in handy.

With the conventions assumed by our framework, the composition template can be rewritten as follows:

```
// functors/compose5.hpp

#include "forwardparam.hpp"

template <typename C, int N>
class BaseMem : public C {
  public:
    BaseMem(C& c) : C(c) { }
    BaseMem(C const& c) : C(c) { }
};
```

```
template <typename FO1, typename FO2>
class Composer : private BaseMem<FO1,1>,
                 private BaseMem<FO2,2> {
  public:
    // to let it fit in our framework:
    enum { NumParams = FO1::NumParams };
    typedef typename FO2::ReturnT ReturnT;
    typedef typename FO1::Param1T Param1T;

    // constructor: initialize function objects
    Composer(FO1 f1, FO2 f2)
      : BaseMem<FO1,1>(f1), BaseMem<FO2,2>(f2) {
    }

    // "function call": nested call of function objects
    ReturnT operator() (typename ForwardParamT<Param1T>::Type v) {
        return BaseMem<FO2,2>::operator()
                 (BaseMem<FO1,1>::operator()(v));
    }
};
```

We reused the ForwardParamT template (see Section 22.6.3 on page 440) to avoid unnecessary copies of functor call arguments.

To use the composition template with our Abs and Sine functors, they have to be rewritten to include the appropriate type information. This is done as follows:

```
// functors/math2.hpp

#include <cmath>
#include <cstdlib>

class Abs {
  public:
    // to fit in the framework:
    enum { NumParams = 1 };
    typedef double ReturnT;
    typedef double Param1T;
```

```cpp
    // "function call":
    double operator() (double v) const {
        return std::abs(v);
    }
};

class Sine {
  public:
    // to fit in the framework:
    enum { NumParams = 1 };
    typedef double ReturnT;
    typedef double Param1T;

    // "function call":
    double operator() (double a) const {
        return std::sin(a);
    }
};
```

Alternatively, we can implement Abs and Sine as templates:

```cpp
// functors/math3.hpp

#include <cmath>
#include <cstdlib>

template <typename T>
class Abs {
  public:
    // to fit in the framework:
    enum { NumParams = 1 };
    typedef T ReturnT;
    typedef T Param1T;

    // "function call":
    T operator() (T v) const {
        return std::abs(v);
    }
};
```

```
template <typename T>
class Sine {
  public:
    // to fit in the framework:
    enum { NumParams = 1 };
    typedef T ReturnT;
    typedef T Param1T;

    // "function call":
    T operator() (T a) const {
        return std::sin(a);
    }
};
```

With the latter approach, using these functors requires the argument types to be provided explicitly
as template arguments. The following adaptation of our sample use illustrates the slightly more
cumbersome syntax:

```
// functors/compose5.cpp

#include <iostream>
#include "math3.hpp"
#include "compose5.hpp"
#include "composeconv.hpp"

template<typename FO>
void print_values (FO fo)
{
    for (int i=-2; i<3; ++i) {
        std::cout << "f(" << i*0.1
                  << ") = " << fo(i*0.1)
                  << "\n";
    }
}

int main()
{
    // print sin(abs(-0.5))
    std::cout << compose(Abs<double>(),Sine<double>())(-0.5)
              << "\n\n";
```

```
// print abs() of some values
print_values(Abs<double>());
std::cout << '\n';

// print sin() of some values
print_values(Sine<double>());
std::cout << '\n';

// print sin(abs()) of some values
print_values(compose(Abs<double>(),Sine<double>()));
std::cout << '\n';

// print abs(sin()) of some values
print_values(compose(Sine<double>(),Abs<double>()));
std::cout << '\n';

// print sin(sin()) of some values
print_values(compose(Sine<double>(),Sine<double>()));
}
```

22.7.3   Reducing the Number of Parameters

So far we have looked at a simple form of functor composition where one functor takes one argument, and that argument is another functor invocation which itself has one parameter. Clearly, functors can have multiple arguments, and therefore it is useful to allow for the composition of functors with multiple parameters. In this section we discuss the implication of allowing the first argument of Composer to be a functor with multiple parameters.

If the first functor argument of Composer takes multiple arguments, the resulting Composer class must accept multiple arguments too. This means that we have to define multiple ParamNT member types and we need to provide a function call operator (operator ()) with the appropriate number of parameters. The latter problem is not as hard to solve as it may seem. Function call operators can be overloaded; hence we can just provide function call operators for every number of parameters up to a reasonably high number (an industrial-strength functor library may go as high as 20 parameters). Any attempt to call an overloaded operator with a number of parameters that does not match the number of parameters of the first composed functor results in a translation (compilation) error, which is perfectly all right. The code might look as follows:

```
template <typename FO1, typename FO2>
class Composer : private BaseMem<FO1,1>,
                 private BaseMem<FO2,2> {
  public:
    ...
    // "function call" for no arguments:
    ReturnT operator() () {
        return BaseMem<FO2,2>::operator()
                 (BaseMem<FO1,1>::operator()());
    }


    // "function call" for one argument:
    ReturnT operator() (typename ForwardParamT<Param1T>::Type v1) {
        return BaseMem<FO2,2>::operator()
                 (BaseMem<FO1,1>::operator()(v1));
    }


    // "function call" for two arguments:
    ReturnT operator() (typename ForwardParamT<Param1T>::Type v1,
                        typename ForwardParamT<Param2T>::Type v2) {
        return BaseMem<FO2,2>::operator()
                 (BaseMem<FO1,1>::operator()(v1, v2));
    }
    ...
};
```

We are now left with the task of defining members Param1T, Param2T, and so on. This task is made more complicated by the fact that these types are used in the declaration of the various function call operators: These must be valid even though the composed functors do not have corresponding parameters.[9] For example, if we compose two single-parameter functors, we must still come up with a Param2T type that makes a valid parameter type. Preferably, this type should not accidentally match another type used in a client program. Fortunately, we already solved this problem with FunctorParam template. The Compose template can therefore be equipped with its various member typedefs as follows:

---

[9] Note that the SFINAE principle (see Section 8.3.1 on page 106) does not apply here because these are ordinary member functions and not member function templates. SFINAE is based on template parameter deduction, which does not occur for ordinary member functions.

```
template <typename FO1, typename FO2>
class Composer : private BaseMem<FO1,1>,
                 private BaseMem<FO2,2> {
  public:
    // the return type is straightforward:
    typedef typename FO2::ReturnT ReturnT;

    // define Param1T, Param2T, and so on
    // - use a macro to ease the replication of the parameter type construct
#define ComposeParamT(N)                                                       \
        typedef typename FunctorParam<FO1, N>::Type Param##N##T
    ComposeParamT(1);
    ComposeParamT(2);
    ...
    ComposeParamT(20);
#undef ComposeParamT
    ...
};
```

Finally, we need to add the `Composer` constructors. They take the two functors being composed, but we allow for the various combinations of const and non-const functors:

```
template <typename FO1, typename FO2>
class Composer : private BaseMem<FO1,1>,
                 private BaseMem<FO2,2> {
  public:
    ...
    // constructors:
    Composer(FO1 const& f1, FO2 const& f2)
      : BaseMem<FO1,1>(f1), BaseMem<FO2,2>(f2) {
    }
    Composer(FO1 const& f1, FO2& f2)
      : BaseMem<FO1,1>(f1), BaseMem<FO2,2>(f2) {
    }
    Composer(FO1& f1, FO2 const& f2)
      : BaseMem<FO1,1>(f1), BaseMem<FO2,2>(f2) {
    }
    Composer(FO1& f1, FO2& f2)
      : BaseMem<FO1,1>(f1), BaseMem<FO2,2>(f2) {
    }
    ...
};
```

With all this library code in place, a program can now use simple constructs, as illustrated in the following example:

```cpp
// functors/compose6.cpp

#include <iostream>
#include "funcptr.hpp"
#include "compose6.hpp"
#include "composeconv.hpp"

double add(double a, double b)
{
    return a+b;
}

double twice(double a)
{
    return 2*a;
}

int main()
{
    std::cout << "compute (20+7)*2: "
              << compose(func_ptr(add),func_ptr(twice))(20,7)
              << '\n';
}
```

These tools can still be refined in various ways. For example, it is useful to extend the compose template to handle function pointers directly (making the use of func_ptr in our last example unnecessary). However, in the interest of brevity, we prefer to leave such improvements to the interested reader.

22.8   Value Binders

Often, a functor with multiple parameters remains useful when one of the parameters is *bound* to a specific value. For example, a simple Min functor template such as

```cpp
// functors/min.hpp

template <typename T>
class Min {
```

```
    public:
       typedef T ReturnT;
       typedef T Param1T;
       typedef T Param2T;
       enum { NumParams = 2 };
       ReturnT operator() (Param1T a, Param2T b) {
           return a<b ? a : b;
       }
};
```

can be used to build a new `Clamp` functor that behaves like `Min` with one of its parameters bound to a certain constant. The constant could be specified as a template argument or as a run-time argument. For example, we can write the new functor as follows:

```
// functors/clamp.hpp

template <typename T, T max_result>
class Clamp : private Min<T> {
  public:
     typedef T ReturnT;
     typedef T Param1T;
     enum { NumParams = 1 };
     ReturnT operator() (Param1T a) {
         return Min<T>::operator() (a, max_result);
     }
};
```

As with composition, it is very convenient to have some template that automates the task of binding a functor parameter available, even though it doesn't take very much code to do so manually.

22.8.1   Selecting the Binding

A *binder* binds a particular parameter of a particular functor to a particular value. Each of these aspects can be selected at run time (using function call arguments) or at compile time (using template arguments).

For example, the following template selects everything statically (that is, at compile time):

```
template<typename F, int P, int V>
class BindIntStatically;
     // F is the functor type
     // P is the parameter to bind
     // V is the value to be bound
```

Each of the three binding aspects (functor, bound parameter, and bound value) can instead be selected dynamically with various degrees of convenience.

Perhaps the least convenient is to make the selection of which parameter to bind dynamic. Presumably this would involve large `switch` statements that delegate the functor call to different calls to the underlying functor depending on a run-time value. This may, for example look as follows:

```
...
switch (this->param_num) {
  case 1:
    return F::operator()(v, p1, p2);
  case 2:
    return F::operator()(p1, v, p2);
  case 3:
    return F::operator()(p1, p2, v);
  default:
    return F::operator()(p1, p2);      // or an error?
}
```

Of the three binding aspects, this is probably the one that needs to become dynamic the least. In what follows, we therefore keep this as a template parameter so that it is a static selection.

To make the selection of the functor dynamic, it is sufficient to add a constructor that accepts a functor to our binder. Similarly, we can also pass the bound value to the constructor, but this requires us to provide storage in the binder to hold the bound value. The following two helper templates can be used to hold bound values at compile time and run time respectively:

```
// functors/boundval.hpp

#include "typeop.hpp"

template <typename T>
class BoundVal {
  private:
    T value;
  public:
    typedef T ValueT;
    BoundVal(T v) : value(v) {
    }
    typename TypeOp<T>::RefT get() {
        return value;
    }
};
```

```
template <typename T, T Val>
class StaticBoundVal {
  public:
    typedef T ValueT;
    T get() {
        return Val;
    }
};
```

Again, we rely on the empty base class optimization (see Section 16.2 on page 289) to avoid unnecessary overhead if the functor or the bound value representation is stateless. The beginning of our
Binder template design therefore looks as follows:

```
// functors/binder1.hpp

template <typename FO, int P, typename V>
class Binder : private FO, private V {
  public:
    // constructors:
    Binder(FO& f): FO(f) {}
    Binder(FO& f, V& v): FO(f), V(v) {}
    Binder(FO& f, V const& v): FO(f), V(v) {}
    Binder(FO const& f): FO(f) {}
    Binder(FO const& f, V& v): FO(f), V(v) {}
    Binder(FO const& f, V const& v): FO(f), V(v) {}
    template<class T>
      Binder(FO& f, T& v): FO(f), V(BoundVal<T>(v)) {}
    template<class T>
      Binder(FO& f, T const& v): FO(f), V(BoundVal<T const>(v)) {}
    ...
};
```

Note that, in addition to constructors taking instances of our helper templates, we also provide constructor templates that automatically wrap a given bound value in a BoundVal object.

22.8.2   Bound Signature

Determining the ParamNT types for the Binder template is harder than it was for the Composer
template because we cannot just take over the types of the functor on which we build. Instead,
because the parameter that is bound is no longer a parameter in the new functor, we must drop the
corresponding ParamNT and shift the subsequent types by one position.

To keep things modular, we can introduce a separate template that performs the selective shifting operation:

```
// functors/binderparams.hpp

#include "ifthenelse.hpp"

template<typename F, int P>
class BinderParams {
  public:
    // there is one less parameter because one is bound:
    enum { NumParams = F::NumParams-1 };
#define ComposeParamT(N)                                                 \
    typedef typename IfThenElse<(N<P), FunctorParam<F, N>,               \
                                       FunctorParam<F, N+1>              \
                     >::ResultT::Type                                    \
            Param##N##T
    ComposeParamT(1);
    ComposeParamT(2);
    ComposeParamT(3);
    ...
#undef ComposeParamT
};
```

This can be used in the Binder template as follows:

```
// functors/binder2.hpp

template <typename FO, int P, typename V>
class Binder : private FO, private V {
  public:
    // there is one less parameter because one is bound:
    enum { NumParams = FO::NumParams-1 };
    // the return type is straightforward:
    typedef typename FO::ReturnT ReturnT;

    // the parameter types:
    typedef BinderParams<FO, P> Params;
#define ComposeParamT(N)                                                 \
        typedef typename                                                 \
                ForwardParamT<typename Params::Param##N##T>::Type \
            Param##N##T
```

```
        ComposeParamT(1);
        ComposeParamT(2);
        ComposeParamT(3);
        ...
    #undef ComposeParamT
      ...
    };
```

As usual, we use the `ForwardParamT` template to avoid unnecessary copying of arguments.

22.8.3   Argument Selection

To complete the `Binder` template we are left with the problem of implementing the function call operator. As with `Composer` we are going to overload this operator for varying numbers of functor call arguments. However, the problem here is considerably harder than for composition because the argument to be passed to the underlying functor can be one of three different values:

- The corresponding parameter of the bound functor
- The bound value
- The parameter of the bound functor that is one position to the left of the argument we must pass

Which of the three values we select depends on the value of P and the position of the argument we are selecting.

Our idea to achieve the desired result is to write a private inline member function that accepts (by reference) the three possible values but returns (still by reference) the one that is appropriate for that argument position. Because this member function depends on which argument we're selecting, we introduce it as a static member of a nested class template. This approach enables us to write a function call operator as follows (here shown for binding a four-parameter functor; others are similar):

```
// functors/binder3.hpp

template <typename FO, int P, typename V>
class Binder : private FO, private V {
  public:
      ...
    ReturnT operator() (Param1T v1, Param2T v2, Param3T v3) {
        return FO::operator()(ArgSelect<1>::from(v1,v1,V::get()),
                              ArgSelect<2>::from(v1,v2,V::get()),
                              ArgSelect<3>::from(v2,v3,V::get()),
                              ArgSelect<4>::from(v3,v3,V::get()));
    }
      ...
};
```

Note that for the first and last argument, only two argument values are possible: the first or last parameter of the operator, or the bound value. If A is the position of the argument in the call to the underlying functor (1 through 3 in the example), then the corresponding parameter is selected when A-P is less than zero, the bound value is selected when A-P is equal to zero, and a parameter to the left of the argument position is selected when A-P is strictly positive. This observation justifies the definition of a helper template that selects one of three types based on the sign of a nontype template argument:

```
// functors/signselect.hpp

#include "ifthenelse.hpp"


template <int S, typename NegT, typename ZeroT, typename PosT>
struct SignSelectT {
  typedef typename
      IfThenElse<(S<0),
                   NegT,
                   typename IfThenElse<(S>0),
                                         PosT,
                                         ZeroT
                                       >::ResultT
                 >::ResultT
      ResultT;
};
```

With this in place, we are ready to define the member class template ArgSelect:

```
// functors/binder4.hpp

template <typename FO, int P, typename V>
class Binder : private FO, private V {
  ...
  private:
    template<int A>
    class ArgSelect {
      public:
        // type if we haven't passed the bound argument yet:
        typedef typename TypeOp<
                    typename IfThenElse<(A<=Params::NumParams),
                                          FunctorParam<Params, A>,
                                          FunctorParam<Params, A-1>
                                        >::ResultT::Type>::RefT
                NoSkipT;
```

```
// type if we're past the bound argument:
typedef typename TypeOp<
                typename IfThenElse<(A>1),
                                      FunctorParam<Params, A-1>,
                                      FunctorParam<Params, A>
                                    >::ResultT::Type>::RefT
        SkipT;
// type of bound argument:
typedef typename TypeOp<typename V::ValueT>::RefT BindT;

// three selection cases implemented through different classes:
class NoSkip {
  public:
    static NoSkipT select (SkipT prev_arg, NoSkipT arg,
                           BindT bound_val) {
        return arg;
    }
};
class Skip {
  public:
    static SkipT select (SkipT prev_arg, NoSkipT arg,
                         BindT bound_val) {
        return prev_arg;
    }
};
class Bind {
  public:
    static BindT select (SkipT prev_arg, NoSkipT arg,
                         BindT bound_val) {
        return bound_val;
    }
};

// the actual selection function:
typedef typename SignSelectT<A-P, NoSkipT,
                             BindT, SkipT>::ResultT
        ReturnT;
typedef typename SignSelectT<A-P, NoSkip,
                             Bind, Skip>::ResultT
```

```
                        SelectedT;
            static ReturnT from (SkipT prev_arg, NoSkipT arg,
                                  BindT bound_val) {
                return SelectedT::select (prev_arg, arg, bound_val);
            }
        };
    };
```

This is admittedly among the most complicated code segments in this book. The `from` member function is the one called from the functor call operators. Part of the difficulty lies in the selection of the right parameter types from which the argument is selected: `SkipT` and `NoSkipT` also incorporate the convention we use for the first and last argument (that is, repeating v1 and v3 in the operator illustrated earlier). We use the `TypeOp<>::RefT` construct to define these types: We could just create a reference type using the & symbol, but most compilers cannot handle "references to references" yet. The selection functions themselves are rather trivial, but they were encapsulated in member types `NoSkip`, `Skip`, and `Bind` to dispatch statically the appropriate function easily. Because these functions are themselves simple inline forwarding functions, a good optimizing compiler should be able to "see through" it all and generate near-optimal code. In practice, only the best optimizers available at the time of this writing perform entirely satifactorily in the performance area. However, most other compilers still do a reasonable job of optimizing uses of `Binder`.

Putting it all together, our complete `Binder` template is implemented as follows:

```
// functors/binder5.hpp
```

```cpp
#include "ifthenelse.hpp"
#include "boundval.hpp"
#include "forwardparam.hpp"
#include "functorparam.hpp"
#include "binderparams.hpp"
#include "signselect.hpp"

template <typename FO, int P, typename V>
class Binder : private FO, private V {
  public:
    // there is one less parameter because one is bound:
    enum { NumParams = FO::NumParams-1 };
    // the return type is straightforward:
    typedef typename FO::ReturnT ReturnT;

    // the parameter types:
    typedef BinderParams<FO, P> Params;
```

```
#define ComposeParamT(N)                                         \
      typedef typename                                           \
              ForwardParamT<typename Params::Param##N##T>::Type \
          Param##N##T
    ComposeParamT(1);
    ComposeParamT(2);
    ComposeParamT(3);

    ...
#undef ComposeParamT

    // constructors:
    Binder(FO& f): FO(f) {}
    Binder(FO& f, V& v): FO(f), V(v) {}
    Binder(FO& f, V const& v): FO(f), V(v) {}
    Binder(FO const& f): FO(f) {}
    Binder(FO const& f, V& v): FO(f), V(v) {}
    Binder(FO const& f, V const& v): FO(f), V(v) {}
    template<class T>
      Binder(FO& f, T& v): FO(f), V(BoundVal<T>(v)) {}
    template<class T>
      Binder(FO& f, T const& v): FO(f), V(BoundVal<T const>(v)) {}

    // "function calls":
    ReturnT operator() () {
        return FO::operator()(V::get());
    }
    ReturnT operator() (Param1T v1) {
        return FO::operator()(ArgSelect<1>::from(v1,v1,V::get()),
                              ArgSelect<2>::from(v1,v1,V::get()));
    }
    ReturnT operator() (Param1T v1, Param2T v2) {
        return FO::operator()(ArgSelect<1>::from(v1,v1,V::get()),
                              ArgSelect<2>::from(v1,v2,V::get()),
                              ArgSelect<3>::from(v2,v2,V::get()));
    }
    ReturnT operator() (Param1T v1, Param2T v2, Param3T v3) {
        return FO::operator()(ArgSelect<1>::from(v1,v1,V::get()),
                              ArgSelect<2>::from(v1,v2,V::get()),
                              ArgSelect<3>::from(v2,v3,V::get()),
```

```
                                  ArgSelect<4>::from(v3,v3,V::get())));
    }
    ...

private:
  template<int A>
  class ArgSelect {
    public:
      // type if we haven't passed the bound argument yet:
      typedef typename TypeOp<
                  typename IfThenElse<(A<=Params::NumParams),
                                      FunctorParam<Params, A>,
                                      FunctorParam<Params, A-1>
                            >::ResultT::Type>::RefT
            NoSkipT;
      // type if we're past the bound argument:
      typedef typename TypeOp<
                  typename IfThenElse<(A>1),
                                      FunctorParam<Params, A-1>,
                                      FunctorParam<Params, A>
                            >::ResultT::Type>::RefT
            SkipT;
      // type of bound argument:
      typedef typename TypeOp<typename V::ValueT>::RefT BindT;

      // three selection cases implemented through different classes:
      class NoSkip {
        public:
          static NoSkipT select (SkipT prev_arg, NoSkipT arg,
                                 BindT bound_val) {
            return arg;
          }
      };
      class Skip {
        public:
          static SkipT select (SkipT prev_arg, NoSkipT arg,
                               BindT bound_val) {
            return prev_arg;
          }
```

```
      };
      class Bind {
        public:
          static BindT select (SkipT prev_arg, NoSkipT arg,
                               BindT bound_val) {
              return bound_val;
          }
      };


      // the actual selection function:
      typedef typename SignSelectT<A-P, NoSkipT,
                                   BindT, SkipT>::ResultT
              ReturnT;
      typedef typename SignSelectT<A-P, NoSkip,
                                   Bind, Skip>::ResultT
              SelectedT;
      static ReturnT from (SkipT prev_arg, NoSkipT arg,
                           BindT bound_val) {
          return SelectedT::select (prev_arg, arg, bound_val);
      }
    };
};
```

22.8.4 Convenience Functions

As with the composition templates, it is useful to write function templates that make it easier to express the binding of a value to a functor parameter. The definition of such a template is made a little harder by the need to express the type of the bound value:

```
// functors/bindconv.hpp

#include "forwardparam.hpp"
#include "functorparam.hpp"


template <int P,          // position of the bound parameter
          typename FO>    // functor whose parameter is bound
inline
Binder<FO,P,BoundVal<typename FunctorParam<FO,P>::Type> >
bind (FO const& fo,
```

```
            typename ForwardParamT
                        <typename FunctorParam<FO,P>::Type>::Type val)
{
    return Binder<FO,
                  P,
                  BoundVal<typename FunctorParam<FO,P>::Type>
                  >(fo,
                    BoundVal<typename FunctorParam<FO,P>::Type>(val)
                    );
}
```

The first template parameter is not deducible: It must be specified explicitly when using the `bind()` template. The following example illustrates this:

```
// functors/bindtest.cpp

#include <string>
#include <iostream>
#include "funcptr.hpp"
#include "binder5.hpp"
#include "bindconv.hpp"

bool func (std::string const& str, double d, float f)
{
    std::cout << str << ": "
              << d << (d<f? "<": ">=")
              << f << '\n';
    return d<f;
}

int main()
{
    bool result = bind<1>(func_ptr(func), "Comparing")(1.0, 2.0);
    std::cout << "bound function returned " << result << '\n';
}
```

It may be tempting to simplify the `bind` template by adding a deducible template parameter for the bound value, thereby avoiding the cumbersome expression of the type, as done here. However, this often leads to difficulties in situations like this example, in which a literal of type `double` (2.0) is passed to a parameter of a compatible but different type `float`.

It is also often convenient to be able to bind a function (passed as a function pointer) directly. The definitions of the resulting `bindfp()` templates is only slightly more complicated than that of the `bind` template. Here is the code for the case of a function with two parameters:

// functors/bindfp2.hpp

```
// convenience function to bind a function pointer with two parameters
template<int PNum, typename RT, typename P1, typename P2>
inline
Binder<FunctionPtr<RT,P1,P2>,
       PNum,
       BoundVal<typename FunctorParam<FunctionPtr<RT,P1,P2>,
                                      PNum
                         >::Type
                >
      >
bindfp (RT (*fp)(P1,P2),
        typename ForwardParamT
                 <typename FunctorParam<FunctionPtr<RT,P1,P2>,
                                        PNum
                           >::Type
                 >::Type val)
{
    return Binder<FunctionPtr<RT,P1,P2>,
                  PNum,
                  BoundVal
                    <typename FunctorParam<FunctionPtr<RT,P1,P2>,
                                           PNum
                             >::Type
                    >
                  >(func_ptr(fp),
                    BoundVal<typename FunctorParam
                               <FunctionPtr<RT,P1,P2>,
                                PNum
                               >::Type
                            >(val)
                   );
}
```

22.9 Functor Operations: A Complete Implementation

To illustrate the overall effect achieved by our sophisticated treatment of functor composition and value binding, we provide here a complete implementation of these operations for functors with up to three parameters. (It is straightforward to extend this to a dozen parameters or so, but we prefer to keep the printed code relatively concise.)

Let's first look at some sample client code:

```
// functors/functorops.cpp

#include <iostream>
#include <string>
#include <typeinfo>
#include "functorops.hpp"

bool compare (std::string debugstr, double v1, float v2)
{
    if (debugstr != "") {
        std::cout << debugstr << ": " << v1
                                       << (v1<v2? '<' : '>')
                                       << v2 << '\n';
    }
    return v1<v2;
}

void print_name_value (std::string name, double value)
{
    std::cout << name << ": " << value << '\n';
}

double sub (double a, double b)
{
    return a-b;
}

double twice (double a)
{
    return 2*a;
}
```

```
int main()
{
    using std::cout;

    // demonstrate composition:
    cout << "Composition result: "
         << compose(func_ptr(sub), func_ptr(twice))(3.0, 7.0)
         << '\n';

    // demonstrate binding:
    cout << "Binding result:     "
         << bindfp<1>(compare, "main()->compare()")(1.02, 1.03)
         << '\n';
    cout << "Binding output:     ";
    bindfp<1>(print_name_value,
              "the ultimate answer to life")(42);

    // combine composition and binding:
    cout << "Mixing composition and binding (bind<1>): "
         << bind<1>(compose(func_ptr(sub),func_ptr(twice)),
                    7.0)(3.0)
         << '\n';
    cout << "Mixing composition and binding (bind<2>): "
         << bind<2>(compose(func_ptr(sub),func_ptr(twice)),
                    7.0)(3.0)
         << '\n';
}
```

The program has the following output:

```
Composition result: -8
Binding result:     main()->compare(): 1.02<1.03
1
Binding output:     the ultimate answer to life: 42
Mixing composition and binding (bind<1>): 8
Mixing composition and binding (bind<2>): -8
```

The main conclusion that can be drawn from this little program is that *using* the functor operations developed in this section is very simple (even though *implementing* them was no easy task).

Note also how the binding and the composing templates interoperate seemlessly. The core facility that enables this is the small set of conventions we established for functors in Section 22.6.1 on page 436. This is not unlike the requirements established for iterators in the C++ standard library. Functors that do not follow our conventions are easily wrapped in adapter classes (as illustrated by our `func_ptr()` adaptation templates). Furthermore, our design allows state-of-the-art compilers to avoid any unnecessary run-time penalty compared to hand-coded functors.

Finally, the contents of `functorops.hpp`, which shows which header files are necessary to be able to compile the previous example, looks as follows:

```
// functors/functorops.hpp

#ifndef FUNCTOROPS_HPP
#define FUNCTOROPS_HPP

// define func_ptr(), FunctionPtr, and FunctionPtrT
#include "funcptr.hpp"

// define Composer<>
#include "compose6.hpp"

// define convenience function compose()
#include "composeconv.hpp"

// define Binder<>
// - includes boundval.hpp to define BoundVal<> and StaticBoundVal<>
// - includes forwardparam.hpp to define ForwardParamT<>
// - includes functorparam.hpp to define FunctorParam<>
// - includes binderparams.hpp to define BinderParams<>
// - includes signselect.hpp to define SignSelectT<>
#include "binder5.hpp"

// define convenience functions bind() and bindfp()
#include "bindconv.hpp"
#include "bindfp1.hpp"
#include "bindfp2.hpp"
#include "bindfp3.hpp"

#endif // FUNCTOROPS_HPP
```

22.10   Afternotes

The STL part of the C++ standard library uses the concept of functors. For example, all algorithms use functors to customize their exact behavior. Many of these functors are so-called *predicates*. Predicates are functions or function objects that return a Boolean value (a value that is convertible to bool). The predicates, in general, should be pure functors; otherwise, unexpected results may occur (see Section 8.1.4 of [*JosuttisStdLib*]).

The C++ standard library also provides several standard functors and adapters for composition. In fact, for every common unary and binary operator a function object is provided. See Sections 8.2 and 8.3 of [*JosuttisStdLib*] for details. However, note that the C++ standard library does not provide enough adapters to support every functional behavior as a combination of function objects. For example, it is not possible to combine the results of two unary operations to formulate a criterion such as "this *and* that." The Boost repository of C++ libraries provides supplementary adapters that fill this gap (see [*BoostCompose*]).

Appendix A

The One-Definition Rule

Affectionately known as the *ODR*, the *one-definition rule* is a cornerstone for the well-formed structuring of C++ programs. The most common consequences of the ODR are simple enough to remember and apply: Define noninline functions exactly once across all files, and define classes and inline functions at most once per translation unit, making sure that all definitions for the same entity are identical.

However, the devil is in the details, and when combined with template instantiation, these details can be daunting. This appendix is meant to provide a comprehensive overview of the ODR for the interested reader. We also indicate when specific related issues are expounded on in the main text.

A.1   Translation Units

In practice we write C++ programs by filling files with "code." However, the boundary set by a file is not terribly important in the context of the ODR. Instead, what matters are so-called *translation units*. Essentially, a translation unit is the result of applying the preprocessor to a file you feed to your compiler. The preprocessor drops sections of code not selected by conditional compilation directives (#if, #ifdef, and friends), drops comments, inserts #included files (recursively), and expands macros.

Hence, as far as the ODR is concerned, having the following two files

```
// File header.hpp:
#ifdef DO_DEBUG
  #define debug(x) std::cout << x << '\n'
#else
  #define debug(x)
#endif

void debug_init();
```

```
// File myprog.cpp:
#include "header.hpp"

int main()
{
    debug_init();
    debug("main()");
}
```

is equivalent to the following single file:

```
// File myprog.cpp:
void debug_init();

int main()
{
    debug_init();
}
```

Connections across translation unit boundaries are established by having corresponding declarations with external linkage in two translation units (for example, two declarations of the global function `debug_init()`) or by argument-dependent lookup during the instantiation of `exported` templates.

Note that the concept of a translation unit is a little more abstract than just "a preprocessed file." For example, if we were to feed a preprocessed file twice to a compiler to form a single program, it would bring into the program two distinct translation units (there is no point in doing so, however).

A.2   Declarations and Definitions

The terms *declaration* and *definition* are often used interchangeably in common "programmer talk." In the context of the ODR, however, the exact meaning of these words is important.[1]

A declaration is a C++ construct that introduces or reintroduces a name in your program. A declaration can also be a definition, depending on which entity it introduces and how it introduces it:

- **Namespaces and namespace aliases:** The declarations of namespaces and their aliases are always also definitions, although the term *definition* is unusual in this context because the list of members of a namespace can be "extended" at a later time (unlike classes and enumeration types for example).

- **Classes, class templates, functions, function templates, member functions, and member function templates:** The declaration is a definition if and only if the declaration includes a brace-enclosed body associated with the name. This rule includes unions, operators, member

---

[1] We also think it's a good habit to handle the terms carefully when exchanging ideas about C or C++. We do so throughout this book.

operators, static member functions, constructors and destructors, and explicit specializations of template versions of such things (that is, any class-like and function-like entity).

- **Enumerations:** The declaration is a definition if and only if it includes the brace-enclosed list of enumerators.
- **Local variables and nonstatic data members:** These entities can always be treated as definitions, although the distinction rarely matters.
- **Global variables:** If the declaration is not directly preceded by a keyword `extern` or if it has an initializer, the declaration of a global variable is also a definition of that variable. Otherwise, it is not a definition.
- **Static data members:** The declaration is a definition if and only if it appears outside the class or class template of which it is a member.
- **Typedefs, using-declarations, and using-directives:** These are never definitions, although typedefs can be combined with class or union definitions.
- **Explicit instantiation directives:** We can consider them to be definitions.

A.3 The One-Definition Rule in Detail

As we implied in the introduction to this appendix, there are many details to the actual rule. We organize the rule's constraints by their scope.

A.3.1 One-per-Program Constraints

There can be at most one definition of the following items per program:
- Noninline functions and noninline member functions
- Variables with external linkage (essentially, variables declared in a namespace scope or in the global scope, and without the `static` specifier)
- Static data members
- Noninline function templates, noninline member function templates, and noninline members of class templates when they are declared with `export`
- Static data members of class templates when they are declared with `export`.

For example, a C++ program consisting of the following two translation units is invalid[2]:

```
// Translation unit 1:
int counter;
```

```
// Translation unit 2:
int counter;                    // ERROR: defined twice! (ODR violation)
```

---

[2] Interestingly, it is valid C because C has a concept of *tentative definition*, which is a variable definition without an initializer and can appear more than once in a program.

This rule does not apply to entities with *internal linkage* (essentially, entities declared with the `static` specifier in the global scope or in a namespace scope) because even when two such entities have the same name, they are considered distinct. In the same vein, entities declared in unnamed namespaces are considered distinct if they appear in distinct translation units. For example, the following two translation units can be combined into a valid C++ program:

```
// Translation unit 1:
static int counter = 2;   // unrelated to other translation units

namespace {
    void unique()          // unrelated to other translation units
    {
    }
}
```

```
// Translation unit 2:
static int counter = 0;   // unrelated to other translation units

namespace {
    void unique()          // unrelated to other translation units
    {
        ++counter;
    }
}

int main()
{
    unique();
}
```

Furthermore, there must be *exactly one* of the previously mentioned items in the program if they are *used*. The term *used* in this context has a precise meaning. It indicates that there is some sort of reference to the entity somewhere in the program. This reference can be an access to the value of a variable, a call to a function, or the address of such an entity. This reference can be explicit in the source, or it can be implicit. For example, a `new` expression may create an implicit call to the associated `delete` operator to handle situations when a constructor throws an exception requiring the unused (but allocated) memory to be cleaned up. Another example consists of copy constructors, which must be defined even if they end up being optimized away. Virtual functions are also implicitly used (by the internal structures that enable virtual function calls), unless they are pure virtual functions. Several other kinds of implicit uses exist, but we omit them for the sake of conciseness.

There are two kinds of references that do *not* constitute a use in the previous sense: The first kind occurs when a reference to an entity appears as part of a `sizeof` operator. The second kind is similar but with a twist: If a reference appears as part of a `typeid` operator (see Section 5.6 on page 58), it is not a use in the previous sense, unless the argument of the `typeid` operator ends up designating a polymorphic object (an object with (possibly inherited) virtual functions). For example, consider the following single-file program:

```
#include <typeinfo>

class Decider {
#if defined(DYNAMIC)
    virtual ~Decider() {
    }
#endif
};

extern Decider d;

int main()
{
    const char* name = typeid(d).name();
    return (int)sizeof(d);
}
```

This is a valid program if and only if the preprocessor symbol DYNAMIC is not defined. Indeed, the variable d is not defined, but the reference to d in `sizeof(d)` does not constitute a use, and the reference in `typeid(d)` is a use only if d is an object of a polymorphic type (because in general it is not always possible to determine the result of a polymorphic `typeid` operation until run time).

According to the C++ standard, the constraints described in this section do not require a diagnostic from a C++ implementation. In practice, they are almost always reported by linkers as duplicate or missing definitions.

A.3.2 One-per-Translation Unit Constraints

No entity can be defined more than once in a translation unit. So the following example is invalid C++:

```
inline void f() {}
inline void f() {}   // ERROR: duplicate definition
```

This is one of the main reasons for surrounding the code in header files with so-called *guards*:

```
// File guard_demo.hpp:
#ifndef GUARD_DEMO_HPP
#define GUARD_DEMO_HPP

...


#endif  // GUARD_DEMO_HPP
```

Such guards ensure that the second time a header file is #included, its contents are discarded, thereby avoiding a duplicate definition of any class, inline function, or template it contains.

The ODR also specifies that certain entities *must* be defined in certain circumstances. This can be the case for class types, inline functions, and non-export templates. In the following few paragraphs we review the detailed rules.

A class type X (including structs and unions) *must* be defined in a translation unit *prior* to any of the following kinds of uses in that translation unit:

- The creation of an object of type X (for example, as a variable declaration or through a new expression). The creation could be indirect, for example, when an object that itself contains an object of type X is being created.
- The declaration of a data member of type X.
- Applying the sizeof or typeid operator to an object of type X.
- Explicitly or implicitly accessing members of type X.
- Converting an expression to or from type X using any kind of conversion, or converting an expression to or from a pointer or reference to X (except void*) using an implicit cast, static_cast, or dynamic_cast.
- Assigning a value to an object of type X.
- Defining or calling a function with an argument or return type of type X. Just declaring such a function doesn't need the type to be defined however.

The rules for types also apply to types X generated from class templates, which means that the corresponding templates must be defined in those situations in which such a type X must be defined. These situations create so-called *points of instantiation* or *POI*s (see Section 10.3.2 on page 146).

Inline functions must be defined in every translation unit in which they are used (in which they are called or their address is taken). However, unlike class types, their definition can follow the point of use:

```
inline int not_so_fast();

int main()
{
    not_so_fast();
}

inline int not_so_fast()
{
}
```

Although this is valid C++, some compilers do not actually "inline" the call to a function with a body that has not been seen yet; hence the desired effect may not be achieved.

Just as with class templates, the use of a function generated from a parameterized function declaration (a function or member function template, or a member function of a class template) creates a point of instantiation. Unlike class templates, however, the corresponding definition can appear after the point of instantiation (or not at all if it is exported).

The facets of the ODR explained in this subsection are generally easily verified by C++ compilers; hence the C++ standard requires that compilers issue some sort of diagnostic when one of these rules is violated. An exception is the lack of definition of a nonexported parameterized function. Such situations are typically not diagnosed.

A.3.3 Cross-Translation Unit Equivalence Constraints

The ability to define certain kinds of entities in more than one translation unit brings with it the potential for a new kind of error: multiple definitions that don't match. Unfortunately, such errors are hard to detect by traditional compiler technology in which translation units are processed one at a time. Consequently, the C++ standard doesn't *mandate* that differences in multiple definitions be detected or diagnosed (it does *allow* it, of course). If this cross-translation unit constraint is violated, however, the C++ standard qualifies this as leading to *undefined behavior*, which means that anything reasonable or unreasonable may happen. Typically, such undiagnosed errors may lead to program crashes or wrong results, but in principle they can also lead to other, more direct, kinds of damage (for example, file corruption).[3]

The cross-translation unit constraints specify that when an entity is defined in two different places, the two places must consist of exactly the same sequence of tokens (the keywords, operators, identifiers, and so forth remaining after preprocessing). Furthermore, these tokens must mean the same thing in their respective context (for example, the identifiers may need to refer to the same variable).

Consider the following example:

```
// Translation unit 1:
static int counter = 0;
inline void increase_counter()
{
    ++counter;
}

int main()
{
}
```

---

[3] Version 1 of the gcc compiler actually jokingly did this by starting the game of Rogue in situations like this.

```
// Translation unit 2:
static int counter = 0;
inline void increase_counter()
{
    ++counter;
}
```

This example is in error because even though the token sequence for the inline function `increase_counter()` looks identical in both translation units, they contain a token `counter` that refers to two different entities. Indeed, because the two variables named `counter` have internal linkage (`static` specifier), they are unrelated despite having the same name. Note that this is an error even though neither of the inline functions is actually used.

Placing the definitions of entities that can be defined in multiple translation units in header files that are `#include`d whenever the definitions are needed ensures that token sequences are identical in almost all situations.[4] With this approach, situations in which two identical tokens refer to different things become fairly rare, but when it does happen, the resulting errors are often mysterious and hard to track.

The cross-translation unit constraints apply not only to entities that can be defined in multiple places, but also to default arguments in declarations. In other words, the following program has undefined behavior:

```
// Translation unit 1:
void unused(int = 3);

int main()
{
}
```

```
// Translation unit 2:
void unused(int = 4);
```

We should note here that the equivalence of token streams can sometimes involve subtle implicit effects. The following example is lifted (in a slightly modified form) from the C++ standard:

```
// Translation unit 1:
class X {
  public:
    X(int);
    X(int, int);
};
```

---

[4] Occasionally, conditional compilation directives evaluate differently in different translation units. Use such directives with care. Other differences are possible too, but they are even less common.

```
X::X(int = 0)
{
}

class D : public X {
};

D d2;   // X(int) called by D()
```

// Translation unit 2:
```
class X {
  public:
    X(int);
    X(int, int);
};

X::X(int = 0, int = 0)
{
}

class D : public X {   // X(int, int) called by D();
};                     // D()'s implicit definition violates the ODR
```

In this example, the problem occurs because the implicitly generated default constructor of class D is different in the two translation units. One calls the X constructor taking one argument, and the other calls the X constructor taking two arguments. If anything, this example is an additional incentive to limit default arguments to one location in the program (if possible, this location should be in a header file). Fortunately, placing default arguments on out-of-class definitions is a rare practice.

There is also an exception to the rule that says that identical tokens must refer to identical entities. If identical tokens refer to unrelated constants that have the same value and the address of the resulting expressions is not used, then the tokens are considered equivalent. This exception allows for program structures like the following:

// File header.hpp:
```
#ifndef HEADER_HPP
#define HEADER_HPP

int const length = 10;

class MiniBuffer {
  char buf[length];
```

```
    ...
};
```

```
#endif   // HEADER_HPP
```

In principle, when this header file is included in two different translation units, two distinct constant variables named `length` are created because `const` in this context implies `static`. However, such constant variables are often meant to define compile-time constant values, not a particular storage location at run time. Hence, if we don't force such a storage location to exist (by referring to the address of the variable), it is sufficient for the two constants to have the same value. This exception to the ODR equivalence rules applies only to integral and enumeration values (floating-point types and pointer types don't fall in this category).

Finally, a note about templates. The names in templates bind in two phases. So-called *nondependent names* bind at the point where the template is defined. For these, the equivalence rules are handled similarly to other nontemplate definitions. For names that bind at the point of instantiation, the equivalence rules must be applied at that point, and the bindings must be equivalent. This leads to a subtle observation: Although `exported` templates are defined in only one location, they may have multiple instances which must obey the equivalence rules. Here is a particularly far-fetched violation of the ODR:

```
// File header.hpp:
#ifndef HEADER_HPP
#define HEADER_HPP

enum Color { red, green, blue };
      // the associated namespace of Color is the global namespace

export template<typename T> void highlight(T);

void init();

#endif   // HEADER_HPP

// File tmpl_def.cpp:
#include "header.hpp"

export template<typename T>
void highlight(T x)
{
    paint(x);   // (1) a dependent call: argument-dependent lookup required
}
```

```
// File init.cpp:
#include "header.hpp"

namespace {  // unnamed namespace!
    void paint(Color c)   // (2)
    {
        ...
    }
}

void init()
{
    highlight(blue);        // argument-dependent lookup of (1) resolves to (2)
}

// File main.cpp:
#include "header.hpp"

namespace {  // unnamed namespace!
    void paint(Color c)   // (3)
    {
        ...
    }
}

int main()
{
    init();
    highlight(red);         // argument-dependent lookup of (1) resolves to (3)
}
```

To understand this example, we must remember that functions defined in an unnamed namespace have external linkage, but they are distinct from any functions defined in an unnamed namespace of other translation units. Therefore, the two paint() functions are distinct. However, the call to paint() in the exported template has a template-dependent argument and is therefore not bound until the points of instantiation. In our example, there are two points of instantiation for highlight<Color>, but they result in different bindings of the name paint; hence the program is invalid.

Appendix B

Overload Resolution

Overload resolution is the process that selects the function to call for a given call expression. Consider the following simple example:

```cpp
void display_num(int);      // (1)
void display_num(double);   // (2)

int main()
{
    display_num(399);       // matches (1) better than (2)
    display_num(3.99);      // matches (2) better than (1)
}
```

In this example, the function name `display_num()` is said to be *overloaded*. When this name is used in a call, a C++ compiler must therefore distinguish between the various candidates using additional information; mostly, this information is the types of the call arguments. In our example it makes intuitive sense to call the `int` version when the function is called with an integer argument and the `double` version when a floating-point argument is provided. The formal process that attempts to model this intuitive choice is the overload resolution process.

The general ideas behind the rules that guide overload resolution are simple enough, but the details have become quite complex during the C++ standardization process. This complexity was driven mostly by the desire to support various real-world examples that intuitively (to a human) seem to have an "obviously best match," but when trying to formalize this intuition, various subtleties arose.

In this appendix we provide a reasonably detailed survey of the overload resolution rules. However, the complexity of this process is such that we do not claim to cover every part of the topic.

B.1   When Does Overload Resolution Kick In?

Overload resolution is just one part of the complete processing of a function call. In fact, it is not part of every function call. First, calls through function pointers and calls through pointers to member functions are not subject to overload resolution because the function to call is entirely determined (at run time) by the pointers. Second, function-like macros cannot be overloaded and are therefore not subject to overload resolution.

At a very high level, a call to a named function can be processed in the following way:

- The name is looked up to form an initial *overload set.*
- If necessary, this set is tweaked in various ways (for example, template deduction occurs).
- Any candidate that doesn't match the call at all (even after considering implicit conversions and default arguments) is eliminated from the overload set. This results in a set of so-called *viable function candidates.*
- Overload resolution is performed to find a *best* candidate. If there is one, it is selected; otherwise, the call is ambiguous.
- The selected candidate is checked. For example, if it is an inaccessible private member, a diagnostic is issued.

Each of these steps has its own subtleties, but overload resolution is arguably the most complex. Fortunately, a few simple principles clarify the majority of situations. We examine these principles next.

B.2   Simplified Overload Resolution

Overload resolution ranks the viable candidate functions by comparing how each argument of the call matches the corresponding parameter of the candidates. For one candidate to be considered better than another, the better candidate cannot have any of its parameters be a worse match than the corresponding parameter in the other candidate. The following example illustrates this:

```
void combine(int, double);
void combine(long, int);

int main()
{
    combine (1, 2);   // ambiguous!
}
```

In this example, the call to `combine()` is ambiguous because the first candidate matches the first argument (the literal 1 of type `int`) *best*, whereas the second candidate matches the second argument *best*. We could argue that `int` is in some sense closer to `long` than to `double` (which supports choosing the second candidate), but C++ does not attempt to define a measure of closeness that involves multiple call arguments.

Given this first principle, we are left with specifying how well a given argument matches the corresponding parameter of a viable candidate. As a first approximation we can rank the possible matches as follows (from best to worst):

- Perfect match. The parameter has the type of the expression, or it has a type that is a reference to the type of the expression (possibly with added `const` and/or `volatile` qualifiers).
- Match with minor adjustments. This includes, for example, the decay of an array variable to a pointer to its first element, or the addition of `const` to match an argument of type `int**` to a parameter of type `int const* const*`.
- Match with promotion. Promotion is a kind of implicit conversion that includes the conversion of small integral types (such as `bool`, `char`, `short`, and sometimes enumerations) to `int`, `unsigned int`, `long` or `unsigned long`, and the conversion of `float` to `double`.
- Match with standard conversions only. This includes any sort of standard conversion (such as `int` to `float`) but excludes the implicit call to a conversion operator or a converting constructor.
- Match with user-defined conversions. This allows any kind of implicit conversion.
- Match with ellipsis. An ellipsis parameter can match almost any type (but non-POD class types result in undefined behavior).

The following contrived example illustrates some of these matches:

```
int f1(int);        // (1)
int f1(double);     // (2)
f1(4);              // calls (1): perfect match
                    //            ((2) requires a standard conversion)

int f2(int);        // (3)
int f2(char);       // (4)
f2(true);           // calls (3): match with promotion
                    //            ((4) requires stronger standard conversion)

class X {
  public:
    X(int);
};
int f3(X);          // (5)
int f3(...);        // (6)
f3(7);              // calls (5): match with user-defined conversion
                    //            ((6) requires a match with ellipsis)
```

Note that overload resolution occurs *after* template argument deduction, and this deduction does not consider all these sorts of conversions. The following example illustrates this:

```
template <typename T>
class MyString {
```

```
  public:
    MyString(T const*);   // converting constructor
    ...
};

template<typename T>
MyString<T> truncate(MyString<T> const&, int);

int main()
{
    MyString<char> str1, str2;
    str1 = truncate<char>("Hello World", 5);   // OK
    str2 = truncate("Hello World", 5);          // ERROR
}
```

The implicit conversion provided through the converting constructor is not considered during template argument deduction. The assignment to `str2` finds no viable function `truncate()`; hence overload resolution is not performed at all.

The previous principles are only a first approximation, but they cover many cases. Yet there are quite a few common situations that are not adequately explained by these rules. We proceed with a brief discussion of the most important refinements of these rules.

B.2.1   The Implied Argument for Member Functions

Calls to nonstatic member functions have a hidden parameter that is accessible in the definition of the member function as `*this`. For a member function of a class `MyClass`, the hidden parameter is usually of type `MyClass&` (for non-`const` member functions) or `MyClass const&` (for `const` member functions).[1] This is somewhat surprising given that `this` has a pointer type. It would have been nicer to make `this` equivalent to what is now `*this`. However, `this` was part of an early version of C++ before reference types were part of the language, and by the time reference types were added, too much code already depended on `this` being a pointer.

The hidden `*this` parameter participates in overload resolution just like the explicit parameters. Most of the time this is quite natural, but occasionally it comes unexpectedly. The following example shows a string-like class that does not work as intended (yet we have seen such code in the real world):

_____

[1] It could also be of type `MyClass volatile&` or `MyClass const volatile&` if the member function was `volatile`, but this is extremely rare.

```
#include <stddef.h>

class BadString {
  public:
    BadString(char const*);
    ...

    // character access through subscripting:
    char& operator[] (size_t);                              // (1)
    char const& operator[] (size_t) const;

    // implicit conversion to null-terminated byte string:
    operator char* ();                                      // (2)
    operator char const* ();
    ...
};

int main()
{
    BadString str("correkt");
    str[5] = 'c';   // possibly an overload resolution ambiguity!
}
```

At first, nothing seems ambiguous about the expression `str[5]`. The subscript operator at (1) seems like a perfect match. However, it is not *quite* perfect because the argument 5 has type `int`, and the operator expects an unsigned integer type (`size_t` and `std::size_t` usually have type `unsigned int` or `unsigned long`, but never type `int`). Still, a simple standard integer conversion makes (1) easily viable. However, there is another viable candidate: the built-in subscript operator. Indeed, if we apply the implicit conversion operator to `str` (which is the implicit member function argument), we obtain a pointer type, and now the built-in subscript operator applies. This built-in operator takes an argument of type `ptrdiff_t`, which on many platforms is equivalent to `int` and therefore is a perfect match for the argument 5. So even though the built-in subscript operator is a poor match (by user-defined conversion) for the implied argument, it is a better match than the operator defined at (1) for the actual subscript! Hence the potential ambiguity.[2] To solve this kind of problem portably, you can declare operator `[]` with a `ptrdiff_t` parameter, or you can replace the implicit type conversion to `char*` by an explicit conversion (which is usually recommended anyway).

It is possible for a set of viable candidates to contain both static and nonstatic members. When comparing a static member with a nonstatic member, the quality of the match of the implicit argument is ignored (only the nonstatic member has an implicit `*this` argument).

---

[2] Note that the ambiguity exists only on platforms for which `size_t` is a synonym for `unsigned int`. On platforms for which it is a synonym for `unsigned long`, the type `ptrdiff_t` is a typedef of `long`, and no ambiguity exists because the built-in subscript operator also requires a conversion of the subscript expression.

B.2.2   Refining the Perfect Match

For an argument of type int, there are three common parameter types that constitute a perfect match: int, int&, and int const&. However, it is rather common to overload a function on both kinds of references:

```
void report(int&);          // (1)
void report(int const&);    // (2)

int main()
{
    for (int k = 0; k<10; ++k) {
        report(k);          // calls (1)
    }
    report(42);             // calls (2)
}
```

In such cases the version without the extra const is preferred for lvalues, whereas the version with const is preferred for rvalues.

Note that this also applies to the implicit argument of a member function call:

```
class Wonder {
  public:
    void tick();            // (1)
    void tick() const;      // (2)
    void tack() const;      // (3)
};

void run(Wonder& device)
{
    device.tick();          // calls (1)
    device.tack();          // calls (3) because there is no non-const version
                            // of Wonder::tack()
}
```

Finally, the following modification of our earlier example illustrates that two perfect matches can also create an ambiguity if you overload with and without references:

```
void report(int);           // (1)
void report(int&);          // (2)
void report(int const&);    // (3)
```

```
int main()
{
    for (int k = 0; k<10; ++k) {
        report(k);            // ambiguous: (1) and (2) match equally well
    }
    report(42);               // ambiguous: (1) and (3) match equally well
}
```

To summarize:
- T and T const& both match equally well for an rvalue of type T.
- T and T& both match equally well for an lvalue of type T.

B.3   Overloading Details

The previous section covers most of the overloading situations encountered in everyday C++ programming. There are, unfortunately, many more rules and exceptions to these rules—more than is reasonable to present in a book that is not really about function overloading in C++. Nonetheless, we discuss some of them here in part because they apply somewhat more often than other rules and in part to provide a sense for how deep the details go.

B.3.1   Prefer Nontemplates

When all other aspects of overload resolution are equal, a nontemplate function is preferred over an instance of a template (it doesn't matter whether that instance is generated from the generic template definition or whether it is provided as an explicit specialization). For example:

```
template<typename T> int f(T);     // (1)
void f(int);                       // (2)

int main()
{
    return f(7);   // ERROR: selects (2), which doesn't return a value
}
```

This example also clearly illustrates that overload resolution normally does not involve the return type of the selected function.

If the choice is between two templates, then the *most specialized* of the templates is preferred (provided one is actually more specialized than the other). See Section 12.2.2 on page 186 for a thorough explanation of this concept.

B.3.2   Conversion Sequences

An implicit conversion can, in general, be a sequence of elementary conversions. Consider the
following code example:

```
class Base {
  public:
    operator short() const;
};

class Derived : public Base {
};

void count(int);

void process(Derived const& object)
{
    count(object);      // matches with user-defined conversion
}
```

The call `count(object)` works because `object` can implicitly be converted to `int`. However, this
conversion requires several steps:

1. A conversion of `object` from `Derived const` to `Base const`
2. A user-defined conversion of the resulting `Base const` object to type `short`
3. A promotion of `short` to `int`

This is the most general kind of conversion sequence: a standard conversion (a derived-to-base con-
version, in this case), followed by a user-defined conversion, followed by another standard conver-
sion. Although there can be at most one user-defined conversion in a conversion sequence, it is also
possible to have only standard conversions.

An important principle of overload resolution is that a conversion sequence that is a subsequence
of another conversion sequence is preferable over the latter sequence. If there were an additional
candidate function

```
void count(short);
```

in the example, it would be preferred for the call `count(object)` because it doesn't require the third
step (promotion) in the conversion sequence.

B.3.3   Pointer Conversions

Pointers and pointers to members undergo various special standard conversions, including

* Conversions to type `bool`
* Conversions from an arbitrary pointer type to `void*`

- Derived-to-base conversions for pointers
- Base-to-derived conversions for pointers to members

Although all of these can cause a "match with standard conversions only," they are not ranked equally.

First, conversions to type `bool` (both from a regular pointer and from a pointer to a member) are considered worse than any other kind of standard conversion. For example:

```
void check(void*);    // (1)
void check(bool);     // (2)

void rearrange (Matrix* m)
{
    check(m);         // calls (1)
    ...
}
```

Within the category of regular pointer conversions, a conversion to type `void*` is considered worse than a conversion from a derived class pointer to a base class pointer. Furthermore, if conversions to different classes related by inheritance exist, a conversion to the most derived class is preferred. Here is another short example:

```
class Interface {
    ...
};

class CommonProcesses : public Interface {
    ...
};

class Machine : public CommonProcesses {
    ...
};

char* serialize(Interface*);          // (1)
char* serialize(CommonProcesses*);    // (2)

void dump (Machine* machine)
{
    char* buffer = serialize(machine);  // calls (2)
    ...
}
```

The conversion from `Machine*` to `CommonProcesses*` is preferred over the conversion to `Interface*`, which is fairly intuitive.

A very similar rule applies to pointers to members: Between two conversions of related pointer-to-member types, the "closest base" in the inheritance graph (that is, the least derived) is preferred.

B.3.4   Functors and Surrogate Functions

We mentioned earlier that after the name of a function has been looked up to create an initial overload set, the set is tweaked in various ways. An interesting situation arises when a call expression refers to a class type object instead of a function. In this case there are two potential additions to the overload set.

The first addition is straightforward: Any member operator () (the function call operator) is added to the set. Objects with such operators are usually called *functors* (see Chapter 22).

A less obvious addition occurs when a class type object contains an implicit conversion operator to a pointer to a function type (or to a reference to a function type).[3] In such situations, a dummy (so-called *surrogate*) function is added to the overload set. This surrogate function candidate is considered to have an implied parameter of the type designated by the conversion function, in addition to parameters with types corresponding to the parameter types in the destination type of that conversion function. An example makes this much clearer:

```
typedef void FuncType(double, int);

class IndirectFunctor {
  public:
    ...
    void operator()(double, double) const;
    operator FuncType*() const;
};

void activate(IndirectFunctor const& funcObj)
{
    funcObj(3, 5);   // ERROR: ambiguous!
}
```

The call `funcObj(3, 5)` is treated as a call with three arguments: `funcObj`, 3, and 5. The viable function candidates include the member operator () (which is treated as having parameter types `IndirectFunctor&`, `double`, and `double`) and a surrogate function with parameters of type `FuncType*`, `double`, and `int`. The surrogate function has a worse match for the implied parameter

---

[3] The conversion operator must also be applicable in the sense that, for example, a non-`const` operator is not considered for `const` objects.

(because it requires a user-defined conversion), but it has a better match for the last parameter; hence the two candidates cannot be ordered. The call is therefore ambiguous.

Surrogate functions are in the most obscure corners of C++ and rarely occur in practice (fortunately).

B.3.5   Other Overloading Contexts

So far we have discussed overloading in the context of determining which function should be called in a call expression. However, there are a few other contexts in which a similar selection must be made.

The first context occurs when the address of a function is needed. Consider the following example:

```
int n_elements(Matrix const&);   // (1)
int n_elements(Vector const&);   // (2)

void compute()
{
    ...
    int (*funcPtr)(Vector const&) = n_elements;   // selects (2)
    ...
}
```

Here, the name n_elements refers to an overload set, but only the address of one function in that set is desirable. Overload resolution then attempts to match the required function type (the type of funcPtr in this example) to the available candidates.

The other context that requires overload resolution is *initialization*. Unfortunately, this is a topic fraught with subtleties that are beyond what can be covered in an appendix. However, a simple example at least illustrates this additional aspect of overload resolution:

```
#include <string>

class BigNum {
  public:
    BigNum(long n);
    BigNum(double n);
    BigNum(std::string const&);
    ...
    operator double();
    operator long();
    ...
};
```

```
void initDemo()
{
    BigNum bn1(100103);
    BigNum bn2("7057103224.095764");
    int in = bn1;
}
```

In this example, overload resolution is needed to select the appropriate constructor or conversion operator. In the vast majority of cases, the overloading rules produce the intuitive result. However, the details of these rules are quite complex, and some applications rely on some of the more obscure corners in this area of the C++ language (for example, the design of `std::auto_ptr`).

Bibliography

This appendix lists the resources that were mentioned, adopted, or cited in this book. These days many of the advancements in programming happen in electronic forums. It is therefore not surprising to find, in addition to the more traditional books and articles, quite a few Web sites. We certainly do not claim that our list is close to being comprehensive. However, we do find that they are relevant contributions to the topic of C++ templates.

Web sites are typically considerably more volatile than books and articles. The Internet links listed here may not be valid in the future. Therefore, we provide the actual list of links for this book at the following site (and we expect this site to be stable):

`http://www.josuttis.com/tmplbook`

Before listing the books, articles, and Web sites, we introduce the more interactive kind of resources that are provided by so-called *newsgroups*.

Newsgroups

Usenet is a large and diverse collection of electronic forums often called *newsgroups*. Some of these newsgroups are *moderated*, which means that every submission is examined in some way for its appropriateness.

A few Usenet groups are dedicated to the discussion of the C++ language. In fact, many of the most advanced techniques presented in this book were first published in some of these groups. In some cases, techniques were developed through collaborative discussion in these groups.

The following Usenet newsgroups discuss C++, the standard, and the C++ standard library:

- Tutorial level C++ (unmoderated)

  `alt.comp.lang.learn.c-c++`

- General aspects of C++ (unmoderated)

  `comp.lang.c++`

- General aspects of C++ (moderated)

  `comp.lang.c++.moderated`

- Aspects of the C++ standard (moderated)

  `comp.std.c++`

If you don't have access to a Usenet newsgroups server, you can use the Google Usenet archive:

`http://groups.google.com`

Books and Web Sites

[*AlexandrescuDesign*]
Andrei Alexandrescu
Modern C++ Design
Generic Programming and Design Patterns Applied
Addison-Wesley, Reading, MA, 2001

[*AusternSTL*]
Matthew H. Austern
Generic Programming and the STL
Using and Extending the C++ Standard Template Library
Addison-Wesley, Reading, MA, 1999

[*BCCL*]
Jeremy Siek
The Boost Concept Check Library
`http://www.boost.org/libs/concept_check/concept_check.htm`

[*Blitz++*]
Todd Veldhuizen
Blitz++: Object-Oriented Scientific Computing
`http://www.oonumerics.org/blitz`

[*Boost*]
The Boost Repository for Free, Peer-Reviewed C++ Libraries
`http://www.boost.org`

[*BoostCompose*]
Boost Compose Library
`http://www.boost.org/libs/compose`

[*BoostSmartPtr*]
Smart Pointer Library
`http://www.boost.org/libs/smart_ptr`

[*BoostTypeTraits*]
Type Traits Library
http://www.boost.org/libs/type_traits

[*CargillExceptionSafety*]
Tom Cargill
Exception Handling: A False Sense of Security
Available at: http://www.awprofessional.com/meyerscddemo/demo/magazine/index.htm
C++ Report, November-December 1994

[*CoplienCRTP*]
James O. Coplien
Curiously Recurring Template Patterns
C++ Report, February 1995

[*CoreIssue115*]
Core Issue 115 of the C++ Standard
http://anubis.dkuug.dk/jtc1/sc22/wg21/docs/cwg_toc.html

[*CzarneckiEiseneckerGenProg*]
Krzysztof Czarnecki, Ulrich W. Eisenecker
Generative Programming
Methods, Tools, and Applications
Addison-Wesley, Reading, MA, 2000

[*DesignPatternsGoV*]
Erich Gamma, Richard Helm, Ralph Johnson, John Vlissides
Design Patterns
Elements of Reusable Object-Oriented Software
Addison-Wesley, Reading, MA, 1995

[*EDG*]
Edison Design Group
Compiler Front Ends for the OEM Market
http://www.edg.com

[*EllisStroustrupARM*]
Margaret A. Ellis, Bjarne Stroustrup
The Annotated C++ Reference Manual (ARM)
Addison-Wesley, Reading, MA, 1990

[*JosuttisAutoPtr*]
Nicolai M. Josuttis
auto_ptr and auto_ptr_ref
http://www.josuttis.com/libbook/auto_ptr.html

[*JosuttisOOP*]
Nicolai M. Josuttis
Object-Oriented Programming in C++
John Wiley and Sons Ltd, 2002

[*JosuttisStdLib*]
Nicolai M. Josuttis
The C++ Standard Library
A Tutorial and Reference
Addison-Wesley, Reading, MA, 1999

[*KoenigMooAcc*]
Andrew Koenig, Barbara E. Moo
Accelerated C++
Practical Programming by Example
Addison-Wesley, Reading, MA, 2000

[*LambdaLib*]
Jaakko Järvi, Gary Powell
LL, The Lambda Library
http://www.boost.org/libs/lambda/doc

[*LippmanObjMod*]
Stanley B. Lippman
Inside the C++ Object Model
Addison-Wesley, Reading, MA, 1996

[*MeyersCounting*]
Scott Meyers
Counting Objects In C++
C/C++ Users Journal, April 1998

[*MeyersEffective*]
Scott Meyers
Effective C++
50 Specific Ways to Improve Your Programs and Design (2nd Edition)
Addison-Wesley, Reading, MA, 1998

[*MeyersMoreEffective*]
Scott Meyers
More Effective C++
35 New Ways to Improve Your Programs and Designs
Addison-Wesley, Reading, MA, 1996

[*MTL*]
Andrew Lumsdaine, Jeremy Siek
MTL, The Matrix Template Library
http://www.osl.iu.edu/research/mtl

[*MusserWangDynaVeri*]
D. R. Musser, C. Wang
Dynamic Verification of C++ Generic Algorithms
IEEE Transactions on Software Engineering, Vol. 23, No. 5, May 1997

[*MyersTraits*]
Nathan C. Myers
Traits: A New and Useful Template Technique
http://www.cantrip.org/traits.html

[*NewMat*]
Robert Davies
NewMat10, A Matrix Library in C++
http://www.robertnz.com/nm_intro.htm

[*NewShorterOED*]
Leslie Brown, *et al.*
The New Shorter Oxford English Dictionary (fourth edition)
Oxford University Press, Oxford, 1993

[*POOMA*]
POOMA: A High-Performance C++ Toolkit for Parallel Scientific Computation
http://www.pooma.com

[*Standard98*]
ISO
Information Technology—Programming Languages—C++
Document Number ISO/IEC 14882-1998
ISO/IEC, 1998

[*Standard02*]
ISO
Information Technology—Programming Languages—C++
(as amended by the first technical corrigendum)
Document Number ISO/IEC 14882-2002
ISO/IEC, expected late 2002

[*StroustrupC++PL*]
Bjarne Stroustrup
The C++ Programming Language, Special ed.
Addison-Wesley, Reading, MA, 2000

[*StroustrupDnE*]
Bjarne Stroustrup
The Design and Evolution of C++
Addison-Wesley, Reading, MA, 1994

[*StroustrupGlossary*]
Bjarne Stroustrup
Bjarne Stroustrup's C++ Glossary
`http://www.research.att.com/~bs/glossary.html`

[*SutterExceptional*]
Herb Sutter
Exceptional C++
47 Engineering Puzzles, Programming Problems, and Solutions
Addison-Wesley, Reading, MA, 2000

[*SutterMoreExceptional*]
Herb Sutter
More Exceptional C++
40 New Engineering Puzzles, Programming Problems, and Solutions
Addison-Wesley, Reading, MA, 2001

[*UnruhPrimeOrig*]
Erwin Unruh
Original Metaprogram for Prime Number Computation
`http://www.erwin-unruh.de/primorig.html`

[*VandevoordeSolutions*]
David Vandevoorde
C++ Solutions
Addison-Wesley, Reading, MA, 1998

[*VeldhuizenMeta95*]
Todd Veldhuizen
Using C++ Template Metaprograms
C++ Report, May 1995

[*VeldhuizenPapers*]
Todd Veldhuizen
Todd Veldhuizen's Papers and Articles about Generic Programming and Templates
`http://osl.iu.edu/~tveldhui/papers`

Glossary

This glossary is a compilation of the most important technical terms that are topic in this book. See [*StroustrupGlossary*] for a very complete, general glossary of terms used by C++ programmers.

abstract class
A class for which the creation of concrete objects (*instances*) is impossible. Abstract classes can be used to collect common properties of different classes in a single type or to define a polymorphic interface. Because abstract classes are used as base classes, the acronym *ABC* is sometimes used for *abstract base class*.

ADL
An acronym for *argument-dependent lookup*. ADL is a process that looks for a name of a function (or operator) in namespaces and classes that are in some way associated with the arguments of the function call in which that function (or operator name) appears. For historical reasons, it is sometimes called *extended Koenig lookup* or just *Koenig lookup* (the latter is also used for *ADL* applied to operators only).

angle bracket hack
A nonstandard feature that allows a compiler to accept two consecutive > characters as two closing *angle brackets* (even though they normally require intervening *whitespace*). For example, the expression `vector<list<int>>` is not valid C++ but is treated identically to `vector<list<int> >` by the angle bracket hack.

angle brackets
The characters < and > when they are used to delimit a list of template arguments or template parameters.

ANSI
An acronym for *American National Standard Institute*. A private, nonprofit organization that coordinates efforts to produce standard specifications of all kinds. A subcommittee called J16 is a driving force behind the standardization of C++. It cooperates closely with the international standards organization (ISO).

argument

A value (in a broad sense) that substitutes a *parameter* of a programmatic entity. For example, in a function call abs(-3) the argument is -3. In some programming communities *arguments* are called *actual parameters* (whereas *parameters* are called *formal parameters*).

argument-dependent lookup

See *ADL*.

class

The description of a category of objects. The class defines a set of characteristics for any object. These include its data (*attributes*, *data members*) as well as its operations (*methods*, *member functions*). In C++, classes are structures with members that can also be functions and are subject to access limitations. They are declared using the keywords class or struct.

class template

A construct that represents a family of classes. It specifies a pattern from which actual classes can be generated by substituting the template parameters by specific entities. Class templates are sometimes called *"parameterized" classes*, although this term is more general.

class type

A C++ type declared with class, struct, or union.

collection class

A class that is used to manage a group of objects. In C++, collection classes are also called *containers*.

constant-expression

An expression whose value is computed at compile time by the compiler. We sometimes call this a *true constant* to avoid confusion with *constant expression* (without hyphen). The latter includes expressions that are constant but cannot be computed at compile time by the compiler.

const member function

A member function that can be called for constant and temporary objects because it does not normally modify members of the *this object.

container

See *collection class*.

conversion operator

A special member function that defines how an object can implicitly (or explicitly) be converted to an object of another type. It is declared using the form operator *type*().

CRTP

An acronym for *curiously recurring template pattern*. This refers to a code pattern where a class *X* derives from a base class that has *X* as a template argument.

curiously recurring template pattern
See *CRTP*.

decay
The implicit conversion of an array or a function to a pointer. For example, the string literal `"Hello"` has type `char const[6]`, but in many C++ contexts it is implicitly converted to a pointer of type `char const*` (which points to the first character of the string).

declaration
A C++ construct that introduces or reintroduces a name into a C++ scope. See also *definition*.

deduction
The process that implicitly determines template arguments from the context in which template are used. The complete term is *template argument deduction*.

definition
A *declaration* that makes the details of the declared entity known or, in the case of variables, that forces storage space to be reserved for the declared entity. For class types and function definitions, this amounts to declarations that include a brace-enclosed body. For external variable declarations, this means either a declaration with no `extern` keyword or a declaration with an initializer.

dependent base class
A base class that depends on a template parameter. Special care must be taken to access members of dependent base classes. See also *two-phase lookup*.

dependent name
A name the meaning of which depends on a template parameter. For example, `A<T>::x` is a dependent name when `A` or `T` is a template parameter. The name of a function in a function call is also dependent if any of the arguments in the call has a type that depends on a template parameter. For example, `f` in `f((T*)0)` is dependent if `T` is a template parameter. The name of a template parameter is not considered dependent, however. See also *two-phase lookup*.

digraph
A combination of two consecutive characters that are equivalent to another single character in C++ code. The purpose of digraphs is to allow the input of C++ source code with keyboards that lack certain characters. Although they are used relatively rarely, the digraph `<:` is sometimes accidentally formed when a left *angle bracket* is followed by a scope resolution operator (`::`) without the required intervening *whitespace*.

dot-C file
A file in which *definitions* of variables and noninline functions are located. Most of the executable (as opposed to declarative) code of a program is normally placed in dot-C files. They are named *dot-C* files because they are usually named with a suffix such as `.cpp`, `.C`, `.c`, `.cc`, or `.cxx`. See also *header file* and *translation unit*.

EBCO
An acronym for *empty base class optimization*. An optimization performed by most modern compilers whereby an "empty" base class subobject does not occupy any storage.

empty base class optimization
See *EBCO*.

explicit instantiation directive
A C++ construct the sole purpose of which is to create a *POI*.

explicit specialization
A construct that declares or defines an alternative definition for a substituted template. The original (generic) template is called the *primary template*. If the alternative definition still depends on one or more template parameters, it is called a *partial specialization*. Otherwise, it is a *full specialization*.

expression template
A class template used to represent a part of an expression. The template itself represents a particular kind of operation. The template parameters stand for the kinds of operands to which the operation applies.

friend name injection
The process that makes a function name visible when it is declared only friend.

full specialization
See *explicit specialization*.

function object
See *functor*.

function template
A construct that represents a family of functions. It specifies a pattern from which actual functions can be generated by substituting the template parameters by specific entities. Note that a function template is a template and not a function. Function templates are sometimes called *"parameterized" functions*, although the latter term is more general.

functor
An object (also called a *function object*) that can be called using the *function call syntax*. In C++, these are pointers or references to functions and classes with a member operator ().

header file
A file meant to become part of a translation unit through a #include directive. Such files often contain *declarations* of variables and functions that are referred to from more than one translation unit, as well as *definitions* of types, inline functions, templates, constants, and macros. They are usually named with a suffix like .hpp, .h, .H, .hh, or .hxx. They are also called *include files*. See also *dot-C file* and *translation unit*.

include file
See *header file*.

indirect call
A function call for which the called function is not known until the call actually occurs (at run time).

initializer
A construct that specifies how to initialize a named object. For example, in

```
std::complex<float> z1 = 1.0, z2(0.0, 1.0);
```

the initializers are = 1.0 and (0.0, 1.0).

initializer list
A comma-separated list of expressions enclosed in braces used to initialize objects (or arrays). In constructors it can be used to define values to initialize members and base classes.

injected class name
The name of a class as it is visible in its own scope. For class templates, the name of the template is treated within the scope of the template as a class name if the name is not followed by a template argument list.

instance
The term *instance* has two meanings in C++ programming: The meaning that is taken from the object oriented terminology is *an instance of a class*: An object that is the realization of a class. For example, in C++, std::cout is an instance of the class std::ostream. The other meaning (and the one that is almost always intended in this book) is *a template instance*: A class, a function, or a member function obtained by substituting all the template parameters by specific values. In this sense, an *instance* is also called a *specialization*, although the latter term is often mistaken for *explicit specialization*.

instantiation
The process of creating a regular class, function, or member function from a template by substituting template parameters with actual values. The alternative sense of creating an *instance* (object) of a class is not used in this book (see *instance*).

ISO
World-wide acronym for International Organization for Standardization. An ISO workgroup called WG21 is a driving force behind the efforts to standardize and develop C++.

iterator
An object that knows how to traverse a sequence of elements. Often, these elements belong to a collection (see *collection class*).

linkable entity
A noninline function or member function, a global variable, or a static data member, including any such things generated from a template.

lvalue
In the original C language, an expression was called an *lvalue* if it could appear on the *left* of an assignment operator. Conversely, an expression that could appear only on the *right* of an assignment operator was called an *rvalue*. This definition is no longer appropriate in modern C and C++. Instead an *lvalue* can be thought of as a *locator value*: An expression that designates an object by name or address (pointer, reference, or array access) rather than by pure computation. Lvalues need not be modifiable (for example, the name of a constant object is a *nonmodifiable lvalue*). All expressions that are not lvalues are *rvalues*. In particular, temporary objects created explicitly (T()) or as the result of function calls are rvalues.

member class template
A construct that represents a family of member classes. It is a class template declared inside another class or class template. It has its own set of template parameters (unlike a member class of a class template).

member function template
A construct that represents a family of member functions. It has its own set of template parameters (unlike a member function of a class template). It is very similar to a function template, but when all the template parameters are substituted, the result is a member function (instead of an ordinary function). Member function templates cannot be virtual.

member template
A *member class template* or a *member function template*.

nondependent name
A name that is not dependent on a template parameter. See *dependent name* and *two-phase lookup*.

ODR
An acronym for *one-definition rule*. This rule places some restrictions on the *definitions* that appear in a C++ program. See Section 7.4 on page 90 and Appendix A for details.

one-definition rule
See *ODR*.

overload resolution
The process that selects which function to call when several candidates (usually all having the same name) exist.

parameter
A placeholder entity that is meant to be substituted with an actual "value" (an *argument*) at some point. For macro parameters and template parameters, the substitution occurs at compile time. For function call parameters it happens at run time. In some programming communities *parameters* are called *formal parameters* (whereas *arguments* are called *actual parameters*). See also *argument*.

parameterized class
A class template or a class nested in a class template. Both are *parameterized* because they do not correspond to a unique class until the template arguments have been specified.

parameterized function
A function or member function template or a member function of a class template. All are *parameterized* because they do not correspond to a unique function (or member function) until the template arguments have been specified.

partial specialization
A construct that declares or defines an alternative definition for certain substitutions of a template. The original (generic) template is called the *primary template*. The alternative definition still depends on template parameters. Currently, this construct exists only for class templates. See also *explicit specialization*.

POD
An acronym for "plain old data (type)." POD types are types that can be defined without certain C++ features (like virtual member functions, access keywords, and so forth). For example, every ordinary C struct is a POD.

POI
An acronym for *point of instantiation*. A POI is a location in the source code where a template (or a member of a template) is conceptually expanded by substituting template parameters with template arguments. In practice, this expansion does not need to occur at every POI. See also *explicit instantiation directive*.

point of instantiation
See *POI*.

policy class
A class or class template the members of which describe configurable behavior for a generic component. Policies are normally passed as template arguments. For example, a sorting template may have an ordering policy. *Policy classes* are also called *policy templates* or just *policies*. See also *traits template*.

polymorphism
The ability of an operation (which is identified by its name) to apply to objects of different kinds. In C++, the traditional object-oriented concept of polymorphism (also called *run-time* or *dynamic* polymorphism) is achieved through virtual functions that are overridden in derived classes. In addition, C++ templates enable so-called *static* polymorphism.

precompiled header
A processed form of source code that can quickly be loaded by the compiler. The source code underlying a precompiled header must be the first part of a *translation unit* (in other words, it cannot start somewhere in the middle of a translation unit). Often, a precompiled header corresponds to a number of header files. Using precompiled headers can substantially improve the time needed to build a large application written in C++.

primary template
A template that is not a *partial specialization*.

qualified name
A name containing a scope qualifier (: :).

reference counting
A resource management strategy that keeps count of how many entities are referring to a particular resource. When the count drops to zero, the resource can be disposed of.

rvalue
See *lvalue*.

source file
A *header file* or a *dot-C file*.

specialization
The result of substituting template parameters by actual values. A specialization may be created by an *instantiation* or by an *explicit specialization*. This term is sometimes mistakenly equated with *explicit specialization*. See also *instance*.

template
A construct that represents a family of classes or functions. It specifies a pattern from which actual classes or functions can be generated by substituting the template parameters by specific entities. In this book, the term does not include functions, classes, and static data members that are parameterized only by virtue of being members of a class template. See *class template*, *parameterized class*, *function template*, and *parameterized function*.

template argument
The "value" substituted for a *template parameter*. This "value" is usually a type, although certain constant values and templates can be valid template arguments too.

template argument deduction
See *deduction*.

template-id
The combination of a template name followed by *template arguments* in *angle brackets* (for example, std::list<int>).

template parameter
A generic placeholder in a template. The most common kind of template parameter are *type parameters*, which represent types. *Nontype parameters* represent constant values of a certain type, and *template template parameters* represent class templates.

traits template
A template the members of which describe characteristics (traits) of the template arguments. Usually the purpose of traits templates is to avoid an excessive number of template parameters. See also *policy class*.

translation unit
A *dot-C* file with all the header files and standard library headers it includes using #include directives, minus the program text that is excluded by conditional compilation directives such as #if. For simplicity, it can also be thought of as the result of preprocessing a *dot-C* file. See *dot-C file* and *header file*.

true constant
See *constant-expression*.

tuple
A generalization of the C struct concept such that members can be accessed by number.

two-phase lookup
The name lookup mechanism used for names in template. The "two phases" are (1) the phase during which a template definition is first encountered by a compiler, and (2) the instantiation of a template. *Nondependent names* are looked up only in the first phase, but during this first phase *nondependent base classes* are not considered. *Dependent names* with a scope qualifier (::) are looked up only in the second phase. Dependent names without a scope qualifier may be looked up in both phases, but in the second phase only argument-dependent lookup is performed.

user-defined conversion
A type conversion defined by the programmer. It can be a *constructor* that can be called with one argument or a *conversion operator*. Unless it is a constructor declared with the keyword explicit, the type conversion can occur implicitly.

whitespace
In C++ this is the space that delimits the tokens (identifiers, literals, symbols, and so on) in source code. Besides the traditional blank space, new line, and horizontal tabulation characters, this also includes comments. Other whitespace characters (for example, the page feed control character) are sometimes also valid whitespace.

Index

Note: Bold page numbers indicate major topics; italic page numbers indicate examples.

->   145
[]   491
>>   206

A

ABC   507
about the book   1
abstract class   **G**507
access declaration   133
actual parameter   91
Adamczyk, Steve   203
ADL   122, **123**, **G**507
Alexandrescu, Andrei   258, 364
AlexandrescuDesign   500
aliasing   420
alignof   **224**
__alignof__   **224**
allocator   52, 284
angle brackets   10, **G**507
    hack   **205**, **G**507
    parsing   128, 205
anonymous union   143
ANSI   **G**507
archetype   **85**
ArgSelect<>   463
argument   90, **104**, **G**508
    conversions   172
    deduction   **167**
      see argument deduction
    derived class   295
    for function templates   **105**

    for template template parameters   51, **111**, 211
    match   488
    named   **285**
    nontype arguments   **109**
    type arguments   **108**
    versus parameter   90
argument deduction   12
    for function templates   13
argument-dependent lookup   122, **123**, **G**508
array
    as template parameter   59
    conversion to pointer   58, 168
    qualification   *351*
Array<>   328
assignment
    with type conversion   45
associated class   123
associated namespace   123
AusternSTL   500
automatic instantiation   141
auto_ptr   394
avoiding
    deduction   **174**

B

back()
    for vectors   *21*, 24
baggage   284
barrier   420
Barton, John J.   174
Barton-Nackman trick   **174**, 177
    versus CRTP   299

base class
    conversion to   494
    dependent   45, 136, 137
    duplicate   287, 449
    empty   289
    nondependent   135
    parameterized by derived class   295
`BaseMem<>`   449
BCCL   500
bibliography   **499**
`binary_function`   284
`bind()`   468
binder
    for function objects   457
`Binder<>`   460, **465**
`BinderParams<>`   461
`bindfp()`   470
`bitset`   44
Blitz++   318, 500
books   **499**
`bool`
    conversion to   392, 494
Boost   500
BoostCompose   500
BoostSmartPtr   500
BoostTypeTraits   501
Borland   155, 342
bounded polymorphism   238
`BoundVal<>`   459
bridge pattern   239
by-reference versus by-value   331
by-value versus by-reference   331

C

call   **418**
    parameter   **13**
call argument
    default   **173**
callback   **417**
CargillExceptionSafety   501
Cfront   163
`char*`
    as template argument   **40**, 209
`char_traits`   284
class   10, 101, **G**508
    associated   123
    as template argument   **40**

definition   480
dependent base   136
inner   227
local   101
name injection   126
nondependent base   135
policy class   **255**
qualification   266, 359
template
    see class template
versus `struct`   87
class template   **21**, 87, **G**508
    as member   **45**, 95
    declaration   22, **95**
    default argument   30, **103**
    full specialization   **190**
    overloading   221
    parameters   **173**
    partial specialization   **200**
class type   87, **G**508
    qualification   266, 359
class type functor   426
client code   245
C linkage   99, 435
code bloat   201
code layout
    control   224
    principles   290
collection class   **G**508
    see container
compiling   74, 153
    models   **141**
    symbol length   79
complete type   143
`complex`   12
`compose()`   447
`Composer<>`   446, **455**
composition
    of function objects   445
`CompoundT<>`   350, 354
concept   75, 78
constant
    true constant   515
constant-expression   91, 107, **303**, **G**508
`const` member function   **G**508
constness
    and smart pointers   390

contact with the authors   **5**
container   **G**508
    as template template parameter   112
    element type   264
context
    deduced   169
context-sensitive   119
conversion
    array to pointer   58, 168
    base-to-derived   494
    derived-to-base   494
    for pointers   494
    for smart pointers   390
    of arguments   172
    sequence   494
    standard   489
    to `bool`   392, 494
    to ellipsis   107, 489
    to pointer-to-member   392
    to `void*`   494
    type promotion   271
    user-defined   109, 489
    with templates   45
conversion-function-id   120
conversion operator   **G**508
Coplien, James   299
CoplienCRTP   501
CoreIssue115   501
covariant return type   216
CRTP   **295**, **G**508
    versus Barton-Nackman trick   299
CSM   279
`<cstddef>`   **4**
curiously recurring template pattern   **295**, **G**509
CzarneckiEiseneckerGenProg   501

D

debugging   74
decay   58, 168, 421, **G**509
    of template parameters   102
declaration   89, **95**, **476**, **G**509
    access   133
    forward   142
    of class template   22
    versus definition   89, **476**
decorated name   418
deduced context   169

deduced parameter   14
deduction   12, **167**, **G**509
    avoiding   **174**
    of initializer   225
default
    argument
      see default argument
    call arguments   **173**
    for template template argument   111
    for template template parameter   111
    nontype parameter   38
default argument
    for call parameters   97
    for class templates   30, **103**
    for function templates   **13**, 207
definition   9, 89, **476**, **G**509
    of class types   480
    versus declaration   89, **476**
demangler   59
dependent base class   136, **G**509
dependent name   119, 121, **G**509
    in using-declarations   **133**
    of templates   **132**
    of types   **130**
deprecated   133
`deque`   52
derivation   135, **285**
derived class
    as base class argument   295
design   229
design pattern   239
DesignPatternsGoV   501
determining types   *278*, *347*, *361*
diagnostics   218
digraph   127, 129, **G**509
    future   206
direct call   **418**
directive
    for explicit instantiation   159
discriminated union   224
domination rule   289
dot-C file   **61**, **G**509
double
    as template argument   **40**, 210
    as traits value   252
    zero initialization   **56**
duo   **395**

recursive   401
Duo<>   397
duplicate base class   287, 449
dynamic polymorphism   **231**, 238

E

EBCDIC   247
EBCO   **289**, *449*, **G**510
EDG   501
ellipsis   107, 358, 489
EllisStroustrupARM   501
e-mail to the authors   **5**
empty()
    for vectors   *21*
empty base class optimization   **289**, *449*, **G**510
empty class object   431
enumeration
    qualification   356
    versus static constant   303
error handling   74
error message   **75**
example code of the book   **5**
exception
    protection   366
    safety   24
expansion
    restricted   174
explicit instantiation   **65**, **159**
    directive   **G**510
explicit instantiation directive   159
explicit specialization   88, 130, 137, **190**, **G**510
explicit template argument   135
export   **68**, **149**, 484
    and inline   69
expression
    constant   107
    for functions   226
expression template   **321**, **G**510
    limitations   340
    performance   340
extended Koenig lookup   140

F

feedback to the authors   **5**
file organization   61
fixed traits   **246**

float
    as template argument   **40**, 210
    as traits value   252
    zero initialization   **56**
formal parameter   91
forward declaration   142
ForwardParamT   440
friend   101, **113**
    function   **114**
    function versus function template   177
    name injection   125, **G**510
    template   **117**
full specialization   *301*, **G**510
    of class templates   **190**
    of function templates   **194**
    of member templates   **197**
func_ptr()   443
function
    call
        see function call
    dispatch table   156
    expression   226
    for types   **263**
    object
        see function object and functor
    pointer   421
    qualification   352
    signature   184
    spilled inline   156
    surrogate   **496**
    template
        see function template
function call   **418**
    operator   417
    syntax   417
function object   **417**, **G**510
    and overloading   496
    binders   457
    class type   426
    composition   445
    value binders   457
FunctionPtr<>   441
FunctionPtrT<>   439
function template   **9**, 87, **G**510
    argument deduction   13
    arguments   **105**
    as member   **45**, 95

declaration **95**
default call argument   97
default template argument   **13**, 207
friend   **114**
full specialization   **194**
inline   **72**
nontype parameters   39
overloading   15, **183**
partial specialization   213
versus friend function   177
functor   **417**, **G**510
and overloading   496
binders   457
class type   426
composition   445
value binders   457
FunctorParam<>   438
fundamental type
promotions   274
qualification   347
future   **205**

G

generated specialization   88
generic programming   **240**
Gibbons, Bill   139, 177, 299
glossary   **507**
greater   429
greedy instantiation   **155**
guard
for header files   479

H

Hartinger, Roland   217
header file   **61**, **G**510
<cstddef>   **4**
guard   479
order   73
precompiled   **72**
<std>   74
<stddef.h>   **4**
heterogeneous collection   238
Hewlett-Packard   139
higher-order genericity   118
holder   **368**
home page of the book   **5**

I

identifier   120
IfThenElse<>   **272**, *273*, *308*, *438*
implicit conversion
for smart pointers   390
implicit instantiation   141
#include
order   73
include file   **G**511
see header file
inclusion model   **63**, **149**
index of the book   **517**
indirect call   **418**, **G**511
induction variables
in metaprograms   309
inheritance   135, **285**
domination rule   289
duplicate base class   287, 449
initialization
of fundamental types   **56**
initializer   **G**511
initializer deduction   225
initializer list   56, **G**511
injected
class name   126, **G**511
friend name   125
inline   **72**
and export   69
inlining   420
inner class   227
Inprise   155
instance   11, **G**511
instantiated specialization   88
instantiation   **11**, 88, **141**, **G**511
automatic   141
diagnostics   218
explicit   **65**, **159**
explicit directive   159
greedy   **155**
implicit   141
iterated   **157**
lazy   **143**
levels   313
manual   160
mechanisms   **141**
model   146

on-demand   141
point   **146**
queried   **156**
recursive   **302**, 313
shallow   **77**
int
   zero initialization   **56**
Internet resources   **499**
introspection   436
intrusive   238
invasive   238
   counter   388
IsArrayT<>   351
IsClassT<>   266, *276*, 359
IsEnumT<>   356
IsFuncT<>   352
IsFundaT<>   347
ISO   **G**511
IsPtrMemT<>   351
IsPtrT<>   350
IsRefT<>   350
iterated instantiation   **157**
iterator   241, **G**511
iterator traits
   for pointers   262
iterator_traits   262, 284

J

Java   227
JosuttisAutoPtr   502
JosuttisOOP   502
JosuttisStdLib   502

K

Koenig, Andrew   122, 140
Koenig lookup   122, 140
KoenigMooAcc   502

L

LambdaLib   502
layout
   control   224
   principles   290
lazy instantiation   **143**

length
   of symbols   79
less   **429**
levels of instantiation   313
lexing   **127**
limit
   levels of instantiation   313
linkable entity   90, 155, **G**512
linkage   **99**
   to C   435
linking   153
LippmanObjMod   502
list   111, 241
list parameters   **222**
literature   **499**
local class   101
lookup
   argument-dependent   122
   for names   121
   Koenig lookup   122, 140
   ordinary   122, 146
   qualified   120
   two-phase   **146**
   unqualified   120
loop
   split   327
   unrolling   314
lvalue   423, **G**512

M

macro   417
make_pair()   59
mangled name   59, 418
manual instantiation   160
map   428
match   488
   best   487
   perfect   489
max_element()   241
maximum
   levels of instantiation   313
   munch   129
member
   as base class   293
   class template   **45**, 95
   function
      see member function

function template   **45**, 95
    initialization   56
    template
        see member template
member class template   **G**512
member function   97
    and virtual   **98**
    as template   **45**, 95
    implementation   24
    pointer to   423
    template   87, **G**512
member template   **45**, 95, **G**512
    full specialization   **197**
    versus template template parameter   259
metaprogramming   203, **301**
    induction variables   309
    reflection   363
Metaware   139, 318
MeyersCounting   502
MeyersEffective   502
MeyersMoreEffective   503
motivation of templates   7
MTL   318, 503
MusserWangDynaVeri   503
Myers, Nathan   258, 284, 299
MyersTraits   503

N

Nackman, Lee R.   174
name   90, **119**, 121
    class name injection   126
    dependent   119, 121
    dependent of templates   **132**
    dependent of types   **130**
    friend name injection   125
    linkage   421
    lookup   **119**, **121**
    nondependent   121
    qualified   119, 120
    two-phase lookup   **146**
    typedef   101
    unqualified   120
name()
    of std::type_info   **58**, *62*, *421*
named template argument   216, **285**
namespace
    associated   123

    template   133
    unnamed   478, 484
nested class   97
    as template   **45**, 95
NewMat   503
newsgroups   499
NewShorterOED   503
NIHCL   243
nondeduced parameter   14
nondependent base class   135
nondependent name   121, **G**512
nonintrusive   238
noninvasive   238
    counter   386
nonreference
    versus reference   58, 168, 331, 493
nontemplate
    overloading   189
nontype argument
    for templates   **109**
    functor   432
nontype parameter   35, **101**
    restrictions   40
null pointer   184
numeric_limits   284

O

ODR   90, **475**, **G**512
on-demand instantiation   141
one-definition rule   90, **475**, **G**512
operator
    ->   145
    []   491
    >>   206
    typeof   215
operator-function-id   120
optimization
    for empty base class   289
oracle   **84**
ordering
    partial   186
    rules   188
order of header files   73
ordinary lookup   122, 146
overloading   15, **179**, **487**
    class templates   221
    nonreference versus reference   493

of function templates   **183**
partial ordering   186
reference versus nonreference   493
templates and nontemplates   189
overload resolution   356, **487**, **G**512

P

`pair`   395, 397
parameter   90, **100**, **G**513
actual   91
ellipsis   107, 358, 489
for base class   45, 137
for call   **13**
formal   91
list of types   **222**
nontype   35, **101**
of class templates   **173**
reference versus nonreference   58, 168, 331
template template parameter   **50**, **102**
type   **101**
versus argument   90
`void`   410
parameterization clause   95
parameterized class   **G**513
parameterized function   481, **G**513
parameterized traits   254
paramter
match   488
parsing   **127**
maximum munch   129
of angle brackets   128, 205
partial ordering
of overloading   186
partial specialization   29, 88, *305*, *331*, **G**513
additional parameters   351
for function templates   213
of class templates   **200**
pattern   239
CRTP   **295**
Pennello, Tom   139
perfect match   489, 492
POD   87, **G**513
POI   **146**, 480, **G**513
pointer
conversions   494
conversion to `void*`   494
iterator traits   262

qualification   350
smart   **365**
to function   421
zero initialization   **56**
pointer-to-member
conversion to   392
function   423
qualification   351
point of instantiation   **146**, 480, **G**513
policy class   **255**, **G**513
versus traits   258
policy traits   **275**
polymorphic object   479
polymorphism   **231**, **G**514
bounded   238
dynamic   **231**, 238
static   **234**, 238
unbounded   238
POOMA   318, 503
`pop_back()`
for vectors   *21*, 24
practice   **61**
precompiled header   **72**, **G**514
prelinker   157
preprocessor
guard   479
primary template   88, **100**, 201, *301*, *305*, **G**514
prime numbers   318
promotion   489
of types   **271**
traits   **271**
property
static   218
traits   275
`ptrdiff_t`   **4**
versus `size_t`   491
`push_back()`
for vectors   *21*

Q

qualification
of array types   351
of class types   266, 359
of enumeration types   356
of function types   352
of fundamental types   347
of pointer-to-member types   351

of pointer types   350
of reference types   350
qualified-id   120
qualified lookup   120
qualified name   119, 120, **G**514
qualifier   268
queried instantiation   **156**

R

RAII   **373**
read-only parameter types   276
recursive duo   401
recursive instantiation   **302**, 313
reference   268
    qualification   350
    to function   421
    to reference   **269**
    versus nonreference   58, 168, 331, 493
reference counting   **379**, **G**514
reflection   363
resource acquisition is initialization   **373**
restricted template expansion   174
run-time analysis oracles   84
rvalue   102, **G**514

S

scanning   **127**
semantic transparency   181
separation model   **68**, **149**
sequence
    of conversions   494
set   428
SFINAE   **106**, *266*, *353*
shallow instantiation   **77**
signature   184
SignSelectT<>   463
sizeof   263
size_t   **4**
    versus ptrdiff_t   491
Smalltalk   238, 243
smart pointer   **365**
    constness   390
    implicit conversions   390
source file   **G**514
spaces   516
specialization   **27**, 88, 141, **179**, **G**514

explicit   88, 130, 137, **190**
full   *301*
generated   88
instantiated   88
partial   88, **200**, *305*, *331*
partial for function templates   213
Spicer, John   203
spilled inlined function   156
split loop   327
square root   305
stack   264
Stack<>   **21**
Standard02   504
Standard98   503
Standard Template Library   139, 240
    see STL
StaticBoundVal<>   459
static constant
    versus enumeration   303
static member   26, 97
static polymorphism   **234**, 238
static properties   218
std::allocator   52, 284
<std>   74
std.hpp   73
std::auto_ptr   394
std::binary_function   284
std::bitset   44
std::char_traits   284
std::complex   12
<stddef.h>   **4**
std::deque   52
std::greater   429
std::iterator_traits   262, 284
std::less   **429**
std::list   111, 241
std::make_pair()   59
std::map   428
std::max_element()   241
std::numeric_limits   284
std::pair   395, 397
std::ptrdiff_t   **4**
std::set   428
std::size_t   **4**
std::stack   264
std::type_info   **58**, 62, *421*
std::unary_function   284

`std::valarray`   342
`std::vector`   21, 241
STL   139, 240, 342
string
   `[ ]`   491
   and reference template parameters   169
   as template argument   **40**, 209
   literal as template parameters   169
StroustrupC++PL   504
StroustrupDnE   504
StroustrupGlossary   504
`struct`
   definition   480
   qualification   266, 359
   versus class   87
Sun Microsystems   156
surrogate   **496**
SutterExceptional   504
SutterMoreExceptional   504
symbol
   length   79

T

tagged union   224
Taligent   139
taxonomy of names   119
template   **G**514
   argument   90
    see template argument
   `export`   **149**
   for namespaces   133
   friend   **117**
   id
    see template-id
   inline   **72**
   instantiation   88, **141**
    see instantiation
   member template   **45**, 95
   metaprogramming   203, **301**
   motivation   7
   name   90, **119**
   nontype arguments   **109**
   of template   27
   parameter   9, **13**, 90, **100**
   partial specialization   29
   primary   **100**, 201
   specialization   **27**, 88

   type arguments   **108**
   union   **96**
`.template`   **44**, 132
   future   207
`->template`   45, 132
   future   207
`::template`   132
   future   207
template argument   90, **104**, **G**514
   array   351
   `char*`   **40**, 209
   class   **40**
   conversions   172
   deduction   **167**, **G**515
   derived class   295
   `double`   **40**, 210
   explicit   135
   `float`   **40**, 210
   named   216, **285**
   string   **40**, 169, 209
template class   87
   see class template
template function   87
   see function template
template-id   87, 90, 104, 120, 132, **G**515
template member function   87
   see member function template
template parameter   **G**515
   array   351
   decay   102
   string literal   169
template template argument   51, **111**, 211
template template parameter   **50**, **102**, *260*
   argument matching   51, **111**, 211
   container   112
   future   211
   versus member template   259
temporaries   322
terminology   **87**, **507**
`this->`   45, **137**
tokenization   127
   maximum munch   129
`to_string()`
   for bitsets   44
tracer   **79**
traits   **245**, *331*, **G**515
   CSM   279

fixed   **246**
for promotion   **271**
for value and reference   331
parameterized   254
policy traits   **275**
`std::iterator_traits`   262
template   **G**515
value traits   250
versus policy class   258
transfer capsule   376
translation unit   90, 150, **475**, **G**515
transparency   180
true constant   **G**515
trule   **376**
tuple   **395**, **G**515
`Tuple<>`   410
two-phase lookup   137, **146**, **G**515
two-stage lookup   **146**
type
arguments   **108**
complete   143
conversion   45
definition   **4**, **27**
see typedef
dependent name   **130**
of container element   264
promotion   **271**
qualification   *278*, **347**, *361*
read-only parameter   276
typedef   **4**, *26*, **27**
name   101
template   **212**
type function   **263**, 403
typeid   **58**, *62*, *421*
`type_info`   **58**, 62, *421*
typename   10, **43**, 101, 130
future   206
`typeof`   **215**
type parameter   10, **101**
type safety   239
`TypeT<>`   *278*, 359
`__type_traits`   363

U

UCN   120
UDC   358
`unary_function`   284

unbounded polymorphism   238
union
definition   480
discriminated   224
qualification   266, 359
tagged   224
template   **96**
universal character name   120
unnamed namespace   478, 484
unqualified-id   120
unqualified lookup   120
unqualified name   120
unrolling loops   314
Unruh, Erwin   301, **318**
UnruhPrimeOrig   504
`UsedFunctorParam<>`   438
`USE_EXPORT`   71
user-defined conversion   109, **G**515
using   10, 133
using-declaration   139
dependent name   **133**

V

`valarray`   342
value
as parameter   35
binders   457
functions   263
value traits   250
VandevoordeSolutions   504
variant type   224
`vector`   *21*, 241
Veldhuizen, Todd   320, 341
VeldhuizenMeta95   505
VeldhuizenPapers   505
virtual
function dispatch table   156
member function   **98**
parameterized   **298**
`void`
as parameter type   410
`void*`
conversion to   494

W

Web site of the book   **5**

whitespace   **G**516

Z

zero initialization   **56**

Also Available from Addison-Wesley

Generic Programming and the STL

Using and Extending the C++ Standard Template Library

Matthew H. Austern

ADDISON-WESLEY PROFESSIONAL COMPUTING SERIES

ISBN 0-201-30956-4
576 pages
©1999

Effective STL

50 Specific Ways to Improve Your Use of the Standard Template Library

Scott Meyers

ADDISON-WESLEY PROFESSIONAL COMPUTING SERIES

ISBN 0-201-74962-9
288 pages
©2001

STL Tutorial and Reference Guide, Second Edition

C++ Programming with the Standard Template Library

David R. Musser, Gillmer J. Derge, and Atul Saini

ADDISON-WESLEY PROFESSIONAL COMPUTING SERIES

ISBN 0-201-37923-6
560 pages
©2001

informIT